SALES
STRATEGY
PLAYBOOK

D1601972

Other Books by Steve W. Martin

Heavy Hitter I.T. Sales Strategy
Heavy Hitter Sales Linguistics
Heavy Hitter Sales Psychology
Heavy Hitter Sales Wisdom
The Real Story of Informix Software and Phil White
Heavy Hitter Selling

SALES STRATEGY PLAYBOOK

The Ultimate Reference Guide to Solve
Your Toughest Sales Challenges

TILIS PUBLISHERS

TILIS Publishers
25401 Alicia Parkway, #L234
Laguna Hills, CA 92653
www.tilispublishers.com

Ordering Information
Orders by U.S. trade bookstores and wholesalers. Please contact Cardinal Publishers Group: Tel: (800) 296-0481; Fax: (317) 879-0872, www.cardinalpub.com.

Cataloging-in-Publication data

Names: Martin, Steve W., 1960-, author.
Title: Sales strategy playbook : the ultimate reference guide to solve your toughest sales challenges
   / Steve W. Martin.
Description: Includes bibliographical references and index. | Laguna Hills, CA: TILIS Publishers, 2018.
Identifiers: ISBN 978-0-999812945 | LCCN 2018953253
Subjects: LCSH Selling. | Marketing. | Business communication. | Success in business.
   | BISAC BUSINESS & ECONOMICS / Sales & Selling / General
Classification: LCC HF5438.25 .M37365 2018 | DDC 658.85--dc23

Printed in the United States of America

First Edition

23 22 21 20 19   10 9 8 7 6 5 4 3 2 1

Cover design: Kuo Design
Interior design and composition: Marin Bookworks
Editing: PeopleSpeak

CONTENTS

Part III: Sales Call Strategy

TOUGHEST SALES CHALLENGES

Use this list to find strategies, tactics, and advice to solve your toughest sale challenges. Source chapters are referenced in brackets.

Do the odds of closing a deal increase with more demonstrations? [135]
How do buyers evaluate vendors and make decisions? [18, 30, 40–41, 102, 130]
How do I become a top salesperson? [6–7, 92–93, 102, 129]
How do I become a trusted advisor? [49–50, 95–99, 102]
How do I become a better negotiator? [70, 78, 99]
How do I become more confident in my forecast? [10, 19–21, 58–59, 67]
How do I become more persuasive? [109–127, 132]
How do I bounce back after a tough loss? [131–135]
How do I call higher in an account? [38–39, 45, 87–90]
How do I conduct client quarterly or annual business reviews? [45]
How do I conduct meaningful discovery when meeting with prospects? [58, 65, 67,84]
How do I control the sales cycle? [20–25, 50, 99]
How do I create a sales strategy? [20–24, 36–41, 47]
How do I cross-sell products? [43]
How do I describe my sales strategy to my sales manager? [20, 22, 47, 79]
How do I determine if I am working for the right company? [1–19]
How do I determine if no decision will be made? [19, 58–59, 67]
How do I determine which decision-maker has the most power? [36, 72–78]
How do I determine which department has the most power? [31–35]
How do I develop a coach or internal champion? [37, 42, 67, 98, 101–103]
How do I differentiate myself and get customers to bond with me? [97–103]
How do I establish trust? [50–55, 62, 101, 133]
How do I expand my presence across the account? [38, 42, 43]
How do I find out if I am winning or losing? [20–21, 36–37, 58–59]
How do I find out if the customer is lying? [104–107]
How do I help my coaches sell my solution to their organization? [37]
How do I know if I will win or lose the deal? [16, 17]
How do I know the purchase is budgeted and approved? [27, 36–37]
How do I make sure the customer will meet with me again? [20, 40, 50–52, 65–66]
How do I meet with and win over C-level executives? [49–50, 54–56, 64–66, 103]
How do I overcome my nervousness? [66,132]
How do I prepare for an account review with my sales manager? [10, 21, 36–39, 47]
How do I present the value of my company, my product, and myself? [40, 52–55, 60, 64, 65]
How do I protect my pricing? [29, 78, 116]
How do I really know where the competition stands in my deal? [15–18]
How do I really understand my client's business? [54, 65, 71, 103]

How do I secure a meeting with a C-level executive? [38–39, 45, 88–89]

How do I structure a meeting with a C-level executive? [66]

How do I qualify the customer and the deal? [58–59]

How do I win over a politically complex evaluation committee? [41, 72–77, 101]

How does meeting with senior executives improve my chance of winning? [135]

How does the underdog beat goliath? [15, 18–25, 29, 41, 72–78, 130]

How influential is our website and what do buyers look at? [30]

If my deal is stalled, what should I do? [19, 23, 25, 36–37, 39]

Should I Introduce my senior executive team members to the client? [135]

Should I focus on sophisticated or less sophisticated buyers? [135]

Should I go after the business or respond to the RFP? [15–17]

Should I answer "blind" RFPs? [135]

What are the best team selling practices? [42, 44, 45, 58, 71, 78, 99]

What are the best questions to ask a prospect and what should I be prepared for? [59–64]

What are the biggest mistakes I should avoid? [12–13, 48]

What are the different sales strategies for enterprise, platform, and point specific sales cycles? [2, 14, 30–35]

What do top salespeople do that I don't? [92–94]

What selling style should I use? [24, 26, 98–99]

What should I do after I lose an important deal? [46, 131]

What should I do during the buyer's journey? [30]

What should I do if I'm losing the deal? [20–23, 39, 47]

What should I say when I meet with a C-level executive? [54, 65–66]

What should I do when I'm stuck with only a single lower-level contact? [38–39]

What's the best day of the week to contact prospects? [86]

What's the best closing strategy? [70]

What's the best email to send to prospects? [87–91, 95]

What's the best negotiation strategy? [78]

What's the best way to penetrate new accounts? [80–91

When does the customer actually make a decision? [16–17, 135]

Where do the best leads come from? [135]

What's the best strategy for approaching procurement, sourcing, and supply chain? [28]

What's the best way to make a presentation? [68–69]

What's the best way to present customer success stories? [64]

What's the best way to sell to the opposite sex? [25–26, 78, 129]

What's the best way to structure sales calls? [44, 49–71]

Why does my sales manager dislike me and what should I do? [8]

Why is the evaluation committee against me? [72–78, 110–114]

SALES RESEARCH FIGURES, CHARTS, AND GRAPHS

Use this list to find sales research figures, charts, and graphs to solve your toughest sales challenges. Page numbers are referenced.

INTRODUCTION

If you are unfamiliar with the concept of a sales strategy playbook, you probably have a few questions. First, what is a playbook and why is it needed? Second, how is it used?

What Is a Sales Strategy Playbook?

A playbook is a strategic document that details the methodology by which salespeople win new customers and expand their presence within existing client accounts, and the tactics to control the customer engagement process. In essence, a sales strategy playbook is the owner's manual that determines how a company will grow sales and prosper.

This playbook serves as a productivity tool for salespeople, sales managers, presales engineers, subject-matter experts, and all their colleagues in their customer-facing organizations. *Sales Strategy Playbook* has four main goals:

- To serve as a road map that provides direction and strategies to grow your business to the next level. The playbook defines the methodology to capture new clients and expand business with existing clients.

- To explain how you should position yourself, communicate with clients, and win over decision-makers at all levels of a customer's organization.

- To provide state-of-the-art information and best practices in a written document so they are accessible to the entire sales organization.

- To be a teaching guide that synchronizes the sales organization. The playbook is a training guide for onboarding salespeople who focus on new clients (hunters), install base account managers (farmers), presales engineers, professional services consultants, and customer service and delivery personnel.

How to Use This Playbook

This is an unusual sales book for four reasons.

1. *It respects the fact that most salespeople don't like to read.* You see, your brain was built for talking. It was not designed for reading. While speaking comes automatically and is a natural part of the brain's development, reading is a skill that must be learned. It requires three different areas of your brain to work together in close coordination. Therefore, *Sales Strategy Playbook* is divided into short chapters of just a few pages, and extensive figures, graphs, tests, and examples will keep your mind engaged.

2. *You can read the book sequentially or read only the chapters that interest you.* This playbook is written "cafeteria style" using a reference guide format. Keep it

close by so you can refer to it when you need guidance, an innovative idea, or advice. Write in this book and highlight passages you find interesting. Make notes in the margins about tactics you plan to try. Bend the corners of pages that are important to you.

3. *The exercises and tests throughout the playbook will help you internalize the concepts, understand your selling style, and learn how your mind is wired to communicate.* The forms used for the exercises are available on my website (www.stevewmartin.com/salesstrategyplaybookforms).

4. *This playbook will help salespeople advance their careers by positively influencing their local office, region, sales organization, and company.* This requires not only winning more business but also having a methodology to explain to others how and why you win.

Based on Extensive Research

Sales Strategy Playbook is based on the knowledge gained from working with hundreds of companies as a sales consultant and trainer. It also is based on extensive research that includes the following:

- Interviews with over one thousand key buyer decision-makers as part of the win-loss analysis research I conduct on behalf of my clients. You will find excerpts from these interviews throughout the book, and they include the interviewee's actual title.

- Industry research on how B2B (business-to-business) buyers select vendors and their perceptions of salespeople.

- Sales research on the attributes of high-performing sales organizations and the personal characteristics of top salespeople.

- Interviews with over one thousand top salespeople and vice presidents of sales who sell for the world's best companies. You will find excerpts from these interviews included in the book.

The subjects covered are also influenced by my personal experiences as a salesperson and vice president of sales. Finally, this playbook incorporates the key concepts from the entire series of Heavy Hitter books about sales strategies for senior salespeople.

PART I

SALES ORGANIZATION STRATEGY

Chapter 1. Sales Organization Stages

The company life cycle starts with an entrepreneurial idea that becomes a reality during the adolescent stage. As the company continues to grow, it enters the adult stage, where the business has established the organizational infrastructure to achieve a measurable market presence and significant revenue growth. The company exits the adult stage and enters the stability of the middle-age stage, where it enjoys sustainable growth balanced with organizational control. As the company continues to age, it enters a senior stage, where the goal is to stay relevant and avoid decline.

Sales organizations can also be classified according to their maturity. Every sales organization can be classified based upon whether it is in a build, compete, maintain, extend, or cull stage. The build stage is when the sales organization is first establishing itself. If successful, it will proceed to a high-growth compete stage and then to a maintain stage that is contingent upon stable, predictable success. As the sales organization ages, it will either extend its prior success and enjoy longevity or suffer decline and be forced into the cull stage, where it must reduce its size. Figure 1.1 shows the interrelationship between the sales organization stages and the company life cycle.

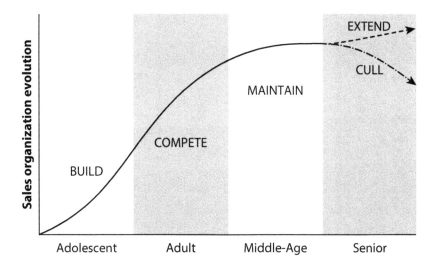

Figure 1.1 Interrelationship between sales organization stages and company life cycle

Sales Challenges

The top sales challenge is always exceeding the monthly, quarterly, or yearly revenue target. However, the sales challenges that inhibit a company from achieving revenue growth vary based on the sales organization stage. This is due to the "push" versus "pull" market characteristics of each stage. For example, in the build stage, a small group of salespeople must push themselves into new accounts and introduce their solution and its benefits. Conversely, a well-known company in the maintain stage is pulled into new sales opportunities because of its market position. Figure 1.2 highlights the different sales organization challenges in the build, compete, maintain, extend, and cull stages.

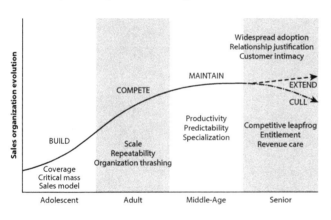

Figure 1.2 Sales organization stage challenges

Build Stage Challenges

In the build stage, the organization is establishing its presence and the foundational infrastructure. The sales engagement model is created and continually refined through the iterative process of meeting with early customers. This is a key learning period based upon trial and error, ranging from deciding what type of salespeople should be hired to

determining the specific messages that appeal to prospective customers.

The top sales challenge in the build stage is creating sufficient sales coverage to push the product into the market. It takes time to hire, train, and build a critical mass of capable salespeople who can penetrate new accounts. During this stage, the sales model is first established, determining whether the sales organization will sell directly via outside field salespeople, over the phone with inside salespeople, or through channel partners.

Compete Stage Challenges

As the sales organization grows, it enters the compete stage and early adulthood. In this stage, the sales organization is engaged with head-to-head competitors, most of whom are well established and typically larger in size. The sales organization continues to grow rapidly with a large injection of new sales team members.

The compete stage challenge revolves around quickly scaling the sales organization so that it can compete effectively against more established competitors in existing markets or grab as much market share as possible in untapped greenfield markets. In this stage, the sales organization begins to develop its collective intuition about where it can win new business and where it is likely to lose. If the knowledge and attributes of how business is won are not instilled into the new salespeople, "organization thrashing" occurs. The new salespeople will chase business they cannot win and waste precious presales resources because there isn't a repeatable sales model. They won't make their quotas and are likely to either be let go or choose to leave because they lack a sufficient pipeline of business to make commissions. In this situation, organization-thrashing occurs because of the continual replenishment of new and underperforming salespeople.

Maintain Stage Challenges

The sales organization enters the maintain stage when the market share between competitors becomes more fixed. Because the market has coalesced around a handful of competitors, the greenfield sales opportunities that existed in the compete stage are gone. Now the company must increase its market share and grow at the expense of the competition.

The sales challenge changes radically during the late compete stage and into the maintain stage. The focus shifts from scaling the organization to maximizing sales productivity by lowering the cost of sales and increasing the average sales price. This may result in moving business from outside sales to inside sales or to less-expensive partner and distributor channels. Another challenge revolves around the predictability of revenue and the size of the sales organization. Since the sales organization is fully staffed and the territory coverage model is complete, the challenge is where to find the additional revenue to meet the growing annual target. Since territories have been split numerous times, the answer revolves around specialization. The sales force is segmented by the size of the company to be called upon, national accounts are segregated, and industry vertical sales specialists covering finance, government, retail, distribution, healthcare, and so on are created.

Extend and Cull Stage Challenges

As the organization continues to age, it enters the extend stage. Here the sales organization's goal is to extend the company's market position by increasing the vendor's strategic importance at existing accounts and to remain competitive so new prospective customers can be won. Conversely, when the sales organization passes the tipping point of effectiveness, it enters the cull stage and is forced to downsize in conjunction with its diminished market presence.

Sales organizations in the extend stage seek to deflect the attacks from compete and maintain stage competitors by extending their presence within existing customer installations. Their challenge is to attain such widespread customer adoption that their solution becomes the de facto standard. From an account management perspective, the challenge is to build irreplaceable customer intimacy by understanding the customer's business issues and goals. Even though superior products might be available from competitors, through the building of strong personal relationships and the sharing of best industry practices, the customer feels justified to continue the relationship as opposed to ending it.

In the cull stage, the company has been leapfrogged by competitors who provide superior offerings. How can a demoralized and marginalized sales force be revitalized? The Darwinian answer is to cull the herd and remove the bottom performers and those with disenfranchised attitudes. The attitude of entitlement must be eliminated for the spark of the competitive spirit to be reignited. Equally important, key existing accounts whose run rate revenue is central to the survival of the company are separated out and placed in "revenue care" programs where they receive dedicated account management, customer support, and executive-level access.

Exercise: Download the Sales Strategy Playbook forms from www.stevewmartin.com/salesstrategyplaybookforms. Print out the sales organization stage figure and plot where your sales organization is on the life cycle curve.

Chapter 2. How Product Complexity Impacts Sales Organization Structure

The complexity of the solution sold is directly related to the evolution of the sales organization. Product sales can be classified by complexity as enterprise, platform, and point-specific. Each sales cycle varies in complexity depending upon the number of individuals and departments involved in the selection process, size of the purchase, and sophisticated nature (implementation requirements, daily operation, and underlying technology) of the solution offered.

Enterprise Sales Trends

Enterprise sales typically involve large capital expenditure purchases that require long sales cycles. Multiple departments of a company and all levels of the organization (C-level executive,

midlevel management, and lower-level personnel) are needed to approve the solution's functionality and its purchase. The Enterprise Resource Planning (ERP) system is an example of an enterprise product.

The enterprise sales cycle requires the establishment of an outside field sales force in the build stage, where each field salesperson is initially responsible for a geographic territory. As the organization moves to the compete stage, the territories are split according to company size, measured by annual revenue or number of employees. The field salespeople are segmented into large account field reps and geography (or "geo") field reps.

During the late adult or early middle-age stage, the territories are split further with the addition of vertical outside field salespeople who call on specific industries such as finance, government, retail, technology, and so on. At this time, new products may be launched to penetrate midmarket accounts. Depending upon the complexity of the solution, the sales force selected to address the midmarket will be either a field-based group located in remote areas or a centralized inside sales group that demonstrates products and closes business solely over the phone. Figure 2.1 shows the progression of the enterprise sales organization structure.

Platform Sales Trends

The platform sale includes a full line of product functionality (or complete stack of technology) that provides a turnkey business solution for the customer. Since it is a user-friendly solution designed for the everyday user and average employee, it is sold directly to

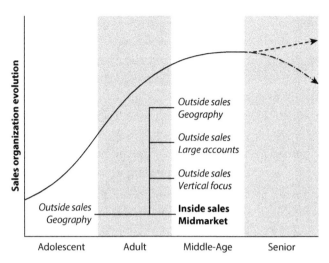

Figure 2.1 Enterprise sales cycle organization evolution

the frontline business users, product operators, and managers. A platform sales cycle might be instigated by the business users within a department and purchased with the blessing of other interested departments. For example, a sales automation solution may be evaluated by the sales department and purchased with the approval of the IT department.

The platform sales cycle shares many of the same characteristics of the enterprise sales cycle. Different departments and all levels of the organization can be involved. The sales cycles are long and there are significant solution costs. However, the sales organization structure may be different depending upon how the solution evolves. At companies where the solution evolves from a point-specific solution in the build stage to a full product platform in the compete stage, it is sold primarily over the phone and

internet. As the organization grows and the company tries to penetrate larger accounts, outside field salespeople are added.

At companies where the complete solution is available and is fully completed during the build stage, it will typically be sold through field salespeople. When the company later offers a pared-down functional solution to address the mid- and SMB (small to medium business) market, it will be sold through inside sales. However, these reps may make field sales calls depending upon the situation. Figure 2.2 shows the platform sales cycle at the adult stage of sales organization development.

Point-Specific Sales Trends

Point-specific sales involve a single solution (or a set of finite complementary functionality offerings) usually targeted to solve the business problems of

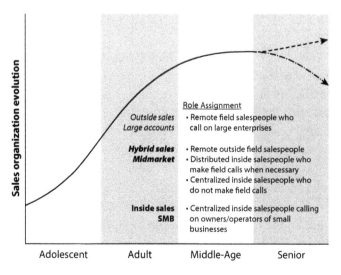

Figure 2.2 Platform sales cycle at the adult stage

a single department within an organization. The purchase decision is typically made by a small number of decision-makers, most likely at the lower level of the organization, with decision approval from midlevel management. For example, a résumé tracking system is a point-specific solution sold to the human resources department.

A point-specific sale can be classified as freeware, simple, or complex. The freeware point-specific sale refers to the initial product available to the user without any cost. For example, customers may serve themselves and download a free product from a vendor's website. This limited-use version of the commercially available product is part of a "land and expand" strategy to establish initial product use and then convert users into paying customers later using inside or outside sales.

The simple point-specific sale is complementary to the customer's existing environment. It is sold as an addition to the way business is being conducted today. The simple point-specific sale primarily utilizes an inside sales model based on geography, which is later verticalized and segmented by company size, with the addition of outside sales field reps calling on large accounts.

The complex point-specific sale may require the customer to break a pre-established relationship with an existing vendor. This entails a "rip and replace" strategy where the existing vendor's products are completely replaced by

newer technology or an entirely different way of doing business. This sales effort requires an outside salesperson and expands over time to include named large accounts and vertical overlay salespeople. Inside sales reps who cover specific verticals, geographies, or midmarket accounts based on company size may be added depending upon the complexity of the product. Figure 2.3 shows the sales organization's evolution and the three point-specific sales cycle types.

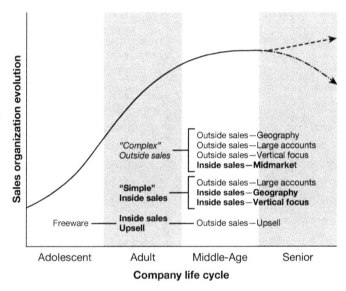

Figure 2.3 Point-specific sales cycle organization evolution

Outside and Inside Sales Staff Shift

According to research I conducted, over twice as many vice presidents of sales reported moving to an inside sales model as opposed to a field sales model as shown in figure 2.4. For 34 percent, the shift was slight, but 12 percent of study participants reported a significant shift from a field sales model to an inside sales model. Twenty-one percent reported a shift from inside sales to a field sales model, including 13 percent

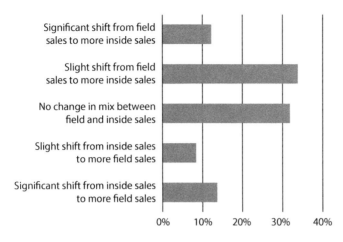

Figure 2.4 Shift in sales staff

Inside salespeople have to be disciplined, make cold calls, follow up, get volume, and close the deals quickly. Outside people have to develop longer-term relationships, as most transactions are larger and require more sales skills and knowledge of the long-term wants, needs, and expectations of the customer.

—Vice President of Sales

who reported a significant shift and 8 percent who reported a slight shift.

Three key factors determine when a sales organization will utilize a field or inside sales model: the sales organization's stage of development, the complexity of the products that are sold, and, to a lesser extent, the sales leader's perception of inside and outside sales model effectiveness. The positive perception of the inside sales model has increased due to many societal shifts, including the technical sophistication of today's buyers and how they research and make buying decisions online.

Today, there is a changing perception among technology sales leaders about the strategic role of inside sales. This is due in part to the benefits sales leaders believe the inside sales model provides in terms of scaling activity, growing the organization, and attacking specific markets. Vice presidents of sales cited several advantages of an inside sales model compared to a field sales model as shown in figure 2.5.

Field sales is more strategic, meeting with C-level executives and developing business innovation to help them grow their business, versus inside, which is higher volume and not as in depth the majority of the time.

—Vice President of Sales

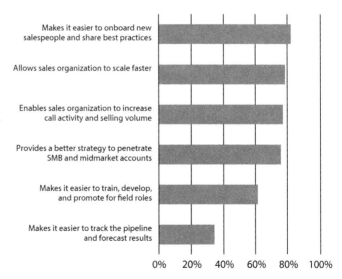

Figure 2.5 Advantages of an inside sales model cited by sales leaders

Chapter 3. Seven Attributes of Great Sales Organizations

What separates great from good sales organizations? After working with hundreds of different companies, I believe the evidence suggests that the best business-to-business sales organizations share specific patterns of organizational structure and behavior. These similarities can be categorized into the seven attributes listed below. Conversely, underperforming or weaker sales organizations tend to be missing some or all of these critical characteristics.

1. *Great sales organizations have strong centralized command and control with local authority.* There is no single greater influence on the success of a sales organization than how the sales leaders create the culture and environment for the people who work for them. In this regard, the best organizations have strong leaders who exercise authoritarian control, dictate team direction, and establish the codes of behavior that all team members must abide by. Although these tenets are used within military units to enforce the chain of command, sales leaders prefer to use motivation and the force of their personal character before employing the power associated with their titles.

   In addition, the senior leadership team typically does not micromanage their sales teams. Instead, independent and autonomous local decision-making operates within the guidelines and protocols established by the leaders. But rest assured, the actions of the sales teams at lower levels of the organization always take into account the goals and desires of the senior leaders.

2. *They have a Darwinian sales culture.* There are two aspects of a Darwinian sales culture. The first is the next hire by the organization is of such high quality and capability that it challenges the more tenured sales team members to perform at the highest level (so that they are not resting on their laurels). The second aspect is that the sales organization is continually "culling the herd" and comparing each member's performance against stringent criteria. Weaker sales team members who do not contribute their revenue share are more quickly let go.

3. *Individuals working for great sales organizations are united against a common enemy.* I have found that the best sales organizations, those that are driven to succeed against all obstacles and odds, have an archrival competitor that they both resent and fear. This is a very important differentiator since it drives individual behavior. As a result, there is a higher win ratio because accounts are pursued with greater preparation, higher intensity, and a life-or-death seriousness.

4. *Members of great sales organizations form a competitive but a cohesive team.* In one sense, a sales organization is an amalgamation of cliques. For example, a sales organization may comprise three areas that include North America, Asia-Pacific, and EMEA (Europe, Middle East, and Africa). Furthermore, North American sales may include three regions:

East, Midwest, and West. Great sales organizations have more than a friendly rivalry between the various regions. Each region is on a mission to prove it is the best. Although all the salespeople and their sales leaders are intensely competitive individuals by nature, they will support their area and regional teammates when needed. It is highly likely that the key sales management leaders have worked with each other before at other companies. They know, like, and respect each other.

5. *They have a DIY attitude.* Many underperforming sales organizations have something in common: the sales organization tends to blame other areas of the organization (engineering, marketing, support, etc.) for its own failings. Members of top performing sales organizations take ownership of their own success and have a "do it yourself" attitude. For example, they will not solely rely on marketing to provide their leads but build their own pipeline without any expectations of leads from marketing. When troubles arise at customer accounts, they will spearhead problem resolution efforts.

6. *They suspend negative belief systems.* Sales is a career in which people experience tremendous highs and lows. Circumstances change very quickly in sales. A competitor's new technology may leapfrog yours. The company whose account you worked so hard to close may want its money back because the product isn't working right. The funnel of deals you may have been counting on for months could disappear in a few minutes.

The sales team members in great organizations live "in the moment," meaning they do not fixate on negative thoughts that prevent them from moving forward and taking action. They are not debilitated by bad news or self-defeating rumors heard through the grapevine.

7. *They exhibit energy and esprit de corps.* While all sales organizations can be defined as a collection of individuals trying to succeed as a team, there is a tremendous amount of peer pressure inside great sales organizations. If a member doesn't achieve his revenue targets, not only did he fail personally, but he also let his team down. On the other side of the coin, when sales team members post great numbers, they are honored and respected by the team. This type of sales culture is very different from an individualistic "every man for himself" environment because it fosters team cohesiveness, morale, and a continually high energy level.

The members of great sales organizations don't believe they are in sales by happenstance. They are professionals who believe they are fulfilling their own destiny. Collectively, as part of an organization they are united for a greater purpose than themselves. While the company's goal may be to go public or reach certain revenue milestones, the greatest sales organizations are on a never-ending mission to prove to the world that they are the best.

Chapter 4. High-Performing Sales Organizations

What separates high-performing sales organizations from average and under-performing sales organizations? To answer this question, I conducted an extensive study consisting of 786 sales professionals. Participants were asked to share their opinions on their sales organization and personal details about their own quota performance.

Twenty-two percent of survey participants included top-level sales leaders such as vice presidents of sales, 14 percent were front-line sales managers who manage salespeople, 17 percent were hybrid sales managers who sell directly to customers and manage other salespeople, and 47 percent were salespeople who carry their own quota.

Study participants were asked to compare their company's year-over-year revenue growth for the past two years and indicate whether annual revenues increased significantly, increased slightly, remained about the same, or declined. Thirty percent of participants indicated they had a high level of revenue growth, 44 percent had slight revenue growth, and 26 percent had revenues that were about the same or had declined. The survey responses were then grouped into high-performing, average-performing, and underperforming categories according to these revenue classifications.

The study results reveal fifteen significant differences between how high-, average-, and underperforming sales organizations perceive themselves, measure performance, staff their organizations, and operate. Below are these key attributes and performance-related metrics that illustrate these differences and the gap between optimum and subpar sales organization performance.

1. *High-performing sales organizations set higher quotas and expect lower quota attainment than average and underperforming sales organizations. As shown in figure 4.1,* 46 percent of

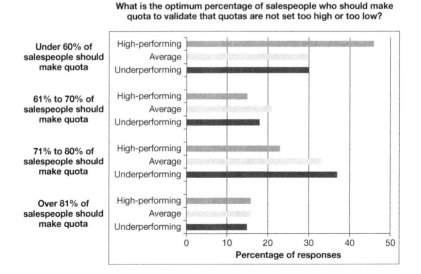

Figure 4.1 Percentage of salespeople who should make quota

members of high-performing sales organizations indicated that less than 60 percent of salespeople should make quota compared to 30 percent of members of both average and underperforming sales organizations. In other words, quota attainment should not be easily achieved and quotas are expected to be aggressively set. Conversely, 52 percent of responses from underperforming sales organizations and 50 percent from average sales organizations indicated that more than 70 percent of salespeople should achieve quota.

2. *High-performing sales organizations hold their team members to a higher level of accountability than average and underperforming sales organizations.* Study participants were asked whether or not they agree with the statement that their salespeople are consistently measured against their quotas and held accountable for their results. Twenty-nine percent of high-performing sales team members strongly agreed with that statement, while only 13 percent of underperforming sales team members did. Fifty-one percent of underperforming members either strongly disagreed, disagreed, or neither agreed nor disagreed with the statement as opposed to only 32 percent of high-performing study participants.

3. *High-performing sales organizations are quicker to terminate underperforming salespeople than average and underperforming sales organizations.* Twenty-four percent of high-performing team members indicated

that salespeople will be terminated for poor performance after one quarter compared to only 5 percent of average and 8 percent of underperforming team members. Eighty-six percent of high-performing team members indicated that a poor performer will be terminated within a year compared to 72 percent of average and 61 percent of underperforming team members. Nine or more quarters are required to terminate an underperforming salesperson according to 16 percent of underperforming and 12 percent of average team members, while no high-performing team members indicated it takes that long.

4. *Sales managers at high-performing sales organizations have higher quota risk pool factors, where the sum of all the quotas of their salespeople is higher than the personal quota they are responsible for.* A sales manager's quota risk pool factor is calculated by adding up all the quotas of the salespeople who report to him together and dividing the sum by his quota. For example, if a sales manager's quota is $10 million and he has ten salespeople who each have a $1 million quota, his quota risk pool factor would be 1. Forty-four percent of sales managers at high-performing companies have a quota risk pool factor greater than 1.25 compared to 26 percent for average and 27 percent for underperforming companies. Fifteen percent of high-performing sales organization managers have a quota risk pool factor greater than 1.75 compared to 5 percent at

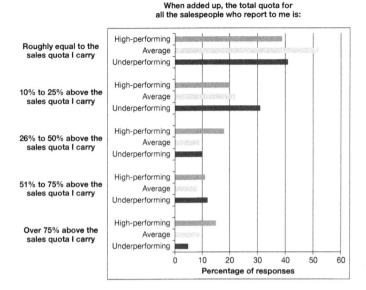

When added up, the total quota for all the salespeople who report to me is:

Figure 4.2 Sales manager quota risk pool factor measurements

underperforming sales organizations as shown in figure 4.2.

5. *High-performing sales organizations are not afraid to aggressively raise year-over-year annual quotas.* Seventy-five percent of high-performing sales organizations raised annual quotas more than 10 percent over the previous year's annual quotas compared to 25 percent for average and 17 percent for underperforming sales organizations. Annual quotas remained the same or decreased for 65 percent of underperforming sales organizations, 48 percent of average sales organizations, and only 14 percent of high-performing sales organizations.

6. *Sales managers at high-performing sales organizations rate the quality of the teams they manage higher than the sales managers at average and underperforming sales organizations.* The study results suggest that declining sales performance is directly correlated to sales talent level. Sales managers at high-performing companies were twice as likely to rate their teams as excellent compared to managers at average and underperforming sales organizations. Seventy-six percent of high-performing sales managers rated their team as excellent or above average compared to 51 percent at average sales organizations and only 49 percent at underperforming sales organizations. Forty-three percent of sales managers at underperforming organizations rated their organization as average and 8 percent below average compared to 23 percent and 1 percent of sales managers at high-performing sales organizations.

7. *Sales managers at high-performing sales organizations indicated their teams have a higher percentage of top performers and a lower percentage of bottom performers than sales managers at average and underperforming sales organizations.* Sales managers at high-performing sales organizations indicated their teams are composed of 45 percent top performers, whereas top performers make up 29 percent of the team for underperforming sales managers. Only 14 percent of the team consist of below-average performers according to high-performing companies

as compared to 24 percent for the managers at underperforming sales organizations.

8. *High-performing sales team members rate the quality of their sales organizations higher than average and underperforming team members.* Twice as many high-performing team members rated their organization as excellent compared to average and underperforming team members. In addition, 78 percent of high-performing team members rated their organization as excellent or above average compared to 51 percent of average and 49 percent of underperforming team members. Only 1 percent of high-performing team members rated their sales organization as below average compared to 10 percent of average and 8 percent of underperforming team members, as shown in figure 4.3.

9. *High-performing sales organizations attract top sales talent through better compensation.* Ninety-one percent of high-performing team members indicated that their compensation was at or above the average of the industry.

Conversely, only 9 percent of high-performing companies paid below market average compared to 29 percent of underperforming organizations. One surprising metric is that 35 percent of both high-performing and underperforming sales organizations compensate above market average. However, based upon the previous three points about performance and the talent quality of sales organizations, it can be interpreted that underperforming companies are overpaying to retain subpar talent, while high-performing companies are willing to pay more to attract top sales talent.

10. *High-performing sales organizations employ a more structured sales process than average and underperforming sales organizations.* Fifty percent of study participants from high-performing sales organizations responded they had sales processes that were closely monitored, strictly enforced, or automated compared to 28 percent from underperforming sales organizations. Forty-eight percent of the participants from

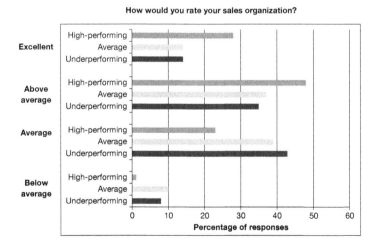

Figure 4.3 Sales organization ratings

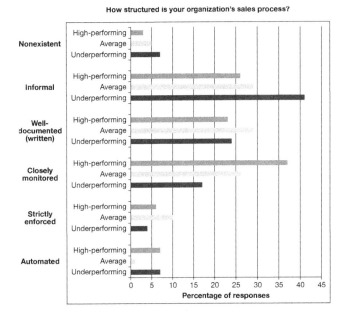

Figure 4.4 Sales process structure ratings

automated compared to their counterparts from average and underperforming organizations. For example, 29 percent of high-performing sales organization study participants indicated their lead follow-up process was closely monitored as compared to 21 percent of average and 22 percent of underperforming sales organizations.

12. *High-performing sales organizations describe their sales culture differently than average and underperforming sales organizations.* Survey participants were asked which of three different descriptions that best describe their sales organization. Were they part of "a cohesive group of like-minded individuals," "a team of seasoned professionals," or "a loose collection of individuals"? Thirty-eight percent of high-performing team members selected "a cohesive group of individuals" compared to 21 percent of average and 23 percent of underperforming team members. Forty-three percent of average team members selected "a team of seasoned professionals" compared to 36 percent of high-performing responses. Only 26 percent of high-performing team members selected "a loose collection of individuals" compared to 37 percent of underperforming and 36 percent of average team members as shown in figure 4.5.

underperforming sales organizations indicated they had nonexistent or informal structured sales processes compared to only 29 percent from high-performing sales organizations as shown in figure 4.4.

11. *High-performing sales organizations more closely monitor their lead follow-up process than average and underperforming sales organizations.* More high-performing study participants indicated their lead process was well-documented, closely monitored, strictly enforced, and

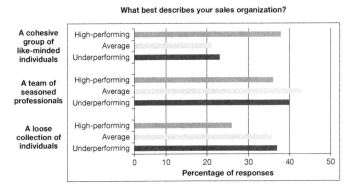

Figure 4.5 Sales organizations' descriptions of their culture

13. *Members of high-performing sales organizations have a different perspective on the factors that separate great from good sales organizations than members of average and underperforming sales organizations.* Study participants were asked to rank seven different factors as to their importance in determining whether a sales organization is good or great. In general, high-performing sales team members placed action-oriented factors at the top of their list, including lead generation and pipeline activity and disciplined sales process and systems usage. Underperforming sales team participants placed more personal skills-based factors at the top of their list, including sales team morale and collaboration, talent of salespeople, and quality of sales leadership as shown in figure 4.6. One interpretation of these results suggests that high-performing sales teams think in terms of strategic sales process management, while underperforming sales teams are more focused on personal sales prowess.

14. *Sales managers at high-performing sales organizations reported a higher percentage of their salespeople achieved their annual quotas than sales managers at average and underperforming sales organizations.* Sales managers at high-performing sales organizations reported that 60 percent of their salespeople achieved their annual quotas as opposed to 49 percent of the salespeople at average sales organizations and 56 percent of salespeople at underperforming sales organizations.

15. *High-performing sales organizations have a higher level of morale than average and underperforming sales organizations.* Fifty-six percent of high-performing team members indicated that their sales organization's morale was higher than most sales organizations' compared to only 11 percent of average and 21 percent of underperforming sales team members. Conversely, 35 percent of underperforming sales team members and 27 percent of average team members indicated that their sales organization's morale was lower than most organizations', while only 4 percent of high-performing team members responded similarly.

High-performing sales organizations	Average sales organizations	Underperforming sales organizations
Lead generation and pipeline activity	Lead generation and pipeline activity	Sales team morale and collaboration
Disciplined sales process and systems usage	Quality of sales leadership	Talent of salespeople
Sales team morale and collaboration	Sales team morale and collaboration	Quality of sales leadership
Quality of sales leadership	Talent of salespeople	Disciplined sales process and systems usage
Talent of salespeople	Disciplined sales process and systems usage	Lead generation and pipeline activity
Training and field support	Training and field support	Training and field support
Integration with marketing, finance, services	Integration with marketing, finance, services	Integration with marketing, finance, services

Figure 4.6 Prioritized factors separating great from good sales organizations

Chapter 5. High-Performing Sales Leaders

All salespeople know the quality of their sales leadership will have a profound impact on their own success, and a recent study I conducted proves this point. Sixty-nine percent of salespeople who exceeded their annual quota rated their sales manager as being excellent or above average. In addition, the quality of the sales organization is directly associated with the quality of sales leadership. Fifty-six percent of salespeople who rated their sales organization as excellent also rated their sales manager as excellent compared to only 3 percent that rated their organization as average.

Given that the best sales organizations have great sales leaders, what separates high-performing sales leaders who exceed their quota from underperformers who miss their quota by more than 25 percent? To find the answer to this question, I asked over four hundred sales leaders (vice presidents of sales and front-line sales managers) to complete an extensive sales management performance study. Twenty-nine percent of participants said they met or exceeded their annual quota last year, while 42 percent attained between 75 and 99 percent. Twenty-nine percent attained less than 75 percent of their annual quota.

I have also had the privilege to interview well over one thousand sales leaders to better understand the impact of management styles and personality patterns on sales success. This combination of quantitative and qualitative research provides interesting insights about the attributes of high-performing sales leaders compared to their less-successful counterparts.

Primary Attributes

There are seven primary attributes of high-performing sales leaders, which are described below in order of priority.

1. *Target fixation.* The best sales leaders are target and deadline driven. In personality testing, top sales managers scored 19 percent higher in the self-discipline facet, 20 percent higher in the success-driven facet, and 27 percent higher in the priority-focused facet than underperforming sales managers. As a result, they have a natural disposition to fixate their team on achieving their revenue goals at the exclusion of all else. They block out distractions and compartmentalize negative news that might sidetrack their team or cause their department to flounder. They keep their team focused and moving forward with a sense of urgency, regardless of the circumstances.

2. *Command instinct.* Great sales leaders establish firm command over their team by exercising the power their title and position entail. For example, they hold the team they manage to a higher level of accountability. Seventy-five percent of high-performing sales managers agreed that their salespeople are consistently measured and held accountable against their quota compared to 58 percent of underperforming sales managers.

    However, their authority is not as autocratically administered as you might think. Rather, it is based upon establishing an environment where sales team members continually seek to prove themselves, thereby driving higher overall departmental performance. The leaders establish this culture using a "carrot and stick" psychological approach. Over-achievers receive praise and public recognition, while underachievers are admonished or ostracized until they redeem themselves. In essence, the command instinct is responsible for creating the peer-pressure and attention-seeking environment that eliminates complacency.

3. *Hiring ability.* The ability to hire quality talent will determine the success or failure of the sales organization. Seventy-two percent of high-performing sales managers rated the sales team they manage as excellent or above average compared to 54 percent of underperforming sales managers. Conversely, 46 percent of underperforming sales managers rated their team as average or below average, while only 28 percent of high-performing sales managers thought so.

   High-performing sales managers build teams that include more top performers and fewer bottom performers. Top-level salespeople are skillful builders of relationships, are persuasive, and have a reservoir of experience they use to control sales cycles. Lower-quality salespeople are not as proficient at closing business. High-performing sales managers categorized their teams as being composed of 44 percent top performers, 44 percent average performers, and 12 percent underperformers. Underperforming sales

managers categorized their teams as 35 percent top performers, 44 percent average performers, and 21 percent underperformers.

4. *Sales intuition.* Sales is a mentor-based profession, and a key differentiator of great sales leaders is their ability to dispense tactical sales advice and add value during customer meetings. While the average sales experience for both high-performing and underperforming sales managers was seventeen years, high-performing sales managers estimated they have achieved their annual quota 88 percent of the time over the course of their career. Underperforming sales managers indicated they have achieved their quota 75 percent of the time. This suggests that the depth of a manager's sales intuition—*the practical knowledge gained from the experiences of participating in sales cycles and managing salespeople*—is directly associated with their success.

5. *Control orientation.* Sales managers who closely monitor and strictly enforce a sales process are more likely to exceed their quota, and the best sales leaders seek to control the daily behavior of their sales teams. Forty-three percent of high-performing sales managers responded that their sales process was closely monitored, strictly enforced, or automated compared to 29 percent of underperforming sales managers. Forty-four percent of underperforming sales managers indicated they had a nonexistent or an informally structured sales process.

6. *Coaching adaptability.* Great sales leaders understand that there is a diversity of selling styles by which salespeople can achieve success. Therefore, they don't employ a one-size-fits-all coaching style. Rather, they adapt their style to suit each individual. The fact that high-performing sales managers had a higher team effectiveness factor than underperforming teams supports these statements.

A team effectiveness factor is calculated by averaging total quota achievement across the number of salespeople on the team. For example, if a team of ten sales reps who each had a $1 million quota sold $8 million in total revenues, the team effectiveness factor would be 80 percent ($8 million of actual sales divided by $10 million of quota). High-performing sales managers averaged an 81 percent team effectiveness factor, while underperforming sales managers averaged 55 percent. One explanation for this significant difference is that high-performing sales managers have a wider range of coaching adaptability.

7. *Strategic leadership.* All sales leaders are battlefield commanders who must devise the organization's sales strategy to defeat the competition. This requires plotting the best course of action to maximize revenue using the most cost-effective sales model. Great sales leaders possess the knowledge to correctly deploy field or inside salespeople, to segment the market into verticals, and to specialize sales teams by product or customer types when

necessary. This helps explain why there was a 51 percent quota performance gap between high-performing and underperforming sales leaders. High-performing sales leaders reported an overall average annual quota attainment of 105 percent compared to 54 percent for underperforming sales managers.

In addition, 77 percent of high-performing sales managers rated their sales organization as excellent or above average compared to 57 percent of underperforming sales managers. Conversely, 43 percent of underperforming sales managers rated their sales organization as average or below average compared to only 24 percent of high-performing sales managers. Simply put, high-performing sales leaders are strategists who build high-performing sales organizations.

Secondary Attributes

The following secondary attributes also play a key role:

- *Political acumen.* One of sales leaders' key functions is to represent the needs of their department and promote important causes to the rest of the company. Deftly understanding the inner workings of their company and knowing how to get initiatives accomplished is an attribute of the best sales leaders. They do not bully other parts of their organization such as marketing, support, or engineering. They tactfully promote their causes internally and know which battles to fight.

- *Inquisitive nature.* The best sales leaders are natural-born investigators. They use their diagnostic questioning skills to ascertain their salespeople's deal knowledge and account standing so they can accurately forecast future revenue. Top sales leaders forecast per their conscience. Regardless of whether they are having a good or bad quarter, they tell it like it is.

- *Information scalability.* Sales leaders are bombarded with a relentless stream of information. Top sales leaders are multitaskers who quickly assess the value and prioritize a wide variety of subjective information, facts, and numbers. They are able to see the big picture while still retaining precise details about important deals. They filter out inconsequential data and distill the complexity surrounding sales situations into actionable directions.

- *Fluid communication.* Top sales leaders are in constant communication with their direct subordinates, bosses, and peers from other areas of the company. They don't wait to hear from someone. Rather, they proactively reach out in order to get a pulse on the situation. In particular, the best vice presidents of sales have extraordinary rapport with the CFO and executive team.

- *Charismatic persona.* Great sales leaders have charismatic personas that motivate individual and team performance through the leaders' emotional, spiritual, and physical presence. They bond with their salespeople through like-minded, empathetic identification about the performance of a job that can be difficult and downright frustrating. They are able to celebrate successes and commiserate about losses. They provide affirmation that the salespeople are part of something larger and more important than themselves.

- *Moral compass.* The behavior of the sales department will closely mirror the conduct of its sales leader. The best sales leaders have an established code of conduct based upon ethical behavior, individual accountability, and a sense of duty to the company and sales organization. They show the direction their moral compass points daily.

- *Ambitious drive.* The desire to attain more responsibility and grow in power is common among top sales leaders. They want to grow their sphere of influence and feel they are equipped to lead the entire organization someday. Ultimately, they seek to become the best and leave a legacy that is long remembered.

- *Product consciousness.* While some types of sales require deep expertise, the best sales leaders are rarely the most product knowledgeable or technically proficient. Rather, they are "product conscious," whereby they understand the product portfolio and know how to apply their knowledge about the customer's business environment in order to direct their team.

- *Fiscal prudence.* The sales leader is the fiscal hall monitor of the sales organization. Top sales leaders spend the company's money wisely, as if it were their own.

It's also important to note that high-performing sales managers had higher quota risk pool factors than underperforming sales managers. A sales manager's quota risk pool factor is calculated by adding together all the quotas of the salespeople who report to the manager and dividing the sum by the manager's quota. For example, a sales manager with a $10 million quota who manages ten salespeople with $2 million quotas would have a quota risk pool factor of two.

The sales organization is unique and unlike any other department of a company. The best sales organizations have strong leaders who exercise control and establish the code of behavior that all team members must abide by. They employ their experiences to determine a strategic direction and coach team members individually. Most importantly, they know how to keep the team on track and focused on winning.

Chapter 6. High-Performing Salespeople

What separates high-performing salespeople who exceed their quota from underperformers who miss their quotas by more than 25 percent? Recent research I conducted along with information gleaned from over one thousand interviews with top salespeople provide interesting insights on this topic.

1. *Verbal acuity.* Verbal acuity can be thought of as a communication level where the meaning, nature, and importance of the words spoken by the salesperson are personally understood by the customer. For a salesperson to establish credibility, messages need to be conveyed at the recipient's communication level, not too far below the level of the words that the customer uses. On average, high-performing salespeople communicate between the eleventh and thirteenth grade level when scored by the Flesch-Kincaid test (see ch. 126) as opposed to the eighth and ninth grade level for underperforming salespeople.

2. *Achievement-oriented personality.* Eighty-four percent of the top performers tested scored very high in achievement orientation. They are fixated on achieving goals and continuously measure their performance in comparison to their goals. Another interesting statistic is that over 85 percent of top salespeople played an individual or team sport in high school. As a result, they are well-equipped to function in competitive environments where self-discipline is a necessity. For example, 52 percent of high-performing salespeople indicated they were power users who take full advantage of their company's CRM technology and internal systems compared to only 31 percent of underperforming salespeople.

3. *Situational dominance.* Situational dominance is a personal interaction strategy by which the customer accepts the salesperson's recommendations and follows his advice. While dominance is commonly associated with brute force, this is not the case in sales. It's simply how people judge others. People are continually sensing whether their position is superior to yours, relatively equal,

or inferior in some way. In turn, this impacts what they say during conversations and how they behave.

A relaxed dominant salesperson speaks freely and guides the conversation as he confidently shares his knowledge and opinions with the customer. An anxious submissive salesperson is forced into reactive behavior, and his tendency is to operate under the direction of the customer, never being in control of the account. Situational dominance test scores of high-performing salespeople averaged 20 percent higher than those of underperforming salespeople.

4. *Inward pessimism.* Over 90 percent of high-performing and underperforming salespeople described themselves as optimists. However, upon further review, I found nearly two-thirds of high-performing salespeople actually exhibit pessimistic personality tendencies. I theorize the explanation for this dichotomy is that salespeople always have to maintain a positive attitude and pleasant demeanor while in front of customers. However, inward pessimism drives a salesperson to question the viability of the deal and credibility of the buyer. Therefore, top salespeople are more naturally driven to ask the customer tougher qualifying questions and are more likely to seek out meetings with senior-level decision-makers who ultimately decide which vendor will be selected.

5. *Sales management impact.* Does a salesperson's manager play a determining factor in achieving success? Study participants were asked whether or not they agreed with the statement, "Outside of setting my quota, my sales manager plays a key role in determining whether or not I make quota." The response from high performers and underperformers was identical. Forty-six percent agreed with the statement and 54 percent were neutral or disagreed with it. However, sixty-nine percent of high-performing salespeople rated their sales manager as excellent or above average compared to 49 percent of underperforming salespeople, indicating there is a correlation between the quality of sales management and quota performance.

Study participants were also asked to rank the attributes of great sales managers. In order of priority, the top three factors for high-performing salespeople were leadership and management skills, practical experience and sales intuition, and communication and coaching skills. The top three factors for underperforming salespeople were industry expertise and product knowledge, communication and coaching skills, and fighting for the team. These results reveal how high-performing and underperforming salespeople utilize their managers differently. Underperformers tend to use their managers to make up for the product and industry knowledge they lack.

Both high-performing and underperforming salespeople are in contact with their sales managers at about the same frequency. For example, 51 percent of high-performing salespeople and 55 percent of underperforming salespeople are in contact with their sales manager all the time during the day. Twenty-eight percent of high-performing salespeople and 20 percent of underperforming are in contact with their manager frequently during the week, while 15 percent of high-performing and 17 percent of underperformers talk to their managers once or twice a week. However, the conversations sales leaders have with top salespeople are quite different from those with underperformers. They are collaborative strategizing sessions about prospective deals while the conversations with underperformers consist of giving directional instructions and validating whether or not daily duties are being carried out.

6. *Sales organization influence.* The research suggests that sales organization morale influences individual sales success. Fifty-three percent of high-performing salespeople rated their sales organization's morale as being higher than most sales organizations'. In comparison, only 37 percent of underperforming salespeople rated their organization's morale higher than most companies'.

Sales organization accountability also influences individual quota achievement. Thirty-nine percent of high-performing salespeople strongly agreed that salespeople at their company are measured against their quota and held accountable compared to only 23 percent of underperforming salespeople. In comparison, 36 percent of underperforming salespeople either disagreed or were neutral about whether salespeople at their company were

measured and held accountable compared to 21 percent of high-performing salespeople.

Finally, the study results indicate that individual sales success is not dependent upon the growth rate of the company the salesperson works for. The percentage of high-performing salespeople was consistent with the percentage of underperforming salespeople across high-growth companies (over 20 percent annual growth), slower-growth companies (5 to 20 percent growth rate), companies with flat revenues, and even companies with decreasing revenues. When all the research above is taken into account, sales performance is more likely dependent on the attributes of the individual and sales environment characteristics than on company-related influences.

Exercise: Take the sales persona test in chapter 92 and compare your answers against those of top salespeople.

Chapter 7. High-Performing Inside Salespeople

I conducted a study to analyze the top factors that differentiate high-performing inside salespeople from underperforming inside salespeople. Nearly two hundred inside salespeople participated in a comprehensive sales performance study by completing an extensive forty-two-question survey. The study goals were to gather quantitative and qualitative information on individual sales performance. Participants were asked to share their opinions and personal details about their own quota performance.

Salespeople were asked to identify what type of salesperson they were and whom they called on. Thirty-nine percent indicated they were "hunters" calling on new accounts. Four percent were "farmers" who were responsible for sales to existing install base clients. Fifty-three percent indicated they were both hunters and farmers. Four percent selected none of the above.

Twenty-six percent of survey participants said they met or exceeded their annual quota last year and were classified as high performers. Forty percent met between 76 percent and 99 percent of their quota and were classified as average performers. Thirty-four percent met 75 percent or less of their quota and were classified as underperformers.

Sales Culture Impacts Performance

An organization's prevailing sales culture can have a significant impact on the performance of its sales team. Thirty-three percent of high-performing inside salespeople rated their sales organization as excellent compared to 21 percent of underperforming inside salespeople. Conversely, 29 percent of underperforming inside salespeople rated their team as average or below average compared to only 19 percent of high-performing inside salespeople.

Sales organization accountability also influences individual quota achievement. Fifty percent of high-performing inside salespeople strongly agreed that salespeople at their company are measured against their quota and held accountable, compared to only 26 percent of underperforming salespeople.

Study participants were asked to rank the importance of different factors in determining whether salespeople achieve their annual quota or not as shown in figure 7.1. Overall, underperformers seem to place greater value on hard work, while high performers place greater value on softer skills and working smarter, not necessarily harder-to-meet quotas.

Impact of Sales Leadership

High-performing inside salespeople rate the quality of their sales leaders more

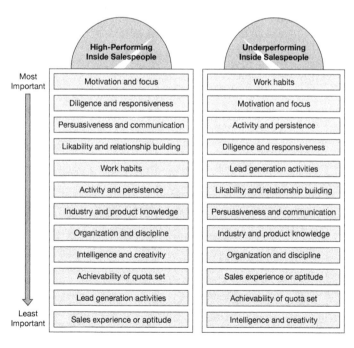

Figure 7.1 Prioritized factors that determine whether inside salespeople make quota

highly. Twenty-six percent of high-performing inside salespeople rate their sales manager as excellent compared to only 10 percent of underperforming inside salespeople. Conversely, 52 percent of underperforming inside salespeople rate their sales manager as average or below average compared to 34 percent of high-performing inside salespeople.

High-performing inside salespeople value different attributes of great sales managers. The biggest difference between high performers and under-performers was their ranking of "practical experience and sales intuition" and "industry expertise and product knowledge" as shown in figure 7.2. High performers ranked practical experience and sales intuition as the most important attribute and industry expertise and product knowledge as the fifth most important attribute, while underperformers believed the opposite, swapping the rankings of those two attributes.

High-performing inside salespeople have a different perception about the impact their sales managers have on their ability to make quota. When salespeople were asked to validate if their sales manager plays a key role in determining whether or not they make quota, 57 percent of high performers strongly agreed or agreed with the statement compared to 34 percent of underperforming inside salespeople. In comparison, 66 percent of underperforming inside salespeople were neutral or disagreed with the statement as opposed to 43 percent of high-performing inside salespeople.

Four Personal Attributes of High-Performing Inside Salespeople

Here are four key personal attributes of high-performing inside salespeople based upon the research results.

1. *High-performing inside salespeople are more likely to be power users of their company's internal systems.* Fifty-six percent of high-performing inside salespeople indicated they were power users who take full advantage of their company's technology and internal systems compared to 34 percent of underperforming inside salespeople. In comparison, 62 percent of underperforming salespeople said they are knowledgeable about their company's internal systems compared to 44 percent of high-performing salespeople. Four percent of underperformers and no high performers said they only use their company's technology and internal systems because they have to.

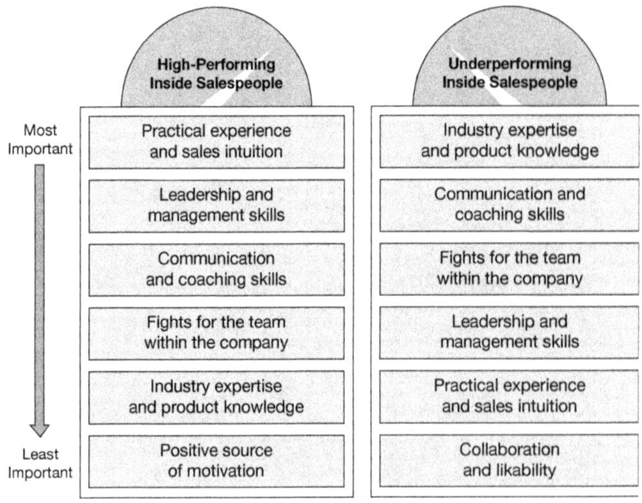

High-Performing Inside Salespeople	Underperforming Inside Salespeople
Practical experience and sales intuition	Industry expertise and product knowledge
Leadership and management skills	Communication and coaching skills
Communication and coaching skills	Fights for the team within the company
Fights for the team within the company	Leadership and management skills
Industry expertise and product knowledge	Practical experience and sales intuition
Positive source of motivation	Collaboration and likability

Figure 7.2 Inside salespeople rank attributes of great sales managers

2. *High-performing inside salespeople are in more frequent contact with their sales managers.* Eighty-seven percent of high performers and 70 percent of underperformers are in contact with their sales manager all the time throughout the day or frequently, multiple times a week. Thirty percent of underperforming inside salespeople are in contact with their sales manager once or twice a week or a couple of times a month compared to only 13 percent of high-performing inside salespeople.

3. *When competing for new accounts, high-performing inside salespeople lose business earlier in the sales cycle.* Sixty-eight percent of high-performing inside salespeople indicated they were most likely to lose a deal early in the sales cycle compared to 54 percent of underperforming inside salespeople. Conversely, 23 percent of underperformers and 9 percent of high performers said they were more likely to lose a deal near the end of the sales cycle.

   One interpretation of these results is that high-performing salespeople know they can work on only a finite number of deals, so they must pursue well-qualified accounts. Therefore, they actually want to lose earlier in the sales cycle so they are free to pursue more new, higher potential deals. Losing at the end of a sales cycle is a greater waste of valuable time, resources, and emotional energy.

4. *High-performing inside salespeople are more likely to find a balance in their use of social media and are more likely to know when the use of social media may not be necessary.* It may be surprising to many that power users of social media are more likely to be underperforming inside salespeople (18 percent) than high-performing inside salespeople (11 percent). On the other hand, average users of social media are more likely to be high performers than underperformers. The social media hype may be causing some salespeople to spend too much time in social channels and not enough time selling.

Chapter 8. Sales Management Styles

The structure and effectiveness of the sales department will mirror the sales management style of its leaders. This is because sales leaders naturally imprint themselves on their organization. Therefore, it can be argued that the vice president of sales is the most important person within a company because he is in charge of its most critical assets: customers and the revenue they generate.

Each vice president of sales has a unique personality. Some are gregarious. Some are assertive. Some are action oriented. But even with their individual differences, they have recognizable patterns of behavior, which have allowed me to catalog their styles of sales management.

I have found that seven management styles are most prevalent: mentor, expressive, sergeant, Teflon, micromanager, overconfident, and amateur. Most likely, a sales leader will use several different management styles and move from one style to another depending on the situation.

To better understand these management styles, I asked vice presidents of sales from leading companies to estimate what percentage of their time they used a particular style and then rank the applicability of the style to their success in their role on a scale of 1 (least important) to 5 (most important). Figure 8.1 is a summary chart of the findings, showing the average results for the study group. A description of each style follows.

Management style	Percent time used	Importance ranking 1 (low) to 5 (high)
Mentor	26%	4.3
Expressive	30%	4.0
Sergeant	18%	3.2
Teflon	10%	2.0
Micromanager	7%	3.3
Overconfident	6%	1.8
Amateur	3%	1.0

Figure 8.1 Sales management styles usage and rating

Mentor

Mentors are charismatic leaders and sales experts who measure their success using three criteria: exceeding revenue goals, creating an environment where the entire team can succeed, and helping all team members realize their individual potential. Mentors are confident in their own abilities and possess the business insight to know what needs to be done and how to do it. On average, study participants reported they used the mentor management style 26 percent of the time. As a driver of success, they gave mentor management style the highest ranking of all the styles at 4.3.

Expressive

Expressive managers are people oriented with a flair for sharing their emotions and amplifying the emotions of those around them. They have a natural ability to put people at ease but are also quite comfortable extolling or admonishing the team. Expressive managers create an environment where a considerable amount of energy is focused on how their organization is thought of and perceived within the company. Study participants indicated they used the expressive style 30 percent of the time and ranked the style's importance at 4.

Sergeant

The sergeant is named after the field sergeant in a military organization. Sergeants develop an intense loyalty to their team, perhaps even greater than their personal loyalty to their company. They are hard workers who are constantly worrying about their "troops." They will even sacrifice their own best interests and tolerate personal hardships if they feel it will benefit their team. The sergeant management style was used 18 percent of the time, and its importance was ranked at 3.2.

Teflon

Teflon managers are pleasant, agreeable, and polite people. However, unlike sergeants, they tend not to have deep personal relationships with their sales team members. Another characteristic of Teflon managers is their ability to stay above the daily fray of politics. Regardless of the situation, Teflon managers are even keeled and rarely frazzled. The Teflon management style was used 10 percent of the time and its importance was ranked at 2.

Micromanager

Micromanagers are the most organized and methodical of all management types.

They have a strong sense of responsibility to their company, and they pride themselves on achieving their revenue goals. They tend to be all-or-nothing thinkers who want things done their way. The micromanager style was used 7 percent of the time and its importance was ranked at 3.3.

Overconfident

Overconfident managers tend to be more self-centered. They are charming and gregarious in public and excellent on sales calls. They tend not to be open to feedback and will get the job done their way and succeed at any cost. The overconfident management style was used 6 percent of the time and its importance was ranked at 1.8.

Amateur

The amateur management style is not necessarily reflective of someone new to sales management. Rather, the style reflects that the person is outside of his comfort zone in a new management role, working with an unfamiliar product at a new company, or in a new industry. As a result, his management style may suffer an identity crisis until he is able to build back his practical sales experience. Study participants indicated they experienced the amateur management style 3 percent of the time and ranked the style's importance at 1.

in the compete stage requires a different skill set than leading a large billion-dollar sales organization in the maintain stage. Culling an inefficient organization requires a specific management style. Nowhere is the sales leader's impact greater than in start-ups, where the vice president of sales must single-handedly build the sales model, recruit the team, and personally persuade customers to buy.

Your Sales Manager Is Your Most Important Customer

Have you ever worked for a sales manager who made you feel uncomfortable? Even though you consistently made your number, you never seemed to earn your manager's respect. Although you made many attempts to improve your relationship, they were all met with indifference. Your sales manager can make your life enjoyable, tolerable, or miserable, and your mental condition is profoundly influenced by this critical relationship. Understanding your sales manager's management style is the key to winning over this crucial person—because your sales manager is your most important customer.

Each of the seven management styles builds a different sales environment because managers hire their "type" of salespeople and establish a culture based upon their belief system and personality. Figure 8.2 lists the seven sales

Which management style is best? This depends upon the sales organization's stage of development. Running a medium-sized $50 million sales department

Management style	Sales force composition	Cultural characteristics
Mentor	Scholarly students	Investigative, consultative
Expressive	Empathetic egomaniacs	Me first, bravado
Sergeant	Sincere soldiers	Loyal, obedient
Teflon	Patient Pollyannas	Optimistic, nice guys and gals
Micromanager	Perfect performers	Repetitive-task orientation
Overconfident	Clever conquerors	Win at any cost
Amateur	Schizophrenic salespeople	Unpredictable, unlikable

Figure 8.2 Sales force culture types

management styles and the characteristics of the sales force environment they create.

Obviously, the cultures a mentor and a micromanager create are different from each other. If you worked for a mentor and suddenly found yourself working for a micromanager, you would have to adapt to a completely different style. Conversely, a mentor doesn't have the same priorities or thought processes as a micromanager. You would lose credibility with a mentor if you treated him like a micromanager. You should implement a strategy to build a long-term relationship based upon your sales manager's style. Let's examine each of the sales management styles and strategies to manage the relationship.

Working with the Mentor Manager

Mentors are confident in their own abilities and possess the business insight to know what needs to be done and how to do it. They believe in accountability and a strict code of ethical conduct, relate well with their team, and motivate by positive encouragement rather than fear. They are comfortable with themselves and are able to maintain perspective and a sense of resolution during tenuous times.

Mentors' philosophy is an extension of their personality. While their demeanor may range from gruff and cantankerous to friendly and personable, they are well liked and act as a unifying force to their sales team members. Although mentors tend to have a very hands-on management style, they don't typically meddle in their team's daily duties. They lead by example instead.

Salespeople want to learn everything they can from mentors, so they adopt a strategy based on being a "scholarly student." They invite their mentors on calls, quiz them about tactics over lunch, or chat with them after hours about their sales experiences. They also extend this strategy to their customers. They want to understand what makes customers tick and the problems they are trying to solve and to befriend them. This becomes the culture of the organization.

Working with the Expressive Manager

Expressive managers are very charming and gregarious individuals who are always ready, willing, and able to discuss personal matters in addition to events at work. They enjoy attention and can be overdramatic, either exaggerating their accomplishments or overstating the prevailing circumstances their team is facing. It could be argued that these "sympathy complaints" are subconscious attempts to secure comfort and affection. Because of their need for constant emotional approval, they can become jealous when others receive recognition.

The long-term strategy to shape the relationship with expressive managers is called "empathetic ego." Empathizing with expressive managers requires sharing their experiences through unselfish listening and continual confirmation that you understand the situation or dilemma. Expressive managers experience tremendous highs and lows; participating in the celebration of the good times is just as important as commiserating during the bad.

A key aspect of the strategy involves protecting expressive managers' egos by supporting their position and validating their worth to others within and outside the sales group. One of the biggest insults to any manager, and expressive ones in particular, is being contradicted in public. Conversely, announcing their successes and broadcasting compliments will yield relationship rewards.

Working with the Sergeant Manager

Sergeants are likable, reliable people who have an intense pride in their work. They have a humble demeanor and will unselfishly pass any praise they receive directly to the team. They wear their emotions on their sleeves, and their team members always know where they stand. While they understand their place in the organization and are confident of their own ability, they still feel somewhat expendable and may suffer from self-doubt. They do not accept criticism easily and will take faultfinding to heart. However, sergeants are typically some of the last people to leave a failing company and may have a history of staying with companies long after the good times have passed.

The strategy for building a successful relationship with a sergeant is based upon "straightforward sincerity." Since sergeants are tell-it-like-it-is people, the communication with them should be open, honest, and candid. For example, sergeants want to know the bad news as soon as possible and don't appreciate it being sugarcoated.

Working with the Teflon Manager

Teflon managers are pleasant, agreeable, and polite people. However, unlike sergeants, you may never really get to know Teflon managers, even after working with them for years. They avoid disclosing personal information or give just enough to be thought of as friendly. From this standpoint, some people will consider them superficial. Another characteristic of Teflon managers is their ability to stay above the daily fray of politics. Yet while they seem cooperative, they are usually very stubborn when it comes to their personal agenda.

Regardless of the situation, Teflon managers are even-keeled and rarely frazzled. They always seem to be in control of their emotions and relate to others mainly in an edited, business demeanor. You will not find these people yelling in the office, and they rarely socialize or develop personal friendships with coworkers. They will share their honest feelings only when there is little personal risk and if sharing this information benefits their business position.

Nothing sticks to Teflon managers. Bad news that would devastate sergeants or expressive managers bounces off them. Teflon managers just keep moving forward and never seem to be depressed or to give up. They enjoy prestige and title and act the part accordingly.

Working for Teflon managers creates an interesting dichotomy because of their personal nonattachment, comfort with solitude, idealized self-image, and desire to remain safe from criticism. Therefore, employ a "patient Pollyanna" strategy to dovetail with these Teflon manager characteristics. Exude a cheerful, pleasant disposition to communicate that everything is okay, even under dire circumstances. Adopt a "politically correct" demeanor, rarely making cynical statements and repressing any open display of anger or disrespect to others. Patience and temperance are virtues Teflon managers appreciate.

Working with the Micromanager

Micromanagers tend to be black-and-white, all-or-nothing thinkers who want things done their way. They may have laboriously created methodical processes for every aspect of their job, most likely having used these same processes at previous companies. Their endless stream of formal and informal regulations sometimes distracts salespeople from achieving results. They tend to hire people who they know will carry out their instructions to the letter, and even though a team member may achieve success, they will criticize that person if it wasn't done their way.

When working with micromanagers, adopt a long-term strategy based upon their concept of the "perfect performance" of an efficient, industrious, and competent salesperson. Working efficiently equals being organized in the mind of a micromanager. Industriousness is akin to a single-minded, business-only attitude toward the job as evidenced by working long hours. A competent salesperson will complete tasks using the established processes. In addition, a constant flow of information is critical to ensure a smoothly functioning world; therefore, overcommunicate by staying in constant touch.

Working with the Overconfident Manager

Overconfident managers are on the opposite end of the humility spectrum from sergeants. They tend to be self-centered and self-absorbed. While charming and gregarious in public, they rarely have deep relationships in private.

Overconfident managers just love to talk about themselves and don't exhibit a great depth of feeling for others. They may boast of past successes and frequently recount stories about these achievements, regardless of whether someone may have heard them before. Not surprisingly, arrogance makes them susceptible to judgmental mistakes. They also enjoy being the life of the party and know how to make any party an unforgettable event. They are typically flashier dressers and very concerned with their appearance.

They will receive strong reactions when they participate in sales situations. Some customers will absolutely love them, while others will have an equally strong opposite reaction. Similarly, overconfident managers will not relate equally well with all members of the team. Rather, they will have a few favorites who resemble them.

They are not open to feedback and are known to get quite defensive when criticized. They will get the job done their way and succeed at any cost. Although they are not exemplary planners, their sheer drive and tenacity make them well suited for roles where they have to launch a new product line or a new company.

Overconfident managers build a sales team of fighting gladiators who possess extraordinary willpower, mental toughness, animated spirit, and intelligence. To be included in this team, Heavy Hitters adopt the "clever conqueror" long-term strategy.

To be a conqueror, you must attack your enemies, be comfortable fighting for the cause, and be unafraid of rankling people in the process because the end justifies the means. You also cannot expose any weakness, such as fear, self-doubt, sadness, or embarrassment. Only the attacker can be victorious; at best, the defender will merely survive.

Working with the Amateur Manager

Amateur managers are the toughest of all the types to work with. While they may make a great first impression, analogous to a great first date, each subsequent date becomes more painful and frustrating. Amateur managers most likely do not have an extensive day-to-day background in sales, are very new to sales management, or lack the ability or temperament to manage a sales force.

Amateur managers fear being judged negatively by their superiors and peers, as well as their subordinates. Therefore, they may perceive the company as unfriendly or hostile. Their fears may also play an interesting part in their decision process. Under stress they become worried and indecisive or they propose so many different solutions that nothing ever happens. Or they may create outlandish plans and elaborate schemes that can't possibly be implemented in the real world. The mood of the sales department is schizophrenic and changes from moment to moment. Sometimes there is cheerful permissiveness, and other times the department is run with iron-fisted authority.

The strategy for working with amateur managers is the opposite of the strategies for all the other management styles. Instead of investing in and building the relationship, you actually search for a way to be released or escape from it. This strategy for liberation from the amateur manager is called "release relationship."

Several different methods can be used to be released from the relationship.

Heavy Hitters could ask for a transfer or reassignment, seek a promotion, quit, or be fired. Each of these is perfectly acceptable. You may be asking yourself, Being fired is acceptable? Absolutely. Heavy Hitters know time is short and do not want to waste their lives. They want to surround themselves with successful people they respect. They have the confidence to stand up for themselves and what they believe in.

Exercise: What style of sales leader do you work for? Do you work for an expressive manager? Is your manager equal parts mentor and overconfident manager? Consider these important points when determining why your relationship with your manager isn't working.

Chapter 9. How Compensation Impacts Sales Organization Performance

Salespeople and sales leaders alike know that compensation can be a strong motivator, but it usually comes at a high budgetary cost. This leads many to ask what the real impact of compensation might be on overall sales professionals' satisfaction and performance.

Top-level sales leaders and sales managers were asked to categorize their company's compensation compared to the compensation of other companies within their industry. Twenty-eight percent indicated their company's compensation was higher than market average, 60 percent were at market average, and 12 percent were below market average

Sales leaders, how does your company's compensation compare to others' within your industry?

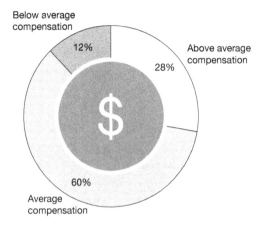

Figure 9.1 Sales leaders categorize their company's compensation

as shown in figure 9.1. Each category of compensation was then analyzed from a number of different perspectives to determine the impact of compensation

Compensation Is Associated with Sales Organization Excellence

Forty percent of sales leaders at companies that compensate above market average rated their sales organization as excellent compared to 16 percent at average compensation and 8 percent at below average market compensation companies. Conversely, 57 percent of sales leaders at companies that compensate below market average rated their sales organization as average or below average compared to 34 percent at average compensation and only 16 percent at above average market compensation companies as shown in figure 9.2.

Thirty-eight percent of salespeople who sell for above market compensation companies rated their sales leadership as excellent compared to only 2 percent of salespeople at below average market compensation companies. Conversely, 22 percent of salespeople at below average market compensation companies rated their sales leadership as below average compared to only 4 percent of salespeople at above average market compensation companies.

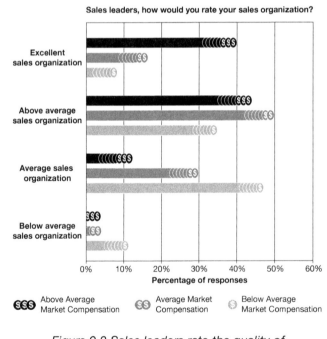

Figure 9.2 Sales leaders rate the quality of their sales organization

on sales organization performance.

Sales Organization Morale Is Directly Tied to Compensation

Sixty-six percent of sales leaders at above average market compensation companies rated the morale across their sales organization as excellent compared to only 21 percent at below average market compensation companies. Conversely, 27 percent of sales leaders at below average market compensation companies rated morale as below average compared to only 4 percent at above average market compensation companies.

Compensation Impacts Sales Organization Culture

Thirty-seven percent of sales leaders at above average market compensation companies described their sales organization as "a cohesive group of like-minded individuals" compared to only 23 percent at below average market compensation companies. Conversely, 42 percent of sales leaders at below average market compensation companies described their sales organization as "a loose collection of individuals" compared to 23 percent of sales leaders at above average market compensation companies.

Companies Where Compensation Was Not Capped Reported Higher Quota Attainment Rates

Seventy-nine percent of sales managers reported achieving their annual quota last year at companies where compensation was not capped compared to 72 percent of sales leaders at companies where compensation was capped. Fifty-one percent of salespeople achieved their annual sales quota at companies

where compensation was not capped compared to 48 percent at companies where compensation was capped. When the impact of capping compensation is analyzed for all study participants, the results suggest companies that achieved lower percentages of their revenue targets were more likely to cap compensation.

The study results substantiate that different sales force compensation strategies can greatly impact the performance and quality of sales organizations. Decisions about whether to cap compensation and whether to pay the sales force above market average, at market average, or below market average can have a substantial effect on revenue growth, company excellence, quality of sales leadership, morale, culture, and quota attainment.

Chapter 10. Research Reveals the Best Sales Forecasters

Predicting the future is difficult, if not near impossible. However, salespeople and their managers are asked to forecast the future all the time. Sales forecasting is an art and a science. It is the combination of metrics, qualitative information, intuition, and best practices. So who are the most accurate sales forecasters, and what separates them from the least reliable? A study of the forecasting habits of more than 350 B2B salespeople and sales managers was conducted to answer this question.

The study results suggest there are three basic types of forecasters:

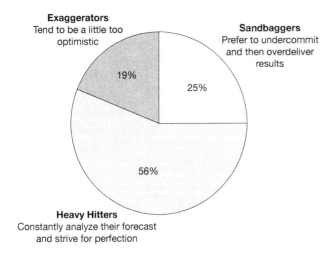

Figure 10.1 Categories of sales forecasters

exaggerators, sandbaggers, and Heavy Hitters. As shown in figure 10.1, 19 percent of the study participants were classified as exaggerators, who are overly optimistic forecasters. They tend to interpret information in their favor. For example, if a customer says, "We understand your product, so there's no reason for you to demonstrate it," exaggerators will interpret this as a positive sign, even though all the other vendors are demonstrating their products.

Exaggerators are happy-ear forecasters who take customers' words at face value. When asked why they have forecasted a particular deal to close, they will say, "The customer told us he likes our solution." They seem to have forgotten the old adage that "all buyers are liars." Exaggerators may also continually paint the future as being incredibly bright. While this quarter might not look so good, the next one is always going to be fantastic.

Twenty-five percent of the participants were categorized as sandbaggers, secretive forecasters who try to get by giving as little information as possible on

the forecast. They figure the less information they give, the less exposure they have to upper management's analysis of their forecast and the associated deal-inspection questions.

Fifty-six percent of the participants were classified as Heavy Hitters, who forecast according to their conscience. They constantly analyze their forecast and strive for perfection. Regardless of whether they will have a good quarter or a bad quarter, they tell it like it is. They ignore the braggadocian, hyped-up forecasts of their teammates and consider it a personal obligation to be honest to themselves, their managers, and their company.

Forecasting accuracy is directly related to the time and effort the forecaster spends calculating, revising, and confirming the forecast during the quarter. Thirty-two percent of the study participants spend one to ten hours on average updating their quarterly forecast, 38 percent spend eleven to twenty-five hours, and 30 percent spend more than twenty-six hours. Heavy Hitter forecasters spend twice as much time updating their forecast during the quarter as exaggerators on average.

Forecasting accuracy varies during the year. For example, 33 percent of forecasts were below the actual revenue number achieved in the first quarter compared to 23 percent in the fourth quarter. Forty-one percent of forecasts were very close to the actual revenue number achieved in the first quarter as compared to 44 percent in the fourth quarter. Twenty-six percent of the forecasts

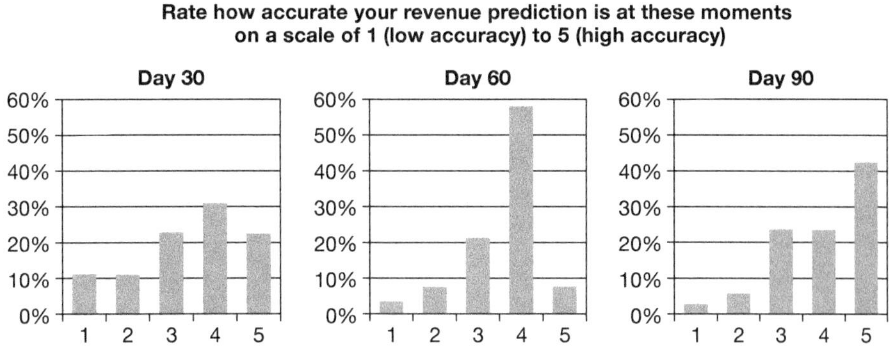

**Rate how accurate your revenue prediction is at these moments
on a scale of 1 (low accuracy) to 5 (high accuracy)**

Figure 10.2 Forecasting accuracy during a typical quarter

were above the actual revenue number achieved in the first quarter as compared to 33 percent in fourth quarter.

Forecasting accuracy also varies greatly during the quarter as shown in figure 10.2. Study participants were asked to rate how accurate their forecast was at key moments during a quarter on a scale of 1 to 5 with 5 being the highest level of accuracy.

Perhaps the most fascinating part of the study was identifying who the most accurate forecasters are. The participants who rated their accuracy as a 5 or a 1 at day thirty ended the quarter with the exact same forecast accuracy of 3.3 on average. Those who rated their accuracy as a 4 ended the quarter at 3.7, while those at 3 ended at 4.4 on average. Meanwhile, the highest accuracy forecasters were those who rated their accuracy as a 2 on day thirty: their accuracy level on average was 4.8 at the end of the quarter as shown in figure 10.3.

What impact do logic and intuition have on forecasting accuracy? Study participants were asked to explain what percentage of their forecast was based upon logic versus intuition. The results indicated that two groups are the most inaccurate forecasters. The least accurate forecasters base their forecasting on 40 percent or less logic and 60 percent or more intuition and 80 percent or more logic and 20 percent or less intuition. Conversely, the most accurate forecasters base their forecast on 50 to 70 percent logic and 30 to 50 percent intuition.

Preparing a complete, accurate forecast is more than a chore that comes with being in sales; it's actually proof that you belong in sales. The best forecasters are Heavy Hitters who use a calculated measure of logic and intuition to predict the future. They spend more time than their counterparts ensuring that their forecasts are correct and cautiously

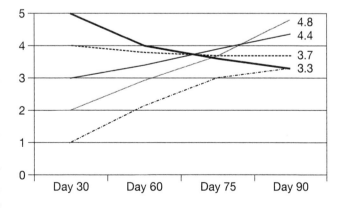

Figure 10.3 Forecast accuracy trends during quarter

approach each quarter being careful not to overcommit and thereby ruin their reputation.

Chapter 11. Statistical Proof You Need a Sales Mentor

Inexperienced salespeople don't know what they haven't seen for themselves. Usually, they gain their experience through the school of hard knocks. Unfortunately, this takes time. But if they emulate a successful practitioner, this time frame can be shortened and the predictability of results can be improved.

A sales mentor's sales intuition has been honed by many years of customer calls; therefore, the mentor's judgment is respected and advice highly sought after. However, in a typical sales organization, role modeling occurs very informally and irregularly. If the sales organization is truly a mentor-based environment, what percentage of salespeople have had sales mentors?

A research study of sales professionals provides the answer to this question. The study results indicate that 54 percent of men and 59 percent of women had a significant sales mentor in their life whom they wanted to emulate or impress. Conversely, 27 percent of men and 28 percent of women did not as shown in figure 11.1.

While the percentages for men and women were very similar, the impacts of having a mentor were quite different. (See chapter 129 for more details on how men and women sell differently.) The measurement of the previous year's average quota attainment shows the greatest impact is for women. Women who had a sales mentor outperformed their counterparts who did not have mentors across the board: vice presidents of sales by 34 percent on average, midlevel sales managers by 3 percent, field sales reps by 29 percent, and inside salespeople by 51 percent. Men experienced positive but lesser results overall: vice presidents of sales who had mentors outperformed their nonmentored counterparts by 12 percent, midlevel sales managers by 16 percent, and field sales reps by 10 percent. The only exception was for male inside sales reps, who were 11 percent below their counterparts as shown in figure 11.2.

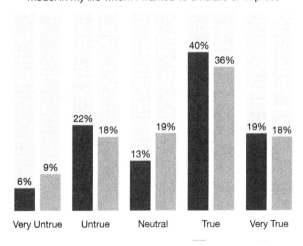

I had a significant sales mentor or sales role model in my life whom I wanted to emulate or impress

Figure 11.1 Sales mentor by gender

These statistics provide direct proof of the benefit of having a sales mentor in your life. Being part of a sales force, you are surrounded by experienced sales experts day in, day out. Take the time to ask them questions and learn from them no matter how knowledgeable you are.

	Previous Year Annual Quota Achievement	
	Men	**Women**
Top-level vice presidents of sales		
No sales mentor	97%	81%
Had sales mentor	109%	115%
Quota Difference	+12%	+34%
Midlevel vice presidents of sales		
No sales mentor	97%	102%
Had sales mentor	113%	105%
Quota Difference	+16%	+3%
Field salespeople		
No sales mentor	100%	58%
Had sales mentor	110%	87%
Quota Difference	+10%	+29%
Inside salespeople		
No sales mentor	99%	86%
Had sales mentor	88%	137%
Quota Difference	−11%	+51%

Figure 11.2 Sales quota attainment by role and mentor

PART II

SALES CYCLE STRATEGY

Chapter 12. Seven Key Mistakes Salespeople Make According to Buyers

Pretend for a moment that you are an experienced buyer who has met with hundreds of business-to-business salespeople. What percentage of the salespeople you have met with over the past year would you say are excellent, good, average, or poor? According to a new study of over two hundred buyers, 12 percent of salespeople were rated excellent, 23 percent good, 38 percent average, and 27 percent poor.

Unfortunately, most underperforming salespeople don't take the time to figure out why they lost a deal or longtime client. They either don't know why they weren't selected or reflexively blame it on factors out of their control. The results from this buyer research provide seven important lessons about the mistakes salespeople make and why they lose business.

1. *They are not trusted or respected.* Customers can think of a salesperson as someone who is trying to sell something, a supplier with whom they do business, a strategic partner who is of significant importance to their business, or a trusted advisor whose advice is followed. Obviously, a trusted advisor enjoys significant advantages over the salespeople competing for the business. However, just 18 percent of the salespeople buyers met with over the past year would be classified as trusted advisors whom they respect.

2. *They can't converse effectively with the senior executives.* While salespeople will frequently meet with lower-level and midlevel personnel at the companies whose business they're trying to secure, the rare conversations they have with C-level decision-makers directly determine whether they win or lose the deal. Therefore, it is critical for salespeople to understand how C-level executives think and to communicate with them in the language they use. Unfortunately, buyers report that fewer than one out of three salespeople can hold an effective conversation with senior executives.

3. *They can't clearly explain how their solution positively impacts the buyer's business.* Buyers amass information that helps them justify their strategic decisions. In other words, a product's strategic value comprises the reasons and arguments buyers provide senior management and others in the company as to why the product should be purchased. Strategic values include increasing revenues, decreasing costs, gaining a competitive advantage, and standardizing operations in order to reduce risk. However, buyers say only 54 percent of salespeople can clearly explain how their solution impacts the buyer's business.

4. *They are too self-centered.* Study participants were asked to choose the primary reason they don't like meeting with salespeople. Their answers reveal that they feel pressured by self-centered salespeople. Forty-four percent believe salespeople are only serving their own agenda, while 25 percent indicated salespeople only care about making the sale. Twenty-three percent of buyers are uncomfortable because it is difficult to say no to salespeople and 8 percent said they're not the type of people they typically associate with. The lesson is clear: instead of focusing solely on revenue, salespeople should concentrate more on helping buyers accomplish their goals.

5. *They use the wrong closing strategy.* Study participants were presented with several closing techniques in order to understand how they would respond. Overall, hard close techniques, such as "This is the last time we'll be able to extend this offer and we need an answer now," were rated least effective. A hard close creates a binary yes-or-no response from the buyer and is associated with a "take it or leave it" mentality. Soft close techniques, such as "If you spend another $100,000 you will receive an additional 10 percent off the entire order," were rated most effective. A soft close is based on a suggestion that leads buyers to believe they are acting of their free will when in fact they have been directed to follow an action. Refer to chapter 70 on closing strategies for more details.

6. *They don't alleviate the risk of buying their solution.* B2B buyers are fixated on risk mitigation because they have been conditioned to be skeptical about salespeople based on past interactions. Therefore, they make vendors respond to immense RFPs (request for proposals), complete laborious evaluation spreadsheets, and document each product feature to prove it exists. The goal is to mitigate risk and reduce the uncertainty associated with selecting a vendor when making a purchase. One of the primary reasons a purchase isn't made after a lengthy evaluation is because the salesperson hasn't alleviated the risk of buying.

Study results show that the tolerance for risk fluctuates by department. For example, the average risk tolerance rate for IT department buyers was lowest at 5 (on a scale of 1 to 10, with 10 being the highest tolerance for risk). Accounting buyers had a 5.1 rating and engineering buyers a 5.5. Conversely, the average risk tolerance rate for marketing buyers was much higher at 7.1 (see ch. 18).

7. *They can't establish a personal connection with the buyer.* There is an equilibrium point where the buyer respects the salesperson's conviction and is not offended by his persistence, which enables the relationship to develop. Buyers cited five key reasons why "chemistry" is absent or a personal connection with a particular salesperson doesn't develop.

- The salesperson was too pushy

- There was a difference in communication styles

- The salesperson's personality was much different than mine

- The salesperson was too eager to befriend me

- There was a difference in age

Most salespeople are very comfortable selling to certain types of people. However, they're far less likely to establish rapport with someone who is wired far differently than themselves. Since they're not exactly sure how to behave, they act in a way the buyer considers too pushy, or they overcompensate by being too friendly.

It's not surprising that 81 percent of buyers indicated they would rather talk with someone who shares their same mannerisms. As a result, buyers will choose the salesperson with whom they develop rapport over others. Ultimately, a salesperson wants to become a communication chameleon. Just as the chameleon changes colors to match its surroundings, the salesperson's goal is to speak the buyer's languages (industry, technical, and job function) in order to change a skeptic into a believer.

Chapter 13. Top Reasons Salespeople Lose

Conducting win-loss studies and learning how product evaluators describe their selection process and why they made their final decision is always fascinating. One of the most interesting parts of these interviews is learning why the competing salespeople lost.

There's a tendency to assume that the losing salespeople lacked the sales prowess that the winner possessed or their product was inferior in some way. However, in the overwhelming majority of the interviews, the evaluators ranked all the competing salespeople and the feature sets of their products as being roughly equal. This suggests that other factors separate the winner from the losers, with some being out of the salesperson's control. These key factors are described below and accompanied by a corresponding win-loss study interview quote.

- *Incumbent advantage.* The incumbent vendor has a huge sales cycle advantage, and the tendency is to win business by default. Based upon my research, the odds of unseating an incumbent vendor are typically about one in five.

   It's a pain to switch vendors. It's a pain to analyze whether you should or not. We naturally prefer working with our existing vendors.

   —Vice President of Purchasing

- *Inability to remove risk.* Customers are never 100 percent sure they are purchasing the right product. Regardless of their confident demeanor, on the inside they experience fear, uncertainty, and doubt. The ability to remove perceived risk plays a key role in determining who wins the deal.

   It sorts itself out pretty fast—those who will and won't make it with us. We are a big company, so there's always a tendency to go with the big players. Who are your proven big-time customers? What resources do you have to get something fixed?

—Chief Operating Officer

- *Lack of C-level executive access.* Because every major purchase involves executive level approval, a salesperson's goal is to connect with a busy executive and conduct a meaningful face-to-face meeting. However, one of the toughest jobs in sales is to penetrate the C-suite, and there is a direct correlation of winning to the number of interactions the salesperson has with executives during the sales cycle.

  Every salesperson is trying to get into my office and explain how their wonderful products will save me tons of money. Very few do because most don't understand what it takes to sit across the table from me.

  —Chief Executive Officer

- *Inadequate business solution focus.* A common theme is that both the winning and losing salespeople knew their products very well. However, winners were better able to prove their value as a business partner with the expertise to solve the customer's problem.

  What's wrong with salespeople is they're typically selling a product. I don't need a product unless it solves one of my business problems.

  —President

- *Ineffective messaging.* Successful communication is the cornerstone of all sales. Winners have the ability to tailor compelling messages that resonate with the evaluators across the organization and decision-makers up and down the chain of command.

  We are a skeptical group, and they lost the deal during their presentation. They said they were different and much better than what we have, but they didn't provide enough proof. What they said didn't really apply to us.

  —Chief Financial Officer

- *Poor presales resources.* The complex sales process is typically a team effort that involves presales technical experts. Losers were often cited as having inferior presales resources and, equally important, the lack of knowledgeable experts who attended meetings throughout the sales cycle.

  The vendor we chose has a group of smart, dedicated, and customer-oriented people. To a great degree, I don't think their products and services are different from their competitors'. They distinguish themselves with their people.

  —Vice President of Supply Chain

- *Lack of an internal coach.* A clear difference between winners and losers is the winners developed an internal "coach" within the account. Coaches are evaluators who provide proprietary information about the selection process and status of the competition and help the salesperson determine his course of action.

Anytime we had a question, the sales rep attacked it. He would get his people on the phone within a day to answer how we could do something. He listened to what we were trying to do and he knew his resources. He earned our trust so we were much more open with him.

—Chief Information Officer

- *Out-of-range pricing.* Time after time, interviewees reported they did not pick the lowest cost option. Savvy evaluators realize there will always be a low bidder. However, there is an acceptable price range the prospect is willing to pay and this can be anywhere from 10 to 25 percent higher than the lowest proposal (depending upon industry and products). Solutions priced outside of this boundary are rarely selected.

    Price is always important, but we did not buy the lowest priced solution. Many other factors, including the fit between organizations, render pricing to a secondary factor. With that said, I never want to buy the highest priced solution.

    —Vice President of Technology

- *They are outsold! Winning salespeople establish their credibility and maintain account control.* Losers operate in a world based on incomplete information and ineffective sales execution.

    I can tell you what makes a bad rep. They don't come prepared when they see me. They don't understand my business. They don't research

what we have in place or understand what challenges we might be facing. Great reps have done their homework, so when they are in my office they can talk to me knowledgeably. They don't tell me they can do things they can't.

—IT Manager

Exercise: Losing is always a frustrating, humbling, and embarrassing event. Think about the last three deals you lost and ask yourself which of the factors above were at the root cause of your loss.

Chapter 14. Enterprise, Platform, and Point-Specific Sales

It is important to define the different types of sales so that you can communicate meaningfully your sales strategy to others. Product and solution sales can be classified by complexity as enterprise, platform, and point-specific. Each sales cycle varies in complexity depending upon the number of individuals and departments involved in the selection process, the size of the purchase, and sophisticated nature (implementation requirements, daily operation, and underlying technology) of the solution offered.

Enterprise Sales

Enterprise sales typically involve large capital expenditure purchases that require long sales cycles. Multiple departments of a company and all levels of the organization (C-level executive, midlevel management, and lower-level personnel) are needed to approve the solution's functionality and its purchase.

Figure 14.1 Enterprise sales cycle

Typically, the enterprise sales cycle starts as a top-down initiative from the highest levels of the organization to midlevel management and lower-level personnel. However, there are decision-makers and evaluators across the organization who will become involved during the sales cycle as shown in figure 14.1.

may be evaluated by the sales department and purchased with the approval of the IT department as shown in figure 14.2. They might see a product demonstration and lobby for its purchase.

Platform Sales

The platform sale typically involves a user-friendly solution that is sold directly to the business area that will use it. A platform sales cycle might be instigated by the business users within a department and the purchase made with the blessing of other interested departments. As opposed to enterprise sales, the wellspring for the platform sales idea typically is from lower level and midlevel personnel within the organization. For example, a sales automation solution

Point-Specific Sales

Point-specific sales involve a single solution (or a set of finite complementary functionality offerings) usually targeted to solve the business problems of a single department within an organization. The purchase decision is typically made by a small number of decision-makers, most likely at the lower level of the organization, with decision approval from midlevel management. For example, a résumé tracking system is a point-specific solution sold to the human resources department as shown in figure 14.3.

There are two categories of point-specific sales: simple and complex. The simple point-specific sale is complementary to the customer's existing environment. The product is sold as an addition to the way business is being conducted today. The

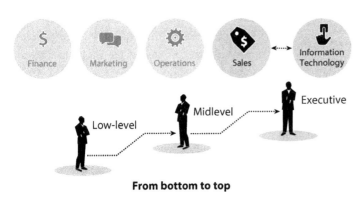

From bottom to top

Figure 14.2 Platform sales cycle

Figure 14.3 Point-specific sales cycle

complex point-specific sale may require the customer to break a pre-established relationship with an existing vendor. This entails a "rip and replace" strategy where the existing vendor's products are completely replaced by newer technology or an entirely different way of doing business. Equally important, you must break the vendor's pre-existing relationship with the customer. As a result, complex point-specific sales are much more difficult to close than simple point-specific sales.

Chapter 15. Should You Pursue the Business?

As a general rule, it is best to be the first salesperson in an account. The chance to understand a customer's environment first, establish relationships, and set the criteria for the selection process is an obvious advantage. However, it's not always possible to find a customer first, and sometimes arriving first doesn't matter. What matters is the strength of your position versus the competition.

You can define your strength compared to your competitor's in one of three ways: you have the advantage, you are equal, or you are out-classed. The three types of strengths are relationship (the personal relationships you have built in the account), product (the functional/technical merits of your product and perception of your company in the marketplace), and personnel (the quality and quantity of people who are at your disposal to work on the account).

Defining your account strength can be tricky. First, the marketing department's job is to pump out volumes of propaganda proclaiming that every aspect of the company and its product is superior to the competition. Your product's true strength can be ascertained only with direct customer feedback gained in past sales cycles.

The second reason is more complex. While salespeople say they are directly responsible for winning a deal, there is a natural tendency to blame losses on something other than themselves. Based on my research, 15 percent of salespeople would admit that losing a deal was because they were outsold, while 27 percent would say it was because of factors outside of their control. The true strength of your competitive position directly correlates to the percentage of deals you win. The only way to accurately gauge how you stack up against the enemy is in head-to-head confrontations.

The decision to pursue an account can be a difficult one. One deciding factor is who has set the tempo in the account—you or a competitor. This is particularly important when your product

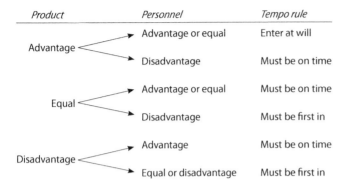

Product	Personnel	Tempo rule
Advantage	Advantage or equal	Enter at will
	Disadvantage	Must be on time
Equal	Advantage or equal	Must be on time
	Disadvantage	Must be first in
Disadvantage	Advantage	Must be on time
	Equal or disadvantage	Must be first in

Figure 15.1 When to pursue the deal

has a long sales cycle that requires a large investment of your time and your company's resources.

Basing the decision on an honest assessment of competitive strength is critical. For example, you should pursue accounts where you have established personal relationships. If you enjoy product and personnel advantages, you should almost always pursue an account, even if you are late into the deal. If you have product and personnel disadvantages, you must be first into the account to win. If you are on equal footing with the competition, you must be on time at the start of the evaluation process to build a relationship advantage. Figure 15.1 illustrates the tempo rules (when you should arrive in accounts) when your products and personnel are at an advantage over, equal to, or at a disadvantage to your competitor's.

Obviously, many combinations are possible. The decision to work on an account or walk away shouldn't be made solely by the salesperson; it's always wise to get outsiders' opinions. The best people to help you make this call are your sales manager and other members of your team who would work on the account with you. Meanwhile, the customer wants to dictate the steps taken during the selection process and keep control of the various vendors so they don't run recklessly through the company.

RFP Response Test

In order to control vendors and objectively compare products, buyers will create detailed request for proposal (RFP) documents that list their business, technical, and operational requirements. In one sense, RFPs are like lottery tickets. Many vendors will respond with a bid, but only one lucky vendor has the winning ticket. In fact, one-third of all RFPs are written with a preferred vendor in mind as explained in chapters 16 and 17. Therefore, the decision about whether or not to respond to the RFP is critical. Here's a test to determine if you should respond. Circle the points next to the statements that are true for the next RFP you're considering responding to.

1. We have never met with the client. 25 points

2. We have met with the client but do not have any significant relationships. 20 points

3. Our product solution fit to the RFP is 85 percent or below. 15 points

4. Winning the business is not strategic to our company. (For example, it is not a marquee account; it doesn't help us enter a new market or create a new solution offering.) 10 points

5. One of our archrivals is currently the incumbent vendor. 10 points

6. The response will require significant time, effort, and resources to complete. 10 points

7. Winning the business is not strategic to the salesperson. (It is not a big revenue deal, important local account, make-or-break deal for the year/quarter.) 10 points

Now total up your score. If your score is fifty or over, you should seriously consider not responding to the RFP. If your score is seventy and over, the general rule of thumb is that you should not respond to the RFP. However, there is an exception to this rule: if you are the market leader or dominant vendor in your industry, you should err on the side of responding to RFPs. Refer to chapter 135 for details.

Setting the tempo is the first step in winning the business. Never forget, the only two appropriate positions to be in at the end of the deal are first place, as the winner, or last place, as the first loser. Every place in between is the result of a judgment error.

The Customer Placebo

The sales cycle has a natural evolution. Customers gather information from each vendor. As they gather more information, one vendor begins to look better than the others, its product sounds like it will work better, and the customers feel that vendor will be a better partner. Naturally, that vendor will enjoy an advantage through the remainder of the sales cycle.

However, customers have a dilemma. They still want to collect information from the other vendors to be 100 percent certain they are selecting the right one. Or they may want to complete the evaluation process to show others in or outside their organization (management, colleagues, consultants, or government agencies) that their evaluation was thorough and fair. As a result, they offer the other vendors the customer placebo.

The customer placebo is present in nearly every sales cycle. One vendor is in a unique position of receiving information from the customer that the other vendors don't receive. As the favored vendor and customer spend more time together, a higher level of rapport is developed. While this happens, the customer presents misleading information to the other vendors about their position in the deal, pretending to be more interested in the products than he actually is. Conversely, he may not share critical information or access to company executives as he does with the leading vendor. Unfortunately, the other vendors continue to spend additional resources, time, and effort on an account they have virtually no chance of winning. Figure 15.2 illustrates the impact of the customer placebo.

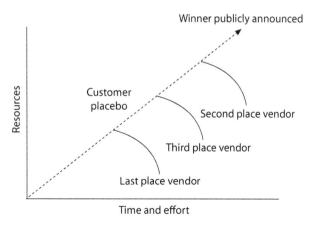

Figure 15.2 The customer placebo

Take a moment to read this scenario before you look at how B2B buyers responded in a study I conducted:

> *You've just sat through hour-long presentations from three different salespeople who work for highly respected companies that are competing for your business. While each salesperson was professional and courteous, you have a favorite company that you would like to do business with. The next day, after the presentations, each salesperson contacts you in order to find out where they stand. What do you do?*

For a moment, put yourself in the position of the buyer. You're meeting with multiple vendors, watching their presentations, and reading their marketing collateral. Each vendor has equally talented, friendly, and professional salespeople who come to your office. However, you can only select one product. How will you behave with each vendor? Will you tell each one the truth? Probably not.

One way to interpret the study results shown in figure 15.3 is to say that 62 percent of prospective buyers are prone to lying. It is basic human nature to want to avoid confrontation. This is particularly true in in-person meetings. Additionally, consider society's implicit guidelines of behavior: we are taught at an early age that if we have nothing nice to say, we shouldn't say anything at all. If the prospective buyer is not interested in the product after meeting with a vendor, it is much more comfortable to offer false expectations to the salesperson over the phone—or just avoid him. Unfortunately, this means the competing salespeople continue to spend time and effort trying to win the business when a decision in favor of one vendor was most likely made early on in the sales cycle.

In addition, 66 percent of B2B buyers agreed with the statement "I try to avoid conflict as much as I can." This desire to avoid conflict permeates sales calls as well. As a result, buyers say things they don't mean and mean things they don't say. Therefore, it can be argued that it isn't what buyers say during the sales call that is important; it's what they don't say.

Know Your Zone

Basically, every deal is in one of three zones: your zone, where you have an advantage; your competitor's zone, where he has an advantage; or open business, which is up for grabs. If you work for the market leader, then more business is in your zone than the competition's, meaning you have a distinct advantage and an easier path to winning the business. Some deals are deep inside your archrival's zone and he has a distinct advantage. You cannot win there, so you shouldn't even try. The remaining deals, representing the lion's share of business, should be

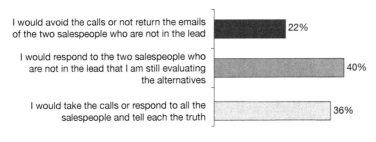

I would avoid the calls or not return the emails of the two salespeople who are not in the lead — 22%

I would respond to the two salespeople who are not in the lead that I am still evaluating the alternatives — 40%

I would take the calls or respond to all the salespeople and tell each the truth — 36%

Figure 15.3 B2B buyer inclinations to avoid telling the truth

hotly contested because there is a path for you to win them. All you have to do is figure it out before your competition.

The zones are predicated on your competitive strengths, including the personal relationships you have built in the account, the functional/technical merits of your product, the perception of your company in the marketplace, and the quality and quantity of people who are at your disposal to work on the account. In your zones there is a natural combination of human chemistry, business synergy, and technical fit between you and the customer.

The attributes of the customer's business and the motivations behind the customer's selection process also influence who has an advantage. Your "sweet spot" is the ideal situation where you are likely to win. The best salespeople know their sweet spot inside and out. One might say, for example, "My sweet spot is packaged-goods companies with $250 to $400 million in annual revenues where the key decision-maker is a gregarious fifty-year-old former factory worker who rose through the ranks to become the plant manager and is now on a mission to increase plant efficiency in order to leave his mark on the company." The more specifically you can describe your zone, the better off you are. Figure 15.4 illustrates the concept of the sweet spot.

Your competitor has a sweet spot as well, and it may be quite close to or far away from yours. Continuing the example from above, the competitor's zone might be billion-dollar-revenue packaged-goods companies where the key decision-maker is an evaluation committee run by an introverted forty-five-year-old who has an extensive financial background. This deal would be plotted on the outside ring of the competitive sweet-spot bull's-eye.

So, what is your zone? Where are you strong and where are you weak? Equally important, ask these same two questions about your competitor before you decide to work on an account.

Minimize mistakes when working on a deal in your zones. Apply your strengths against the competition's weaknesses in open accounts. Stay out of deals deep in the competitor's zone. Salespeople who willingly compete on the enemy's terrain are only fooling themselves. Sales managers who mandate that salespeople go after accounts deep in the competition's zone are just plain foolish.

Exercise: What is your sweet spot? Take a moment to define your ideal prospect, where you specifically have a distinct competitive advantage. Be sure to think about the specific selection process scenarios where you are more likely to win. Compare the key deals you are working on to this description.

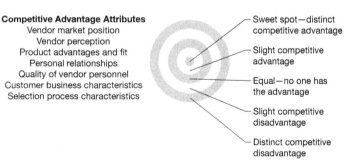

Competitive Advantage Attributes
Vendor market position
Vendor perception
Product advantages and fit
Personal relationships
Quality of vendor personnel
Customer business characteristics
Selection process characteristics

Sweet spot—distinct competitive advantage

Slight competitive advantage

Equal—no one has the advantage

Slight competitive disadvantage

Distinct competitive disadvantage

Figure 15.4 Competitive bull's-eye showing the sweet spot

Chapter 16. Key Moments Sales Cycles Are Won or Lost

The three basic types of sales cycles are renewal, persuasion, and creation deals. Renewal deals involve selling more products and services to existing customers or trying to close a multiyear contract coming up for renewal (such as a three-year agreement). Persuasion deals are extremely competitive customer evaluations that typically involve the customer creating an RFP or similar document. In these deals you are usually competing against your archrivals. Finally, in creation deals you target and penetrate a new account to get the customer to use your products for the first time, with the hope the customer will make a much larger purchase in the future.

Each sales cycle requires a different strategy. In renewal deals the goal is to execute a justification strategy, where the customer experiences the benefits from using the solution and working with the vendor to justify renewing the relationship. The salesperson should employ a "sales virus" strategy, where the salesperson continually spreads out to meet everyone in the customer's organization, across all departments and at all levels. He addresses all outstanding issues and provides excellent customer care, ensuring the widespread adoption of his solution and its use to the fullest extent by all users.

A critical time occurs six months to one year before the actual renewal date. Figure 16.1 shows when the customer begins the decision-making process and decides whether or not to research new vendors or stay with the existing solution. The people in the company who are responsible for the use and operations of the product, along with procurement and senior management, ask critical questions about the vendor and solution:

1. Do procurement department governance practices require that the product or service be periodically put out for a new bid?

2. Is a better solution available?

3. Does the expense warrant continued use of the product or service?

4. Could we obtain the same product or receive the same service for less money from another supplier?

5. How responsive and helpful is the customer service?

6. How professional is the account management?

7. How is the overall company relationship?

8. How difficult is it to replace the current vendor's product or service?

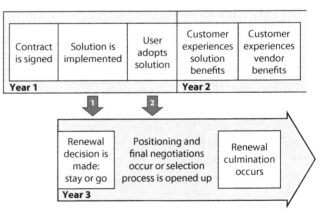

Figure 16.1 Renewal/add-on sales cycle with two key moments identified

The first key sales cycle moment is when the customer decides whether to stay with the current vendor. The answers to the questions above will determine if the company will start a new vendor selection process. The purpose of client quarterly and annual business reviews (see ch. 45) is to ensure the vendor has an accurate pulse on each of these topic areas and the client is satisfied. If the decision is made to retain the vendor, then the second key sales cycle moment occurs during the contract and negotiation process. If members from the client's legal, procurement, and management team do not feel the vendor is acting reasonably in good faith, then they will collectively decide to open the selection process up and entertain bids from new vendors.

Persuasion sales cycles are quite different because they are based on the transmission and receipt of information. In essence, they are a series of response-based sales calls where the customer compares your answers to his questions against those from your competitors. As a result, all the salespeople involved in the deal are continually saying to the customer, "We are the best because . . ."

The persuasion sales cycle has four critical moments as shown in figure 16.2. The first is prior to the start of the sales cycle. The first salesperson to build relationships and influence the selection process criteria obviously has a huge advantage. The second most important moment is the vendor presentation. Why? Because this is one of the few moments during the entire sales cycle when the entire evaluation team, all the key influencers, and senior executives are present. In some cases, it is your only opportunity to win over the senior executives.

Therefore, your presentation has to be persuasive to differentiate yourself from the competition and be flawlessly executed. Since the customer will see presentations from every competitor in a very short period of a week or so, the decision is frequently made then but not publicly announced until much later.

The third most important moment is the vendor interview. This is one of the few chances you have to develop relationships and uncover the political structure of the account. Asking questions is an excellent way to demonstrate your technical knowledge and domain expertise and provide evidence that you know the best practices of your industry. Questions show your competency and the quality of your company.

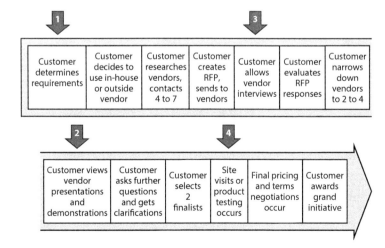

Figure 16.2 Persuasion sales cycle with four key moments identified

The fourth most important moment is after the customer narrows down the solutions and decides to complete hands-on testing of the product finalists or make site visits to existing customer installations. This will determine which vendor wins when the competition between vendors is extremely close.

Creation sales cycles are the opposite of the information-based persuasion sales cycle. They are hypothesis sales based upon establishing trust where the salesperson says to the customer, "We can help you do X better. Let us come in and prove it." The salesperson's goal is to win a "beachhead" deal and get the customer to start using his company's product or start a small project to validate the solution. The hope is that the project will be successful and culminate with a big purchase.

The creation sales cycle is based upon establishing trust. Unlike the persuasion sales cycle based upon persuasive words, the creation sales cycle is based upon completing actions that create trust, build respect, and form alliances with employees who will promote the solution within their organization. Every interaction is intended to build momentum behind the project's initiative. There are product demonstrations designed to create initial interest and follow-on demonstrations to rally support and validate the breadth of the solution. Figure 16.3 shows the typical steps of the creation sales cycle with the two key moments identified.

A real-world ROI (return on investment) analysis should be provided to internal coaches so they can position the purchase as an investment, as opposed to an expense, to their peers and company leadership. The most important moment during the creation sales cycle is when the ROI analysis is accepted by the evaluators and then presented to the senior management. Ideally, you would like to copresent the ROI justification along with your internal coaches. However, you will most likely not be present at this closed-door meeting. Therefore, you must ensure that the ROI is accurate and not so overinflated that all credibility is lost.

Their ROI model was way off. Frankly, our people don't even want to deal with them.

—Vice President of Business Development

The second most important moment is when the company tests your product, service, or proof of concept idea. Advancing to an initial deployment is directly dependent upon the magnitude of success of the evaluation and whether or not the customer's expectations were met. Therefore, the criteria that determine success must be identified and

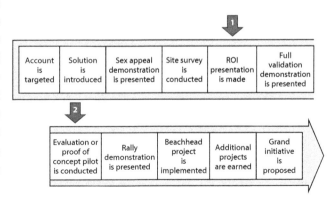

Figure 16.3 Creation sales cycle with two key moments identified

agreed upon beforehand in writing. A full project plan should be developed so that adequate resources are assigned by both parties and the execution is carefully managed in order to minimize risk.

Chapter 17. Spot Turning Points to Avoid Wasting Time

All the competing salespeople put time, effort, and energy into winning a deal. The customer does too. However, every type of sales cycle (add-on/renewal, creation, or persuasion) has a critical moment, or "turning point," where it is won or lost. In some cases, the turning point is easy to spot. For example, a salesperson may be presenting his solution and encounter a deal-breaking objection that he is unable to overcome.

Even though the customer remains cordial for the rest of the meeting, a turning point has occurred and the deal is lost. From the salesperson's perspective the deal has just stalled. However,

the customer has already made a decision, but since he hasn't reached the conclusion of the evaluation process, he hasn't publicly announced it. In most cases, the turning point occurs when the salesperson isn't present. It's in casual hallway conversations or internal emails that selection team members share opinions that influence vendors' futures. The only outward sign that a turning point has occurred is the perceptible change in deal momentum as evidenced in figure 17.1.

You probably noticed the term "buzz kill" on the graph. This represents the person, business reason, political issue, or technical obstacle that causes momentum to turn downward. Ninety out of one hundred times you will not recover from a buzz kill. The graph shows that the buzz-kill moments happened at different times during the sales cycle for the losers. The first loser started in the lead but quickly lost momentum. He tried to rally back into a competitive position but wasn't able to do so and gave up knowing he couldn't win. The other two losers thought they experienced a stalled deal, which is actually worse. After the buzz-kill moment the customer spent less effort and energy investigating their solutions. He met with them less often than with the winner because he was losing interest. Unfortunately, these salespeople continued to try to resurrect their momentum far longer than the first loser.

Some companies won't let salespeople stop working deals even though

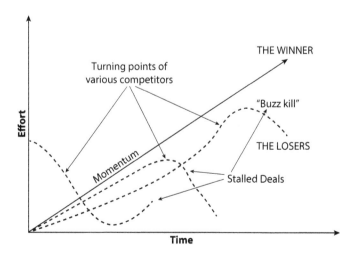

Figure 17.1 Turning points of various competitors

buzz kill has occurred. You may even be familiar with the following drill, which I call the "walk of shame." All the various sales managers meet with the rep and theorize about all the possible ways to win. Then they mandate that the selling continue even though the salesperson knows working on a deal past a buzz kill is a waste of time.

Usually, it is the salespeople themselves who will decide on their own to continue the walk of shame. Since they have invested so much time, energy, and emotion into the deal, they find it impossible to let it go. This is particularly true for salespeople who have neglected to build up a pipeline of future business opportunities.

Time takes on an additional dimension of meaning during the sales cycle. Usually, we think of time as a continuum. We spend most of our mental energy thinking about the immediate tasks before us. We typically don't consider time to be a finite resource. There's always tomorrow, next week, next month, or next year. During the sales process, time is not just minutes and days; it is actually a measure of deal momentum. Therefore, increasing momentum in a deal represents good or positive time, and backward momentum is bad or negative time. Heavy Hitters keep the negative time they spend on deals to a minimum.

Time is a salesperson's enemy because time is finite. On average, there are thirty days in a month and ninety days in a quarter. Time is the governor that determines how many deals can be worked and where effort should be focused. The relentless march of time creates artificial deadlines by which deals must be won. Time is a precious resource that must be conserved, respected, and above all, used to your advantage.

Your most valuable asset is your time. First, in order to protect your time you must be able to recognize when a buzz kill occurs during sales calls. Second, if you are unsure why you are losing momentum during sales calls, bring along your manager or someone else and ask that person to help you identify buzz-kill moments.

> *There was a company that I liked at the beginning, and we were just not going to give it to them. We went through the whole procedure, making sure all the boxes were checked off by a panel of people.*
>
> —Chief Financial Officer

Unfortunately, I have some very frightening news to share with you. Approximately 30 percent of the time the winner of the persuasion sales cycle was determined before the "official" selection

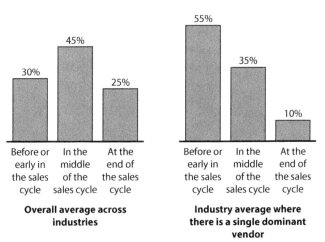

Overall average across industries

Industry average where there is a single dominant vendor

Figure 17.2 When customers make up their minds

process started. Another 45 percent of the time, customers had already made up their minds about whom they were going to buy from about halfway through the process. That means, 75 percent of the time, customers had made their decision by halfway through the process. Only 25 percent of the time did customers make their final decision at the end of the selection process. Therefore, if you are not clearly in the lead at the midpoint of the selection process, the odds are that you are going to lose. These numbers are even worse in industries where there is one dominant vendor who has overwhelming market share. Where this is the situation, 55 percent of decisions are made before the selection process starts. Figure 17.2 illustrates this point.

Here's another frightening fact. In the overwhelming majority of cases, the decision wasn't even close between the top two choices. Even though customers had made up their minds, they still caused all the other salespeople to jump through a series of hoops for nothing, wasting their valuable time, resources, and mental and emotional energy.

Exercise: Recall your last three major wins and losses. What was the most impactful turning point during each sales cycle? Was the turning point different for each win and loss? Were there similar patterns for all the wins and all the losses? Most likely, these turning points will happen again in the future. Write down the buzz-kill moments of the deals you recently lost and prepare a counteractive strategy for each so history doesn't repeat itself in the future.

Chapter 18. Department and Industry Risk Tolerances

Put yourself in the position of the experienced evaluator who has met with hundreds of salespeople. What percentage of salespeople would you say are excellent, good, average, or poor? Overall, study participants rated 12 percent of salespeople as excellent, 23 percent good, 38 percent average, and 27 percent poor as shown in figure 18.1.

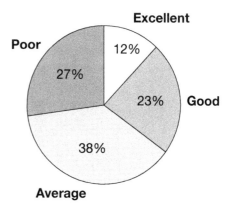

Figure 18.1 B2B buyers' rating of salespeople

Think about those figures for a moment. What are the implications of nearly two-thirds of B2B salespeople being considered average or poor? This situation creates an aversion to risk because evaluators have been conditioned to be skeptical and not to trust salespeople in general. Therefore, they'll make every vendor respond to immense RFPs and complete laborious spreadsheets—each product feature and operation has to be fully documented to prove it exists. They'll require meticulous hands-on evaluations of each product

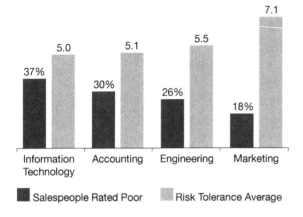

Figure 18.2 B2B departmental buyer ratings of salespeople and risk tolerance

and painstakingly documented findings. The goal is to mitigate risk and reduce the uncertainty associated with selecting a vendor and making a purchase.

When you look at ratings of salespeople from the perspective of departmental buyers, a pattern emerges. Evaluators who are part of IT, engineering, and accounting are more critical of the salespeople than those from less-scientific or process-oriented departments such as marketing. Since the analytical buyers have advanced degrees in the sciences (computers, finance, engineering, etc.), they are more likely to be skeptical and consequently more demanding of salespeople. This should not be a surprise since they've had years of systematic education followed by a business career that was heavily focused on scientific methods and data analysis.

Another interesting pattern occurs when

tolerance for risk is analyzed by department. There seems to be a correlation between the ratings of salespeople and the tolerance for risk. Specifically, a higher negative rating of salespeople is inversely related to the department's tolerance for risk. For example, IT personnel rated 37 percent of all salespeople as poor and their risk tolerance average was the lowest at 5 (on a scale of 1 to 10). Conversely, marketing personnel rated 18 percent of salespeople as poor and their tolerance for risk rating was much higher at 7.1. It can be inferred from these metrics that these two departments will interact with salespeople and analyze vendors in different ways with varying levels of due diligence. Figure 18.2 shows how buyers' poor perception of salespeople is inversely related to their appetite for risk.

The tolerance for risk also varies greatly by industry as well, as shown in figure 18.3. Dynamic, creative, trend-oriented industries such as fashion, entertainment, and real estate have the highest risk tolerance averages. More

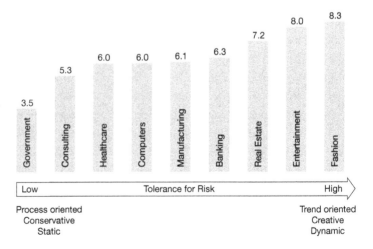

Figure 18.3 Industry risk tolerance

conservative, static, and process-oriented industries such as government, consulting, and healthcare have the lowest risk tolerance averages. Again, this validates that different industry types interact with salespeople and analyze vendors in different ways with varying levels of due diligence.

Evaluators will go to great lengths to reduce the risk of buying. They might list their needs in documents that are hundreds of pages in length. They might hire consultants to verify that they are making the right decisions. And they'll conduct lengthy evaluations to test prospective products, talk to existing users of the products, and complete pilot testing to ensure the products work as advertised—all in an effort to eliminate their fears, reduce their uncertainties, and eliminate risk. The B2B buyer is fixated on risk mitigation.

Chapter 19. How to Predict When No Decision Will Be Made

The real enemy of salespeople today isn't their archrivals; it's no decision. What prevents a prospective customer from making a purchase even after he has conducted a lengthy evaluation? The reasons may surprise you.

Regardless of the prospective customer's confident demeanor, on the inside he is experiencing fear, uncertainty, and doubt while making his selection. The stress this creates serves as the key factor in determining whether or not a purchase will be made. Therefore, all salespeople need to understand this lowest common denominator of human decision-making—they need to understand the nature of stress.

From a psychological perspective, stress shortens attention spans, escalates mental exhaustion, and encourages poor decision-making. From an organizational perspective, when anxious evaluators experience too much stress, they typically suffer analysis paralysis. They are too overwhelmed with information and contradictory evidence to make a decision.

It's the salesperson's responsibility to anticipate and defuse the main sources of customer stress during the selection process. These are informational stress, vendor selection stress, budgetary stress, evaluation committee stress, corporate citizenship stress, and organizational stress.

Informational Stress: Is the Information Being Presented Truthful?

We live in very skeptical times in which information presented by the media and experts is continually challenged and constantly debunked. In addition to being subject to the general cynicism of our society, most customers have had negative experiences with salespeople sometime in the past. Therefore, customers are always in the stressful position of separating fact from fiction. Meanwhile, even the most ethical salesperson carries the burden of proving he's telling the truth.

Worse yet, as the sales cycle progresses, competing vendors may try to escalate FUD (fear, uncertainty, and doubt) in the customer's mind about the wherewithal of the competitors and the capabilities of their products. For example, competitors will try to sabotage one another with facts such as unfavorable performance metrics, missing functionality, and tales of unhappy customers. In turn, the attacked competitors will provide the customer with believable information that contradicts the original attacks. Therefore, the sales cycle naturally disintegrates into a quarrel between salespeople and this scenario helps set the stage for no decision to be made.

Vendor Selection Stress: Is the Tug of War between Vendors Equal?

One of the biggest problems during the sales cycle is that the difference between most products is extremely small. Compounding this problem is that everyone is presenting the same basic messages to the customer. Take a moment and visit the home page of your company's website and those of your two biggest competitors. You'll see that the words and claims are basically interchangeable. There tends to be a higher no-decision rate where product differentiation is extremely small. Since all the competing products share the same basic features, functions, and benefits, evaluation team members may take longer to make their decision or postpone it indefinitely.

Budgetary Stress: Is the Money Available and Justified to Be Spent?

Whether a purchase is actually made is directly related to the perceived risk versus the anticipated reward. A company's budgeting process is designed not only to prioritize where money is to be spent but also to remove the fear of spending it. Here's a quote from a senior executive decision-maker I interviewed that explains this point:

There are two main criteria for deciding on whether or not to make the purchase. One is value to the company as measured by return on investment and how it compares to other projects being considered. Then there are strategic projects that are critical to our long-term success such as protection of our brand or improving customer satisfaction. While projects may be approved initially for further evaluation, a cross-functional team of senior executives reviews the final recommendation and whether the money should be actually allocated and released.

Every initiative and its associated expenditure is competing against all the other projects that require funds. Purchases are continually reprioritized based upon emergencies and in response to changing conditions. For example, when new executive leaders join organizations, one of their first acts may be to freeze major expenditures and reevaluate all requests. The bad news is that a salesperson may have worked on a deal for most of the year only to find out that it was never truly budgeted.

Evaluation Committee Stress: Why Can't We Agree?

Whenever a company makes a purchase decision that involves groups of people, the final decision is influenced by self-interests, politics, and group dynamics. Tension, drama, and conflict are normal parts of group dynamics because decisions are not typically made unanimously. As members promote their own personal agendas, the interpersonal conflicts can cause the decision-making process to stagnate and stop. Other selection team members may not be 100 percent certain they are picking the right solution. All of this uncertainty encourages no decision.

> *If I don't believe the business case, then I reserve the right to exercise my veto. Even though another executive wants to do it, I have to believe the business case or I will resist it. It's not like I have an ax to grind with IT, R&D, marketing, or sales, but I have to remain independent and wear my corporate hat. I also have the duty to say no when the level of change represents an unacceptable level of risk.*
>
> —Vice President of Finance

Corporate Citizenship Stress: Is It in the Best Interest of the Company?

While customers inherently want to do what's in the best interest of their company and to be good corporate citizens, the fundamental dynamic of corporate-employee loyalty has changed.

Today, business is a "survival of the fittest" world where employment is never guaranteed and loyalty frequently goes unrewarded. In some situations, prospective buyers can feel continual pressure to put their individual needs before the company's.

Even after a formal evaluation process, the likelihood that a purchase will not be made jumps tenfold when the solution recommended is not aligned to a company's goals and direction. This is frequently the case with projects and purchases that are instigated by lower levels of an organization as they bubble up the chain of command for review. There is not a compelling business case to drive the purchase forward so it never garners senior-level support.

Organizational Stress: How Do My Colleagues Perceive Me and Should We Really Do It?

Peer pressure is a powerful influencer of group dynamics, and evaluators are constantly worried about how the purchase decision will reflect on them. Senior executives are worried about what investors, the board of directors, and members of the leadership team think about them. And of course, they want their employees to respect them as well. Mid-level managers suffer competitive pressure because all are striving to advance in their careers and move upward in the organization. Lower-level personnel are continually seeking to prove themselves to their managers.

> *After five months, we finished the selection process and had to build a business case and present it to our board because of the significant dollar value of the contract. They had only given an initial approval to complete the study. At the time, it felt like they were putting us through a meat grinder. We had to show pricing for the vendors, explain why we selected the more expensive solution, detail the implementation risks, and what the world would look like afterward. I was unsure the project would be approved after all the time and effort.*
>
> —Chief Information Officer

Whether from above, below, or the same level in an organization, coworkers are continually evaluating the behavior, success, and failures of those tasked with the decision-making process. Obviously, this exerts pressure on the evaluators to make the right decision and not to make a decision if there isn't an obvious choice or clear-cut direction. This results in the decision-makers' second-guessing themselves because they are continually asking, How do my colleagues perceive me and should we really do this?

Exercise: The first step to determining the likelihood of no decision being made is to conduct a stress test. Pick an account and rate each of the six stress factors on a scale from 1 (low stress) to 5 (high stress), circling the applicable level of stress.

Name of Account: _____

	Low			High	
Informational stress	1	2	3	4	5
Vendor stress	1	2	3	4	5
Budgetary stress	1	2	3	4	5
Evaluation committee stress	1	2	3	4	5
Corporate citizenship stress	1	2	3	4	5
Organizational stress	1	2	3	4	5

Add up your points and compare the results to the categories below.

22 points and over	High likelihood of no decision
17- 21 points	Medium likelihood of no decision
16 points and under	Low likelihood of no decision

Graphing your scores will help you visualize the stress levels and where a counteractive strategy needs to be employed to alleviate stress. In the example shown in figure 19.1, the selection committee can't unanimously agree on a decision because the respective sales teams have presented their solutions effectively. Faced with this situation, employ flanking strategies (see ch. 39) such as arranging for the prospect to visit customers to see their results, offering to conduct a pilot project so they can experience the product firsthand, or inviting them to visit your corporate office and tour your factories. The goal of these flanking strategies is to provide additional information that pulls the decision to your side.

Customers are stressed out. They don't know whom or what to believe. They are under immense peer pressure, and they are torn between doing the right thing for the greater good of the company and acting in their personal best interest. To make matters worse, the vendors increase the pressure by injecting claims of their superiority and accusations about their competitors' inferiority. For all these reasons it's no surprise that no decision is the top competitor today.

However, there's one last thing you should know about buyers. Sixty-nine percent said they feel like they have to double-check things such as lightswitches, stovetops, and door locks to see if they are off or secure. Buyers exhibit obsessive-compulsive tendencies in which they seek perfectionism and an excessive need to control their environment. These tendencies create even more stress when they have to select between salespeople and their products. The added stress shortens attention spans, escalates mental exhaustion, and encourages poor decision-making.

Customers dread having to verify the information presented by vendors. Salespeople will exaggerate, describing a product's benefits as greater than they really are and talking about larger-than-life results their product cannot deliver. Customers know it's their responsibility to discount such claims and validate that the facts are as they have been represented. They are the watchdogs of their pocketbooks and organizations, and this is a tremendous responsibility. It is the salesperson's most important responsibility to defuse this stress by establishing trust.

Exercise: Take a moment to graph the levels of stress for the most important account you are working on right now.

Thirteen Tactics to Overcome No-Decision and Stalled Deals

Here are sales tactics you can employ to keep deals moving forward,

1. *Call high!* The best tactic to overcome no decision is to secure the backing of senior-level executives at the account you're trying to close. Through their support, you can garner new momentum and a dead deal can be resurrected.

2. *Enlist your coach (specifically, your guide and emissary).* A fundamental premise reiterated throughout this book is the necessity of having

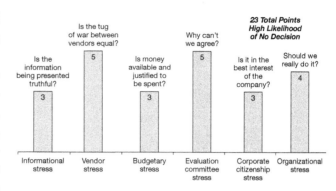

Figure 19.1 Graph of no-decision tendencies

someone within the prospective client's company who coaches you with a constant, accurate source of information that reveals the customer's internal politics. Moreover, the goal is to develop impassioned supporters (guides and emissaries as explained in chapter 37) who will defend you when you aren't around and promote your solution because they are compelled to do so.

3. *Utilize real-world proof points.* Conduct a pilot project so the prospect can experience the real benefits of using your product. Take the prospect to see successful customer installations and witness your product in action. Invite the prospect to user group meetings and conferences where he can have unedited conversations with actual users of your product.

4. *Provide independent validation.* Use information such as industry analyst reports, independent product reviews, and unbiased benchmark results to justify the value of your solution and validate your claims.

5. *Become a sales virus.* Employ a "sales virus" strategy, where the salesperson continually spreads out

to meet everyone in the customer's organization, across all departments and at all levels. See chapter 39 on flanking strategies for different tactics that can be used.

6. *Fall back to a smaller position.* In chapter 70 we review the concept of fallback positions, alternatives you prepare ahead of time to present if the customer rejects your primary closing strategy. Perhaps your initial deal is too big or the scope of your project too large. In this case, cut it back so that it is a smaller purchase and easier to implement. In other situations, divide and conquer: split the project implementation into smaller chunks that can be accomplished more easily by different groups of people.

7. *Mitigate risk versus reward.* Provide free usage for a period of time, guarantees, contractual performance clauses, money-back no-risk purchase agreements, and extended payment terms to mitigate the risk of buying.

8. *Understand the exact objections.* Make sure you specifically identify the exact objection that is preventing your deal from moving forward, and don't assume it is because your price is too high. Once the objection is clearly identified, fully document how you address the objection in a logical and methodical manner. Deliver your arguments in person, via email, and through your coaches to key decision-makers.

9. *Neutralize naysayers.* It's frequently said that a happy customer will tell another person about his or her experience, while an unhappy customer will tell ten. That adage applies to the evaluators who are plotting against you. Naysayers can be ordered to change their position, persuaded to change their position, or neutralized and taken out of the decision-making process. Take an honest objective look to understand their position. Put yourself in their shoes and ask yourself what would cause you to change your mind.

10. *Offload the effort and timing.* A frequent objection to moving forward with a new product or service is that there are bandwidth limitations because of a lack of resources, personnel, or time to train the team to use your solution. When faced with this circumstance, create a holistic proposal that offsets this objection with services, training, and more vendor managed responsibilities.

11. *Consensus conquers.* In today's business world, the boisterous and willful collective voice of all the evaluators and end users can overcome the single tongue of the senior executive dissenter who is blocking the sale. Senior decision-makers are prone to make the politically correct decision and buy rather than risk alienating their entire team.

12. *Conduct a flanking strategy session to get wider, higher, and deeper.* Conduct a flanking brainstorming session as described in chapter 39 and determine the flanking strategies that can be used that have the highest likelihood of success.

13. *NEGU: Never ever give up.* Timing can be everything. Many times a no

decision is really just a delay so don't abandon the account. I've interviewed over one thousand top salespeople and one of the most important things they all have in common is persistence.

Chapter 20. Sales Strategy Is Based on Account Control

Take a moment to write down your definition of "sales strategy" in one or two sentences.

I've asked thousands of salespeople to complete this exercise and can't recall ever hearing or reading the exact same description twice. Some answers focus on the sales process, such as "Prospecting, qualifying, differentiating my solution, and closing." Some emphasize the client relationship, such as "Building trusted relationships," while others the outcome, "Showing customers how they can improve their business and save money." While none of the answers are wrong, this exercise proves that each individual salesperson defines sales strategy in his or her own way.

Sales strategy can be defined as the overriding plan to win the customer's business by establishing and maintaining account control. The goals are to neutralize competitors' advantages and place them in a defensive position while always anticipating "no decision" and motivating the customer to buy.

The strategy is based upon executing a series of customer interactions (sales calls, presentations, demonstrations, and so on) and maneuvers. Maneuvers (such as phone calls, letters, and emails) are specific actions intended to move a salesperson to the next interaction.

Although maneuvers are typically small steps, they can have a great impact on the deal. Maneuvers include facts and other proof points that put the customer's mind at ease and motivate him to meet with you again. For example, let's say a customer is looking at a competitor's product and hesitates to meet with you. One maneuver is to email the customer an industry article that rates your product better than the competition. After reading the article, the customer decides to let you present your solution. The idea is you have to maneuver into position to make the next interaction. Maneuvers prevent you from remaining at the same stage in the sales cycle or being eliminated. Figure 20.1 illustrates the interrelationships between strategy, goals, customer interactions, and maneuvers.

The sales cycle is a sequence of action points, such as sales calls,

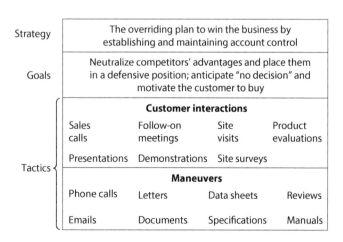

Strategy	The overriding plan to win the business by establishing and maintaining account control	
Goals	Neutralize competitors' advantages and place them in a defensive position; anticipate "no decision" and motivate the customer to buy	

Tactics:

Customer interactions

Sales calls	Follow-on meetings	Site visits	Product evaluations
Presentations	Demonstrations	Site surveys	

Maneuvers

Phone calls	Letters	Data sheets	Reviews
Emails	Documents	Specifications	Manuals

Figure 20.1 Sales strategy, goals, and tactics

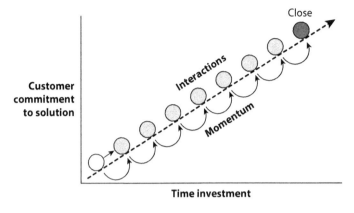

Figure 20.2 Sales cycle interactions and momentum

demonstrations, surveys, and site visits. However, each party has different goals. Your competitors are trying to eliminate you from the next customer interaction. Meanwhile, you are a suitor courting a customer into forming a long-term relationship, akin to a marriage. You accomplish this by scheduling interactions to explain your advantages and the merits of your company. The successful outcome of each interaction provides the opportunity to build momentum in the account, as evidenced by the customer's commitment to spend more time with you through additional interactions as shown in figure 20.2.

Customers have a different set of goals for meeting with salespeople. Relationships are expensive and involve investments of valuable time and money. Customers have to spend time to determine whether a product's characteristics are as they have been represented. They have to spend time evaluating other suitors to determine whether they are picking the best possible partner. They have to spend time learning to use the new products they select, implementing them, and most likely, fixing product problems. In addition, customers have to acquire the solution and pay ongoing

fees for support. They want to make sure they are selecting the best partner and have found their perfect match.

Earning the Right to Meet Again

All salespeople want to develop close personal relationships with buyers. However, 74 percent of B2B buyers said they have only cordial relationships with the salespeople they do business with because they're just too busy. Here are strategies to ensure you're able to secure the next meeting.

- *Discovery.* A successful first touchpoint discovery session sets the stage for the entire sales cycle. Discovery is more than trying to qualify the customer's budget, time frame, and need. It's methodically proving you approach solving problems differently than the competition by asking intelligent questions (see chs. 59 and 67).

- *Domain expertise.* Think about all the knowledge you and the colleagues within your company can provide the customer. The number one cause for "one and done" customer calls is the prospect doesn't receive anything of value in exchange for spending time to meet with the salesperson.

- *Data.* Research, trends, and comparisons of their industry, company, and competition provide prospective customers the incentive to meet again.

- *Deep dive assessment.* Everyone wants to learn more about their industry, profession, and themselves.

If you perform a study of the client's business you are guaranteed to be invited back to share the results.

- *Hold back.* Don't core dump all your product details and give away your industry knowledge all at once in the first meeting. Have patience and hold back information you know is of interest to the prospect for later. Plan how you will release these insights over time.

- *Demeanor.* Are you a "contagious" salesperson? Does your presence excite customers and have an appeal that makes them feel at ease? Always assume the customer is burned out and bored. Tell him a provocative story that captures his imagination and makes him want to meet with you again. After all, if you aren't excited about what you do for a living, why should the customer be?

Account Control Chart

During a long sales cycle of several months it's easy to focus on individual battles and lose sight of winning the war. The sales cycle is reduced to a series of interactions without an overriding strategy. You become fixated on the next interaction, proceeding from the initial call to the sales presentation, from the presentation to the demonstration, and from the demonstration to the product evaluation. The moment you work on an account without a strategy, you relinquish account control. Worse yet is when the details of the battles—where, when, and how they will be fought—are out of your control because they are determined exclusively by the customer or even a competitor.

Meanwhile, competitors are trying to outdo and sabotage you with their own maneuvers. For example, they provide the customer with believable information that contradicts yours. Therefore, the sales cycle naturally disintegrates into a "he said–she said" type of quarrel. This leaves the customer not only confused but sometimes in analysis paralysis from receiving too much contradictory information, which sets the stage for the dreaded "no decision."

If you find yourself in an account bickering with a competitor, take a step back and ask yourself, What is my strategy to win the account? Is the customer or competition controlling my interactions? Most importantly, am I winning the business? You can chart your position in an account depending upon the amount of information you acquire and the level of rapport you develop with the decision-makers and influencers. Figure 20.3 illustrates how to determine your bearings and correlates to your competitiveness to win the business using an account control chart. You are in the position of being blind, competitive, or in control.

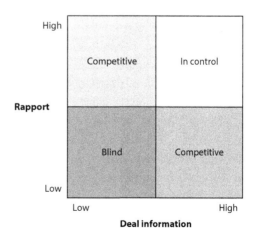

Figure 20.3 Account control chart showing sales cycle quadrant positions

The vertical axis measures the amount of rapport you enjoy with a customer. For example, in a brand new account you would have low or no rapport. A high rapport account would be one where you have personal friendships based on many years of interactions with the customer. The horizontal axis measures the amount of truthful information being shared by the customer. This is an assessment of the quantity and quality of the information you have uncovered and includes unique information the competition doesn't receive.

The "blind" quadrant is where you have little information about the deal and little rapport has been established. You usually find yourself in this unenviable position at the beginning of every new sales cycle. Your immediate goals are to collect information by discovery and start developing rapport. As the sales cycle progresses, if you are unable to collect pertinent information or develop significant rapport, you should stop working the deal.

The amount of information salespeople receive from customers will vary. For example, the evaluation criteria could be extremely well documented. A request for proposal may be three hundred pages long with descriptions about the customer's environment and detailed questions for the vendor to answer. However, this is only the external aspect of the product selection. The internal politics of the selection process isn't publicly revealed. It's by establishing relationships and rapport that salespeople learn the inner workings of the customer.

In the lower right-hand quadrant, you have lots of information but little rapport. The objective is to move quickly to establish relationships and create rapport. Without relationships, the likelihood of winning the deal decreases as the sales cycle progresses. In the upper left-hand quadrant, you have established rapport but have a low level of information about the customer's requirements or a high level of uncertainty whether the deal will happen.

For example, you may have painstakingly developed relationships within the applications group of the IT department of a Fortune 100 company. However, because of the IT department's size and bureaucracy, the application group is unsure of the project's direction and approval. Therefore, even though rapport is high and the application group has identified technical needs, the knowledge of whether there is a deal to be closed is low.

Ultimately, you want to be in the "in control" quadrant. Here, you have established rapport and you receive proprietary information that the other vendors don't. In addition, an interesting paradigm shift occurs in the vendor-customer relationship. The customer begins working with the vendor as a long-term partner while still in the sales cycle. For example, this occurs when issues arise about the functionality of the product and the customer works with the vendor to find an acceptable solution. This shift from being treated like one of the vendors to becoming part of the customer team is very noticeable.

You move from quadrant to quadrant as the sales cycle progresses. Moving from the blind quadrant to a competitive quadrant marks forward progress in the deal. During the sales cycle, you can also experience setbacks that move you back into the position of being blind. For example, if your coach suddenly leaves the company or is reassigned, you are blind again.

An implicit strategy is associated with your position in every quadrant. In each quadrant, execute a strategy that counteracts a competitor or corrects a weakness in your current position. The quadrant strategies shown in figure 20.4 are retreat, attack, confront status quo, leverage relationships, and maintain account control.

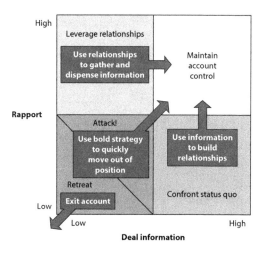

Figure 20.4 Strategy associated with each account control quadrant position

Retreat

It takes a lot of discipline to walk away from an account that has involved a heavy investment of time, energy, and emotions. Knowing when to retreat from an account where there is little chance of winning is just as important as knowing when you will win. It makes no sense to work on deals where your involvement is not wanted or appreciated. As I like to say, "The salesperson with the poor pipeline continually tries to pry the customer's front door open with his broken foot."

Attack

You will lose the deal if you remain in the attack position for longer than the beginning of the sales cycle. The attack position dictates that the salesperson execute a bold strategy to immediately move from this position. You can attack the customer's business model and processes to make him think differently. Attack the customer's selection process and show him his methodology will not result in the best possible decision. Identify important research steps he is missing and other key considerations that should be included. Bypass the established evaluation process and present your case directly to the customer's key executives. Motivate the customer to spend time with you through a variety of tactics including price discounts, service level guarantees, and other valuable concessions.

Attack the competition and furnish unbiased comparison information that shows you're better. This can include unsuccessful customers, critical industry analyst comments, negative press reports and reviews, and published third-party benchmarks that contrast performance. Provide benchmarks that prove your performance is better. Whatever the attack, it must be bold to interrupt the sales cycle: create fear, uncertainty, and doubt (FUD) and focus the attention back on you. Finally, the attack must be done in the most professional way possible so as to not alienate the customer.

Confront Status Quo

In the confront status quo position, the salesperson has a high amount of information but little customer rapport and few, if any, substantial relationships. In this position, use information to draw

attention to your solution to build relationships. Think about all the different
types of information you can provide a
prospective client:

- Latest industry trends
- Metrics and statistics to benchmark
  and improve the prospect's business
  performance
- Best practices and practical advice
  from current customers
- Information about direct competitors
  and top-performing companies in the
  prospect's marketplace
- The impact of new technologies and
  related products on the bottom line
- Developments in other parts of the
  organization
- Guidance to minimize risk during the
  selection process
- Information about the other vendors
  that are being evaluated

Utilize a wide range of colleagues to help
you disseminate information and infil-
trate the account, such as presales engineers, consultants, sales management,
company leaders, and channel partners
with pre-existing relationships.

Leverage Relationships

In the leverage relationships position,
execute a "high and wide" strategy to
build deeper relationships up and down
the chain of command and across all
departments of the company. Through
these different relationships you are able
to gather information to assess your
position, and the interactions enable
you to execute your sales cycle strategy. Most importantly, you can develop

internal coaches to serve as your eyes
and ears when you are not around.

Your coach (aka internal champion)
can introduce you to other key decision-
makers and influencers involved in the
selection process. These introductions
take advantage of the theory of attached
relationships, where the salesperson is
attached to an existing relationship and
bestowed with the same qualities, such
as standing, character, and reputation.
Assuming the introductory relationship
is positive, the salesperson is automatically thought of in the same manner.

The Seven Account Control Requirements

Only one competing vendor can be in
control of an account at a time. In this
position you try to protect yourself from
the attack strategies of competing vendors. Strive to fortify your personal relationships to deflect the other vendors.
Through the natural strength of this position, take the high ground over the other
vendors by engaging in only positive tactics that demonstrate integrity or directly
influence the selection process. You are
in harmony with the customer and the
customer will defend you against others. Once in this quadrant, the goal is to
stay there for the remaining stages of the
sales cycle.

The seven requirements associated
with account control are as follows:

1. Intimate knowledge of the selection
   process, along with the negotiation
   and procurement processes after the
   finalist has been chosen

2. Ability to influence the selection process or direct stages of the customer's evaluation

3. Trusted relationships and rapport with evaluation team members and other key sales cycle influencers

4. Ability to persuade people involved in the selection process to follow your advice and recommendations and disseminate information on your behalf

5. Privileged intelligence about the politics of decision-making and who is for or against your solution

6. Accurate information about your account standing and whether you are winning or losing

7. Access and rapport with senior executives who must approve and pay for the purchase

In chapter 21 we'll review how to chart your position and create an account control spider chart. This will help you determine areas of account control strength and weakness at a specific account.

> *It's not the number of deals you are working on that's important; it's the number of deals you are in control of.*
>
> —Top Salesperson

Chapter 21. How to Create an Account Control Spider Chart

Time takes on an additional dimension of meaning during the sales cycle. Usually, we think of time as a continuum. We spend most of our mental energy thinking about the immediate tasks before us. We typically don't consider time to be a finite resource. There's always tomorrow, next week, next month, or next year. During the sales process, time is not just minutes and days; it is actually a measure of deal momentum. Therefore, increasing momentum in a deal represents good or positive time, and backward momentum is bad or negative time.

We can plot our momentum in an account over time using an account control quadrant chart. Figure 21.1 is an example of positive momentum at an account. Notice the advancing position from the blind quadrant in January to the competitive quadrant in February, representing that more significant relationships were developed. Then in late March there is forward movement to the in control quadrant, reflecting that the salesperson is positioned to win.

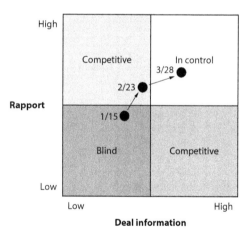

Figure 21.1 Account control quadrant chart showing positive momentum

Exercise: Visit www.stevewmartin.com/salesstrategyplaybooktemplates and download the account control quadrant chart. Select the key deals you are working on and chart your position in each account going forward.

We can also chart our level of account control and likelihood of winning the business and overcoming customer inertia, which results in no decision being made. In chapter 20 we reviewed the seven requirements to maintain account control. First, we rank the seven account control criteria on a scale of 1(low) to 10 (high).

___ 1. Intimate knowledge of the selection process, along with the negotiation and procurement processes after the finalist has been chosen

___ 2. Ability to influence the selection process or direct stages of the customer's evaluation

___ 3. Trusted relationships and rapport with evaluation team members and other key sales cycle influencers

___ 4. Ability to persuade people involved in the selection process to follow your advice and recommendations and disseminate information on your behalf

___ 5. Privileged intelligence about the politics of decision-making and who is for or against your solution

___ 6. Accurate information about your account standing and whether you are winning or losing

___ 7. Access and rapport with the senior executives who must approve and pay for the purchase

Then we rank the following:

___ Overall ability to beat the competition and overcome no decision.

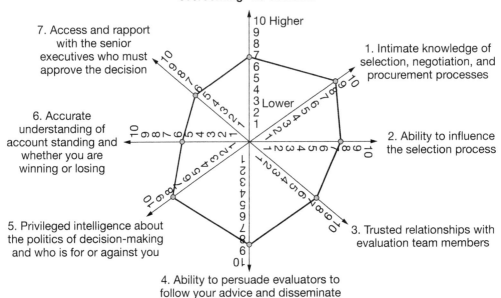

Figure 21.2 Account control spider chart showing radius measurements

Next, we plot the numbers on an account control spider chart and draw lines between the requirements as shown in figure 21.2. The smaller the web, the greater the odds of losing (or no decision), while the larger the web the higher the likelihood of winning. Just like the spider wants its web as big as possible, you want your web to become larger and larger over time. Wherever the dots on the radial lines (known as spider web radii) are low, these ratings require immediate action to correct. In figure 21.2, accurate understanding of positional strengths and weaknesses and rapport with senior executives are too low.

Exercise: Download the account control spider chart from www.stevewmartin.com/salesstrategyplaybookforms and complete spider charts for the most important accounts you are working on.

Chapter 22. Win More Business Using an "Indirect" Approach

For decades, business-to-business selling has been conducted in basically the same way. Salespeople directly approach customers armed with facts, features, and the benefits of their products to persuade customers to buy. However, customer decision-making has changed and today's buyers are smarter and more sophisticated than ever. In addition, your competitors have not sat idly by. They're focused on defeating you so they have educated themselves about your products and sales tactics. Sales success in today's times requires a new way of thinking about sales strategy. The

question is, What is the right strategy for today?

In his classic book *Strategy,* famous military historian Liddell Hart detailed the "indirect" approach to war. In painstaking detail he described the superiority of the indirect approach over the direct approach, using examples throughout the history of warfare. He theorized that the outcome of every major war from Roman times through World War II could be attributed to the approach the parties selected. Instead of a brute force direct attack to overwhelm the enemy, the victors always chose to battle indirectly. When forced to fight, the indirect approach involves using surprise, intelligence, logic, psychology, and human nature to exploit the enemy's weaknesses.

Hart argued that the indirect approach was not solely a war strategy but also an influential philosophy that could be applied wherever opposition to new ways of thinking exists. He said, "The direct assault of ideas provokes a stubborn resistance, thus intensifying the difficulty of producing a change of outlook. The suggestion that there is a bargain to be secured is far more potent than any direct appeal to buy."[1] Below, you will find seven principles of the indirect approach and their business-to-business sales application.

1. *Employ psychology.* The first and foremost principle is that the indirect approach is a psychological operation ("psy-op" in military jargon) based upon understanding, predicting, and influencing human nature. In sales, winning requires earning the trust, respect, and friendship of another human being. The victor

builds the strongest customer relationship while inflicting mental and emotional trauma on his enemies. The secondary psychological goal is to elevate the enemy's combat fatigue and skepticism about winning because a halfhearted warrior is more than halfway to losing.

2. *Control your destiny.* During a long sales cycle of several months or more, it's easy to focus on individual battles and lose sight of winning the war. The sales cycle is reduced to a series of battles without an overriding grand strategy. Salespeople become fixated on the next customer interaction, proceeding from the initial sales call to the sales presentation, then on to the product demonstration and evaluation. However, all salespeople are like generals who should create a strategy to win their wars long before the first battle begins. Successful military leaders are in control of their destiny. They preplan how and where they will attack in accordance with the resources at their disposal. Victorious commanders achieve their objectives through calculated maneuvers to gain the advantage and countertactics to neutralize the enemy's advantages.

3. *Know your enemies.* How well do you know your competitors? How much time do you spend studying their websites, products, and marketing collateral? Do you take the time to perform an honest win-loss analysis after each engagement? Most salespeople argue that they simply don't have enough time for these types of activities. However, history repeats itself for those who don't learn from the past.

4. *Be the first on the battlefield.* As a rule, it is always best to be the first salesperson in an account. The chance to understand a customer's environment first, establish relationships, and set the criteria for the selection process are obvious advantages. But if you work for an underdog company that competes against industry favorites, being the first on the battlefield is the difference between success and failure.

5. *Use spies to provide privileged information.* Nearly twenty-five hundred years ago Chinese general Sun Tzu wrote about the indirect strategy when he said, "Knowledge of the enemy's position can only be obtained from other men. Hence, the use of spies."[2] These words are still true today. In order to win any complex sale you need proprietary information that only a spy can provide. These spies are members of the selection team, other company employees, or even business partners. They provide valuable information about the internal machinations of the selection process and inform you about the thoughts of the various selection team members. Without a spy, you never know how well you are positioned in an account or what the enemy's next move will be.

6. *Understand how the objective is organized.* All battlefield commanders need location-based information so they can map the way to reach their objective. Similarly, salespeople need a complete understanding of how the evaluators are organized within their company because political power during the decision-making

process goes far beyond the lines and titles on an organization chart.

If you are involved in selling an enterprise solution, you already know the importance of understanding the inner workings of the various departments within a company. Your product might be purchased by the information technology department and used by accounting and manufacturing. Therefore, it's critical to map out the political interrelationships between evaluators and their respective departments of the organization (see chs. 31–35).

7. *Create turning points.* The indirect approach is based upon creating turning points that cause enemies to lose momentum they can never regain. Like war, every deal has a critical moment, or turning point, that determines the winner and the loser. In sales, information can be used to create turning points that eliminate competitors. Your expertise on the customer's industry, understanding of best practices, knowledge of unflattering facts about your archrival, and the willingness to raise critical issues the customer is unaware of can be used to create turning points.

For the sales warriors of the business world today, the difference between being hailed as a hero or branded a failure hinges on winning. But in order to win, you must know the steps it takes to develop a winning strategy. Winning is everything in sales as it is in war. In the words of indirect approach practitioner General George Patton, "If everyone is thinking alike, then someone isn't thinking."[3]

Chapter 23. Positional Tactics to Gain Account Control

All B2B sales are intense, high-stakes, very personal battles between two individuals or two groups of people: you and your competition. The victor will savor the spoils of winning while the loser experiences humiliation and sometimes much worse.

A variety of positional tactics can be employed to establish and maintain account control. These tactics are either directed at a vendor to lessen his leadership position or executed to improve the salesperson's position in the account. This list is by no means all-inclusive of the possible options. Rather, it is provided to help you brainstorm on ideas to gain account control.

*   *AWOL.* "Absent without leave" is a term for when a person of responsibility abandons his or her duties and disappears without permission or explanation. In sales, it quite often makes sense for salespeople who suspect they are losing to go AWOL and disappear. Doing so forces an interested customer to pursue the salesperson. For example, when the customer asks for information, the salesperson will not provide it until he gets the information or commitments he wants in return. Doing nothing sometimes frustrates the members of the selection team who are working against the salesperson as it forces them to spend additional time dealing with this disruptive person. Other times, it is exactly what they would like to have happen as

they want the salesperson and his solution to quietly disappear.

- *Bombardment.* In the sales vernacular, "bombardment" refers to the tactic of sending a constant stream of technical information, business justification material, and company marketing propaganda to the various levels of personnel within the account you are trying to win. Senior executives should receive short, high-level summary information, such as press articles or one-page industry analyst reviews. Midlevel managers should be sent more detailed case studies from other successful customers and case-use white papers. Low-level, hands-on product evaluators should receive data sheets and detailed implementation guides. Bombardment is an excellent "beachhead tactic" to use when you are trying to develop some recognition and credibility with particular individuals you have yet to meet during the sales cycle.

- *Camouflage.* Salespeople employ the camouflage tactic by enlisting a member of the selection team or other key influencer to disseminate positive information about their solution and negative information about competitors while they remain hidden in the background. A very simple example of a camouflage is asking an internal champion or coach to casually endorse your product to the CIO over lunch.

- *Competitor ambush.* Perhaps the most effective sales example of ambushing the competition is telling a prospect about the competition's customers who have dumped their products and

switched to yours. Even a competitor who is way ahead in the lead can lose his position when the customer hears these enormously destructive stories.

- *Deep battle.* Deep battle is an appropriate sales tactic when you sense a selection committee is aligned against you and fear its recommendation to senior management. The goal of deep battle is to use a coach—a friend on the inside—to introduce you to the ultimate and final decision-makers, the bully with the juice and emperor who exist in every account (see ch. 36). You want a chance to plead your case in person. A salesperson may also ask the president, vice president of sales, and other senior executives from within his company to blindly call their counterparts at the customer's company. If the tactic is successful, you will have neutralized the selection committee's power and have a chance to win the deal. If the tactic fails (which is often the case), you will have alienated the committee and therefore lost.

- *Land mine.* A land mine is a premeditated action that is intended to stop a competitor as he tries to engage and gain momentum with the customer. What type of land mine will you execute? Will you lie in wait until that competitor makes a statement you know you can clearly contradict and ruin his reputation in the process? Will you demonstrate functionality that your opponents can't match? Are you going to tell the customer about a new, unreleased product; provide third-party objective opinions; or disclose negative information about a competitor based upon your own experiences? When will the land mine be set? Will it be during the big sales presentation on the third PowerPoint slide or in an informal meeting with the customer?

- *Left flank (logic).* Flanking is a battlefield movement that consists of changing one's position to gain an advantage. The left-flank tactic is based upon logic and information. Flanking to the left refers to the tactic of changing the customer's selection criteria or raising a critical issue the customer is unaware of. It is named after the left side of the brain, the part that is analytical and invokes rational reasoning and deductive logic.

- *Parting shot.* A parting shot is a sharp, telling remark or critical communication made by a salesperson to strike a blow at the decision-makers' confidence. Examples include warnings about failed customer installations, critical memorandums sent to executives about the selection team members' competence, or predictions about the future failure of the project.

- *Pincer attack.* In sales, the two pincers that crush your opponents are relationships and information. When customers like you personally and believe your product to be the best (whether real or imagined), you are placed in the advantageous position of being able to control and edit the information flowing to and from the other vendors. This lopsided combination of personal friendships and information superiority are pincers that crush the competition.

- *Right flank (people).* The right-flank sales tactic is associated with the people involved in the decision process. It is named after the right hemisphere of the brain, which is dominant for facial recognition, spatial abilities, and visual imagery. A right-flank movement is focused on finding coaches within an account. Coaches are individuals who seem to like you, are receptive to your position, and appreciate your company. For example, you might make a right-flank maneuver and go around your main contact within an account in order to set up a meeting and establish a relationship with a more powerful decision-maker.

- *Scorched earth.* This tactic involves using any means necessary to stop the deal from happening. At this point, you are only trying to prevent the other vendors from winning. This is an extreme measure of last resort. Examples include calling the customer's senior management and explaining that the selection process was biased because decision-makers had improper relationships with the winning vendor, complaining to interested outside parties (regulatory boards, media outlets, financial investors, and the general public) about misconduct during the selection process, seeking legal action to stop the purchase, and offering to provide your product at a greatly reduced price or even for free.

- *Shield.* The shield tactic involves developing advocates (guides and emissaries described in chapter 37) within an account who shield and protect you from the slings and arrows of your competitors and from naysay-ers within the company. The stron-gest of these shields is provided by a senior executive—president, CFO, CIO, or vice president—who is back-ing your solution. Regardless of your advocates' direct involvement in the selection process, the private opin-ions of these powerful people work behind the scenes to ward off known rivals and unseen internal detractors.

- *Smoke screen.* The smoke screen tac-tic is based upon an indirect strategy. For example, salespeople schedule meetings to discuss product func-tionality when in reality they are using these meetings to discern the per-sonal biases of decision-makers.

  Salespeople may change the topic of conversation during a sales call to a strong point in order to avoid a discussion about a deficiency. They provide customers with detailed information or technical specifica-tions about their products' strengths in order to divert attention from the products' known weaknesses.

- *Sniping.* Not everyone on the cus-tomer's selection committee will be enamored with you and your solu-tion. Occasionally an individual may be so ardently opposed to you and your company that that person must be taken out of the selection process altogether. Sniping involves lying in wait for the perfect moment to dis-credit and take out a detractor. For example, a lower-level employee who is voicing opinions against you must be removed from the sales process. You instill fear in the senior executives that the project will be unsuccessful with this person on the team. Sniping is very uncomfortable to do, but there are times when you must silence your opposition.

- *Stalking.* Contrary to common sense, some salespeople are actually able to hound the customer into purchasing their solution. They will not abandon the account or leave the decision-makers alone until the customer buys from them. The relentless, unapolo-getic hounding and stalking of the customer is a very risky approach as it can backfire as well.

- *Team crossfire.* The team crossfire tactic involves using other people that are part of your sales team to help you win a deal. It may include other members of your company, such as your presales system engi-neer, implementation consultants, or business partners, who have a vested interest in your winning. You fire away at the competition together. It's a logic-based sales tactic designed to cause doubt in the customer's mind about another vendor's capabilities while bolstering your position.

- *Tempo.* The tempo tactic involves using the element of time to gain an advantage. In some sales situations a rapid full force response with your best resources in the quickest pos-sible time is best. "Rapid" means the ability to move quickly before an adversary can react. "Full force" can be defined as the ability to domi-nate an adversary both physically and psychologically. In other situa-tions, it is necessary to spread out and lengthen the selection process. Offering to complete a detailed on-site study of the customer's busi-ness, inviting the customer to make site visits to other installations, and taking the customer on a tour of your corporate headquarters are great examples of tempo tactics. These events allow you to demonstrate your expertise, and they give you additional time to build the personal relationships you need to win.

- *Unload the bus.* This involves applying as many personnel resources as you can to an account. Sales calls are an opportunity to demonstrate company strength, and the salesperson may ask his support team (subject-matter experts, system engineers, consultants, product managers, sales managers, company executives, and so on) to attend.

- *Vendor cross-examination.* The vendor cross-examination tactic seeks to force adversaries to answer uncomfortable questions about their products, companies, and reputations. You want the customer to interrogate them about their faults on your behalf. At other times, you want to influence the sales cycle such that the customer creates unnecessary and unimportant steps that keep the other vendors busy responding to minutiae.

- *Wedge issues.* The wedge issues tactic is based on the repetition of key differentiating information. Let's say you have advantageous benchmark information that shows your product is faster than your opponent's solution, which happens to be in the lead. At every possible opportunity, you harangue the customer about the implications of poor performance, the technical differences between the products that cause poor performance, how much unnecessary equipment would need to be purchased to rectify the performance problem, and the business impact of poor performance. You continually hammer on performance in order to create an opening, a wedge or gap between the leader and the customer, where you can begin to spread your company's story and your product's benefits to the decision-makers.

Different positional tactics can be employed together to drive a successful outcome. For instance, a meeting can be set up under the guise of one topic using the smoke screen tactic when the goal is really to gain access to a specific person (right flank) and influence that person to change the logical selection criteria (left flank) by reciting key wedge issues.

Chapter 24. The Three Components of Sales Strategy Creation

Sales strategy is defined as the overriding plan to win the business by establishing and maintaining account control. The goals are to neutralize competitors' advantages and place them in a defensive position, while always anticipating "no decision" and motivating the customer to buy. The strategy is based upon executing a series of customer interactions (sales calls, presentations, demonstrations, and so on) and maneuvers. Maneuvers (such as phone calls, letters, and emails) are specific actions intended to move a salesperson to the next interaction.

Sales strategy creation can be broken down into three components. The first component is the different sales cycle factors that define the type of account you are trying to win. The second component is the account control components that serve as the framework to create and execute the strategy. The final component is the purpose behind customer interactions during the sales cycle as shown in figure 24.1.

Sales cycle	Account control	Customer interaction
Type of product Point-specific Platform Enterprise	**People involved in decision** Politics of decision-making Buyer personas Human nature of decision-making	**Build rapport and relationships** Likability and harmonious communication Trusted advisor relationship
Type of sales cycle Renewal/add-on Persuasion Creation	**Process of engagement** Established sales process Sales intuition and pursuit knowledge Positional tactics based on competition	**Establish situational dominance** Professional differentiation Influencing of opinions and beliefs **Gather information** Discovery and competitive perceptions Deal qualification and triangulation
Type of buyer Intra-departmental Consolidator Consulter Responder Bureaucrat	**Product and company positioning** Value, ROI, and proof points Best practices and successful clients Business compatibility	**Educate** Learning styles and information dissemination Handling of objections and changing opinions
Key evaluators Coach Bully with the juice Emperor	**Provocation versus alignment** Alignment with customer's thought process Transformation of customer's thought process Provocation of customer's thought process	**Motivate action and close** Achievement of sales call goal and outcomes Mutual understanding and purchase motivation

Figure 24.1 Sales strategy elements

Sales Cycle Components

The sales cycle components include the complexity of the product you sell and whether it is point-specific, platform, or enterprise. As discussed in chapter 14, each sales cycle varies in complexity depending upon the number of individuals and departments involved in the selection process. The sales strategy will be dependent upon the sales cycle type and whether it is a renewal or add-on, persuasion, or creation.

Strategy is predicated upon the type of buyer and which area of the company is driving the decision. Buyer types can be classified as intradepartmental or enterprise (interdepartmental). Intradepartmental buyers are purchasing a product that will be used solely within their department, so they have complete decision-making authority. Enterprise buyers are selecting a product that a variety of departments will use, so more decision-makers are involved. Enterprise

buyer types include the consolidator, consulter, responder, and bureaucrat (see chs. 31–34). Key evaluators play important roles during the selection process such as a coach, bully with the juice, and emperor (see chs. 36–37). Finally, strategy is predicated upon knowing whether you are behind or in control.

Account Control Components

The second element of strategy is the account control components. The grand strategy should always be based upon an approach to influence the people, politics, and customer's selection process through the strategic positioning of your company and product's unique proof points.

People Involved in Decision

It is critical to identify all the members of the evaluation team and the extended network of influencers and deal approvers in an account. Beyond titles and reporting structure, also seek to understand the politics of decision-making and how group decision-making will impact the outcome. The complex interrelationships between evaluators and their behavior in group settings are unique to every sales cycle. Specifically, identify each individual buyer's persona (see chs. 73–77) to understand how he processes and transmits information, the ability of that person to influence the evaluation group, and the political power each wields. This information is used to plan and execute sales tactics.

Process of Engagement

Most companies have identified a sales process to serve as a framework for the sales organization to engage potential clients. This playbook provides a step-by-step guide for how the salesperson manages the buying process. The sales process is unique to companies and tailored to the solutions they sell. Figure 24.2 shows examples of the sales engagement process for an on-premises

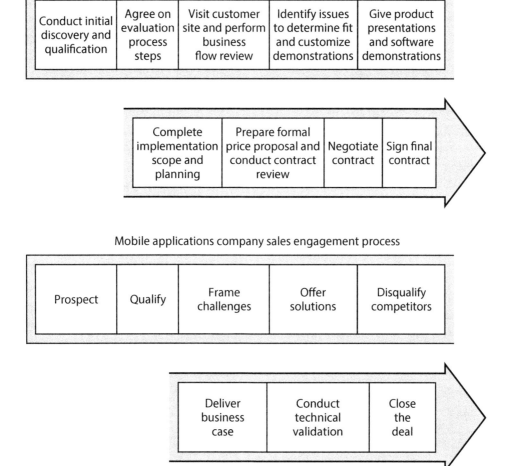

Figure 24.2 Different sales process engagement examples

software and mobile application company. The sales process is part of sales cycle strategy, not the sales strategy in itself.

The sales engagement processes serve as the blueprint by which the salesperson is ideally working new accounts. However, the salesperson has the difficult task of applying these steps in the real world. The value the salespeople add to the process is their pursuit knowledge and sales intuition based upon previous sales cycle experiences. Sales intuition is the process of comparing a series of past experiences against current circumstances. Think of sales intuition as a highly developed model for making decisions and a powerful heuristic engine constantly learning from every sales call. When a salesperson invokes his intuition, he can recognize account standing and select the best positional sales tactics (see ch. 23) to gain the leadership position.

> *Vendor A came in with quite a few people, and from day one they studied our business processes. Then they came back with a demo that really tried to match as much of our process as possible. They also prepared a very thorough RFP response with lots of material about services and references. They showed us they were organized, had real-world experience, and had a high level of professionalism.*
>
> —Vice President of Technology

Product and Company Positioning

To stand out you have to be different. You need a more sophisticated approach that differentiates your solution in the minds of customers. You can't *tell* customers you're unique, different, and one of a kind. You must *demonstrate* it to them, starting with the framework to position your product and company.

Logical arguments alone, no matter how well you present them, will not change skeptics into believers. Finessing customers to change their opinions requires an appeal to their human nature. The positioning of your company and product starts by understanding the strategic, operational, political, and psychological value you provide the evaluators (see ch. 40). This is communicated as you describe how you can solve their problems better than other competitors as the foundation of your sales strategy.

Sales strategy is based upon the creation of intellectual, logical, and psychological appeal. The goal is to build credibility with the prospect by methodically explaining background information, facts behind your business approach, and your technical superiority that will ensure the prospect's success. Sales strategy requires clearly defining the business problem that needs to be solved (or the opportunity that can be created), the cause of the problem (or reason for the opportunity), the possible options that can be utilized to solve the problem (or achieve the opportunity), and the goal realized when the problem is solved (or when the opportunity is realized).

One of the key budgeting factors (see ch. 27) that determines which projects will be approved is the investment payback period. Projects are prioritized by return on investment. Two good rules of thumb are to never assume a purchase is budgeted and always presume evaluators need your help to justify their purchase internally. Do not expect them to build the business case on their own. Equally important, you don't want your business case presented again. You want to be the person who presents the ROI justification to the key company leaders.

One of the biggest problems most salespeople have is they are too eager to tell the customer about their products. They do not build a story line that piques customer interest. Instead of launching into the product line and technical aspects of the products, the focus should be on the success of existing clients and the best practices you provide. Customer examples are very important. Presenting examples from companies that mirror the prospect's business objectives has a powerful impact.

Your strategy should be based upon diagnosing the customer's situation using an unbiased third-party point of view. Do you understand the customer's problem and have the credibility to recommend a solution? Do you understand how to solve their problem from the strategic, operational, and financial perspective (including all costs, ROI, and payback scenarios)? Have you provided real-world results from your existing clients and other tangible evidence that your solution is better than the others? If so, then you have shown your business compatibility and demonstrated you are a fit.

Provocation versus Alignment

The drive to take command of a situation is instrumental to a salesperson's success. Just as a doctor must sometimes prescribe a painful treatment to heal a patient, in some sales situations you must control prospective customers to help them. Conversely, at other accounts you must align with their business strategy and follow their decision-making process explicitly. In the next chapter we'll review when to align, transform, or use provocation to interrupt and change the customer's thought process.

Customer Interaction Components

Salespeople work with the unpredictable part of the sales process: people. Their job is to formulate an interaction strategy based upon the people who comprise the organizations they are trying to sell to. This is one of the most important aspects of sales strategy that the salesperson controls.

Every customer interaction can have different purposes. At the foundation are personal likability and rapport. Rapport is a special relationship between two individuals based upon harmonious communication. The salesperson's job is to build rapport with a wide variety of people across the company. You have to communicate with lower-level staff, mid-level managers, and most importantly, C-level executives. To do so, you need to change your demeanor and speak different languages depending upon the person you are meeting with. You wouldn't think of talking to a CFO as you would a computer programmer. The CFO and programmer have entirely different buyer personas that influence how they select products.

The purpose of the interaction is to establish situational dominance where the customer follows your advice. You also want to gather and triangulate information to qualify the opportunity and educate the customer in his learning style to overcome objections. Finally, you need to use the appropriate closing strategy to realize the goal of the sales call. Each of these customer interaction topics is covered in part IV, New Account Penetration Strategy and part V, Personal Sales Strategy.

Chapter 25. When to Use Provocation, Transformation, or Alignment Selling Styles

In some sales situations, it is necessary to align with the customer's thought process in order to win. These customers are experienced and knowledgeable about their business and technical fields. They are specialists who have buyer personas (see chs. 72–77) that command authority and demand respect. The vetting process they employ is designed to screen out unqualified vendors who don't conform to their established business principles or fit their technical environment. For example, an IT department that spent millions of dollars implementing SAP, Microsoft, or Oracle solutions will probably not entertain vendors that aren't integrated with these solutions.

There are other situations where the customer's thought process must be transformed and gently shaped over the course of the sales cycle. This is based on developing rapport with the customer to gain the control position. For example, one top salesperson I studied was an extremely curious person by nature. Like a plane crash investigator, he continually analyzed small pieces of information to construct the entire puzzle. He placed himself in the customer's shoes to understand his problems and know when and why he would buy. He was an extremely independent person driven to know how things worked and was not comfortable until all the i's were dotted and the t's were crossed. Gradually, over the course of the sales cycle, he gained the customer's respect as a trusted advisor. He was then able to shape the customer's thought process by sharing his expertise, prescribing cures, and suggesting corrective actions.

It may be necessary to divert and separate the customer from his existing thought process and change his way of thinking to stand out from the competition. This requires a realignment of his beliefs through provocation by challenging his preconceived ideas, biases, or decision-making methodology. For example, another top technology salesperson I studied had a strong situational dominance instinct, which includes the propensity to take command in social settings (see ch. 99). He was a verbal warrior who said exactly what was on his mind. However, he was not reckless about his words. Rather, he used them with precision to reach the core of the customer's psyche and reveal the hidden biases and silent objections that are always in the back of someone's mind. He was an accomplished conversationalist who was able to persuade customers to change.

The sales linguistic term for this type of mental reorientation is "pattern interruption" (see ch. 82). The pattern interruption engages the customer and provokes open-mindedness. The goal of a pattern interruption is to break the customer's current mode of thinking by detaching pre-existing thoughts.

Detaching can be an effective tool in situations where you want to change a behavior quickly. For example, when you greet someone, you will cheerfully say, "How are you doing?" The automatic response is "fine" or "okay." It is the expected and anticipated response attached to that particular question. Let's pretend the response is "My dog just died." This answer is completely opposite from the expected response. Immediately, you would be detached from being cheerful and become somber or apologetic.

As shown in figure 25.1, you can be in alignment with the customer's thought process on how he will solve the problem in order to achieve the goal. By building rapport and earning the customer's trust you can gradually transform his thought process over time. Or you can perform a pattern interruption early in the sales cycle and completely change the customer's thought process.

The following analogy explains the difference between alignment, transformation, and provocation. A customer wanted to buy a comfortable pen from you because he planned to write a book. A salesperson using alignment might say, "We have a wide range of pens for sale, but this is our most popular because of its ergonomic grip and it will last longer since it contains 30 percent more ink." A salesperson using transformation would say, "Let me study how you write. Based upon this information, I will recommend not only the right pen but also the paper and pencils that would work best for you." A salesperson employing provocation would say, "What you really want is an iPad. It does so much more than a pen. You can write, edit your thoughts on the fly, and record them for easy retrieval. But most importantly, you can instantly share your important insights with people all over the world via the internet."

Situational dominance is a personal communication strategy by which the customer accepts your recommendations and follows your advice. In every account, you have an important choice to make. Will you provoke and challenge the customer to think differently about the future by changing how he does business and uses technology? Will you remain adaptable and selectively challenge or align yourself depending upon specific topics as the sales cycle progresses? Or will you try to align yourself to his current thought process and the manner in which he does business or uses technology today?

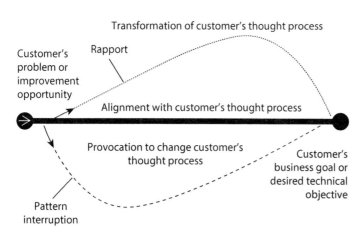

Figure 25.1 Alignment with, transformation of, and provocation to change the customer's thought process

Figure 25.2 represents the sliding scale of situational dominance.

The Five Ps of Provocation

Be forewarned, if you employ provocation incorrectly there is a high likelihood that you will alienate the customer. You will have lost momentum that cannot be regained and, for all intents and purposes, have lost the deal. Therefore, keep these five *P*s of provocation in mind.

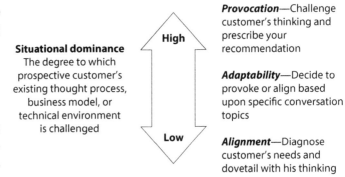

Situational dominance
The degree to which prospective customer's existing thought process, business model, or technical environment is challenged

Provocation—Challenge customer's thinking and prescribe your recommendation

Adaptability—Decide to provoke or align based upon specific conversation topics

Alignment—Diagnose customer's needs and dovetail with his thinking

Figure 25.2 Sliding scale of situational dominance

- *Principle driven.* The use of provocation should be based on your core principles and moral compass. In other words, your ethical values require you to question the customer's decisions or direction. You are morally obligated to stop the customer from making a mistake.

- *Planned in advance.* A successful provocation strategy is planned in advance and thought out ahead of time. Winging it and flying by the seat of your pants will usually fail.

- *Purposely initiated.* Provocation is not applied equally to every sales situation. It is purposely initiated when the circumstances require it.

- *Plainspoken.* Provocation cannot be delivered using words you don't feel comfortable with and a demeanor the customer doesn't respect. It should be delivered in a candid, forthright, direct, honest, transparent, open, straightforward, unambiguous way.

- *Personally detached.* No one wants to be bullied, intimidated, or forced to do something. Similarly, provocation should never be confused with aggressiveness or threatening behavior. Provocation should be delivered with sincerity and personal detachment from emotional excitement because situational dominance is not based upon physical or emotional dominance.

What is the natural situational dominance tendency among salespeople? In order to find the answer to this question, two hundred outside field salespeople were given a situational dominance test. Half of the salespeople were responsible for new account sales (also called "hunters") and the other half were responsible for install-base sales with existing clients (also known as "farmers"). Test scores indicate that the situational dominance tendency was higher for hunters and lower for farmers. Seventy-five percent of hunters had high or average situational dominance while 43 percent of farmers had slightly below average or low situational dominance as shown in figure 25.3.

	New account field salespeople	Existing client field salespeople
High situational dominance	28%	11%
Average situational dominance	47%	46%
Slightly below average situational dominance	18%	33%
Low situational dominance	7%	10%

Figure 25.3 Situational dominance test results for field salespeople

How Customers Perceive Provocation

There is a delicate balance between a salesperson being considered a valuable advisor whose advice is sought out versus alienating the customer by challenging his direction and belief systems. The following quotes are from customers who seek to change their business model. They need the help from outside their organization. They seek provocation from vendors in order to accomplish strategic change. Therefore, a high level of situational dominance should be employed by the salesperson working on these types of accounts.

As I look at our business, I see our people have been here a really long time. In other words, we have our own version of the truth, and what we know is what we know. We don't have a lot of insight into best practices from other companies. We wanted their sales team to tell us if there was a better way of doing processes and being more efficient. We would like them to come to us with recommendations and game-changing advances.

—Vice President of Manufacturing

Your people will tell you what you want to hear. It's a little bit like being the emperor who wore no clothes. What I need out of a partner is not just someone who will do what I tell them to do. I need someone who knows as much or more about the marketplace, who can shape my thinking and requests so they can provide the most value.

—President

We classify projects into three different categories; growth, run, and transformation. Transformation projects change the way we do business or establish new ways of doing business that we have never done before. Growth refers to organic year over year growth and run is the base infrastructure needed to run the business. The transformation projects are the most complex and we'll engage our network of vendors to help us plan and successfully complete them.

—Vice President of IT

Never forget you are probably selling to the individuals who charted their current strategic direction and selected the technology they use today. Therefore, there are times when the best strategy is to be aligned with them. For example, the following quotes are from customers who are not amenable to provocation. Rather, they seek solutions that complement their existing thought processes. These selection processes tend to be more tactical as opposed to strategic and usually involve less complexity. These sales cycles are better suited for the alignment or adaptable levels of situational dominance.

We wanted a vendor who was a fit to our business. We are a financial services company that is pretty dynamic in the way we operate, so we had to have a partner who was willing to work in our environment. We are looking for the firm that will understand our business. We are successful because of our business model, not the way any vendor operates. We are looking for the partner who comes to the table and says, "Okay, I get it and we're going to work with you and not impact your business model."

—Chief Information Officer

I've had many conversations where a salesperson said, "Did you think about this?" or "We can improve that better than what you're doing." This is simplistic thinking to some extent. There isn't a true understanding of the analysis and decision points that resulted in where we are today. Their assumptions are based upon false pretenses.

—Vice President of IT

Vendor A was trying to focus on the bigger picture and we were trying to tactically solve a problem. Their PowerPoint slides showed this grand vision and how all the pieces fit together, and we kept saying we're not doing that, we only want this piece right now. They couldn't

bring the conversation from the whole architecture of end-to-end solution to just talking specifics about one product. I tried to tell the salesperson a couple of times I felt like he was missing it with the approach he was taking. He kind of heard and kind of not.

—Vice President of IT

It is important to understand that people are open to different levels of change. Based upon win-loss sales cycle research, 20 percent of customers are genuinely open to change. Forty-five percent can be persuaded to change, while 35 percent are extremely resistant.

Chapter 26. What Selling Styles Do Buyers Prefer?

The selling style you use with a particular client will determine whether or not you gain situational dominance. With this in mind, what selling style do prospective buyers prefer? A study of B2B buyers shows that 40 percent preferred a salesperson who listens, understands, and then matches his solution to solve their specific problem, while 30 percent like a salesperson who earns their trust by making them feel comfortable that he will take care of their long-term needs. Another 30 percent want a salesperson who challenges their thoughts and perceptions and then prescribes a solution that they may not have thought of or didn't know about as shown in figure 26.1.

There are differences based upon whether the buyer is male or female. Figure 26.2 shows that when the results are

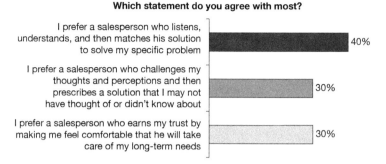

Which statement do you agree with most?

I prefer a salesperson who listens, understands, and then matches his solution to solve my specific problem — 40%

I prefer a salesperson who challenges my thoughts and perceptions and then prescribes a solution that I may not have thought of or didn't know about — 30%

I prefer a salesperson who earns my trust by making me feel comfortable that he will take care of my long-term needs — 30%

Figure 26.1 B2B buyer selling style preferences

analyzed by gender, women preferred the salesperson who makes them feel comfortable and takes care of their long-term needs. Men preferred the salesperson who understands and then matches a solution to solve their specific problem. Other differences between selling to men and women are covered in more detail in chapter 130.

There are also significant differences in selling preferences by industry. While banking and manufacturing preferences were fairly evenly split among all three styles, buyers in the government vertical unanimously selected a salesperson who listens and solves their specific needs. The technology vertical had the highest percentage of respondents who preferred a salesperson to challenge their thinking at 40 percent. Conversely, government and consulting verticals had the lowest percentages; only 20 percent of the consulting industry wanted a salesperson to challenge them. Buyers in the real estate

vertical don't want to be challenged at all. At 50 percent, they had the highest percentage of respondents who preferred a salesperson who earns their trust and will take care of their long-term needs.

From a departmental perspective, 15 percent of accounting and 19 percent of information technology department members want to be challenged, while 43 percent of engineering department members do. Over 50 percent of marketing, information technology, and engineering department members prefer a salesperson who listens and matches his solution to solve their specific needs. The sales department members equally preferred a salesperson who listens and solves their needs and one who challenged them, while human resources was equally split across all three selling styles.

There's an interesting explanation for selling style preferences that is based on whether the buyer is comfortable with

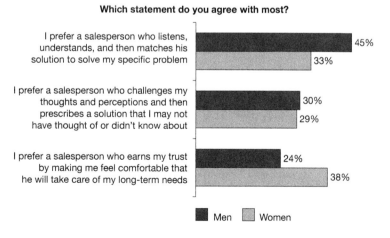

Which statement do you agree with most?

I prefer a salesperson who listens, understands, and then matches his solution to solve my specific problem — Men 45%, Women 33%

I prefer a salesperson who challenges my thoughts and perceptions and then prescribes a solution that I may not have thought of or didn't know about — Men 30%, Women 29%

I prefer a salesperson who earns my trust by making me feel comfortable that he will take care of my long-term needs — Men 24%, Women 38%

■ Men □ Women

Figure 26.2 Buyer selling style preferences by gender

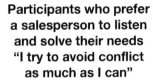

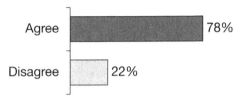

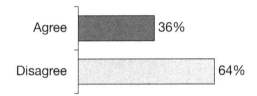

Figure 26.3 What motivates B2B buyer behavior

conflict as shown in figure 26.3. Seventy-eight percent of participants that preferred a salesperson who listens and solves their specific needs agreed with the statement "I try to avoid conflict as much as I can." Conversely, 64 percent of participants who preferred a salesperson who challenges their thoughts disagreed with the statement and are comfortable with conflict.

Now let's examine how buyers responded to this scenario:

Three salespeople gave you presentations about the products their companies offer. After the presentations you determine that all of the products are very similar in functionality and price. Which salesperson would you rather do business with?

- A professional salesperson who knows his product inside and out but is not necessarily someone you would consider befriending

- A friendly salesperson who is likable and proficient in explaining his product

- A charismatic salesperson whom you truly enjoyed being with but

is a not the most knowledgeable about his product

Sixty-six percent of survey participants selected the friendly salesperson, 23 percent the professional salesperson, and 11 percent the charismatic salesperson as shown in figure 26.4.

While the top selection of buyers from every industry was the friendly salesperson, it is interesting to note that the entertainment and fashion industries had the highest percentage of charismatic salesperson responses, and the manufacturing and healthcare industries had the highest percentage of professional salesperson responses. The reality is that prospective customers will choose to do business with someone who is likable over one who is solely considered professional or another one who is more charismatic. The reason behind this is that they want to feel comfortable communicating with the person and they value this characteristic the most. For instance, 81 percent of buyers would rather talk with someone who has the same mannerisms as they do.

Now take a moment to answer the following question: Which statement do you agree with most?

Three salespeople gave you presentations about the products their companies offer. After the presentations you determine that all of the products are very similar in functionality and price. Which salesperson would you rather do business with?

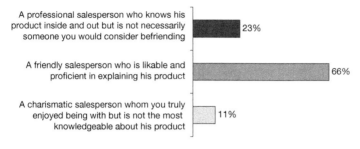

Figure 26.4 The type of salesperson that is preferred when products are similar

- Likability is an important differentiator between me and my competitors.

- Sometimes you have to point out that what customers are doing is wrong and proverbially tell them their "baby is ugly."

- Challenging the customers' point of view can make them feel too uncomfortable.

According to my research as shown in figure 26.5, when salespeople who achieved over 125 percent of their previous year's quota were asked about which statement they agreed with most, 49 percent indicated that likability was an important differentiator between them and their competitors. Conversely, 45 percent agreed with the statement "Sometimes you have to point out that what customers are doing is wrong and proverbially tell them their 'baby is ugly.'" In other words, sometimes you have to be provocative and confront customers' belief systems. This statement is indicative of someone who naturally exhibits situational dominance. Finally, 6 percent concurred with the statement that challenging the customer's point of view will make customers feel too uncomfortable. They aren't naturally inclined to be situationally dominant.

Situational dominance is a personal communication strategy by which the customer accepts your recommendations and follows your advice (see ch. 99). The drive to take command of a situation is instrumental to a sales professional's success. Just as a doctor must sometimes prescribe a painful treatment to heal a patient, in some sales situations you must control prospective customers to help them. Conversely, at other accounts you must align with their business strategy and follow their decision-making process explicitly. In every account, you have an important choice to make. The answer you selected above is a preliminary indicator of your natural level of situational dominance.

Most interestingly, the salespeople in each of these answer groups gave

Which statement do you agree with most?

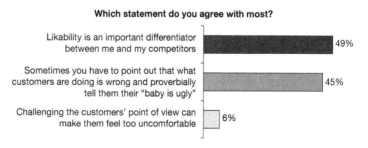

Figure 26.5 Sales philosophy characteristics of salespeople who achieved over 125 percent of quota

completely different reasons when asked why they are most likely to lose a deal. "I might have thought I was in a better position than I was" was the top answer for those who said likability was an important differentiator. "I was outsold" was the top answer for those who said you have to point out that what customers are doing is wrong. "Something outside of my control made it impossible to win" was the top answer for those who said challenging customers can make customers feel uncomfortable.

Chapter 27. Client Budgeting and Project Approval Processes

If you are involved in selling enterprise, platform, or point-specific solutions, you know the importance of understanding the inner workings of the various departments within a company. Your product might be purchased by the IT department and used by accounting and manufacturing. It might be selected by accounting and used by marketing and other areas of the organization. Or it could be selected solely by accounting for its internal use within the department.

Many purchase decisions require multiple departments to become involved. It's critical to map out the interrelationships of the departments within an organization, and most importantly, the power of the C-level executive who heads the department involved in the selection process. The organizational structure also determines who will sponsor the project and fund the purchase.

One of the most important sales questions is, "Where will the money come from to make the purchase?" In some cases, the answer is easy to find out while in others it is much harder to ascertain. In general, purchases can be classified as either "lights on" or "strategic innovation."

Lights-on purchases typically have to do with the ongoing operation of the business and existing infrastructure that is budgeted on an annual basis. For example, each department prepares an annual budget that includes ongoing costs, expenditures for anticipated growth, and money set aside to replace capital items that wear out or become obsolete during the fiscal year. Lights-on expenditures include planned expenditures that are allocated in the annual departmental budget and unplanned expenditures, which require money to be reallocated from the

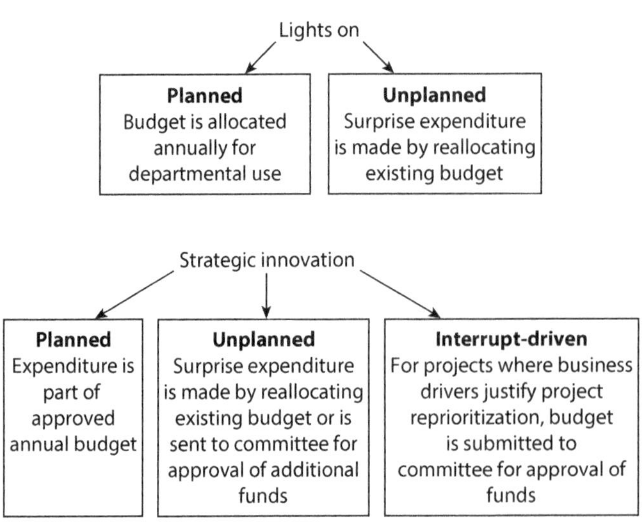

Figure 27.1 Different budget classifications

existing budget. These surprise expenditures may be the result of a drastic change in the business, such as an acquisition or any type of emergency.

We have a three-year plan that we update on a regular basis. The IT steering committee is made up of our senior executives that validate the prioritization of projects and approves the funding based upon business value and return on investment. When there is an unforeseen IT need or requirement imposed upon us that requires a major IT initiative, we essentially rob Peter to pay Paul. The projects that aren't started yet are evaluated and put on hold because overall funding is finite.

— Chief Information Officer

Organizations constantly search for strategic innovation to increase their revenues and drive down operating costs. Strategic innovation projects are budgeted on an annual basis but also can be added during the course of the year to the list of business initiatives. Strategic innovation has a larger scope and the projects impact the entire company. As a result, there is a cross-functional committee comprised of senior leaders from all areas of the organization that approve and prioritize which initiatives will be undertaken. Strategic innovation projects can include approved and planned expenditures for

the year, unplanned surprise expenditures that require funds, and "interrupt-driven" initiatives, where business drivers justify the expenditure. Figure 27.1 shows the different types of budgeting.

The type of products that garner executive attention are those that help set strategic direction. These solutions enable the execution of a long-term strategic plan or immediate business benefits in a short payback time frame. The business innovation these projects provide creates efficiencies that generate money to the bottom line or significantly increase topline revenues.

There is a continual reprioritization of projects during the year as more interrupt-driven projects are approved. Let's apply this model to the IT department. IT initiatives that have already been blessed by the cross-functional approval committee are tabled and delayed until the funds and the resources to complete the project are available. Or they may be canceled entirely. In the example shown in figure 27.2, ten strategic projects have been approved for the

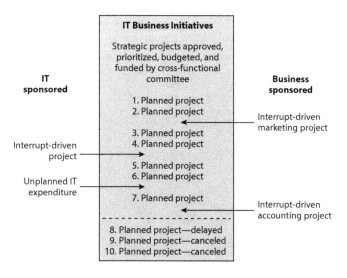

Figure 27.2 Strategic IT initiative planning showing delayed and canceled projects

current year. However, during the year three additional interrupt-driven initiatives and an unplanned IT expenditure caused project eight to be delayed until next year, and projects nine and ten had to be canceled.

> *When you are talking about large projects, the decision is made at the senior executive level. We have a number of governance committees that once projects have been identified as business cases, they are put through a process where we align resources based upon a supply-and-demand model. From there, they are brought to the senior executives and each project is rated on a number of dimensions such as risk, costs, and customer impact. If there's an idea raised by the business that says we can save millions if we do this project for a million, we may hit the pause button on an existing project in order to reallocate resources. We have actually done this on two large projects this year. If we believe the return is so significant, we will go out and hire additional resources as to not impact the other projects.*

—Chief Information Officer

Chapter 28. Procurement Is Different Than Sourcing and Supply Chain

Titles are very important as they reveal an organization's structure. I am continually amazed at the lackadaisical attitude many salespeople have about understanding the organizational structure of the companies they call on. When they are asked what a person's title is, they will answer, "manager," or something equally nebulous, when they should answer, "manager of application security who reports to the director of application development, who, in turn, reports to the vice president of business applications, who works for the CIO." Knowing the exact titles of the contacts you interface with during the purchasing process and whether they report to procurement, sourcing, or supply chain is critical.

Understanding the different philosophies between procurement, sourcing, and supply chain is important. Sourcing and supply chain buying professionals tend to be more sophisticated than general procurement buyers. They are knowledgeable about lean manufacturing techniques and can be certified in Six Sigma systems and principles. Procurement, sourcing, and supply chain are related to the sophistication of the company's purchasing requirements, the type of products the company creates, and the organizational complexity as shown in figure 28.1.

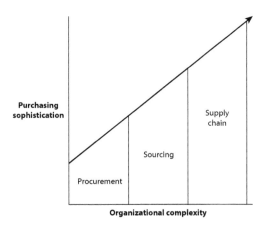

Figure 28.1 Purchasing organization department types

The procurement department's orientation is to consider the products it buys to be commodities. Products are basically interchangeable because there is little differentiation between the competing vendors' offerings. Therefore, price becomes the most important evaluation criterion. Sourcing is more innovative and open to input and recommendations from vendors. As a result, vendors are evaluated holistically, in a different context than procurement—based upon the overall potential of the relationship and its benefits. The supply chain is strategic to the business. The focus is on high-level company objectives at the direction of the senior-most levels of the company. The department establishes mutually beneficial strategic relationships with the vendors who can help it achieve its goals. Note the different orientation in the following quotes from procurement, sourcing, and supply chain managers.

My rule in dealing with salespeople is I like to dictate the relationship.

—Procurement Manager

If we are asking for XYZ today, show us you can do it cheaper than our current supplier. But from there, how can we both grow? What cost saving ideas and innovations can you bring to us? Never forget, I'm measured by the money I save the company, from my planned versus actual budget. There's always constant demand to reduce costs. Procurement is more tactical on the day-to-day basis. They execute by the parameters set by sourcing. Sourcing is identifying what we do and how we do it. What are the business requirements we have and how do we change the dynamics of what we are doing today? I qualify suppliers, assess risk mitigation, and establish supplier relationships.

—Director of Sourcing

I explained we had three main objectives for the manufacturing of the product. These objectives were passed down by senior management to put on the supply chain. The objectives were to have flexibility, flow, and velocity. Obviously, with a supply base that is 3,000 miles from the facility it is more difficult to accomplish.

—Supply Chain Manager

Companies that provide products or solutions that are embedded into products face another challenge. Whom should they call on and when do they need to contact them? During the product development phase, the prospective customer is open to innovation and the strategic involvement of vendors. As the product is defined and prototyped and

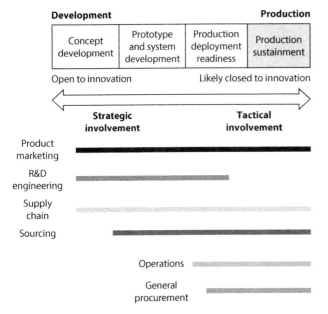

Figure 28.2 When departments are involved in product development

Chapter 29. The Truth about Price and Decision-Making

Price plays an important role in every sales cycle. Since it is a frequent topic during customer conversations, salespeople can become fixated on the price of their product and believe they have to be lowest. However, decision-makers have different propensities to buy, and the importance of price falls into three categories. Thirty-eight percent of buyers studied were "price conscious" and product price was a top decision-making factor. Forty-two percent were "price sensitive" and product price was secondary to other decision-making factors such as product functionality and vendor capability. Finally, 20 percent of buyers were "price immune," meaning they bought the products they want, as shown in figure 29.1. In this case, price becomes an issue only when the solution they want is priced far higher than the others being considered, typically above the 15 to 25 percent range.

the company prepares for its release, the customer is less likely to innovate and is not open to the strategic involvement of vendors. However, the customer may be open to the tactical involvement of vendors who offer improvements with very little change effort and risk.

Figure 28.2 shows product development stages and when the various departments within an organization become involved. During the concept development stage, product marketing (product management, brand management, and so on) and engineering (research and development) drive vendor decisions while supply chain issues are considered. As the concept becomes reality, sourcing and operations are involved. Note the time frame difference between general procurement versus sourcing and supply chain. Figure 28.2 should be interpreted as a general guideline because departmental involvement varies greatly by product type and from industry to industry.

Figure 29.1 Price as a deciding sales cycle factor

Price is always important, but what is the cultural fit between the organizations? Who has the ability to execute? What is our risk with the vendor? It clearly has some impact, but it is not the most important deciding factor. I would say we probably weight price at about 25 percent. However, when you get into double digit differences in price between vendors, then it starts to become material.

—Chief Information Officer

Price sensitivity is different for each company and industry. For example, industries that operate on very small gross margins, such as retail, tend to be price conscious. Conversely, industries where technology or the creation of intellectual property is a core part of the business, such as technology, legal, finance, and banking, tend to be less price conscious. Figure 29.2 shows the industry and departmental pricing classifications based upon an extensive study of B2B buyers who were asked to describe their pricing decision scenarios and questions. Consider these classifications as general guidelines because every situation is unique.

	Industry	Department
Price Immune	• Government	• Engineering
Price Sensitive	• Banking • Technology • Consulting	• Marketing • Sales
Price Conscious	• Fashion • Healthcare • Real Estate • Retail	• Accounting • Human Resources • IT • Manufacturing

Figure 29.2 Price sensitivity by industry and department

On the surface, it may seem contradictory that government is price immune. However, government buyers are personally not fixated on price. They know their procurement policy is based on the lowest bid or they will justify sole sourcing the purchase to get the exact product they want. So the issue of price is somewhat moot.

By the middle of the sales cycle, after the presentations, the group knew who they wanted to go with. The company we chose came out way ahead of the number two and we didn't go with the cheapest solution either. But we didn't want to make that known to them because in the event we couldn't make the negotiation work with our top pick, we could go back to number two.

—Corporate Manager

As a salesperson, you are constantly being compared to your competitors. But in reality, you and your company are being compared to all the vendors that they are doing business with. The purchasing departments are continually evaluating your company's product performance, customer service, and support of their account. Price is only one component of measurement and in most cases not the most important as indicated in this quote below from a C-suite level executive.

We rank vendors not only by spending but more importantly by strategic significance or if they are commodity-type vendors. This measure is how we feel how critical it is to maintain their services to our company, how easy it would be to

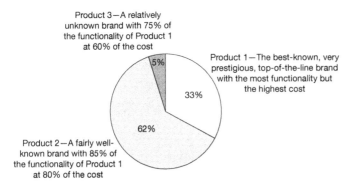

Let's say you are going to select an expensive product that you use every day from one of three on the list below. Which one would you choose?

Product 3—A relatively unknown brand with 75% of the functionality of Product 1 at 60% of the cost

Product 1—The best-known, very prestigious, top-of-the-line brand with the most functionality but the highest cost

5%
33%
62%

Product 2—A fairly well-known brand with 85% of the functionality of Product 1 at 80% of the cost

Figure 29.3 Buyer inclinations to purchase prestigious versus lesser-known brands

replace them, and what role their organization takes in helping us determine our strategy for our business. Now every vendor wants to be classified as strategic whether or not they deserve it. The worst place to be is to be thought of as a commodity vendor because we are going to grind you down on price because there is no value add.

In most industries there is a single company that dominates its market. In comparison to its competitors, it has a much larger market share, top-of-the-line products, greater marketing wherewithal, and more company cachet. For salespeople who have to compete against these industry giants, life can be very intimidating indeed.

However, the study results provide some much-needed good news in this regard. Evaluators aren't solely fixated on the market leader and are more willing to select second-tier competitors than one would

expect. In fact, only 33 percent of participants indicated they prefer the most prestigious, best-known, top-of-the-line brand with the highest functionality and cost. Conversely, 62 percent said they would select a fairly well-known brand with 85 percent of the functionality at 80 percent of the cost. However, only 5 percent would select a relatively unknown brand with 75 percent of the functionality at 60 percent of the cost of the best-known brand as shown in figure 29.3.

Not surprisingly, the answer to this question was different based upon industry. Fashion, banking, and real estate had the highest propensity to select the best-known, top-of-the-line product, while manufacturing and healthcare had the lowest.

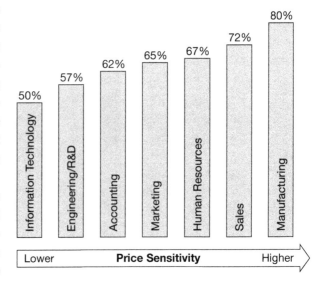

Figure 29.4 Departmental preferences to purchase lesser-known brands

From a departmental perspective, the information technology and engineering departments had the highest number of respondents who would select the best-known, top-of-the-line product followed by accounting and marketing as shown in figure 29.4. Conversely, manufacturing, sales, and human resources would be most likely to buy lesser-known brands with slightly reduced functionality if they were priced accordingly.

Now let's examine the impact of price when the functionality of the challengers' products is greater than that of the best-known company. The percentage of buyers who will buy the industry leader drops to 24 percent, while the percentage that will buy the least expensive product increases by over 25 percent as shown in figure 29.5. This proves that for three-quarters of buyers, a relationship exists between functionality and price.

Finally, the composition of the evaluation team will impact the price the customer is willing to pay. Specifically, men and women have different propensities to pay. Therefore, it is imperative you review the evaluation committee decision-making tendencies in chapter 130 and buyer personas in chapters 72–77.

Chapter 30. The Buyer's Journey and Impact of Vendor Websites

Every major B2B purchase progresses through four sales cycle stages, and different types of influencers determine which vendor is in the lead at each stage.

- *Buyer research stage.* The customer conducts independent research on the vendors, underlying technologies, and methodologies via the internet, analyst reports, product reviews, industry news, member associations, and elsewhere.

- *Product stage.* Based upon the research, the buyer contacts a select number of vendors and meets with their salespeople to learn more about the products. The buyer is validating the initial research and augmenting his knowledge of the respective products through interactions with each salesperson competing for the business.

- *Business stage.* As the sales process progresses, the buyer assesses which vendors offer the best business value and are a philosophical fit for the business.

- *Political stage.* The last stage is making a final decision between the top two or three vendors. The final decision is typically influenced by many political factors beyond the attributes evaluated in the product and business stages.

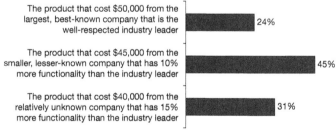

Let's say you are making a product selection from three competing companies. Which one would you pick?

The product that cost $50,000 from the largest, best-known company that is the well-respected industry leader	24%
The product that cost $45,000 from the smaller, lesser-known company that has 10% more functionality than the industry leader	45%
The product that cost $40,000 from the relatively unknown company that has 15% more functionality than the industry leader	31%

Figure 29.5 Buyer inclinations to select products based upon price and functionality

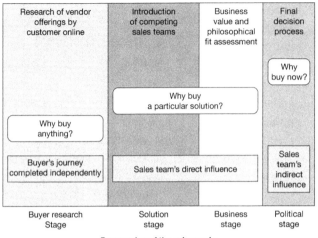

Figure 30.1 The buyer's journey and progression of the sales cycle

Study participants were asked, "Do vendor websites influence the final vendor selection you make?" Overall, 61 percent of study participants said the websites definitely influence their final decision, while 37 percent indicated they somewhat influenced their final decision. Only 2 percent said websites had no influence at all. In addition, these percentages were nearly identical across all departments.

Vendor websites are most influential at the beginning of the sales cycle in the buyer research stage. While the influence of internal politics and evaluation group dynamics become more important as the sales cycle progresses as illustrated in figure 30.1.

The importance of the vendor's website varies throughout the sales cycle. Early on, the website plays a pivotal role as evaluators decide which vendors are qualified. In the product stage, the majority of information is transmitted from the sales teams directly to the customer and the website serves as a validation checkpoint. The website's importance increases during the business and political stages as senior-level executives who weren't part of the evaluation team review the findings and recommendation as shown in figure 30.2.

What aspects of a website do evaluators consider most influential, and do the answers differ by industry? Study participants were asked to rate how eight different website topics influence their purchase decisions. The top three items for banking, computers, and consulting industries were the same: customer testimonials and success stories, competitive comparisons by industry analysts, and positive news/reviews by press and periodicals. The

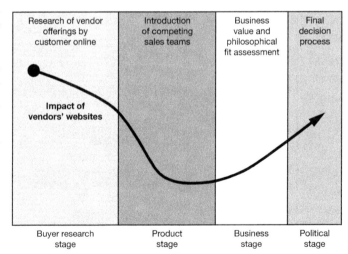

Figure 30.2 The relative impact of vendors' websites on the progression of the sales cycle

You are selecting between two different companies and looking at their respective websites. What influences your purchase decision?

	ALL	Banking	Computers	Consulting	Entertainment	Fashion	Government	Healthcare	Manufacturing	Real Estate
Detailed technical information such as data sheets and manuals	**59**	51	62	59	58	45	**63**	50	68	63
Positive reviews/news by press and periodicals	**70**	69	72	70	73	73	60	61	**69**	78
Competitive comparisons by industry analysts	**73**	74	74	72	72	73	67	74	76	72
Customer testimonials and success stories	**70**	67	80	71	69	75	52	**71**	70	68
Company background and history information	**48**	48	48	46	47	57	**70**	33	49	55
Best practices and insights that might be found on a blog	**57**	52	58	57	60	48	57	64	61	58
The look and feel of the website	**67**	62	60	67	**70**	85	53	**66**	75	60
The quality of the leadership team and interviews with key execs	**54**	57	56	52	51	60	40	30	58	**72**

Figure 30.3 Buyers rank website attributes by industry

top three items for entertainment and fashion industries were the same; the look and feel of the website, competitive comparisons by industry analysts, and positive news/reviews by press and periodicals.

Manufacturing and healthcare were also the same: the look and feel of the website, customer testimonials and success stories, and competitive comparisons by industry analysts. The top three aspects for government were unique and included company background and history information, detailed technical information such as data sheets and manuals, and competitive comparisons by industry analysts. Finally, real estate was the only industry to include quality of the leadership team and interviews with key execs in their top three.

The full list is shown in figure 30.3 with the top three aspects highlighted (one-hundred-point scale where the higher numbers are more important and the top three ranked items are shown in bold).

Your website is more than an online reference platform; it's an extension of the sales force. It sets the stage to ensure the salespeople are invited to participate in the customer's evaluation. It provides validation while salespeople discuss products and business capabilities with prospective clients. It provides affirmation to the senior-level decision-makers whom the sales force may never meet that they can confidently move forward with their purchase.

Chapter 31. The Consolidator Enterprise Buyer Type

Enterprise sales cycles typically involve large capital expenditure purchases that require long sales cycles. Multiple departments of a company and all levels of the organization (C-level executives, midlevel management, and lower-level personnel) are needed to approve the solution's functionality and its purchase. The consolidator buyer type is typically associated with enterprise sales cycles where the purchase will impact many areas of the company.

Consolidators are departments that have C-level executives who seek to increase their power, authority, or control within their organization. To grow their sphere of influence, they launch grand initiatives, major company-wide projects that affect the operations of other departments.

The planning and creation of a grand initiative are at the direction of the department's executive leadership. This type of project does not typically percolate up from lower-level personnel through the chain of command; it is driven down from the top and out to the rest of the company.

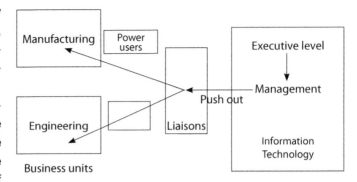

Figure 31.1 Consolidator enterprise buyer type

Figure 31.1 illustrates the consolidator's flow of power. In this example, the vice president of the information technology department has decided to drive an initiative to move all applications and programs off the company's aging mainframe computers onto new, less-expensive cloud-based applications. After making this executive decision, he mandates that his direct managers fulfill his wishes. These direct reports assemble teams to plan the project and evaluate the vendors. The business liaisons who report back to the information technology department gather information from the various departments, schedule vendor demonstrations with departmental power users, and serve as intermediaries between the various departments during project implementation.

Liaisons have an important role. Business liaisons' official function is to ensure a department is working well and satisfies the needs of the other departments within the organization. Business liaisons are the people who translate business needs between departments. In larger companies, common business liaison titles are "business analyst," "project manager," "facilitator," and "technical consultant." In smaller companies, the role of liaison usually is filled by departmental managers.

In one sense, every department within a company is a customer of every other department. And every department has very sophisticated users of the services of other departments. For example, the sales department has sales operations staff members who depend upon information from the finance department. The manufacturing department has technical personnel who use information from research and development.

The employees who fill the positions described above are called "power users." To accomplish their departmental roles, power users are required to have an intimate knowledge of their department as well as other departments. They must use the systems, information, equipment, or resources from another department to complete their jobs. Typical power users might have titles that include "specialist," "technician," "support," "administrator," or "leader."

Notice that the boxes representing manufacturing and engineering are smaller than the information technology box and that the business liaisons box is larger than the power users boxes. This indicates who is more dominant and has superior power. The sizes of the boxes are different in the illustrations of the other types of departmental buyers.

> The objectives for this project were passed down from the senior-most level of our company. This project was fast-tracked with an aggressive completion date so we selected a vendor who we knew could get the job done based on our previous experiences with them.
>
> —Director of Information Technology

The underlying motivation behind grand initiatives like this one is usually power, whether it's to gain more, consolidate it, or decrease that of other leaders and their departments within the organization. In the example above, the information technology department is exercising its power over manufacturing and engineering. Sometimes a grand initiative is an executive-level coup, an internal revolution intended to change the way the company operates. For example, a business leader takes the initiative to buy a turnkey SaaS (software as a service) cloud solution to avoid being at the mercy of IT. Many times, this is a well-orchestrated conspiracy in the guise of a logical business project. Other times, this is an act of revenge against an intercompany archenemy.

Consolidators are typically a salesperson's dream because they have a propensity to make things happen. "Big-bang consolidators" tend to buy the equipment and services they need to complete a grand initiative all at once. "Cautious consolidators," on the other hand, purchase the products and services they need piecemeal, taking one small step at a time in order to prove their project's success. Be forewarned, you should be tracking key executives when they switch jobs because they are definitely leaders who want to consolidate their power during their first six months on the new job.

Chapter 32. The Consulter Enterprise Buyer Type

The second type of enterprise sales cycle buyer is the consulter. Consulters are departments that have the characteristics and attributes of a consultant to their organization. They seek to understand the problems of other departments and offer recommendations on how those problems can be solved using their services.

They proactively share their proprietary knowledge and departmental expertise or offer unsolicited advice to other departments in an attempt to show how they can improve efficiency. Therefore, they are continually polling the other departments; seeking opportunities to promote their services; and pushing out their ideas, philosophies, and opinions. Liaisons are vitally important to consulters because they are gatherers and disseminators of information. As a result, liaisons have more power and influence with consulters than they do with consolidators.

Consulters are more prevalent in massive multibillion-dollar companies than in smaller organizations. The C-level executives are less powerful than their counterparts in the consolidator model, so

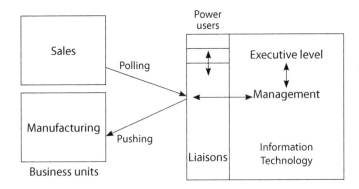

Figure 32.1 Consulter enterprise buyer type

they have to achieve their desired outcomes through finesse rather than brute force. Since consulters are constantly seeking customers for their services, the power users are more likely to be within the consulter's department than in another business unit.

> *We quite often find ourselves in the position of being the functional champion, proactively showing solutions to the business it can help. We're always saying "Hey, could this help you?" We want their people to see something so we can get some champions behind it.*

—Vice President of Information Technology

Figure 32.1 shows the information flow of a consulter department. In this example, the information technology department liaisons are constantly polling the business units for their needs and pushing out information they believe is beneficial.

For example, a liaison (see ch. 31) may seek out and meet with the vice president of sales, who expresses his dissatisfaction with the timeliness of the sales forecasting system. The liaison takes this information back to his department, and it travels up the chain of command to where a decision is made to investigate new sales forecasting solutions. Conversely, a liaison may hear about an exciting new technology from the chief technology officer. The liaison schedules a meeting with the technology vendor to learn more information. He then sets up meetings with his constituents (power users of his department's services) in manufacturing to explain how the new technology may improve their operations.

Like a consultant hired on an hourly basis, consulters seek to continually validate their benefits and justify their existence to their customers. Selling to consulters differs from selling to consolidators because consulters enjoy the company of other consultants. They need vendors who will represent them professionally to their business user community.

Chapter 33. The Responder Enterprise Buyer Type

The third type of enterprise sales cycle buyer is the responder. Responders are weaker departments that operate under the direction of stronger departments. The department that is the primary decision-maker (such as a consolidator; see ch. 31) might need the approval of another department (responder) to make the purchase or its assistance to implement it. Usually, the primary decision-making department funds the purchase.

Therefore, it is critical that the sales and customer interaction strategy focus on the primary decision-making department first. For example, the finance department would select the financial application it wants to use and IT would bless the decision and help implement it.

Vendor A understood our needs and came to us with ideas and suggestions, "What about this? What if? Next year you will be this size and here is what you'll need." They were telling us what we should be doing instead of what we thought we should. The other two vendors were very technical and described their solutions using technical jargon. The IT guys liked it, but the business guys were like, "What are you talking about?" We selected the company that did a much better job getting to the nontechnical guys.

—Director of Supply Chain

Many times, responders are literally under attack from the business units because their needs are being unmet. In some cases, the business units have been disappointed by the responders' past blunders. As a result, responders tend to be treated disrespectfully and suffer from a lack of departmental esteem. Whereas consolidators seek to gain power and consulters seek to proliferate their services, responders are just trying to minimize the risk associated with a business unit's purchase and survive.

Vendor A is well connected in the financial organization. They tend to sell to the CFO. Probably 90 percent of Vendor A's sales have been driven by the CFO. You have to learn who makes decisions in the organizations you serve and how you connect to them. Vendor B focuses on the IT people. While Vendor B hires good salespeople, they don't think about hiring salespeople who can connect with CFOs and business leaders.

—Executive Director of Supply Chain Systems

Figure 33.1 illustrates the power flow of a responder when the finance department is unhappy with some IT applications. Once again, the sizes of the boxes reflect the departments' dominance and control. The power users can be very influential in the responder model. In this example, IT is the whipping boy of finance, constantly enduring the department's criticisms. Important power users in the finance organization complain to management that their needs aren't being met. In turn, senior executives dictate their needs to midlevel managers, who relay the message to IT liaisons (intermediaries who interact with other departments).

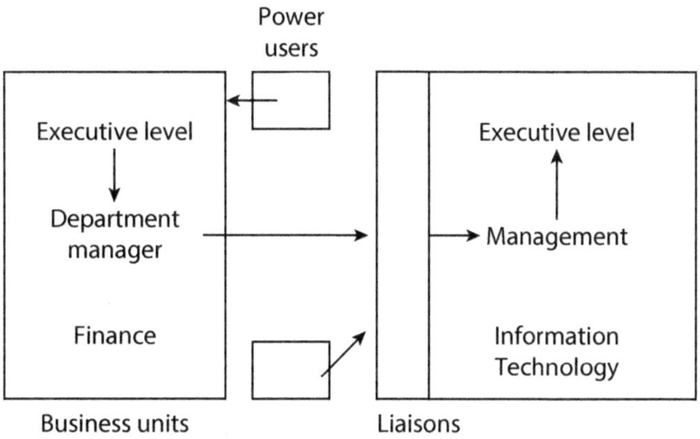

Figure 33.1 Responder enterprise buyer type

In this instance, the liaisons' main goal is to run interference on behalf of their department, sorting out the most important requests while trying to maintain a semblance of departmental decorum. For issues of extreme importance and urgency, senior executives of a business unit will contact their counterparts in IT directly and tell them to get something done. The power is clearly on the business unit side.

When selling to a responder, you must sell to all levels of the primary decision-making department as well as the power users. Using the example in figure 20.1, you must win over the finance department and ensure the IT department is comfortable blessing the finance department's decision.

Chapter 34. The Bureaucrat Enterprise Buyer Type

The final type of enterprise sales cycle buyer is the bureaucrat whose priority is to maintain the status quo through rules, regulations, and delaying tactics. The features of a bureaucrat are secretiveness, a response system that reflexively rebuffs demands made upon the department, and the centralization of administrative activities around the senior leader, the archbureaucrat.

> *The usual disaster is the IT department gets railroaded into doing twelve projects and only has resources for eight. My role is to prevent that from happening, which can make you rather unpopular.*
>
> —Vice President of Information Technology

The environment is structured similarly to a military command and control hierarchy that stamps out innovative thinking from lower levels of the department and hinders the free flow of information. The bureaucratic monarchy considers other departments outsiders and issues edicts that must be complied with for fear of consequences.

Figure 34.1 illustrates the shield that bureaucratic buyers erect around their department. In this example, IT dictates to the manufacturing department what products it will use. Meanwhile, the engineering department's recommendation is rejected, even though it is in the best interest of the company. One point to note is the lack of liaisons; the bureaucrat buyer is inwardly focused and less concerned about sensing the needs of other departments.

The four enterprise buyer types (consolidator, consulter,

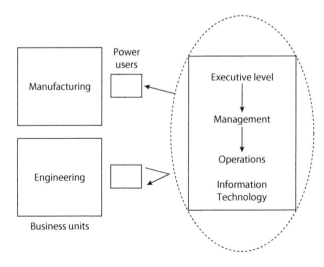

Figure 34.1 Bureaucrat enterprise buyer type

responder, and bureaucrat) have different orientations toward the operation of their departments. They buy products in different ways and for completely different purposes. It also is important to understand that a department can be different types of buyers depending upon the project. An IT department may be a consolidator for one project it is championing and a consulter on another. For example, the finance department may be driving a project to complete Sarbanes-Oxley compliance and the IT department is a responder. Conversely, the IT department could be the consolidator when driving new electronic data interchange technology that the finance department will use.

Chapter 35. How Organizational Power Impacts Enterprise Sales Cycles

You must determine a project's wellspring to know to whom and how to sell your solution. For example, at one company, every employee had to undergo ergonomics training on the proper way to use computers. Based on this information, you might assume that the driver behind this company-wide initiative was the human resources department and its vice president of human resources. However, the CFO instigated this project so the company would qualify for reduced insurance premium rates.

The power of C-level executives and departmental leaders follows a pattern of behavior

that reflects an evolution of power. When they join a new company, they are typically consolidators who are on a mission to establish authority by laying out their agenda of changes and the projects that are necessary to implement that change (which involves making purchases). This is one of the major reasons why you should keep track of executives on the move in your industry and be the first to call on them.

A leader who has been at a company for many years has an entirely different motivation for becoming a consolidator. He wants to leave his mark on the organization. He wants to be remembered by his employees and colleagues in his industry. Over time, a consolidator will lose power. The projects and initiatives he championed will have less-than-spectacular results and fail to live up to their hype. As a result, he has to change his style and demeanor within the organization to accomplish his goals and becomes a consulter. As he continues to lose organizational power he becomes a responder. In an effort to get some power back, he becomes a bureaucrat C-level executive, as figure 35.1 illustrates.

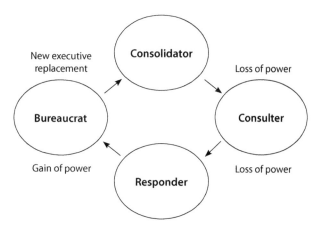

Figure 35.1 Evolution of C-level executive power

Finally, the executive team tires of working with the difficult bureaucrat and the members make a decision to change the departmental leader. They hire a new C-level executive who has a vision, a plan, and the power to change the department. The new executive is a consolidator, and the whole process repeats itself.

Promote the Executive's Evolution of Power

Your products and services can help the consolidator gain more power, the consulter and responder become consolidators, and the bureaucrat maintain independence. An important element of your competitive advantage is recognizing the true power position of the senior executives who are involved in the sales cycle. Since every executive has authority associated with his title, it's natural for salespeople to assume every leader is a powerful consolidator. But it's just not the case in the real world.

Exercise: Here's a quick exercise to help you understand where you win and why you lose. Write down the company names of your last five wins and note whether they were intradepartmental or enterprise buyer types. Intradepartmental buyer types have complete decision-making authority because the product being purchased will be used solely within their department. Enterprise buyers are selecting a product that a variety of departments will use, so there is more decision-making complexity. Determine whether each enterprise buyer was a consolidator, consulter, responder, or bureaucrat. Then write down the same information for five major losses or

no-decision deals. Quite often, you will find the losses were with completely different organizational buyer types than the wins. For example, if most of your wins were with consolidators, most of your losses were probably with another type, such as consulters or responders.

Chapter 36. Identifying the Bully with the Juice and the Emperor

Whenever a company makes a purchase decision that involves a team of people, self-interests, politics, and group dynamics will influence the final decision. Tension, drama, and conflict are normal parts of group dynamics because purchase decisions are not typically made unanimously.

One finding from hundreds of sales cycles I have analyzed is that one member of the selection team was able to exert will and determine the vendor that was selected. I have coined the term "bully with the juice" for this person. This is simply a description of a person who will tenaciously fight for his cause in order to get his way. This person isn't afraid to be politically incorrect or ruffle some feathers to ensure his personal desires are met.

Four different characteristics of the people involved in the product selection process can be measured as displayed in figure 36.1. The vertical axis shows a person's insistence that things be done his way. This is called being a "bully." A bully will get his way at any and all costs. A bully is not afraid to be politically incorrect as well.

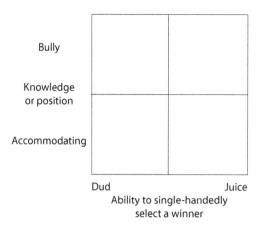

Figure 36.1 Characteristics of evaluators

"Bully" is not necessarily a negative term, nor does it mean that the person is physically intimidating. It is simply a description of a person who will tenaciously fight for his cause in order to get his way. People are more likely to be bullies when they have an elevated status within the evaluation team. The status could be the result of their domain expertise or their title and the authority it commands.

At the other end of the spectrum are people who are accommodating. They are apathetic about whatever solution is purchased. The degree to which people are bullies or accommodating depends on the effect the purchase decision has on them personally, their span of control, their position in the company, or their ability to perform their jobs.

On the horizontal axis are the concepts of "juice" and the "dud." Simply put, juice is charisma. But even this definition is too simple. Some people are natural-born leaders. They have an aura that can motivate and instill confidence. That's juice. Juice is fairly hard to describe, but you know it when you see it. People who have juice do not necessarily act like superheroes, nor are they always the highest-ranking people involved in an evaluation.

Instead, they are the ones who always seem to be on the winning side. Only one member of the customer's evaluation team has the juice. Single-handedly, he imparts his own will on the selection process by choosing the vendor and pushing the purchase through the procurement process. He can either finalize the purchase terms or instruct the procurement team on the terms that are considered acceptable. With large enterprise purchases, the bully with the juice is usually at the senior management level. To succeed, you will need sponsorship at this level. With smaller point-specific sales, the bully with the juice is typically a lower-level hands-on evaluator.

Duds are named after the ineffective fireworks they represent. Sometimes the fuse of a firework will burn down, but nothing will happen. Other fireworks may be very big but produce disappointing results. Duds talk big but take little action. "Accommodating duds" are people who do not take an active role in the sales process. Even worse are "dud bullies," who pretend they have juice but don't. You may not realize who they are until it's too late.

For all the people involved in the sales selection process, you need to calculate their amount of juice and their propensity to be bullies. For example, John, Jim, Karl, and Rich are plotted by a salesperson who sells large-scale computer data storage equipment in figure 36.2. John is the senior purchasing agent. Jim is a network administrator. Karl is the director of information technology, and Rich is the CIO. They are going to make a $350,000 purchase.

Bully
Knowledge or position
Accommodating
John
Rich
Jim
Karl
Dud
Juice
Ability to single-handedly select a winner

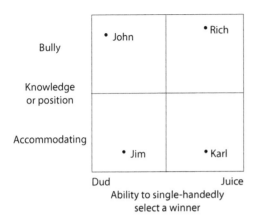

Figure 36.2 Plotting individual assessments to identify the bully with the juice

As shown in the figure, John is a dud bully, Jim is an accommodating dud, Rich has the juice, and Karl is accommodating to him. Even though Jim and Karl might conduct the vendor evaluations, their decision can be overridden by Rich. While they might have a vested interest in ensuring that their favorite vendor wins, you can assume their recommendation will match Rich's preference. His will may be imposed on the evaluation process through brute force or by finesse. Either way, his preference is "bullied" into the decision.

When thinking about all the evaluation committees you have been a part of
There is always one member of the committee who tries to influence the decision his way
35%
There is usually one member of the committee who tries to influence the decision his way
55%
Occasionally, there is one member of the committee who tries to influence the decision his way
9%
Rarely or never, there is one member of the committee who tries to influence the decision his way
1%

Figure 36.3 The occurrence of the bully with the juice according to buyers

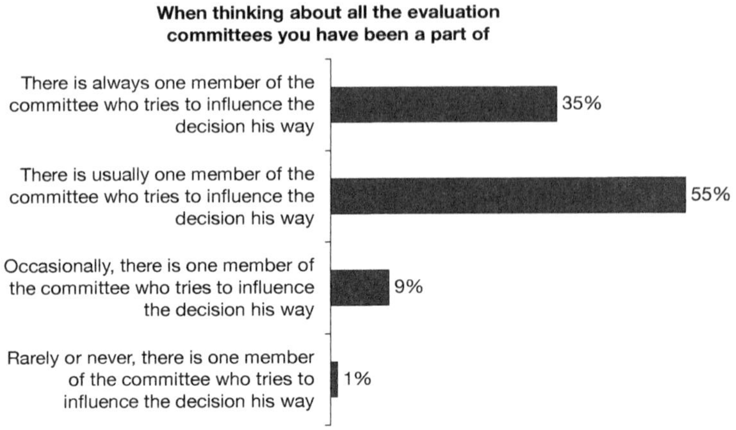

However, Rich, the CIO who has the juice, probably doesn't care which toner cartridges are purchased for the company's laser printers. He will be accommodating and support the decision of the people who make that decision. Someone else has the juice for the procurement of toner cartridges.

> *We tried to build consensus, but it was my money. That's what it came down to. I wanted to consider everyone's needs, but at the end of the day, it was my decision.*
>
> —Vice President of Marketing

Now let's assume Rich is making a $3.5 million software purchase. Once again, he is the bully with the juice and the evaluation team's recommendation matches the vendor he wants. However, he can't make a purchase of this magnitude by himself. It must be blessed by the "emperor."

In ancient Rome, the emperor would decide whether or not a beaten gladiator would live by gesturing with a thumb up or down. Today, the life or death of enterprise purchases is decided in much the same way by a company president, CEO, chairman, board of directors, or capital expenditure committee that has no personal attachments or vested interests in the purchase. This individual or group will decide whether the funds should actually be spent. This

emperor will give a thumb up or down to release the funds to make the purchase, even though an exhausting evaluation of many months or even years may have been conducted by lower level personnel.

> *The initial decision was no. The leadership committee didn't believe the contribution margin was high enough. I went back three months later and had it approved after talking with a number of their customers and building a better business case.*

— Vice President of Customer Care

Two of the most important people in every sales cycle are the bully with the juice and the emperor. These people will ultimately make and approve the decision. Therefore, it is imperative that you truly understand the decision-making process. Who is the bully with the juice? Will an emperor have to ultimately approve the decision? Whether you are selling a product in only one or two sales calls or two dozen or more, you must always validate who the bully with the juice and the emperor are.

To quantify how often there is a bully with the juice from the perspective of evaluation team members, I conducted an extensive study on B2B buyers and asked them about their selection committee experiences. Overall, 90 percent of respondents confirmed that there is always or usually one member of the committee who tries to influence the decision his way as shown in figure 36.3.

The occurrence of the bully with the juice varies based upon vertical industry. Finance, technology, and government verticals had the highest number of responses, indicating that there is always one committee member who tries

to influence the decision, while manufacturing and entertainment had the next highest number.

How often is the bully with the juice successful in getting the outcome he wants? In other words, what percentage of the time does the particular vendor he is promoting actually get selected? Eighty-nine percent of participants said the bully with the juice is successful most of the time, while 11 percent selected some of the time as shown in figure 36.4. In practicality, it can be said that a salesperson doesn't have to win over the entire selection committee, only the bully with the juice.

What percentage of the time does the vendor whom the "bully with the juice" is promoting get selected?

Most of the time — 89%
Some of the time — 11%

Figure 36.4 How often the bully with the juice is successful

The real enemy of salespeople today isn't their archrivals; it's no decision. What is it that prevents prospective buyers from making a purchase even after they have conducted a lengthy evaluation process? Every initiative and its associated expenditure is competing against all the other projects that are requesting funds.

Do the departments of a company have different abilities to push through their purchases and defeat the company's bureaucratic tendency not to buy? Let's look at the profiles of the various departments in terms of how they ranked their group leadership ability as a predictor of their department's ability to promote their internal agenda.

Departments were ranked according to the percentage of department members who strongly agreed with the statement "I am often a leader in groups." Sales was highest at 50 percent followed by IT at 33 percent, engineering at 29 percent, marketing at 22 percent, accounting at 22 percent, and human resources was at zero. In addition, here are the rankings B2B buyers gave when asked which departments were most powerful as evidenced by their ability to get new business initiatives approved: (1) sales, (2) marketing, (3) engineering/R&D, (4) manufacturing/operations, (5) IT, (6) accounting, and (7) human resources.

Beyond their formal titles and their positions on organization charts, people take on specific roles when they are part of a selection committee. Some will take control of the group and steer the decision toward their preference. Based on the research results, you would expect sales, IT, and engineering to have more internal clout to push through their projects as opposed to marketing, accounting, and human resources. Therefore, the former are better departments to sell into from the salesperson's perspective. As a president of a company once told me during a win-loss interview, "At the end of the day, a project will or won't get approved depending upon who is pushing it."

Group dynamics are very complex and often revealing. One way to identify the bully with the juice is by observing people's behavior during presentations and meetings. In chapter 124 we review how a pecking order is communicated by where people sit during meetings. Whether at a round table or in a classroom setting, the person with the most juice and greatest ability to bully will usually take the dominant seating position. This dominating behavior is also evidenced in meeting interactions. To explain this, we need to introduce the concept of the "participation pie" as shown in figure 36.5.

Usually, the person who interacts the most will be the bully with the most juice. This is particularly true when the bully with the juice is a domain-expert manager who is very technical: he or she is in charge and wants everyone to know it. Be forewarned that you may observe a different behavior when the bully with the juice is a business-expert manager. He or she may choose to remain silently hidden in the back of the room.

Dud bullies will be very active meeting participants. However, the more they participate, the more it becomes obvious that they do not have the stature or expertise they think they do. We have all been in meetings where people like this are contradicted or even publicly chastised by members of their own team. Dud bullies confirm the old adage "It is better to keep your mouth shut and be suspected of being a fool rather than open it and confirm suspicions."

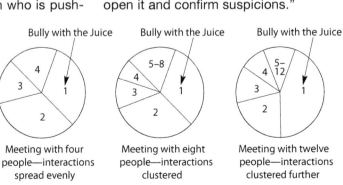

Meeting with four people—interactions spread evenly

Meeting with eight people—interactions clustered

Meeting with twelve people—interactions clustered further

Figure 36.5 Participation pie charts

Another key aspect of the participation pie is how the number of attendees affects the level of participation. In meetings with up to four members, the amount of time each person spends interacting and asking questions is relatively equal. As the group grows to eight people, the interactions become clustered around several people. In larger groups, up to twelve people, the majority of interactions are usually among a few individuals.

Every group meeting presents the opportunity to understand the internal machinations of the customer's selection process. Pay attention to who is dominating the conversation and build a participation pie as the meeting progresses.

Exercise: The bully with the juice is the single most important decision-maker during the selection process. Once a product is selected, the emperor then decides whether or not to actually make the purchase. Review the top three deals you are currently working on and identify the bully with the juice and emperor by name and title. Compare titles and note whether they're different or the same. Evaluate the relationship you have with each person and list the action steps you can take to strengthen it. Similarly, list the action steps you can take to meet the bully with the juice and emperor in accounts where you haven't met them.

Chapter 37. Developing an Internal Coach

One of the most important sales cycle objectives is to develop a constant, accurate source of information that reveals the internal machinations of the

customer's internal politics, vendor decision-making process, and vendor preferences or prejudices. For many years, the term "coach," also known as an internal champion or advocate, has been used by all types of salespeople, selling every conceivable solution, to define the person who provides this inside information. Coaches are individuals who provide accurate information about your standing, let you know how you are faring at the account or during the sales cycle, and expose internal and external competitive threats to you.

Sometimes salespeople believe they have a coach when in reality they don't. Heavy Hitters know they have a coach when the person not only provides them with accurate information but also helps them by fighting for their cause. A true coach will represent and promote your solution and services to their colleagues and, even better, to their senior executive leadership. Finally, the information coaches provide is accurate. Figure 37.1 shows the different types of coaches and their respective numeric ranking with the highest number indicating the strongest and most desired as coaches.

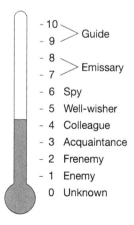

Figure 37.1 Types of coaches and their numeric ranking

Each type of coach is described below:

- *Unknown.* Someone within the account you have never met is considered an unknown. The danger with not knowing a person is that you have no idea how he or she perceives you personally, your company, or the solution you provide. Therefore, this places you in a position of risk.

- *Enemy.* An enemy is someone who is against you, your product, or company. Enemies have either publicly stated their views against you or you have learned through private conversations with others within the account that they are against you. They could have a favorite vendor they would rather work with or be a detractor of the project you are part of. Regardless, they don't like you (or members of your team) and are most likely plotting against you.

- *Frenemy.* A frenemy is someone who befriends you so that you think he or she is a supporter. In reality, the frenemy is only acting the part and is truly an enemy who is against you. Frenemies are extremely dangerous because they lull you into a false sense of security that you are winning when they are really coordinating a plan to defeat you.

- *Acquaintance.* An acquaintance is someone whom you've met in the past but you don't have any significant relationship with. While acquaintances recognize you, you have no idea whether they truly like you or not and don't know their personal thoughts about the solutions you provide or how you're performing.

- *Colleague.* A colleague is someone whom you may have met during the sales cycle or even meet with on a regular basis but the relationship is strictly professional. So colleagues do not share intimate details of the behind-the-scenes politics within their company. Rather, they are performing their duties and the focus of their interactions with you are strictly business and nonpersonal.

- *Well-wisher.* Well-wishers talk to you on an intimate, friendly basis. They provide information that you may even consider proprietary. However, well-wishers are extremely amiable people and may be providing the same information to other vendors competing for the business.

- *Spy.* Spies are observers who provide you information about the internal machinations of the selection process. Unlike well-wishers, acquaintances, or frenemies, the inside information they provide is reliable, accurate, and timely. They report the thoughts of the various selection team members and the movements of other vendors. A spy is the weaker type of coach when compared to an emissary and guide.

- *Emissary.* Emissaries are spies who not only provide you with their personal observations but disseminate information on your behalf as well. They act like agents who have been sent on a personal mission and serve as a diplomatic representative for the cause they represent. They'll lobby their colleagues and promote you and your solution to others within their company when you're not around. Emissaries have a deeper, more personal connection to you than weak spies do. They're confidants who have a vested interest in you winning so they are willing to take more risks on your behalf rather than spies who won't publicly support your cause or proclaim their personal preferences aloud.

- *Guide.* Guides are trusted friends who will courageously defend you and your solution when you are not around to do so yourself. Guides are considered your best friends. Not only are they confidants who provide all the inside details about the internal politics of decision-making, but they also help you plan and execute your strategy to win the business. The best guides are usually seasoned employees. They may have worked at the company for quite some time and understand how to get things done. They have the business acumen and the experience to provide adept advice on how to win the deal and get the contract signed. Most importantly, after helping devise the winning game plan, they play an integral part in executing it.

The ideal coach is the person with the highest authority or influence involved in the selection process. When this person becomes the coach, you will enjoy a unique advantage. For example, let's assume Rich, the CIO who is making the $350,000 purchase decision as described in chapter 36, is your internal champion and is ranked as a guide. You are in a great situation to win!

However, the coach could be anybody inside the customer's company or even outside the company, such as a consultant working on the project or channel partner who has established relationships. All of these advisors share a common characteristic. They have a selfish reason for wanting you or your company to win. This reason may range from the simple fact that they like you to the belief that your solution will help them gain power, prestige, or authority because of the complicated nature of internal politics.

Here are some interesting metrics that prove the importance of having a coach. Figure 37.2 shows an analysis of the type of coach the winning salesperson had developed for persuasion and creation sales cycles (see ch. 16).

	Persuasion Sales Cycles	Creation Sales Cycles
Guide	55%	75%
Emissary	30%	23%
Spy	12%	2%
No Coach	3%	

Figure 37.2 Types of coach for persuasion and creation sales cycle wins

Quite often, salespeople mistake someone for a coach when in fact the person isn't a loyal compatriot. You should always have a certain level of paranoia about your coach. Is he or she secretly coaching the competition? Is he or she acting as your eyes and ears when you are not around? Is he or she truthfully telling you about what the other vendors are up to and about the preferences of the various selection committee members? Is he or she providing privileged and proprietary information to you that the other vendors aren't receiving?

One of your most important goals is to develop a trusted coach—hopefully, a guide. Obviously, the more coaches you have inside an account, the better the quality and quantity of information you will receive. The information you receive from these confidants can be used to determine your standing in an account and help determine your course of action. Being at the mercy of a single person is a risky position to be in. What if your coach is wrong?

How to Develop a Coach

Think about all the relationships you have in your life—deep close relationships with friends you have known most of your life, casual relationships with colleagues and coworkers, and new relationships with customers. Regardless of how they were formed, all relationships share similar underlying characteristics. In order to recruit an internal champion, it is first necessary to understand the nature of friendships.

A big difference exists between a friend and an acquaintance. An acquaintance is someone with whom you have a cordial relationship. While the relationship is friendly, the unspoken understanding is that neither person will demand significant time of the other to maintain the relationship. Conversely, a friend is someone who unselfishly invests time to maintain the relationship and derives enjoyment from doing so. An acquaintance is someone you know slightly, a well-wisher with whom you may have pleasant lunches and other social get-togethers. A friend is a trusted sympathizer and, more importantly, an active helper.

Who are your friends? Most likely they are in your same age group, you share similar backgrounds, or you live in the same geographic area. You also probably share similar values and motivations and have complementary personalities.

The term personality refers to all aspects of a person's individuality. While everyone's personality is as distinct as a fingerprint, some traits of behavior can be classified to help understand a person's attitude, habits, and conduct.

The process for developing friendships has three major characteristics, and these characteristics can also be utilized to develop a coach. First, two people have an "intersecting activity." Second, a "kinship in communication" is established. Third, they are motivated to bond with each other as a result of value systems called "benefactions." Let's examine each of these characteristics further to understand how to develop an internal champion coach.

Intersecting Activities

All people have outside interests, hobbies, and personal pursuits by which they display their personalities, beliefs, and values. Think about all the potential non-business-related subjects you can discuss with your customers: cars, movies, wine, college, pets, marriage, professional sports, child rearing, and investments (see ch. 52).

Each intersecting activity also has a unique language. In order to have a meaningful conversation about an intersecting activity, you need to understand its language. For example, a conversation about stock investing requires an understanding of terms such as "price earnings ratio," "market cap," and "stock shorting." Through the use and understanding of these common terms, rapport is established.

You can easily identify intersecting activities of customers by observing how they have decorated their cubicles or offices. Pictures of family vacations, mementos, awards, degrees, and other personal artifacts convey their interests and the attributes of their personality.

Always engage the customer in a personal conversation about the intersecting activities you have in common. By doing so, you develop rapport with the *entire* person, not just the *business* person—building the foundation of a personal friendship that sets you apart from the competition. This mutual interest sets the stage for developing a personal relationship and ultimately a coach.

Kinship in Communication

In part V, Personal Sales Strategy, we review how your ability to communicate effectively with customers is imperative for building rapport. In fact, the sales linguistics definition for rapport is "harmonious communication." Equally important, your communication style directly impacts whether or not a person will become your coach. People will bond with someone new when the flow of communication is natural, comfortable, and enjoyable.

Remember, meaning comes not only from what you say but how you say it. Therefore, try to adjust your vocabulary to resemble, sound, and feel like the customer's. Coordinate your posture, speech, breathing, and movements to mirror the customer's. By doing so, you develop rapport and a deeper level relationship.

Customer Benefactions (the Benefit from Taking Action)

Customers purchase products that increase their happiness, esteem, power, or wealth. They rationalize these psychological decisions with logic and facts. The term "benefaction" refers to the

psychological benefits that determine a person's actions. Four core psychological drives determine selection behavior and greatly influence whether or not the client will become your internal champion.

These four benefactions are well-being, pain avoidance, self-preservation, and self-gratification. Physical well-being, the will to survive, is one of our strongest desires. It weighs heavily in the minds of customers. Making customers feel their jobs are safe in your hands is a top priority. Ideally, you would like them to believe that the competitive vendors are actually threats to their livelihood. Customers are equally concerned with maintaining their mental and emotional well-being.

When something is hurting you badly, the desire to eliminate the source of pain can be all-consuming. Pain is one of the best purchase motivators because customers are forced to act quickly and decisively to eliminate it. Customers bond with people who will help them eliminate their pains and troubles.

Self-preservation, the third core psychological drive, is the desire to be recognized for our unique talents while still belonging to a group. Customers and salespeople alike naturally seek the approval of others. Customers purchase items that they believe will enhance their stature and protect their group position. They not only want to be respected by their peers but also want to become group leaders. Naturally, salespeople want to be pack leaders too.

Self-gratification is our desire to put our own needs before everyone else's. Customers will go to great lengths to purchase something that makes them feel better about themselves and superior to others. Egos drive the business world.

When considering developing some-one into a coach, always ask yourself the question, What is this person's bene-faction? In other words, what is driving this person's behavior and how will I help him or her achieve this goal? And how do the person's various individual benefactions mesh? Even though a wide range of benefactions is possible, each is all individually personal and self-cen-tered. Here are two examples of how the customer's behavior is explained using benefactions.

Beverly wants to implement a new cutting-edge technology. By adding this valuable skill set to her resume, she will be able to command more money in the marketplace.

- She wants more money in order to buy a home for her family.

- By knowing this new technology, she has the security of having a market-able skill.

- The industry periodicals and her friends are enamored with this new technology and she's tired of feeling left out.

- There's power in knowledge. Know-ing something her colleagues don't puts her in a superior position.

Matt is a project leader who wants to select a particular technology solution because it is successfully used by so many other well-known companies.

- A successful project is an opportu-nity to demonstrate his value to the company. He wants to keep his job during these difficult economic times.

- He's risk-averse and feels that if he can control the selection of the technology for the project, it will be successful.

- He can share tips with and leverage the experience of other local users of the product.

- If the project is successful, he'll earn the promotion he's always wanted.

Map out the needs of all the people involved in the account and hypothesize about their benefactions. You are search-ing for confidants who have a vested interest in using your products because it will help them attain their physiological, safety, belonging, or esteem needs.

Frame the conversations in terms of fulfilling these needs. In the first example, your strategy with Beverly is to reiterate how cutting-edge your solution is. Pro-vide collateral materials such as indus-try articles, press announcements, and technical documentation that confirm your technological advantage. Capital-ize on her belonging needs by introduc-ing Beverly to your other customers and inviting her to your annual customer user group meeting. Provide access to your company's subject-matter experts to re-emphasize your innovation and technol-ogy offering uniqueness while acceler-ating her ability to learn it. Help Beverly become knowledgeable and powerful. In turn, Beverly will associate her success with yours and this will motivate her to become your coach.

In the second example, demonstrate to Matt that your solution is the least risky by providing thorough product demonstrations, an on-site evaluation, and ongoing implementation meetings. Customer references and site visits will also provide independent validation. If Matt feels confident your solution will work, he will defend it against solutions he believes are dangerous or pose an unsafe risk. He is motivated to support it and will coach you on what you need to do internally to close the business.

There are many ways to develop a coach. Always try to understand people's personal pains, objectives, and motivations within their organization. Show that you are genuinely interested in their success and that you have equal skin in the game for the common objectives. Understand their work history by reviewing their LinkedIn profile and find common personal and industry connections. Socialize with them online and in a nonwork environment setting whenever possible. Treat them as if you'll be friends for life.

Exercise: Human behavior is complex, and every individual is unique in his or her own way. Think about the last five accounts you've won. Who was your coach? Why did that person support you? When you're done listing your reasons, check to see if they are on the list below.

---

37 Reasons Someone Becomes Your Coach

1. The person likes you.
2. The person likes your company.
3. The person likes your solution/ services.
4. The person dislikes the other salespeople.
5. The person dislikes the other companies.
6. The person dislikes the other solutions/services.
7. You provide the person the highest probability of success.
8. You enable the person to get a promotion and move up the ladder.
9. You help advance the person's career within the industry.
10. You enable the person to make more money.
11. You enable the person to meet his targets or achieve his personal MBO (management by objective) program bonuses.
12. You provide the least amount of risk.
13. You protect the person's job.
14. You make the person's life easier.
15. Your solution involves less work and the person is tired of working hard.
16. Your solution enables the person to learn something new technically or business-wise.
17. Your solution helps make the person more marketable.
18. The person is bored and you are exciting.
19. The person is returning a favor to you.
20. The person sympathizes with the situation you're in.
21. The person wants to work for your company or one of your other customers someday.
22. You make the person more powerful.
23. You provide the person with the ability to be a leader of a group of peers.
24. You provide the person industry or competitive knowledge.

25. You socialize with the person.

26. You massage the person's ego and treat the person with the respect he deserves.

27. You are part of the same community.

28. Your solution allows the person to do something he hasn't been able to.

29. Your solution allows the person to control the environment more.

30. Your solution makes the person happy.

31. Your solution allows the person to get revenge on someone else in the organization.

32. Your solution is less expensive, so the person will have money left over for other projects.

33. The person is familiar with your company and has used its products in the past.

34. The person is deeply concerned about the well-being of the department or company and believes you are the best long-term solution.

35. The person wants to break away from past practices and company traditions.

36. The person is tired of working with the current vendor or frustrated by how the current vendor's product operates.

37. The person is not satisfied with the level of support he is receiving from his current vendor.

Help Your Coach Sell Internally

Don't assume your coach knows how to sell your product internally. Specifically, ask if the coach needs help and what type of help is needed. Is it a more detailed ROI justification? Is there a particular decision-maker who needs to be won over? Try to identify beforehand the roadblocks and obstacles your coach will face. Provide step-by-step instructions on what he should do by explaining exactly how your other customers pushed through the project or purchase.

Usually, there's only one chance to push through a major purchase, so stress the importance of strategizing together on the internal sell. Go so far as mapping out the organization and walking through who the supporters and detractors are. If there are internal presentations to be made, offer to take part, create the presentation, or test run the presentation with your coach. Stay in continual contact and monitor your coach's progress.

You need someone inside the company who will fight on your behalf. You work with this person like a trainer works with a boxer. The trainer prepares the boxer for his prizefight by teaching him how to attack and defend himself against his opponent. During the actual fight, the boxer will come back to his corner bruised and battered. The trainer's job is to provide support and make the boxer feel like a world champion again so he can get back into the ring.

Exercise: Developing a coach is a necessary step required to establish and maintain account control. Coaches are individuals who provide accurate information about your account standing, account politics, and competitive threats to you. They want you to win and succeed; they're your friend and ally. Review the top three deals you are currently working on and honestly assess whether or not you have a coach versus an acquaintance or colleague by ranking the people in each account from one to ten. List the action steps you can take to develop a coach or improve the strength on the one you have.

Chapter 38. WHD (Wider, Higher, Deeper) Account Expansion Strategy

The WHD (wider, higher, deeper) client expansion strategy is based upon extending your reach, recognition, and relationships throughout a prospective or existing client's organization. The strategy is predicated on developing a wider footprint across the organization so that key decision-makers and important influencers understand the full breadth of the products and services you provide and how these solutions might be used within their department. Equally important is informing them about where your products are used within other parts of their organization and the resulting success those departments have had. We'll focus on developing a wider footprint in this chapter.

Another key element of the WHD strategy is navigating higher within accounts to the senior-level decision-makers who initiate strategic projects and decide which vendors they will use to help them achieve their critical goals. This topic is reviewed in chapter 39. Finally, at the foundation of the strategy is the never-ending quest to build deeper client relationships across the organization, which is covered in chapter 42.

Regardless of the size and complexity of the organization you are selling to, you can classify people within every department into three basic categories of responsibility: product, management, and executive. Most likely, your solution is targeted at one of these categories. Your initial contact with the account and most frequent interactions with the customer will also be within one of these categories. Let's take a moment to define and understand the nuances of these categories.

Product Category

The *product* category includes those individuals who work hands on with your product. These people use a vendor's products to create a new product for their company. For example, a computer programmer creates an application (product) by using programming tools provided by a vendor. A telephone operator creates communication (product) by using telephone equipment provided by a vendor. A security officer safeguards assets (product) by using surveillance equipment from a vendor. People within the product category may have "administrator," "analyst," "technician," "specialist," or "engineer" in their titles. Or their titles will explain exactly what they do, such as "buyer," "mechanic," or "receptionist."

Management Category

The management category provides direction to each of the various departments of the organization. Typically, people at this level may have "director," "manager," "supervisor," or "leader" somewhere in their title. While many different management styles exist, there are two fundamental types of department managers, the "domain expert" and the "business expert." The domain expert managers achieved their position by being the most knowledgeable person within their department. For example, a network manager may have been promoted to a management position because of his troubleshooting expertise. The maintenance supervisor may have been the most talented mechanic. The accounts payable manager may have previously been the most knowledgeable clerk. Domain experts are the "alpha," or dominant resource, that all the other members of the group consult for technical advice.

Meanwhile, business expert managers are responsible for representing their department to the other departments within the company. While they are still technical, they rely heavily on the technical opinions of a few key members of their team to make decisions.

Executive Category

In larger companies, the executive category is composed of people who have the word "president" or "chief" in their titles, such as vice president, chief information officer (CIO), chief technical officer (CTO), chief marketing officer (CMO), or chief human resources officer (CHRO). In smaller companies, the category also includes individuals with "executive director" in their title.

Each category of responsibility has a different orientation toward the operation of the department. The executive category ensures the department is coordinated with the business strategy and

major initiatives. The management category leads ongoing projects, day-to-day operation of the departments, and supervision of the people responsible for products. Meanwhile, the product category is focused on the microcosm of the department.

Different areas of responsibility within the department require different technical aptitudes, and this impacts who leads the organization and manages the individual departments. For example, the most technically astute network engineer is very likely to be promoted to manage the networking department. He is classified as a domain expert manager. However, it is unlikely he will become the executive-level CIO, as it requires business and political acumen to reach the top. In general, more of the executive-level leaders have business expert manager backgrounds. However, certain departments require deep technical expertise, such as the security management department. In this case, a domain expert manager who was an information security specialist may become the chief information security officer. Figure 38.1 illustrates this concept.

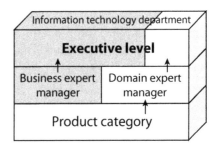

Figure 38.1 Leadership by domain or business expertise

Wider Footprint

Before you can develop a wider footprint, you need to gain a clear understanding of how the department you are working with is organized. First, identify all the employees by name, exact title, and organization reporting structure and create an organization footprint chart. It is critical to identify all the department members and the network of influencers and approvers in an account. Beyond titles and reporting structure, also seek to understand the politics of decision-making and how group decision-making will impact your outcome. The complex interrelationships between the different people and levels within the department are unique in every account.

Once you have created an organization footprint, color code the people according to how you think they perceive your company, products, and services

(for example, green for good, yellow for neutral, red for negative, and white for unknown). Next, grade your relationships using the coach rating defined in chapter 37. (This rating is based on the strength of the relationship and represented as a number on a scale of zero to ten.) Also identify the bully with the juice and the emperor as described in chapter 36. In addition, include the LinkedIn profile URL for each person. An example of a simplified organization footprint chart is shown in figure 38.2

The chart shows a common occurrence. The salesperson is selling a solution to the application development department and has strong support from that team (Miranda Lambert, Jamey Johnson, and Jason Aldeen). However, there is neutral support from John Cash, the emperor at the executive level. In addition, Ray Hubbard, the director of financial systems, is an enemy and a key influencer of John Cash. The salesperson is in a position of risk as the emperor may not approve the application development department's recommendation, even though it is made by the bully with the juice who chose the vendor.

The second step is to develop a footprint map of the entire department. For example, the financial systems group in the previous example resides in the application services

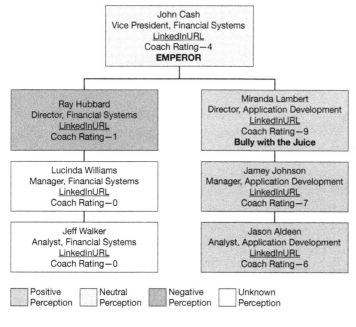

Figure 38.2 Organization footprint chart showing coach ratings and buyer perceptions

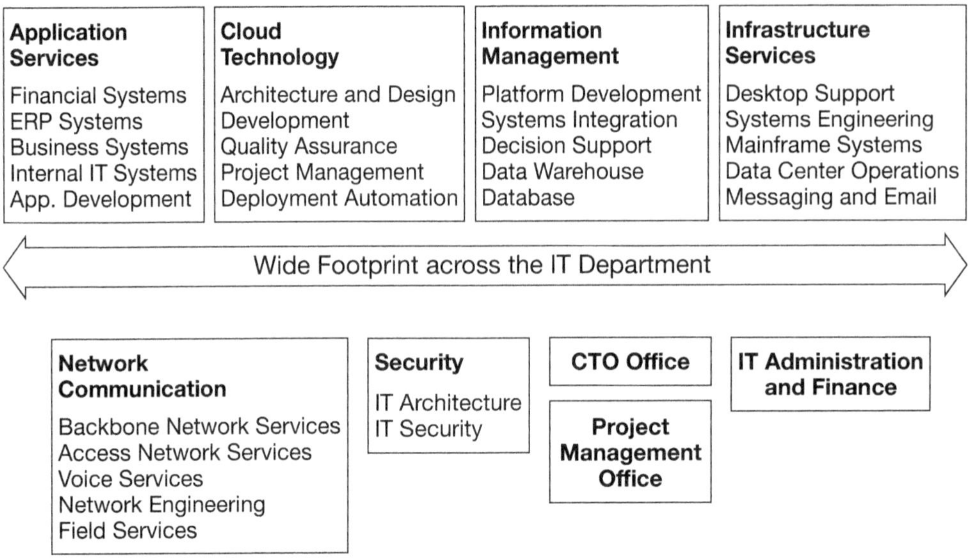

Application Services	**Cloud Technology**	**Information Management**	**Infrastructure Services**
Financial Systems ERP Systems Business Systems Internal IT Systems App. Development	Architecture and Design Development Quality Assurance Project Management Deployment Automation	Platform Development Systems Integration Decision Support Data Warehouse Database	Desktop Support Systems Engineering Mainframe Systems Data Center Operations Messaging and Email

Wide Footprint across the IT Department

Network Communication	**Security**	**CTO Office**	**IT Administration and Finance**
Backbone Network Services Access Network Services Voice Services Network Engineering Field Services	IT Architecture IT Security	**Project Management Office**	

Figure 38.3 Developing a footprint map of an entire department

group of the IT department as shown in figure 38.3.

Then begin creating organization charts for other areas of the company where there are potential opportunities (or better yet, have your coach supply you with organization charts). Identify the people who might need the products you provide today and those who might be interested in the solutions you will offer in the future. Build an organization footprint chart for each opportunity like the previous example for the financial systems department.

Corporate Control, Independent, and Interdependent Organizations

Fortune 1000 companies have complex organization structures, and departments can be organized by division, line of business, or geography under the oversight of a global corporate group. The interrelationship of the various organizations will influence which solutions are purchased and deployed. The "corporate control" environment is where the corporate group sets guidelines and standards that ultimately determine which products will be used at the subsidiary organizations. For example, the IT department at the corporate headquarters in the United States may overrule the purchase decision being made at the IT department in the United Kingdom. "Independent" organizations are able to use their discretion and buy the products they prefer. Using the previous example, the UK IT department can purchase the products it likes. "Interdependent" organizations are more integrated. They promote and cross-pollinate ideas, methodologies, products, and technology among the organizations. Figure 38.4 shows an example for the IT function, but it equally applies to all other departments such as finance, manufacturing, marketing, and purchasing.

The sales effort focus must be concentrated at different locations depending on the organization's structure. Corporate control accounts must have a concerted effort at headquarters. All divisions and operations should be called on at interdependent accounts. Meanwhile, independent accounts can be sold to individually.

Penetration Strategies

Once the key decision-makers and evaluators have been identified within other departments and at the other business units, it is time to create a penetration strategy to introduce yourself, your company, and your solution offerings. Begin outreach campaigns to the key decision-makers based on the specific offering they would be interested in, providing relevant industry information, demonstrations, webinars, and lunch-and-learn sessions. The goal is to gain an initial meeting and then build a meaningful relationship using the tactics described below. (For a detailed messaging strategy review, please read part IV, New Account Penetration Strategy.)

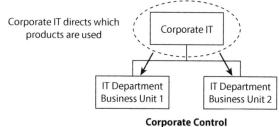

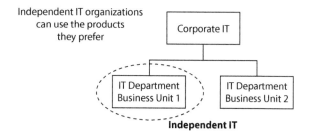

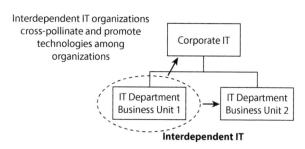

Figure 38.4 Example of corporate control, independent, and interdependent organizations

- Recruit your "green" supporters and coaches for introductions. Let them know your desire to reach out to other areas of the organization and seek their advice. Ask for introductions where possible and let them know ahead of time that you will be contacting others within their organization. Always keep them posted on your progress.

- Utilize your product's value proposition to introduce yourself. Put yourself in the prospective client's shoes and create introductory messaging around each person's personal goals,

problems, departmental challenges, and opportunities for improvement. Hypothesize about the pain points the person is experiencing and show each person that you provide a cure.

- Leverage existing success where you've done business before in the organization. Even though the people you contact are part of the same organization, never assume they know who you and your company are and that they are already your client. Rather, assume they don't have any idea of the products and services you provide. Create an introductory overview showing the people you work with, the projects you've completed for them, and the successful results they enjoyed from using your products. Send the overview directly to your contacts or share it with them over LinkedIn.

- Execute the LinkedIn network strategy (see chs. 91 and 95) to connect with target contacts. Continually share articles and post relevant information with your network. Send direct in-mail messages with invitations where appropriate. Invite your contacts to demonstrations, lunch-and-learn sessions, webinars, and meetings with your company's subject-matter experts and senior executives.

- Conduct flanking strategy brain-storming sessions (see ch. 39) with your team. Assign tasks based upon people's role and approach the new opportunity from multiple directions.

There are three important points to remember when developing a wider footprint within an organization. First, you must believe in what you're doing. Your efforts cannot be based upon half-hearted motivations. You must have a conviction that you and the solutions you offer can uniquely help the client.

Second, your attempts to contact someone new will take time. In essence, you are running a political campaign that will take several months and in many cases over a year. While you obviously want to generate immediate interest, you need to set your own expectations so you don't get frustrated by a lack of results and stop campaigning.

Third, the reason why an executive doesn't respond to your message is not

that he or she is disinterested or too busy. Do not misinterpret a lack of response and assume he or she doesn't want your solution. Rather, consider it your fault because you didn't send the right message. While you didn't get the message right this time, you should also know that you will get it right over time. Therefore, you should never be bashful about contacting the person again. However, you must send a different type of message or history will surely repeat itself.

Chapter 39. Flanking Strategies When You're Stuck at the Wrong Level

The WHD (wider, higher, deeper) strategy defined in chapter 38 is predicated on not becoming "single-threaded," where you are tied to only one contact at an account as shown in figure 39.1. The typical scenario is that a salesperson is locked into a monogamous relationship with a lower-level contact. Therefore, the salesperson is unable to access key decision-makers as shown below. Instead, the goal is to employ an expansion strategy to establish as many relationships at the highest levels of the organization as possible through flanking strategies.

Flanking is a strategic movement that consists of changing one's position to gain an advantage. The first step in determining which flanking strategy to employ is conducting a brainstorming session with the entire new-business sales team (salesperson, presales engineer, sales manager, senior sales leadership, and product subject-matter experts) or existing client account team (account manager, consulting personnel, and account

management lead-
ers). During this ses-
sion, the account
is reviewed and the
situation discussed.
Next, the strategy is
chosen and the tacti-
cal execution plan is
defined. This details
what specific actions
will be taken and the
personnel responsible
for executing them.

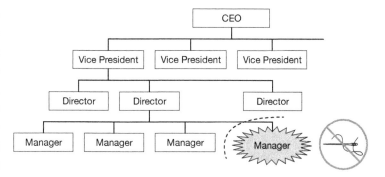

Figure 39.1 Single-threaded account relationship at the wrong level

The strategy chosen is based upon the unique situation and circumstances that are particular to the account and includes left and right flanking strategies.

- *Left-flank (logic) strategies.* The left-flank strategy is based upon logic and information. Flanking to the left refers to a series of different tactics for changing the customer's selection criteria or raising a critical issue the customer is unaware of. It is named after the left side of the brain, the part that is analytical and invokes rational reasoning and deductive logic. Information transmitted during left flanking can include the following:

  - Latest industry trends

  - Metrics and statistics to bench-mark and improve the prospect's business performance

  - Best practices and practical advice from current customers

  - Information about direct competi-tors and top performing compa-nies in the prospect's marketplace

  - Product demonstrations and eval-uations that prove improvements

    - The impact of new technologies and related products on the bot-tom line

    - Developments in other parts of the client's organization

    - Guidance to minimize risk during the selection process

    - Information about the other solu-tions that are being evaluated

- *Right-flank (people) strategies.* The right-flank sales strategy is associ-ated with a series of different tactics to reach the various people involved in the decision process. It is named after the right hemisphere of the brain, which is dominant for facial recognition, spatial abilities, and visual imagery. A right-flank move-ment is focused on finding coaches who are internal champions within an account. These are individuals who seem to like you, are receptive to your position, and appreciate your com-pany. For example, you might make a right-flank maneuver around your main contact within an account in order to set up a meeting and estab-lish a relationship with a more power-ful decision-maker. Some examples of the people who may be involved in a right-flank maneuver to get to the CXO are shown in figure 39.2.

Figure 39.2 Right flanking utilizes relationships to meet senior-level decision-makers

The flanking strategy chosen must be executable in the real world, and a key consideration is the determination of the likelihood of success. Below is a list of flanking tactics that is by no means inclusive of all the possible options. Rather, as you read each option, try to determine if it's based on left or right flanking (or in some cases both).

- *Barter.* Offering to provide the person you are calling on something of value in exchange for securing access to a senior executive. The object of value could be a proof of concept, free trial products, subject-matter expertise, valuable technical data, consulting services, favorable licensing terms, or anything else your company can offer.

- *Bombardment.* Sending a constant stream of business justification information, high-level summary information such as press articles or industry analyst reviews, and customer-related information to the C-level executives.

- *Brand attachment.* Leveraging your brand affinity to reach C-level executives. For example, you could reveal to the executives that they are using your product or services themselves or using another product that your company made possible ("Every time you access your favorite website from home, you're on our network.").

- *Coach introduction.* Using your coach (internal champion) to introduce you to the C-level decision-makers.

- *Company/business review.* Offering to conduct a site survey or business analysis and provide the analysis to the C-level executives (see ch. 45).

- *Corporate site visit.* Inviting C-level executives to visit corporate head-quarters to meet key executives and hear about the latest business and technology innovations.

- *Customer site visit.* Incenting C-levels executive to conduct a site visit with a key customer at their invitation.

- *Deep battle.* Using your president, vice president of sales, and other senior executives from within your company to call their counterparts at the customer's company.

- *Direct appeal.* Providing a detailed explanation directly to the C-level executive as to why he should meet with you. The explanation should include the knowledge and experiences you've gathered from working on his account (or within his industry) that justify the need for a meeting.

- *Heart to heart.* Having a sincerely honest conversation with your key contacts as to why they will not elevate your presence and introduce you and your solution to the C-level executives of the company.

- *Hostage.* Not granting a request or withholding something of importance to your lower-level contact until he orchestrates the meeting you request.

- *Internal referral.* Finding an internal referral from another part of the company or division within the company who will introduce or validate you and your solutions.

- *Irresistible offer.* Proposing a solution that is so compelling from a price, terms, and time-frame standpoint that it will garner C-level attention.

- *It's our discovery process.* From the very first meeting, setting the stage so that the customer knows that a key part of the discovery process is meeting with C-level executives. The purpose of these meetings is to ensure that the two organizations are a fit by validating their long-term vision, short-term goals, and key day-to-day requirements.

- *Key event.* Inviting C-level executives to attend a strategic event (annual client summit, local business event, forum, trade show meeting, or road show).

- *Lateral executive.* Approaching a C-level executive who is at the same level as the one you are trying to reach at the company to gain advice and an introduction.

- *Mutual customer introduction.* Asking a current customer to take the initiative and contact C-level executives on your behalf.

- *Prevention.* Setting the stage from the initial customer meeting by explaining that the process entails the mutual meeting of respective senior executives.

- *Recruitment of administrative assistant.* Executing a coordinated campaign to win over the executive's administrative assistant and request an introduction.

- *SME (subject-matter expert) leverage.* Using your company's key business and technical subject-matter experts to create a meeting opportunity.

- *Social outing.* Inviting C-level executives to attend a significant social outing.

- *Third-party introduction.* Seeking advice from and leveraging your company investors, board of directors, industry partners, consultants, vendors, or salespeople (from other companies) who know or have previously done business with the target company.

- *Value affirmation.* Meeting with your key contacts to ascertain the legitimacy of your value proposition and refining it so that it appeals to the C-level executives.

- *X-factor.* Developing a strategy associated with the unique combination of circumstances that are specific to the account.

The flanking strategy examples are given to facilitate the brainstorming process for your strategy session. It's important not to limit yourself to the examples on this list. Think outside the box and start flanking because the worst place to be is single-threaded!

Build Situational Dominance and Do Not Break Character

A critical point of any flanking strategy is that it must build or maintain your situational dominance. Your personal selling strategy is to establish situational dominance, and in every customer interaction you will find yourself in one of three places. You can be in a submissive position, where you are not respected and the customer rejects or ignores what you say because you're not respected. You can be in an equal position, where the customer respects you and is interested in hearing what you have to say. Finally, you can be in a situationally dominant position, where the customer accepts your arguments, internalizes them, and then acts on them. Your goal of your flanking strategy is to achieve and then keep situational dominance (see ch. 99).

The goal is to "maintain character" by continually exhibiting a high standard of professionalism with the prospective client across all your customer-facing organizations: sales, account management, consulting, and so on. Conversely, you never want to "break character," which occurs when a team or someone within the organization does not maintain a high standard of professionalism. For example, camping out in the hallway in front of someone's office in an effort to to see a C-level executive breaks character and lowers situational dominance. Reaching out to a senior executive with an inappropriate or inconsequential message does as well. This is why every flanking strategy to be executed must be approved by the brainstorming team in order to validate that it does not lower situational dominance or break character.

Here are a few more important points to keep in mind. The material and message you send should vary according to the level of the personnel in the account you are trying to penetrate.

Senior executives should receive short, high-level summary information, such as press articles, one-page reviews, and short case studies about their industry or companies you are doing business with. Save the company brochure, white papers, data sheets, and other detailed information for the midlevel and lower-level personnel.

Think about all the different types of items you can send to potential contacts other than a standard introduction. You can send interesting news clippings and serious-sounding industry updates that help validate your marketing claims. You can send details about your success within their company via email. Most importantly, whatever emails or messages you send should be professionally written with perfect grammar. They should be customized to the recipient's interests or problems and reinforce your situational dominance.

How to Conduct a Flanking Strategy Session

Here are the step-by-step instructions for conducting a flanking strategy session.

1. *Identify the strategy leader, executive sponsor, and scribe.* The flanking strategy leader will lead the strategy session and ensure all the action items that are created from the session are executed. For every account, there should also be an executive sponsor who oversees the strategy session and ensures the stakeholders from the various areas of the organization are involved and engaged. Finally, a scribe will complete the flanking strategies action plan as shown in figure 39.3.

2. *Determine the session attendees.* The strategy session should include key members of the sales, account management, and services organizations who are involved with the account. In addition, other team members can be invited, including company executives and applicable subject-matter experts. However, it is important to keep the number of attendees to a manageable number, preferably no more than six attendees.

3. *Conduct the session.* The typical strategy session agenda is shown below.

   A. *Account overview—The strategy leader provides a summary of the account, including the following information:*

   - Account overview and current account standing.
   - Discussion of primary contact relationship and why the sales team is stuck at a particular level.
   - Walk-through of account organization chart with key targets identified.

   B. *Round-robin flanking strategy identification—The strategy leader solicits flanking strategy ideas from each attendee.*

   - Each attendee presents ideas in order of strongest to weakest.

- After an idea is introduced the pros and cons are discussed.
- The scribe records each idea on the flanking strategy action sheet. It is assigned an owner who will execute it along with a target date of completion and a predicted success percentage.
- Once all the ideas are exhausted, the entire list of flanking strategies is prioritized for a final time.

4. *Execute the flanking strategy.* The strategy leader and executive sponsor monitor the execution and success of the items on the flanking strategy action plan.

Chapter 40. Psychological, Political, Operational, and Strategic Value

Establishing rapport is the only way to learn the true inner workings of a customer's selection process. In order to build customer rapport, you must demonstrate the value of your products, your company, and yourself. You must be able to convince the customer of the unique psychological value, political value, operational value, and strategic value you provide.

Great companies are consumed with value add. It's not just selling their product but helping you understand what is happening in the industry, having regular

Priority	Flanking Description	Owner	Target Date	Predicted Success %	Completed Date
1					
2					
3					

Figure 39.3 Flanking strategy action plan

touchpoint meetings with the team, reviewing the road map, and sharing your knowledge of what your organization can do to help us execute our strategy. For me, strong companies have this ingrained in their culture. They share information, don't ask for orders.

—Senior Vice President

Psychological Value

At the root of every decision is one of four psychological values. People buy products they believe will help them fulfill deep-seated psychological needs: satisfying the ego, being accepted as part of a group, avoiding pain, and ensuring survival. All the other outward appearances of a customer's decision-making process—the analysis, return-on-investment calculations, and other internal studies—are the means to achieving an overriding psychological goal. Therefore, the psychological value is the most important value when it comes to purchasing decisions.

I have interviewed more than a thousand customers as part of the win-loss studies I conduct for my clients. The most important finding from these studies is that human nature is the ultimate decision-maker for nearly every major decision. While the customer may have publicly recited a laundry list of rational reasons to justify the decision he made, he truthfully revealed in private that politics, self-interests, and personal emotions were responsible for the selection in the end.

Customers do not establish vendor relationships based upon the best business judgment; rather, they judge

vendors based upon who establishes the best business relationships. A C-level executive I interviewed said it best: "We made it clear that we weren't buying a brochure or data sheet. For that matter, we weren't even buying a product. We were buying a long-term relationship with another company and, equally important, the team of people from that company whom we would have to work with on a day-in, day-out basis."

Customers purchase products that increase their happiness, esteem, power, or wealth. They rationalize these psychological decisions with logic and facts. For example, a vice president of a manufacturing company may explain that he wants to buy supply chain software because it will save a million dollars a year when, in reality, he is making the purchase to show the CEO that he is a prudent businessman. The desire to impress the CEO (the benefit) drives the software purchase (the action). The term "benefaction" refers to the psychological benefits that determine a person's actions.

Four core psychological drives determine selection behavior. These four benefactions are well-being, pain avoidance, self-preservation, and self-gratification. Physical well-being, the will to survive, is one of our strongest desires. It weighs heavily in the minds of both customers and competitors. Making customers feel their jobs are safe in your hands is a top priority during sales calls. Ideally, you would like them to believe (whether it is true or not) that the competitive solutions are actually threats to their livelihood. Customers are equally concerned with maintaining their mental and emotional well-being. When something is hurting you badly, the desire to eliminate the source of pain can be all-consuming. Pain is one of the best purchase motivators because customers are forced to act quickly and decisively to eliminate it.

Companies experience different kinds of pain all the time. Nuisances can create dull aching pains in every department, such as a temperamental copy machine. Throbbing pains may reappear occasionally, like internet service providers that go down momentarily every few months. Stabbing pains require immediate attention, for example, when the order-entry system is down and products can't be shipped and sales cannot be made. Companies can live with dull aches and cope with throbbing pains as necessary. But the stabbing pains receive immediate attention and dictate budgeting.

Self-preservation, the third core psychological drive, is the desire to be recognized for our unique talents while still belonging to a group. Customers and salespeople alike naturally seek the approval of others. Customers purchase items that they believe will enhance their stature and protect their group position. They not only want to be respected by their peers but also want to become group leaders. Naturally, salespeople want to be pack leaders too.

Self-gratification is our desire to put our own needs before everyone else's. Customers will go to great lengths to purchase something that makes them feel better about themselves and superior to others. Egos drive the business world.

Political Value

The second most important value, political value, involves organizational power. Many people think that power

is dependent upon title and that the way work gets done in organizations is through hierarchical authority. However, this is not usually the case. Power is the ability to influence the environment for your own benefit. It is often used to get your way when diplomacy, consensus building, and negotiation fail. For example, while I have parental authority over my children, they have their own types of powers and associated strategies to get their way. Sometimes they will band together and recruit their mother to support their cause in order to override my authority. Companies operate in much the same way.

Your product provides customers the opportunity to achieve political power. It may enable them to increase their authority, help them become indispensable to the company, allow them to satisfy an internal powerbroker, or enable them to maintain authority. Interdepartmental coordination always involves the use of power. Your product can make someone more powerful, or for those seeking to become more influential, it can provide much needed visibility that enables them to be in contact with the company's powerbrokers.

Operational Value

The third most important value is operational value. People's success in an organization is dependent upon the success of their department's operations. Therefore, every department has inherent pressure to accomplish projects that successfully add operational value.

The ways that operational value is determined are quite diverse. An ambitious manager might consider your product's operational value to be the ability to successfully complete the department's project that enables his department to proliferate its services throughout the company. Another customer might prize satisfying internal customers in other departments, and operational value to some might be found in products that enable them to resist change. For example, a bureaucratic IT department might add a new internet interface to its existing mainframe rather than replace the entire system.

You can also think of operational value in terms of the customer's résumé—a list of all his successful projects and accomplishments. After the customer purchases your solution, what accomplishment or milestones would he add to his résumé?

Strategic Value

Strategic value, the fourth value, is based upon the appearance of rationality and impartiality. However, customers do not seek information that will help them make an objective strategic decision; they amass information that helps them justify their preconceived ideas of strategic value. In other words, your product's strategic value comprises the reasons and arguments evaluators give to senior management and others in the company as to why the product should be purchased, regardless of whether the reasons are real or imagined.

	Consolidators	Consulters	Responders	Bureaucrats
Psychological value	Self-gratification	Physical well-being	Self-preservation	Pain avoidance
	Fulfill desire to achieve	Satisfy will to survive	Gain approval of others	Avoid painful change
Political value	Consolidate power	Become indispensable	Draft off the powerful	Maintain authority
Operational value	Enable the grand initiative	Proliferate service offerings through organization	Reactively accommodate internal customers	Do as little as possible
Strategic value	Gain competitive advantage	Improve quality	Improve customer satisfaction	Standardize operations
	Increase revenues	Decrease costs	Improve productivity and efficiency	Maintain ease of business

Figure 40.1 Different values for different enterprise buyer types

The seven basic types of strategic value enable customers to

- Gain a competitive advantage (increase market share, enter new markets, defeat competition)
- Increase revenues
- Decrease costs
- Increase productivity and efficiency
- Improve customer satisfaction
- Improve quality
- Standardize operations (increase ease of business and mitigate risk)

Some customers will say that a purchase provides a competitive advantage or will enable them to increase revenues. Others might argue internally that a purchase will save money in the long run. Some will show how customer satisfaction will be improved or detail improvements in operational efficiency.

Enterprise buyer types perceive value differently. Consolidators will say that a purchase provides a competitive advantage or will enable them to increase revenues. Consulters might argue that a purchase will save money in the long run. Responders will show how customer satisfaction will be improved, and bureaucrats will detail improvements in operational efficiency. Figure 40.1 summarizes how consolidator, consulter, responder, and bureaucrat enterprise buyer types view each of the four different types of value.

Exercise: Write down your psychological, political, operational, and strategic value to the customer. During customer interactions, present your solution to the potential buyer based upon these four values. You must communicate that *you* and *your solution* can help solve critical department problems, help the customer become an expert and an internal source of knowledge, and help him become successful and more powerful, and that you are providing a safe, long-term solution.

Chapter 41. Logic versus the Human Nature of Customer Decision-Making

To understand the impact of logic and human nature on decision-making, let's study Bob, a college-educated professional with a doctorate in computer science. Successful in his career, he has become the CFO of a Fortune 500 company. Bob is a smart businessman who employs sound business practices and possesses the acumen to get to the top of the corporate ladder.

Let's say Bob is facing two very important decisions. The first decision involves making a multimillion-dollar technology purchase for the division he runs. The second decision involves proposing marriage to Maggie, his girlfriend of nine months. Bob approaches each of these decisions in a very different way.

For the business decision, he first conducts an in-depth study of the inefficiencies of his current infrastructure. Next, he presents his findings with an internal rate-of-return study for replacing the old equipment with state-of-the-art machinery to the senior management team of the parent company. Then he performs a detailed analysis of the various equipment vendors and makes a final selection.

Getting married is one of life's most important decisions. Bob has fallen in love with Maggie. He feels good being with her, thinks about her often, and looks forward to their time together. She has the qualities he admires, and when compared to girlfriends of the past, she is the best. Bob decides he will ask her to marry him.

However, as he moves forward in his decision-making process, an unexpected change in Bob's thought process occurs. The subconscious mind, the self-regulating system designed to prevent us from making unwise choices, is on vigilant watch. It drives Bob to perform a "gut-check" of the rational, logical information regarding the equipment purchase. Beyond the facts and figures, does the decision feel right? He second-guesses himself and asks whether the move will help or hurt his career.

Conversely, the emotional high associated with the idea of marriage is tempered by reality. He now evaluates Maggie's little habits that he once thought were cute with a more rational eye. He studies other aspects of their relationship with equal intensity. Figure 41.1 illustrates the changing nature of decision-making.

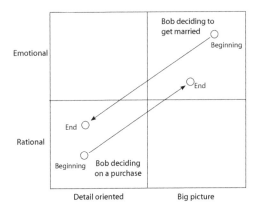

Figure 41.1 The changing nature of decision-making

Anticipate the impact of the subconscious mind during the sales cycle and take it into account during sales calls. The customer with whom you had a "red-hot" initial sales call will suddenly turn cold and fail to respond to your follow-up calls. The prospect who has established an elaborate selection process will ultimately be influenced by emotions. Knowing this ahead of time, you can plan to use different types of words that correspond to a logical, emotional, and psychological appeal in interactions with your customers.

Do salespeople truly understand the impact of human nature on the sales cycle? In a recent study I asked over one thousand salespeople to answer the following question: "I would say that most buyers base their final purchase decision on ___ percent logic and reason versus human nature (emotion/politics/personal biases)." Their responses are shown in figure 41.2.

Now let's compare the results to what buyers actually think when they were asked, "Let's say you have to choose between two similar vendors with products that are very similar in features, functionality, and price. Would your final decision be based on logic or instinct?" The results are shown in figure 41.3. A comparison of answers shows that salespeople intuitively understand how prospective buyers behave in general. The only difference is that customers are slightly more instinctive than salespeople believe. Furthermore, customers can be divided into logical and instinctual decision-makers.

Two very important points need to be made about the groups of logical and instinctual decision-makers. First, both groups conduct their evaluations in the same basic manner with the same level of due diligence. Therefore, it is difficult for salespeople to determine which type of decision-maker they are dealing with

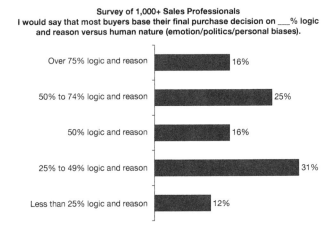

Figure 41.2 Salespeople's ratings of how buyers use logic versus human nature to make buying decisions

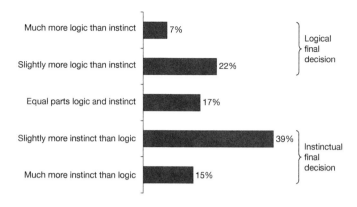

Figure 41.3 Survey of buyers showing how they use logic and human nature in decision-making

early in the sales cycle. Second, the groups gravitate to different types of vendors.

The instinctual decision-maker has a higher tendency (44 percent) to select the better-known top-of-the-line goliath vendor, while the logical final decision-maker is far more open (69 percent) to selecting lesser known brands. A theory behind this is that instinctual final decision-makers will play it safe and follow the herd within their industry. Conversely, reason and common sense motivate the logical decision-makers to purchase the most efficient solution.

Exercise: Take a moment to answer a question before you read further. Which of the following subjects would you say was your favorite when you were in school?

- ☐ Art
- ☐ History
- ☐ Language or composition
- ☐ Math
- ☐ Physical education
- ☐ Science

There is another facet of decision-making where salespeople and evaluators are quite different. Of the sales professionals who achieved over 125 percent of their annual quota last year, 29 percent selected history as their favorite school subject, 23 percent selected science, 23 percent selected math, 13 percent selected physical education, 9 percent selected language and composition, and only 3 percent selected art as shown in figure 41.4. Their answer reveals a lot about how they process information, think, and make decisions.

The subject you selected in the exercise is an important indicator of your selling style and how you process information and develop your sales intuition. Sales intuition is the ability to correctly

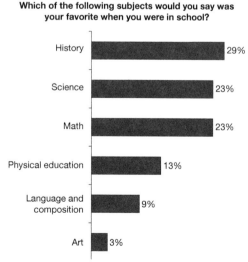

Figure 41.4 Favorite school subject of salespeople who achieved over 125 percent of previous year's annual quota

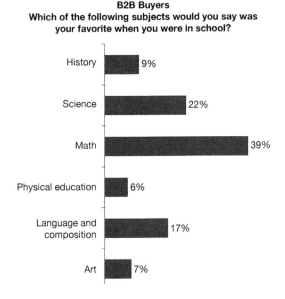

B2B Buyers
Which of the following subjects would you say was
your favorite when you were in school?

- History — 9%
- Science — 22%
- Math — 39%
- Physical education — 6%
- Language and composition — 17%
- Art — 7%

Figure 41.5 Favorite school subject of buyers

read and anticipate a customer's actions. You can think of your sales intuition as a highly developed model for making decisions and a powerful heuristic engine that is constantly learning from the past. It is the process of comparing a series of past experiences against current circumstances.

History is based upon the study of important events, times, people, and places from the past. Obviously, learning from the past is an important method for making well-informed decisions in the future. Therefore, it should not be surprising that history was the top selection. In essence, history is based on a form of storytelling, and this is indicative of a person's strong verbal orientation. Equally important, history lovers tend to possess a characteristic I refer to as situational curiosity, and this impacts their sales success. This is the personal desire to understand all the different aspects of a sales situation—the who, what, when, where, and why the customer will buy.

Science is the process of discovery and exploration based upon a systematic methodology of observation, measurement, and testing. Through this process science lovers attempt to organize the chaos that occurs naturally during the sales cycle. This requires the ability to think about the future hypothetically. Their sales intuition is developed based upon a more cerebral orientation, where the interpretation of results tends to be more quantitative than the method used by the qualitative history lover.

Math is based upon formulas, frameworks, and regimentation. It is indicative of absolute thinking where results are either black or white, all or nothing. Math lovers have an analytical orientation that is consumed with predictable outcomes based upon concrete terms. In which level of the sales organization is this type of thinking most relevant—the sales rep level, midlevel management, or top-level vice president of sales? More top-level vice presidents of sales selected math than did any other sales role, and this makes sense when you think about the complexity of sales forecasting.

Physical education (sports) and sales share a lot of the same characteristics. Each requires hard work, perseverance, sacrifice, and personal discipline. More importantly, each is based upon preparing oneself—physically, mentally, and strategically—for the long run, whether it is an entire season or a fiscal year. Being in sales takes a single-minded drive to achieve a goal and this is indicative of someone who is action oriented.

It requires an intensely competitive personality and the willingness to make a commitment and personal sacrifice to win. The habit of putting in long hours, whether on a baseball diamond, on a football field, on a tennis court, or in a swimming pool, parallels the habits of successful salespeople.

Language and composition and the arts are based upon self-expression that tends to be associated with mental, spiritual, and social well-being. When compared to math and science, the creative orientation is quite the opposite. These subjects are concerned with empathy, emotional expression, and out-of-the-box thinking. They strengthen their sales intuition through deep, personally sophisticated customer conversations.

What are the favorite subjects of buyers? The results from a study of B2B buyers is shown in figure 41.5. Thirty-nine percent preferred math and there's a big difference between a historian and mathematician. Also, twice as many buyers prefer language and composition and art, and half as many prefer physical education. There are huge differences in the thought processes of an artist and a scientist, a historian and an athlete, or a linguist and a mathematician. Be forewarned, there are also significant differences between the favorite subjects of men and women (see ch. 129).

Unfortunately, sales organizations today are making two common mistakes. First, all the salespeople are taught to deliver the same message in the same way even though buyers communicate, learn, process information, and make decisions in vastly different ways. Second, most sales training time is spent only on having salespeople memorize logical facts about the company, product, and

competitors. Little or no training is given on the development of sales intuition when in fact, a salesperson's intuition is responsible for guiding him to say or do the right thing at the right time.

Chapter 42. Ten Principles for Developing Deeper Client Relationships

Ever-increasing business challenges and a rapidly changing business landscape require salespeople to create deeper, more meaningful relationships than in the past. Your purpose is to help your clients solve their short-term problems and fulfill their long-term mission. With this goal in mind, ten guiding principles for developing deeper client relationships are described below and shown in figure 42.1.

1. Customer intimacy
2. Excellence
3. Curiosity
4. Knowledge
5. Communication
6. Openness
7. Innovation
8. Expertise
9. Measurement
10. Friendship

Figure 42.1 Principles for developing deeper client relationships

1. *Customer intimacy.* Continually seek to understand what your customers need, build stronger relationships, and excel in customer service by providing valued solutions on time within their budget. You never want to let them down and should think of their challenges as your opportunities because you are inherently optimistic.

2. *Excellence.* Always maintain focus on superb execution in order to meet your clients' expectations. Continually streamline how you interact with them and strive to improve their efficiency in order to save clients money.

3. *Curiosity.* While responsiveness is always foremost in your mind, always try to understand the root causes behind each specific request clients make. Moreover, don't limit yourself to performing only within the scope of your role as a salesperson or by solely thinking about the task at hand. Rather, be naturally curious about all aspects of the clients' operations. Ask a lot of questions and listen more than you talk. By doing so, you'll uncover additional areas where you can help clients improve their operations and leverage your expertise.

4. *Knowledge.* Since your company's strength is the collective knowledge gained from years of experience while working with a wide variety of companies and challenging environments, share this knowledge freely with your customers and educate them on best practices, industry trends, and the latest technical developments. You are here to help their organization maximize their value to their customers and prevent them from taking the wrong course of action.

5. *Communication.* Use clear, concise client communication. Comprehension should always be your top-of-mind concern when you speak or write. Every email, meeting, conference call, report, and presentation is an important interaction that is a direct reflection of your brand. The better you communicate, the more credibility you have.

6. *Openness.* Since we are confident in our company and ourselves, we don't think our ideas are always the best. Therefore, we are open to change and always explore new ideas. If we fail, we accept responsibility and make corrections so it doesn't happen again. While failure is always humbling, we believe it provides a meaningful opportunity to learn and improve.

7. *Innovation.* Think outside the box when presented with a problem. Don't automatically recommend solutions. Instead, tap into your own past experiences or seek advice from colleagues and those in your network of subject-matter experts to find the optimal solution.

8. *Expertise.* Become personally committed to improving your skills and stay on top of the latest technologies and goings-on in your industry. Keep current so you can have relevant conversations with your clients.

9. *Measurement.* Objectively measure all aspects of your performance and your client's success, and provide detailed feedback to the customer in a professional manner. Know where you stand and have an accurate understanding about how you, your products, and customer support are doing.

10. *Friendship.* Stay grounded and do not take yourself too seriously. Life's short. Have fun and enjoy being a positive presence that makes the people around you feel better about themselves. Friends think about

friendships over the long term. There-fore, they are honest, considerate, and respectful. You want everyone within your client's organization to become a close friend.

Ultimately, you want to develop these ten principles with everyone you work with and become irreplaceable. By doing so, you will embed yourself into accounts with deeper value and sophisticated relation-ships that insulate you from internal and external threats. Clients cannot replicate all the different types of value you provide; therefore, they are less likely to consider swapping your solution with the competi-tion's, they are less inclined to haggle with you over the price of your services, and it is far more difficult to replace you with lower-priced competitors.

Exercise: For each of the principles above, create a list of actions you can take to improve the relationship with your key clients. Strategize with your manager and colleagues and solicit their ideas as well. Update your action list on a regular basis. Keep track of the actions that are most impactful and use them with other accounts.

Chapter 43. Cross-Selling Strategy

What is a cross-selling strategy? Let's pretend you're buying a book online from Amazon. You search and find the book you want to buy. As you scroll down the page for more details, Amazon presents two related books and bundles them together for one convenient price. This is an example of a cross-selling strategy.

A cross-selling strategy consists of introducing your different solution offer-ings to existing clientele. Unlike the Ama-zon example, where the cross-selling strat-egy is based on a one-time transactional event, your strategy should be based on a never-ending campaign to introduce your solutions to all the other departments within the client's company along with all the entities that are related to the organiza-tion (for example, remote geographic loca-tions and separate divisions).

A fundamental premise of the cross-selling strategy is that your attempt to penetrate another area of a client's orga-nization will take time. In essence, you are running a political campaign that will most likely take several months, and in some cases over a year, to complete. While you obviously want to generate immediate interest, you need to set your own expec-tations so you don't get frustrated from a lack of results and stop campaigning. Your campaign ends only when the cus-tomer buys the solutions you've proposed or specifically tells you to stop contacting him. The five cross-selling strategy exe-cution steps are defined below.

1. Determine Opportunity Areas and Title Targets

The first step is to analyze the organiza-tion and related entities in order to pick the key areas where one of your solution offerings would be applicable. In chapter 38 we reviewed the strategy to develop a wider footprint across the organization by mapping out key decision-makers and important influencers. Next, you deter-mine the title targets in each opportunity area. These are people who have spe-cific titles that typically purchase your products. You want them to become knowledgeable about the full breadth of the solutions you provide and how they might be used within their department. For example, if you sold fraud prevention technology your title targets might include the chief risk officer and the fraud manager who work in the fraud and risk department and the chief information security officer from the IT department. Ideally, you would like your coaches (see ch. 37) to provide you with the organization charts and contact data, but you cannot rely on them exclusively. You have to use investigative research to find the key contacts just as a salesperson would when trying to penetrate a new account (see ch. 84).

2. Select the Campaign

The second step is to create a campaign that will introduce a specific solution from your portfolio to the title target. The strongest campaign will be for the solution that solves both an immediate business problem and fulfills a future business goal or requirement. This has the highest sense of urgency. The second strongest campaign is for one that solves an immediate problem, while the weakest one is based on enabling a business goal sometime in the future as shown in figure 43.1.

Figure 43.1 Selecting the campaign to reach a title target

3. Create the Outreach Messages

The best outreach messages pique the title targets' interest, build your credibility, and hook them on why they should meet with you. Put yourself in the targets' position and theorize on the strategic, operational, political, and psychological value your solutions provide them. Refer to chapters 87–90 for specific types of outreach messages. Most importantly, use SCAR (situation, challenge, action, and result) to format customer success stories to explain how you've helped other areas of their company (see ch. 64). You can create an effective outreach message that is centered upon a business problem, industry theme, or goal you know the targets want to achieve.

4. Select the Outreach Channel

You can use a variety of outreach channels to contact the title target during the course of a campaign.

- *Internal referral.* Introductions from existing clients are your most powerful campaign channel. Your client can introduce you to other key decision-makers and influencers in other departments. These introductions take advantage of the theory of attached relationships, where you are bestowed with qualities such as standing, performance, and reputation as a result of an existing relationship. Assuming the introductory relationship is positive, you will be thought of in the same manner.

- *Email.* Email is universally the preferred method by which the prospective customers would have you contact them. See chapter 85 for details on when to send an email.

- *LinkedIn.* LinkedIn is an important networking channel as described in chapter 91. Connect with all your contacts at current and past clients. Send a personalized invitation whenever you meet someone new who might be of value to your network. This includes new contacts at existing client companies, partners, salespeople, and consultants you meet on a daily basis. Continually send articles, announcements, and case studies to your network. Make sure your profile is fully developed and meets the standards described in chapter 95.

- *Phone call.* The odds of connecting with the person you are trying to reach via a phone call are extremely low, so you will most likely go to voice mail. Most salespeople don't leave a compelling message so the target won't bother calling back. You must be able to leave a succinct message. In no more than twenty-five seconds, you must identify who you are and why the customer should call you back. Your message must be delivered in a clear, commanding, yet approachable tone.

- *Letters.* Any letter sent by snail mail must meet one important condition: it, and associated collateral that is sent to the target, must be unique and compelling. The material and message you send should vary according to the level of personnel you are trying to reach. Senior executives should receive short, high-level summary information, such as press articles, one-page reviews, and short case studies about your internal implementation or companies within

their industry whom you are doing business with.

- *Drop-ins.* Unannounced stop-bys at someone's cubicle or office can be viewed positively or negatively depending upon the individual. Typically, higher level personnel won't welcome the interruption. In addition, you don't want to break character (see ch. 44).

- *Lunch-and-learn talks.* Extending a nonthreatening invitation to your targets to attend a catered lunch at the client's office to learn about an emerging technology, a hot trend, or best practices based upon your experience with other clients can be a very effective tactic.

- *Demonstration/training days.* Another tactic is to reserve a conference room at the client's office for the day and selectively invite team members to stop by for a demonstration or offer a free class on a skill set they would value.

- *Audit/site analysis.* You could offer to perform a study of how the department is performing a task or operation and then present the results compared with industry standards and provide improvement recommendations.

- *Proof of capability/concept.* Seeing is believing, and you could extend an offer to conduct a pilot project utilizing your products or services.

5. Rest and Then Repeat with a New Campaign Message

It's easy to make two critical mistakes when you try to cross-sell to prospective customers. You might either contact them once and stop if you don't get a response or contact them way too often. It's easy to mistakenly believe you are gaining mind share and acceptance by sending an introductory email every other week. However, the opposite is true. You are devaluing and diluting your message. The only exception to this rule is posting your message on LinkedIn, and this is because the LinkedIn feed is viewed optionally.

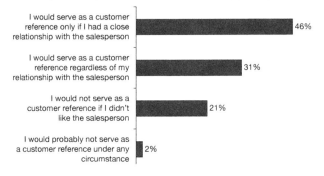

Figure 43.2 Likelihood that customers will recommend a product

Therefore, you need rest breaks consisting of weeks or months where you do not contact the customer directly. After the rest period has ended, you start another campaign with a series of three entirely new messages.

Why Won't My Client Make an Internal Introduction for Me?

The reality is that customers are not all that inclined to recommend a product if they don't have a close relationship with their account manager as shown in figure 43.2.

There are several possible reasons for this scenario. Obviously, a less-than-happy client will not recommend a vendor that has not met their standards. However, assuming your client is relatively satisfied, here are some other possible reasons.

- *Unacceptable risk.* The person believes recommending your company internally could jeopardize his job security, current standing, or future potential. First and foremost,

the solution you are asking to be introduced has to be within the domain expertise of your company. If it falls way outside of your core competencies (as described on your website or from previous discussions), the perceived personal risk may be too high for the person to promote it internally.

- *Inappropriate ask.* Organizations are complex political structures where hierarchies are respected. Asking a low-level contact in the purchasing department to reach out to senior executive leaders of other departments may not be politically correct unless your contact knows the people himself.

- *Service dissolution.* The client may believe the additional demands on you will diminish your capability to successfully deliver products and services to him. In addition, the client may personally fear becoming marginalized.

- *No motivation.* The client may not wish to have any additional visibility into his department and how it is operated. In other words, he wants to fly under the radar and avoid the prying eyes of other departmental leaders (and, respectively, the vendors used).

Why Didn't the Internal Prospect Respond to My Outreach Message?

It's reasonable to expect up to three weeks for a response to your email or solicitation. If a customer doesn't respond, put yourself in his position and theorize why you didn't hear back from him. Did you send an email that was basically an infomercial or did you laboriously explain technical details? Fight the urge to explain too much. Instead, structure the message so the customer finds it enticing or better yet, try to reach the person through another channel. In addition, make sure your outreach is well written, professional, and at the same level of verbal acuity of the prospect (see chs. 44 and 126). Finally, don't assume the client isn't interested in your products. It might just be an issue of timing, so continue your campaign to recruit the target.

Chapter 44. Customer Meeting Guidelines

The way you present yourself to new and existing clients is directly influenced by the industry you're in and the type of products or services you sell. For example, selling a hot new technology for a start-up in Silicon Valley is very different from selling services for a big consulting firm in New York City. In essence, you have to take on the role that is in character with the company's public image. For example, the services salesperson would be out of character wearing a T-shirt and jeans, and

the high-tech salesperson would be out of place in a three-piece suit.

"Breaking character" occurs whenever a salesperson (or company colleague) says something, does something, or acts in a way that breaks the customer's belief in him and damages his credibility. Breaking character can occur in a sales call, during any part of a sales cycle, or over the course of the customer's journey after becoming a client. For example, a salesperson calls on a prospect and closes the account. Then the consulting services team members begin implementation. Finally, the account is transferred to an account manager when it goes into production. Any individual involved at each of these steps could break character and jeopardize the account.

The goal is to "maintain character" by continually exhibiting a high standard of professionalism with clients across all customer-facing organizations: sales, account management, implementation, and support. When this is done, the client enjoys a consistently positive experience while transitioning from a prospect to a client. Conversely, breaking character occurs when a team or someone within the organization does not maintain these standards of professionalism.

Specifically, the interactions across the customer-facing areas of the organization should be synchronized. This means everyone should be of the same mind culturally and speak from the same page with consistent communication quality when interacting with customers. Instead of having a loose collection of individuals who do as they see fit, specific customer interaction protocols are established including well-defined escalation processes. There is a cohesive

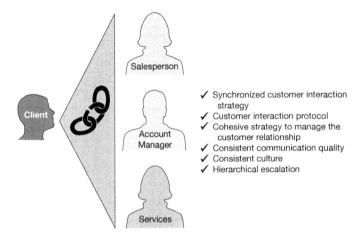

Figure 44.1 Breaking character can occur anytime during the customer's journey by any customer-facing team member

methodology by which all areas of the company work together to manage the account, based on a consistent experience across every part of the organization, because if one area breaks character, then the entire chain that binds the client to the company is broken as shown in figure 44.1.

I want to share with you a very important lesson I've learned after conducting thousands of customer role-plays with salespeople as part of the process of researching their company. I played the part of an interested prospect, and they presented their company and answered my questions as typically done in an initial meeting that lasts anywhere from thirty minutes to an hour. I am continually surprised at how many times salespeople inadvertently say something negative about their company, products, or themselves and don't even realize it. For example, they'll say their company is not that good at doing X when they should be saying that their company is best known for their specialty of doing Y. *Maintaining character means you never demean yourself, your company and its products,* or your career and the industry you are part of in front of customers!

Types of Customer Meetings

Whether you're dealing with a new prospective customer or an existing install base client, the goal is to employ a WHD (wider, higher, deeper) expansion strategy to increase your product and awareness footprint (see ch. 38). Ideally, you should create a meeting calendar in order to plan and execute the WHD strategy with meetings conducted at all levels of the client's organization. The calendar should include strategic relationship meetings between the respective executive teams where both parties review their company's future direction. These meetings can be scheduled on a quarterly or annual basis either on-site or at an annual user group meeting (see ch. 45). Regular meetings between the respective midlevel management teams should be held where the overall account standing and progression is reviewed and areas of risk and opportunities discussed. Finally, daily and weekly meetings between the respective operations teams to discuss project details should be conducted as shown in figure 44.2.

Team Selling: Client Meeting Guidelines to Maintain Character

A key aspect of maintaining character is subscribing to the philosophy of "we" that is predicated on teamwork, collaboration, and ownership when meeting

Figure 44.2 Types of customer meetings

with clients. For example, refer to your company as "our company," not "the company," when in front of clients. You can adopt the following client meeting guidelines to ensure we transmit the message of ownership, personal responsibility, and overall professionalism in every interaction.

1. *We respect colleagues.* Quite often, several team members will be attending a client meeting. We always observe these meeting protocols. First, all team members always defer to the colleague in attendance with the highest title and rank. We always invite the senior-most person to speak and solicit this person's comments during the course of the meeting. Second, we show respect for our colleagues and never interrupt them while they are talking or talk over them. In addition, we do not directly contradict what they have said in front of the client. For example, instead of saying "I don't think that will work here," we would say, "Here's another idea we should also explore."

2. *We never demean.* People naturally want to be around optimistic people, and we strive to avoid negativity. First

and foremost, we never say anything demeaning about the client's company or anything condescending about anyone who works at the company. In addition, we never demean our company in any way, either indirectly or directly, during a conversation with the client. Likewise, we never demean any part of our organization or anyone within our organization.

3. *We set a meeting goal and specific outcome.* The first step toward conducting a successful sales call is to determine your goal and outcome for the meeting. Start the meeting by announcing the meeting goal and exactly what it is you want to accomplish along with how long you expect the meeting to last. For example, "The goal for today's meeting is to review all the open support tickets for this project, and I expect the meeting to last sixty minutes."

   Moreover, too many meetings end without any definitive results. First meetings with customers are short and the time passes quickly. Therefore, it is important to identify a specific outcome of the meeting beforehand so you can judge whether you have achieved your goal. Professional athletes understand specific outcomes, and, for example, a basketball coach will ask the team to mentally rehearse cutting down the net after they win the championship before the big game. Your specific outcome may be to have the customer tell you at the end of the meeting "That was a great review, and it sounds like all the support issues are under control."

4. *We prepare and synchronize.* Hold a premeeting with other team members before the customer meeting so that everyone understands our strategy to achieve our meeting goal. Provide an update about the client so everyone understands the client's current situation and then we brainstorm on the issues (or opportunity) the client is experiencing, our position on the issue, and the course of resolution. Provide an overview about all the people from the client's company who will be in attendance and their perception of us along with their coach rating (see ch. 37).

5. *We control the agenda and socialize it.* The person who creates the agenda inherently controls the meeting. Wherever possible, we create the agenda and socialize it with meeting attendees by sharing it with them anywhere from a couple of days to a couple of weeks in advance of the meeting. The more important or difficult the meeting is expected to be, the better off you are sharing the agenda with the key client attendees in person. These private premeetings can prevent public embarrassments.

6. *We have a confident demeanor.* Your personal demeanor (how you conduct yourself and behavior) speaks volumes. Regardless of the situation, keep a calm and confident demeanor. Most of all, do not get defensive. Stay positive. This is a critical lesson. When confronted by someone who disagrees with your opinion, it's okay to disagree without being disagreeable. Remember, this is business— it's not personal.

7. *We handle questions professionally.* One of the hardest things to do in all of sales is handle tough questions from skeptical, condescending, or hostile customers. Customers ask two basic types of questions in general. Some are very specific questions about an issue, while others are more general about a broad topic. In both instances, make sure you understand the question before answering it. Either rephrase the question in your own mind with your own words and repeat it to the questioner aloud or ask the questioner to further explain what he meant before answering. Don't be too eager to give an answer to a question that wasn't even asked.

   Since most meetings and sales calls are conducted with groups of people, you should also give a little background information with your answers to ensure everyone understands the topic. Don't assume everyone understands the issue or is up to speed on the subject being discussed.

8. *We are passionate.* Showing honest enthusiasm for your client's business will permeate through the client's mind. As a result, they'll think of you first when they have a problem to solve. The most persuasive people are passionate about the company they work for and what they do for a living.

9. *We pay attention to the details.* Always show up on time out of respect for

the client. Come prepared with supporting materials such as reports and handouts. Assign one member of your team the duty of taking notes. Make sure everyone knows the dress code because every business has a unique culture.

10. *We continually rate rapport.* At the heart of every successful client meeting are mutual trust, the competence of the participants, and the development of rapport. Rapport is a special relationship between two individuals based upon harmonious communication (see ch. 71).

Chapter 45. Quarterly and Annual Business Review Meetings

After you have been managing an existing client's account for many months or years, it's natural to become "single-threaded" where almost all your interactions are with a single point of contact. Usually, this is a lower-level person in the organization and your interactions tend to focus solely on daily issues and top-of-mind tasks. As a result, you are placed in a position of risk because other vendors are continually telling leaders at the higher levels of the organization how much better off they'd be if they replaced you.

Holding client quarterly business review and annual business review meetings (abbreviated QBRs and ABRs) is a key flanking strategy designed to preempt this precarious situation. The meetings' ultimate goal is to justify the continued use of your solutions with decision-makers at all levels of the company and across the stakeholder departments that use and pay for the solutions you provide.

What Clients Qualify for QBRs and ABRs?

Because of the time, effort, and resources required to conduct ABR and QBR meetings, they are reserved for specific types of clients as shown in figure 45.1. Both QBRs and ABRs should be considered mandatory for key accounts. Key accounts are tier-one, top-revenue accounts that determine whether or not you will achieve your revenue target.

Selective meetings	Mandatory meetings
Static accounts—Selective ABR meetings depending upon future business potential. Static accounts are tier-two revenue accounts that consistently buy your solutions but in smaller volume than tier-one accounts.	Key accounts—Mandatory QBR, ABR, and even MBR (monthly) meetings. Key accounts are tier-one, top-revenue accounts that determine whether or not you achieve your revenue target.
Trailing accounts—Very selective ABR meetings depending upon immediate business potential. Trailing accounts are tier-three revenue accounts where business has fallen off or minimal purchases have been recently made.	Strategic accounts—Mandatory ABR meeting depending upon client importance. Strategic accounts are clients that are important from a marketing, competitive, or product development perspective, regardless of the amount they spend now.

Figure 45.1 QBR and ABR meeting selection guidelines

ABRs are also mandatory for strategic accounts. Strategic accounts are clients that are important from a marketing, competitive, product development, or potential revenue growth perspective, regardless of how much money they spend now. ABR meetings should be selectively conducted with static accounts depending upon future business potential. Static accounts are tier-two revenue accounts that consistently buy your solutions but in smaller volumes than tier-one accounts. ABR meetings should be very selectively conducted with trailing accounts. Trailing accounts are tier-three lower-revenue producing accounts where business has fallen off or minimal purchases have recently been made.

The Six Underlying Principles for Conducting QBRs and ABRs

Most salespeople mistakenly do not structure, plan, prepare, and execute QBR or ABR meetings with the level of sophistication that is required. Rather, they conduct them in the same manner as they would an operations meeting with lower-level staff. Unfortunately, they miss the opportunity to develop more strategic relationships with C-suite executives and midlevel managers. In order of priority, here are six underlying principles for conducting QBR and ABR meetings.

1. Develop Customer Intimacy in Order to Identify Additional Business Opportunities

The foundation of the successful QBR and ABR meeting is based on developing customer intimacy through research, relationships, results, and reporting. First, you must conduct "organizational" research to understand the client's overall business condition, the important issues it is facing, and the initiatives it is undertaking. Review their press releases, news articles, financial disclosures, and analyst reports. The goal of the organizational research is to gain the following:

- Knowledge of how the client's business is organized and operates

- Understanding of the client's recent trends, news, initiatives, and company direction

- Understanding of the client's industry and market position and what competitors are doing

The meeting also provides you the opportunity to build confidential friendships with the contacts you regularly meet with and create new relationships with employees of the company whom you don't normally have access to.

Equally important, the meeting provides the opportunity to analyze and explain the successful results the customer is achieving by using your products or services. Ideally, you want these success points to be broadcast virally throughout the organization. Therefore, they must be quantified and reported in interesting documents or slides that are easy to share.

A natural by-product of a successful QBR or ABR meeting is the identification of other business opportunities within the client's company. The overview research enables you to identify the business problems and new initiatives where your products or services add value to the client's business. Strong relationships lead to internal referrals and result in follow-on meetings. Quantifying your results helps you control and disseminate positive messaging about your company and the solutions you provide.

2. Ascertain Account Standing up, down, and across the Organization

The meeting also provides you an important opportunity to learn how the different areas of the company and the various levels (from C-suite executives to midlevel management and lower-level personnel) perceive your company, solutions, support, and team members. Prior to the meeting, you should conduct "personnel" research consisting of premeeting interviews and online surveys with questions specifically asked to ascertain a true picture of your account standing. Questions and topics should include

- Satisfaction with products, services, customer support, account management, and the company overall

- Specific causes for any low satisfaction ratings and examples of gaps in product functionality or service levels

- Advice and recommendations for improvements

These interviews and surveys also provide an important interaction that enables you to learn more about the individuals along with their future business plans and departmental initiatives. Equally important, they help solidify your understanding of decision-making politics. If your survey response rate is very low, consider making it anonymous to boost responses.

3. Develop Internal Coaches as Part of Your Strategy to Build a Trusted Advisor Relationship

Throughout this playbook, I have reiterated the importance of finding a coach who serves as your internal champion as a necessary step to closing business. A coach is an individual who provides you privileged, proprietary, and accurate information about the politics within an account. A coach serves as your friend and ally who helps position you as a trusted advisor within the account. Equally important, your friendship with a coach will block out other competitors.

4. Establish and Reinforce the Concept of "Relationship Justification"

One of the main reasons incumbent vendors become vulnerable and are ultimately replaced is because they don't secure relationship justification. Relationship justification is achieved when the customer's benefit from using a solution and experience working with a vendor justify continuing the relationship. The QBR or ABR create the opportunity to demonstrate another important aspect of value you provide. They show you have a professional methodology for managing clients.

At these meetings you can show your company's level of commitment and the depth and breadth of your organization. In effect, you want to demonstrate you are one with the client and perform better than the other vendors. Moreover, the meeting provides an opportunity for senior leaders of both companies to share ideas, brainstorm on problems, and philosophize about their industry. Therefore, don't attend the QBR or ABR meeting alone. Structure the meeting to include your senior leaders and subject-matter experts, and match the types of personnel from the two organizations. The QBR or ABR meeting is the means by which you can secure face time with key senior-level leaders who must ultimately set the budgets and approve the purchases of your solutions. You want to be sure they clearly understand how you have delivered value to their organization.

5. Rank and Compare the Client's Maturity Level and Recommend Improvements

How does the customer's usage of your products or services compare to that of other clients? Customers migrate through a life cycle of adoption starting at a beginning stage and then moving to a developing stage an intermediate stage, and advanced stages of maturity. The meeting should provide best practices and recommendations to help the client move to the next stage of development. In addition, the client should be shown a vision for the future and a product road map for success. In turn, this will help promote usage, spending, and widespread adoption of the other solutions and services you provide.

6. Design the Meeting Takeaways so They Create a Viral Presence within the Client's Organization

In many respects, you should think of the meeting as part of a long-term marketing campaign to expand your presence wider, higher, and deeper within the account. Realistically, not everyone will be interested or will be able to attend the QBR or ABR. Therefore, the material you cover has to be professionally documented and include eye-catching graphics that easily communicate the main topics that were covered. For example, where problems have been experienced in the past, charts showing quantifiable progression should be included.

Customers should look forward to receiving the takeaway report because they will learn something new about themselves and how their company compares to others.

Key Role Assignments

Typically, the account manager acts as the *meeting leader,* who facilitates the session. In this role, the meeting leader keeps the session on track, controls the timing, and is responsible for ensuring follow-up items are assigned and acted upon. The meeting leader solicits customer attendees' thoughts and reactions as each subject area is presented. It is very important that the other members of the meeting leader's team defer to him in order to position him as the focal point of account management and control.

Another important meeting role is that of the *scribe*. The scribe takes notes to record issues, follow-up action items, and any commitments that are made. In addition, there should be a *meeting sponsor* assigned from the client's company. Ideally, this person has a vested interest in the success of the meeting and a positive perception of your company and solution. Typically, the meeting sponsor is from sales or client success management. Strategize with this person to determine which client personnel should attend along with who will complete the following meeting details.

1. Determine who should attend the meeting.

2. Conduct the premeeting research to determine account standing (client satisfaction survey, areas of risk and opportunity, supporters, and the possible actions of detractors).

3. Construct the agenda.

4. Create the invitation.

5. Send the invitation and agenda to the right people.

6. Coordinate the meeting logistics.

7. Create the meeting presentation and takeaways.

8. Create the meeting follow-up survey.

There's a fine line between not having enough client participation and having far too much. The bigger the meeting, the more unwieldly it can become to manage.

In addition, it's always a good practice to preview the materials you plan to present with the meeting sponsor and your coach in order to fine-tune the presentation and avoid unwanted surprises.

Sample Meeting Topics and Agenda

The topics covered in the QBR or ABR meeting typically include a session kick-off; an account status overview; metrics, trends, and rankings; best practices recommendations; a company update; and a client vision road map as outlined in figure 45.2. This meeting isn't a lecture

Session Kickoff. Introduction of attendees and review of the agenda and objectives for the session. Discussion of meeting methodology, preparation steps, and research.

Account Status Overview. High-level assessment of where the account stands that includes completed milestones and proof points showing accomplishments.

Metrics, Trends, and Rankings. Metrics from the vendor's perspective that provide a snapshot of current performance and historical trends. Metrics from the client's perspective showing how the customer ranks in comparison to other clients or industry-published statistics.

Best Practices Recommendations. Real-world examples that provide specific recommendations on how the client can improve product usage, streamline business processes, and drive profitability.

Company Update. New information including recent company developments, financial results, customer success stories, and industry reports that help the client understand your company's direction and success to validate the client's commitment to your company.

Client Vision Road Map. Discussion about the future partnership that maps out the vision of where you and your client are headed together, whether it be through new products, additional services, or entirely new ventures.

Post-Meeting Survey and Takeaways. Meeting takeaways including eye-catching graphics that easily communicate the topics that were covered. Online survey where attendees can anonymously rate the quality of the meeting, share their thoughts, and provide advice on how to improve future meetings.

Figure 45.2 Quarterly and annual business review meeting structure

meeting where participants sit idly by. Rather, it should be interactive, where client attendees can express their opinions and ask questions. Please note that the order of these topics is dependent upon each client's unique situation.

Session Kickoff

The kickoff includes an introduction of attendees and review of the agenda and objectives for the session. The meeting methodology, preparation steps, and research completed prior to conducting the meeting are also discussed.

Account Status Overview

The overview should be a high-level assessment of where the account stands. You can think of this section somewhat like a doctor explaining the results from a medical test that includes both good and bad news. At accounts where client satisfaction problems are pervasive, this should include a review of open problems, outstanding issues, and problem resolution steps. Items that convey a sense of progress such as successful resolution and action reports should be presented. The account status should include completed milestones and other successful proof points showing accomplishments. It's also important to allocate

time so the client attendees can express their points of view on the account status as well.

Metrics, Trends, and Rankings

The metrics to be presented vary widely depending on your industry and the products and services you provide. Here are some examples:

Average lead time	Managed inventory levels
Average response time	Number of defects
Billing breakdowns	Open support tickets
Calculated savings	Orders placed
Contract milestones	Past-due invoices
Cost/spending analysis	Portfolio performance
Customer service calls	Product returns
Deployment locations	Product usage
Employees trained	Project planning schedules
Industry comparisons	Sales by SKU, foot, and so on
Labor savings	Service level contracts
Lead times	Volume rebates

Metrics can be analyzed and presented from two perspectives. The first is from the vendor's perspective, which provides a snapshot of current performance and historical trends. These metrics provide a deeper level of analysis than the account status overview. You should highlight areas of positive improvements that objectively show your accomplishments.

The second is from the client's perspective. Part of the analysis should include how the customer ranks in

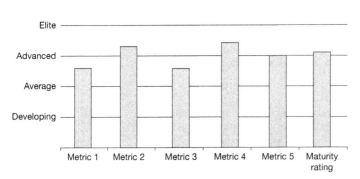

Figure 45.3 Client maturity rating

comparison to other clients or industry-published statistics. Figure 45.3 illustrates how these metrics can be presented in order to define the customer's overall maturity level rating. Customers migrate through a life cycle of adoption starting at a beginning stage and then moving to a developing stage and then advanced stages of maturity. In this example, the customers are classified as developing, average, advanced, and elites. This client's maturity rating is slightly above advanced.

Best Practices Recommendations

Before I ever have my first conversation with prospective clients, I will review the list of the hundreds of companies I have worked with and write down key best practices and experiences from previous engagements that might be of help to them. Similarly, you should share your personal knowledge from working with your other clients along with all of the best practices from your company's customer base and subject-matter experts. Customers love to learn what other companies are doing and hear game-changing ideas. Share real-world examples and provide specific recommendations on how they can improve product usage, streamline business processes, and drive profitability.

Company Update

Think like a journalist who has to keep readers informed. Review your website and recent press releases, product pages, industry information, and customer success stories. Read your annual and quarterly financial reports. What is new or has recently changed, and how does it impact your client? What

information can you share that helps the client understand your company's direction and success?

Client Vision Road Map

It's a good idea to end the meeting with a discussion about the future partnership. First, what new initiatives are on the client's horizon, and where else does the client's company need help with its operations today and tomorrow? Second, what exciting developments is your company working on, and where can you partner together in the future? Finally, you should map out the vision of where you and your client are headed together, whether it be through new products, additional services, or entirely new ventures.

Post-Meeting Survey and Takeaways

Create a viral presence in the client's organization by providing meeting takeaways including eye-catching graphics that easily communicate the topics that were covered. Send an online survey where attendees can anonymously rate the quality of the meeting, share their thoughts, and provide advice on how to improve future meetings.

Important Advice

The QBR or ABR account management meeting process differentiates you from the competition. Therefore, it should be presented to new prospects during the selection process as well. Both hunters and farmers should be able to present it. Professional brochures and data sheets should be created to explain your QBR and ABR program just as if it was another product your company offered to the marketplace.

Chapter 46. Key Questions to Ask after a Loss

While losing to competitors is painful, losing to the dreaded "no decision" is even worse: we spent time, effort, and resources on an account where the selection team couldn't even make a decision. Whether losing to competitors or to no decision, true loss analysis starts by asking fundamental questions that are inherent to every sale.

Did We Establish and Maintain Account Control?

Sales strategy can be defined as the overriding plan to win the business by establishing and maintaining account control. The goals are to neutralize competitors' advantages and place them in a defensive position while always anticipating "no decision" and motivating the customer to buy. However, only one competing vendor can be in control of an account at a time, and that vendor is the winner at the end of the sales cycle (see ch. 20).

Did We Sell to the Bully with the Juice?

Some people are natural-born leaders. They command respect, and people tend to follow their lead. Such a person is the bully with the juice. In every deal, there is typically one person who is the bully with the juice and the key evaluator (see ch. 36).

It is imperative to identify with absolute certainty who is the bully with the juice. Obviously, a top priority is to meet this decision-maker in order to understand his needs, ascertain biases, and persuade the person to choose your solution. If you can't determine who is the bully with the juice, you should be prepared to lose. Likewise, always assume the bully with the juice is meeting with your competitors.

Did We Have a Coach in the Account?

All successful sales involve a salesperson being coached through the evaluation process by an internal spy. You need a coach within the account to win the deal. This person is a constant source of accurate information revealing the internal machinations of the customer's selection process (see ch. 37).

The ideal coach is the person with the highest authority or greatest influence who is involved in the selection process and who guides your strategy and helps you execute it. When this person becomes a coach, the salesperson will enjoy a unique advantage. However, the coach could be anybody inside the customer's company or even someone outside the company, such as a consultant involved in the selection process and the implementation of the winning vendor's product.

Did We Sell Our Logical and Psychological Value?

Unfortunately, we have been trained to think of customers and ourselves as rational decision-makers who use logic and reason exclusively. However, every major purchase decision can be traced to one of four psychological roots: the will to survive, the desire to avoid pain, the need to gain the approval of others, and the desire to satisfy selfish egos (see ch. 40).

When you sell based solely upon logic, you are destined to lose because the logical reasons people give for buying products are only rationalizations that enable them to justify the expenditure. The successful influencer is the one who appeals to the four psychological motivators and understands the politics of group decision-making

Did We Truly Know the Key Executive Decision-Maker's Business Motivations and Values?

Heavy Hitters always delve beneath the surface, the technical and business criteria, to uncover individual motivations. Customers may have their "official" reasons for purchase decisions; however, there is also an "off the record" truth. The final decision is really driven by the desire to fulfill self-centered needs on the part of a few individuals. Therefore, like a psychologist, Heavy Hitters concentrate on eliciting the deep feelings and desires from the "patient." In this case, they are trying to determine the principles, standards, incentives, and priorities of the key senior executive decision-makers (see chs. 35 and 54). Always in the back of their minds is the question, What is driving these people's behavior, and how will my product help them create their initiatives or control their pains?

Did We Know the Decision-Maker's Fantasy?

All sales involve selling the fantasy that a product is going to make the customer's life easier, save the customer money, or enable the customer to make more money (see ch. 103). The feature set of your product validates the fantasy elements of your story and promotes the customer's fantasy. During the sales cycle, your goal is to communicate how

you can turn your customer's fantasy into a reality, but only when your product is selected.

Selection team members also have personal fantasies. Maybe they want to master new technology to enrich their resumes. Maybe they want to earn bonuses for cutting costs or increasing revenue. Maybe they want to be perceived as heroes within the company or spend more time at home and less at work. Everyone has a personal fantasy that is associated with the procurement of a product. Top salespeople understand this and align their strategy with personal fantasies. They don't just recite product features, benefits, and specifications. They position psychological value to block competitors and differentiate themselves.

Did We Take the Customer's Word at Face Value?

For a moment, let's put ourselves in the position of the customer. As the customer, you are going to meet with multiple vendors, watch their presentations, and read their marketing collateral. Each vendor, most likely, has equally talented, friendly, and professional salespeople who come to your office. However, you will select only one product. Given that, how will you behave with each vendor? Will you tell each one the truth? Probably not (see chs. 15, 104, and 107).

It is basic human nature to want to avoid confrontation. This is particularly true when you are meeting in person, face to face. In addition, our society has implicit guidelines of behavior. We are taught at an early age that if we have nothing nice to say, then we shouldn't say anything at all. Therefore, it is much more comfortable for the prospect to say something he thinks you want to hear than the actual truth.

Did We Recognize the Turning Point?

Every deal has a critical moment or turning point that determines the winner and the losers (see ch. 17). In some cases, the turning point is easy to spot. For example, a salesperson may be presenting a solution and encounter a deal-breaking objection that he is unable to overcome. Even though the customer remains cordial for the rest of the meeting, a turning point has occurred and the deal is lost. In most cases, the turning point occurs when the salesperson isn't present. It's in casual hallway conversations or internal emails that selection team members share opinions that influence vendors' futures. This proprietary information is revealed only when you have an internal spy.

Did We Misinterpret Information or Misread the Prospect?

The sales cycle is a formalized information-and-activity exchange. Customers are trying to gather enough information about vendors in order to determine if they are appropriate long-term partners. Meanwhile, salespeople are trying to gather enough information about the customer in order to determine if they can win the deal. Information is communicated back and forth, and each message that is sent must also be received and interpreted correctly (see chs. 58 and 59).

However, an obstacle is inherent in this process. Each message is subject to a person's interpretation and filtering. Some information is ignored, some

information is misinterpreted, and some information is generalized. Therefore, do you really know if your arguments were interpreted correctly? More importantly, did you interpret your customer's messages correctly (see ch. 108)?

Did We Follow Our Sales Intuition?

Successful salespeople are continually cataloging their successes and failures. They store patterns of individual and company behavior and link them to the sales process. From this base of intuitive knowledge they are able to decide which deals to work on and create and execute account strategies. It's your sales intuition that's responsible for predicting the future. While you have learned that you must be persistent and energetic to succeed, sometimes it is far more important to listen to your sales intuition so you don't continue to work on deals when you're not in control and have lost all momentum (see chs. 16 and 20).

Did We Have the Right Closing Strategy?

While it is ingrained in all salespeople to ask for the business, many salespeople don't formulate a complete closing strategy that is based on a primary closing strategy, fallback positions, and an appropriate delivery technique. Your primary closing strategy should be based upon securing the main objective, which could be to agree upon a final price or negotiate final purchase terms. You also need fallback positions, alternatives you prepare ahead of time to present should the customer reject your primary closing strategy. Buyers prefer specific types of sales delivery techniques and a study that shows which closing strategies are most effective from their point of view can be found in chapter 70.

Should We Have Pursued the Business in the First Place?

Many salespeople are trying to complete an unnatural act because they never had a real opportunity to win. In the final analysis, a deal is either in our zone where we have an advantage, in the competitor's zone where they have an advantage, or it is truly up for grabs (see ch. 15). Heavy Hitters constantly try to triangulate (see ch. 58) their position by answering these questions: Is there a deal? Am I winning? Whom do I have to watch out for, and what can ruin this deal?

Chapter 47. Sales Strategy Statements and Planning Checklist

"If you can't describe it, it doesn't really exist" is one of my favorite sayings. This statement is particularly true for salespeople who have to explain their sales strategies to their managers and other senior executives within their company. Salespeople who can't explain the strategy to win an account most likely don't have one. They're usually focused only on the next sales call, not the overriding plan to win the business by establishing and maintaining account control.

Sales Strategy Statements

Sales strategy statements provide a structured framework to explain one's sales strategy by describing the sales cycle, account control, and customer interaction components, as described in this part of the playbook. Following is an example of a sales strategy statement. It begins with a high-level review of the sales cycle component factors, such as the sales cycle type, buyer type, and key decision-makers, in the first paragraph. The elements of account control, such as decision-making politics, ROI positioning, and provocative proof points, are covered in the next paragraph. Finally, the key upcoming customer interactions are reviewed along with the goals and motives behind them.

> We are working on a $450,000 enterprise deal with Coca-Cola. Since this is a creation sales cycle, no decision is our biggest competitor. Therefore, we must create a consolidator buyer type, which requires the senior leaders of the organization to actively promote this project within the organization. This requires selling at the highest levels of the company. Specifically, we must ensure Mark Jones, the vice president of supply chain, is aligned with the project as he is the emperor who will ultimately approve the purchase. A key decision-maker is Mary Cranston, the senior supply chain director. She is the bully with the juice and her backing of the project is an absolute necessity. Without her internal support and promotion, this deal will stall out and not happen.
>
> A key goal of our strategy is developing Mary into our coach, ideally a guide. Right now, we rate her as an emissary coach. Because her persona type is an analytical straight shooter, our consulting team will perform a complete site survey in order to create a comprehensive ROI payback

analysis model and full implementation timeline proposal. Since our enemy is that they maintain the status quo, we have to position our solution with concrete proof points that we can improve their operations.

We have three key meetings scheduled this month. We're taking Mary Cranston and her team on a site visit to see our installation at Anheuser Busch's St. Louis plant. We'll be able to spend two full days building relationships with Mary and her team on the 7th and 8th. During the week of the 14th we're conducting our site survey of their facility, which provides a great opportunity to understand the political landscape and discover possible detractors. Finally, we are planning on presenting our initial proposal and ROI analysis to Mary privately at the end of the month. We want to be able to review it with her and get her feedback. It's critical she is comfortable with the numbers and approves our recommendations. She has told us she will schedule a meeting with Mark Jones shortly thereafter, and we'll copresent the project findings to him. We'll need our key senior leadership team members to attend this meeting in order to develop executive-level relationships. Our goal is to gain Mark's approval and then complete the contract execution process by the end of the quarter.

Every deal a salesperson works on is unique. Each deal involves different people with unique personalities, one-of-a-kind customer requirements and selection processes, and extraordinary decision-making politics. Therefore, the strategy and tactical plans to win each

account should be unique as well. The salesperson who employs the same tactics for every account is making a mistake. Your sales strategy should fit the specific circumstances of the deal you are working on, not the other way around.

Exercise: While it's easy to update someone about the current status of an account, it requires concentration, mental energy, and a framework to actually define a sales strategy. Create a sales strategy statement for an important account you are working on, describing it in terms of sales cycle, account control, and customer interaction components.

Sales Strategy Preparation Checklist

The diligence with which you prepare your strategy to win an account will directly determine if you win the deal. The victor controls the sales cycle, maps out the political landscape of decision-makers, uses tactics to outmaneuver enemies, and outsmarts competitors with arguments that disarm, neutralize, and render their claims ineffectual. Use the following checklist to help you prepare for your next sales strategy. (Source chapters are referenced in brackets.)

- [ ] What's my initial account strength, and are my product, personnel, and company at an advantage, equal, or at a disadvantage to the competition's? [15]
- [ ] Is the deal far outside my zone, or was my RFP response score test over fifty? [15]
- [ ] Is this a renewal/add-on, persuasion, or creation sales cycle? [16]

☐ What buzz-kill moment should I prepare for? [17]

☐ Has a turning point already occurred that will prevent me from winning? [17]

☐ What is the likelihood of no decision being made, and was the stress test score over twenty-two? [19]

☐ What tactics will I use to motivate the customer to buy and overcome no decision? [19]

☐ What steps will I take to establish account control? [20]

☐ What is my quadrant position on the account control chart? [20]

☐ What does my account control spider chart look like, and what are the weakest radii? [21]

☐ How will I employ the indirect approach and create a turning point? [22]

☐ What positional tactics will I employ to gain account control? [23]

☐ What is my sales strategy statement? [24]

☐ Will I use provocation, transformation, or alignment? [25]

☐ What's the customer's budgeting process, and is this a planned, unplanned, or interrupt-driven purchase? [27]

☐ Is the customer price conscious, price sensitive, or price immune? [29]

☐ For enterprise sales cycles, is the buyer a consolidator, consulter, responder, or bureaucrat? [31–34]

☐ Who is the bully with the juice, and what is our relationship to him? [36]

☐ Who is the emperor, and what is our relationship to him? [36]

☐ Who are our coaches, and what are their coach rating classifications and their numeric rankings? [37]

☐ What benefactions are behind the customer's motives? [37]

☐ Have we created an organization footprint chart? [38]

☐ Is this a corporate control, independent, or interdependent organization? [38]

☐ What different types of flanking strategies will we use? [39]

☐ Should we conduct a flanking strategy session? [39]

☐ What are the psychological, political, operational, and strategic values I provide to the customer? [40]

☐ What actions will we take to build deeper client relationships? [41]

☐ For existing clients: How will we conduct annual and quarterly business review meetings? [45]

When you take the time to think about all the items on the checklist, you are planning your sales cycle strategy with precision—something your competition is incapable of doing or won't take the time to do.

PART III

SALES CALL STRATEGY

Chapter 48. Why B2B Buyers Don't Like Salespeople

Why don't B2B buyers like meeting with salespeople? What are their perceptions of the salespeople they meet, and how do they ultimately choose between them? To answer these questions, I asked over two hundred business professionals who evaluate the products and services their companies use to participate in a research project. Study participants completed an extensive seventy-six-part survey on a variety of subjects to assess their personality tendencies and were asked to provide opinions on real-world sales scenarios. The goal of this research project was to understand what's really on customers' minds.

Study participants were asked to choose the primary reason they don't like meeting with salespeople. Their answers, shown in figure 48.1, reveal they feel pressured because salespeople are self-centered. In addition, buyers are uncomfortable because it is ingrained within every salesperson to ask for the business at the end of a sales call, and most buyers don't enjoy saying no.

The primary reason I don't enjoy meeting with salespeople is:

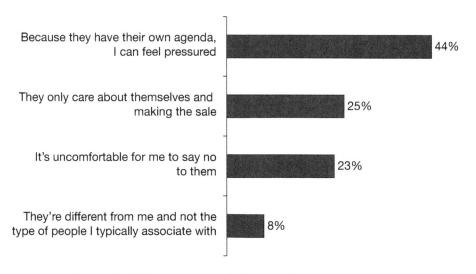

Figure 48.1 Why buyers don't like meeting with salespeople

You have a unique chance to start relationships with exceptional people who will become customers and sometimes friends. A sincere concern for the customer's outcome is required to create an authentic relationship. You should concentrate more on helping customers accomplish their goals rather than focusing on your agenda.

Salespeople Give a Canned Pitch and Don't Listen to Buyer Requirements

Communication challenges and language-based deficiencies are the most frequent shortcomings cited by buyers who meet with salespeople. The conversations salespeople have with buyers are quite complex. They consist of verbal and non-verbal messages sent consciously and subconsciously. Successful customer communication is the foundation of all sales; the words salespeople speak define them. However, since salespeople talk all the time, they underestimate the complexity of communication and take the process for granted. As a result, they tend to repeat the same pitch to every prospect. Figure 48.2 shows how buyers rank the shortcomings of salespeople.

Differences in Communication Style and Personality Can Alienate Buyers

In every good sales call, there is an equilibrium point where the buyer respects the salesperson's conviction and is not offended by his persistence. Pushy salespeople quickly alienate prospective buyers because they don't develop rapport. Rapport is a special relationship between individuals based upon harmonious communication. Buyers will choose to work with the salesperson who develops rapport over those who don't.

Buyers were asked to complete the following sentence: "When you meet with a salesperson and there is not a personal connection or 'chemistry' it is

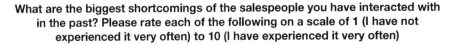

What are the biggest shortcomings of the salespeople you have interacted with in the past? Please rate each of the following on a scale of 1 (I have not experienced it very often) to 10 (I have experienced it very often)

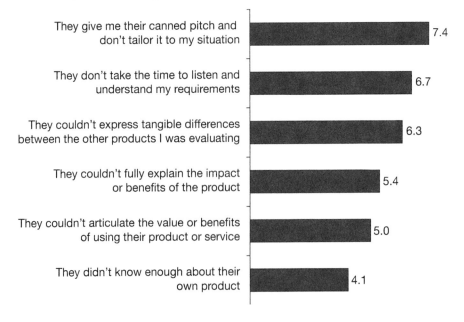

Figure 48.2 Buyers' ranking of salespeople's shortcomings

usually because"; here are the top six selections:

1. They are too pushy.
2. There is a difference in communication styles.
3. Their personality is much different than mine.
4. They are too eager to befriend me.
5. There is a difference in age.
6. There is a difference in gender.

In addition to lack of rapport, other factors may prevent greater sales success. Most likely, you are very comfortable selling to specific types of people; however, you're far less likely to establish rapport with someone who is wired differently. Since you're not exactly sure how to behave, you may act in a way the buyer considers too pushy or overcompensate by being overly friendly.

You may have taken debate, public speaking, and communications classes while in school. These likely focused on hard skills, such as the memorization and presentation of structured arguments, which may not be very helpful to salespeople. Anyone can recite facts. Two people can say the very same words with entirely different results. Mastering the soft skills—building rapport with skeptics, understanding how people process and interpret information, and framing your ideas within a buyer's personal desires—is what ultimately makes someone influential.

Salespeople Want to Develop Relationships but Buyers Are Too Busy

A sales call is a scheduled communication event in which each party has different goals. The salesperson's main goal is to gain continued access to the prospective buyer and start a relationship. But the buyer has a different set of goals. Relationships are expensive and involve investments of valuable time. Buyers have to spend time to determine whether a product's characteristics are accurately represented, they must evaluate vendors to find the best possible partner to solve a business problem, and they must learn and implement the new product. Obviously, they're very busy. Therefore, when salespeople meet with buyers, it's best to provide a wealth of information in the most economic amount of time as shown in figure 48.3.

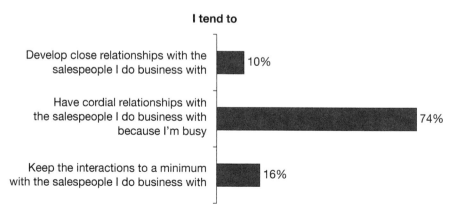

I tend to

Develop close relationships with the salespeople I do business with 10%

Have cordial relationships with the salespeople I do business with because I'm busy 74%

Keep the interactions to a minimum with the salespeople I do business with 16%

Figure 48.3 Buyers are too busy for close relationships with salespeople

The relationships between salespeople and buyers is complex. An invisible boundary exists between the seller and buyer. Both the seller and buyer edit their language and hide their true feelings or try to keep the conversation at a nonpersonal level. It's the salesperson's job to remove this boundary and create a friendship.

Chapter 49. Sales Call Strategy Using Sales Linguistics

Customers today are smarter. Information is not only easier to find but available in greater detail than ever before. In addition, technology has become a way of life. Via the internet, customers can research products, prices, and opinions. Our cars, appliances, and toys have become computerized tools. Collectively, this has raised the level of sophistication (and skepticism) of the customers we must converse with and sell to. Power is definitely in the hands of today's buyers and the situation will only continue to get worse.

Your competitors have not sat idly by either. They've educated themselves about your products and sales tactics, and they're more focused on defeating you than ever. Fortunately, they usually believe the best way to defeat you is by frontal attack based upon their product features, when in reality, using language to build customer relationships is the winning strategy.

This strategy requires differentiating yourself from the competition by building a stronger relationship with the customer than the competition through the words you speak. Customers can think of you as a salesperson who is trying to sell something, a supplier with whom they do business, a strategic partner who is of significant importance to their business, or a trusted advisor whose opinions on business and personal matters are sought out and followed. Obviously, a trusted advisor enjoys significant advantages over a salesperson.

Language is studied in many well-established fields. Sociolinguistics is the study of language use in society and social networks. Psycholinguistics is the study of how the mind acquires, uses, and represents language. Neurolinguistics is the study of how brain structures process language. Today, an exciting new area of study called "sales linguistics" applies aspects from these fields to the conversations salespeople have with customers. The goal of sales linguistics is to understand how salespeople and their prospective customers use and interpret different languages during the decision-making process. There are seven different types of sales call languages shown below:

1. *Word catalog language.* The mind's method for receiving and interpreting information based upon the three sensory channels—visual, auditory, and kinesthetic (see chs. 110–113).

2. *Internal dialogue language.* The never-ending stream of communication inside the mind that represents honest, unedited, and deep feelings (see ch. 107).

3. *Physical language.* Also known as body language, the nonverbal communication that is constantly being

emitted by the customer's body posture (see chs. 106, 123–124).

4. *Intersecting activity language.* Interests, hobbies, and personal pursuits by which the executive displays his personality, beliefs, and values (see ch. 52).

5. *Technical specification language.* The androgynous, nonpersonal, and technical communication that is based upon the nomenclature and technical terms of the executive's industry (see ch. 53).

6. *Business operations language.* The language that is specific to the daily running of the executive's business and his role in the organization (see ch. 54).

7. *Confidential language.* The most powerful trust-based language by which the customer explains his personal needs, desires, and plans along with the strategy by which he hopes to fulfill them (see ch. 55).

While we'll talk about these languages in more detail, let's spend a moment to review the internal dialogue language. Your internal dialogue is the never-ending conversation you have with yourself. It's repeating the words of this sentence to you now. It is very dominating. It's always on, always engaged, and always talking to you. It drives the language you speak to prospective customers during sales calls as well as your actions. Your customer's internal dialogue is equally active.

When you make a sales call, you are not talking to people. You are actually talking to their internal dialogues. Understanding this will help you conduct successful sales calls because your main concern is a customer's state of mind. Remember that the words customers actually say represent only a fraction of their true feelings.

There are three pillars of persuasion: the logic and reason of what you are saying, the personal connection you establish, and the psychological appeal of you and your solution. These pillars shown in figure 49.1 impact customers differently. Logic and reason appeals to the conscious or "controllable" mind while your psychological appeal impacts the subconscious or "uncontrollable" mind.

The nature of conversational themes depends upon the nature of your relationship. Salespeople engage the customer in friendly conversation, suppliers talk about their products' capabilities and attributes, strategic partners discuss business matters, and trusted advisors talk about future plans along with the people and politics behind them.

In addition to conversational themes, you need to master the seven different languages used by salespeople and customers during sales calls. These languages can be divided into two

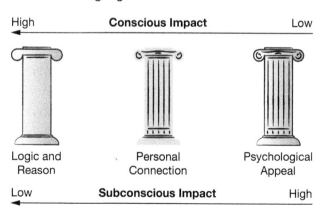

Figure 49.1 The three pillars of persuasion

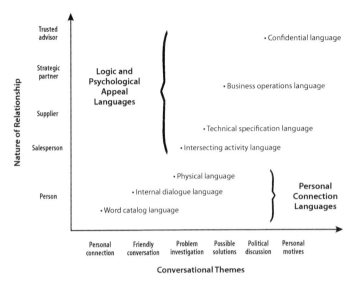

Figure 49.2 Ideal progression of languages during sales calls

that everyone is speaking a common language. However, no universal language exists because everyone's mind is so distinct. People actually talk in many diverse languages. Therefore, if you want to communicate more persuasively and learn how to make lasting impressions, you should learn to speak each of the different languages listed in figure 49.3.

To differentiate yourself from the competition, you must speak more impactful languages with your customers. The ideal progression during sales calls is to quickly establish a personal connection with the customer and then progress through the

categories. The lower-level languages are responsible for the personal connection between people and consist of the word catalog language, internal dialogue language, and physical language. The higher-level languages are logic and psychological appeal languages. They consist of the intersecting activity language, technical specification language, business operations language, and confidential language. Figure 49.2 represents these languages and their associated conversational themes.

Please note that the personal connection languages are each reviewed in-depth in part V, Personal Sales Strategy. In this section we'll cover the higher-level logic and psychological appeal languages.

When you strike up a conversation with customers, you probably believe

Confidential language	The most powerful trust-based language by which the customer explains his personal needs, desires, and plans along with the strategy by which he hopes to fulfill them
Business operations language	The language that is specific to the daily running of the customer's business and his role in the organization
Technical specification language	The androgynous, nonpersonal, and technical communication that is based on the nomenclature and technical terms of the customer's industry
Intersecting activity language	Interests, hobbies, and personal pursuits by which the customer displays his personality, beliefs, and values
Physical language	Also known as body language, the nonverbal communication that is constantly being emitted by the customer's body posture
Internal dialogue language	The never-ending stream of communication inside the mind that represents honest, unedited, and deep feelings
Word catalog language	The mind's method for receiving, interpreting, and transmitting information based on the three sensory channels—visual, auditory, and kinesthetic

Figure 49.3 The seven sales call languages

higher-level logic and psychological appeal languages with the ultimate goal of having the customer speak the confidential language with you.

> *Are you talking generically or specifically? Tell me how you are going to help our business. Tell me how you are going to help our factories. Tell me how you are going to help our employees. I've had salespeople come rolling in my office with some bright idea and say that it is really great. But until I understand you and until you understand me, I'm not going to buy.*
>
> —Chief Executive Officer

Chapter 50. The Trusted Advisor Sales Goal

The first step toward conducting a successful sales call is to determine your goal and outcome for the meeting. The ultimate goal for the sales call is simple: you want the customer to expose his internal dialogue to you—the unedited discussion inside the mind that represents a person's deepest feelings (see ch. 107). You want the customer to honestly explain what he is trying to accomplish and why he is doing it from a business and, more importantly, personal standpoint. You want the customer to tell you about his personal needs and career desires along with how he plans to fulfill them. You want him to trust you and speak confidentially to you.

What Is Trust?

Trust can be thought of as a person's confidence in someone or something. The concept of trust is based on the future, as well as a track record of the past. For instance, I trust my wife and I trust that the sun will rise tomorrow. Because I've been married for decades and the sun has risen every day of my life, I have confidence that both won't disappoint me in the future. Trust is perceived as a factual emotion, meaning it's tangible to the person experiencing it because it's true.

Different types of trust are created based upon contrasting emotions and experiences.

- *Authoritative trust.* Trust that is due to a person's stature—for example, when a patient trusts a doctor's judgment. Salespeople with deep industry, business, or technical domain expertise develop authoritative trust with their clients.

- *Earned trust.* Trust that is earned by actions, habits, commitments, and honesty—for example, when two people start dating and earn each other's trust over time. Salespeople earn the customer's trust during the sales cycle through consistent demonstrations of their character.

- *Faith-based trust.* The belief that a future goal, dream, or aspiration will occur because of a trusted relationship—for example, when a person makes a donation to Feeding America because he or she is committed to ending hunger in the United States. Customers will grant faith-based trust when they believe a salesperson and his solution are the means to achieving an important objective.

- *Intrinsic trust.* Trust that is naturally developed as part of a relationship—for example, when children intrinsically trust their mothers. Salespeople who have worked with a client for a long period of time develop intrinsic trust.

- *Symbolic trust.* Trust that is associated with a representation, metaphor, or symbol—for example, I'm a University of Southern California faculty member, and alumni I meet trust me when they learn this. Salespeople who work for very respected companies also enjoy symbolic trust when they meet customers who formerly used their products.

Characteristics of a Trusted Advisor Relationship

There's a pecking order in the relationships between buyers and the salespeople they meet with. At the lowest level, buyers meet with a person who is solely trying to sell them something. Buyers consider the salespeople involved in these selfish interactions to be of poor quality. In fact, buyers classify 26 percent of the salespeople they meet with in this category. Next is the average salesperson and buyers place 44 percent of salespeople in this category. Higher up the pecking order is the supplier with whom the customer is doing business with regularly. Then there is a strategic partner. This is an important relationship that is considered critical to the customer's business. At the highest level is a trusted advisor. Only 18 percent of the salespeople will achieve this trusted advisor status according to buyers.

Here are the characteristics of a trusted advisor relationship.

1. *The salesperson has attained situational dominance* (see ch. 99). In a trusted advisor relationship, the salesperson is not a submissive servant who quickly accommodates every request. Rather, the salesperson is respected and in a dominant position. The customer listens to the salesperson's advice and acts on his recommendations.

2. *The relationship is based on collaborative ambition.* Both parties are ambitious and want to enjoy career success. They have chosen to work together in order to achieve independent and mutually beneficial outcomes. On the flip side, the stability and safety of the relationship reduces detrimental risks to their careers.

3. *The relationship is based on honesty.* Neither the salesperson nor the customer edit himself or hides behind his respective role. Both parties naturally express themselves in an open and honest way.

4. *It is a quid-pro-quo relationship.* It's not a one-sided relationship where one party does all the giving and makes all the effort. There's a balance between give and take that neither party will let get out of line. There's an implied agreement based on the concept of a favor for a favor.

5. *It is a confidential relationship.* Trust between both parties is paramount. Therefore, confidentiality is a requirement that cannot be violated.

6. *It is an unselfish relationship.* Of course, the seller wants to sell and

the buyer needs to buy. But both parties are unselfish in that they look out for the other. They are considerate of the situation each is in and honor their relationship by upholding their commitments.

7. *It is a monogamous relationship.* Loyalty is at the foundation of every serious relationship. It's impossible to have a trusted advisor relationship when the customer is buying from the salesperson's archrivals and the salesperson has personal relationships with the customer's enemies because he's doing business with them.

8. *It is a forward-thinking prescriptive relationship.* The nature of people in long-term relationships is that while they may wax philosophically about the past, they are constantly thinking about the future. In a trusted advisor relationship, the salesperson should not only be fixated on the present but always proactively planning for the future and finding areas for improvement.

I look at vendors by measuring three important aspects. One, the relationship and that starts with the point-person who owns the account. Two, what they do for our day-to-day business. Do they deliver on their value proposition? Three, what kind of innovation can they bring to the table? It's not about keeping the lights on because that is what all the vendors can do. When I think about a partner as opposed to a vendor, I think about those three things.

—Chief Information Officer

Here's the interesting part about a trusted advisor relationship. A strong personal friendship between the salesperson and customer may or may not exist. While it's advantageous, a close friendship is not a requirement. On the other hand, mutual respect is a must, and this is evident in the topics of conversation between the salesperson and the customer. As figure 50.1 shows, the conversational themes start with establishing a personal, friendly connection, followed by investigating the problem and discussing possible solutions. Ideally, the conversation will flow into an off-the-record talk about the politics of the customer's organization and personal ulterior motives.

The Personal Outcome

This may sound counterintuitive, but you are not meeting with the customer to sell anything. Your goal is to become a trusted advisor by asking questions and

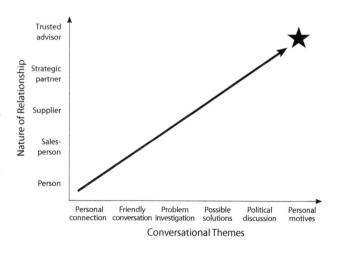

Figure 50.1 Trusted advisor goal

intently listening to the answers so that you can apply your expertise to solve the customer's business problems or complete his initiatives.

You might be worried that this important sales call may be your only chance to meet with the customer; therefore, you feel you *must* explain to him how wonderful your company and products are. However, if you go into this meeting with the intention of selling something, you'll be proven right: it will be the last time you get on his busy calendar.

Never forget that although you are excited about the meeting, the customer isn't that excited about your products and not all that interested in your marketing pitch. He's seen them and heard them before, and they all seem the same. You will be granted continual access if you can demonstrate how you can help solve his business problems and help him achieve his personal ambitions.

Unfortunately, the majority of sales call conversations never reach the confidential language (see ch. 49). The discussion gets stuck at the technical specification language or the business operations language. Usually, this is because the salesperson is too busy talking about his products and what they do instead of what the customer wants to change. At other times, this is by design because the customer doesn't trust and believe the salesperson enough to speak frankly and share his thoughts with him.

Moreover, too many meetings end without any definitive results. First meetings are short and the time passes quickly. Therefore, it is important to identify a specific personal outcome of the meeting beforehand so you can judge whether you have achieved your goal.

Professional athletes understand personal outcomes. Sprinters will visualize an entire race and see themselves on the winner's stand receiving the gold medal. College basketball coaches will ask their teams to mentally rehearse cutting down the net after they win the national championship.

Your personal outcome may be to have the customer tell you at the end of the meeting "It sounds great. Send me your proposal." In this example, you create a mental picture of the person and hear those words being said as he shakes your hand. You can measure the success of the call based upon what actually happens and how closely that matches this visualization.

The tactical objectives for the meeting can be quite diverse. The objective could be to *gather* information and find out how you are perceived versus the competition or other details about the selection process. It could be to *impart* information about your products or make a special pricing offer. It could be to *create* relationships or *influence* opinions. It could be to *negotiate* terms and conditions.

Whatever the tactical objectives for your meeting may be, you should define the words the customer must say to know that they have been achieved. You want to hear the customer say something definitive like "You are our preferred solution" or "Yes, we have a deal," not "We are still evaluating options" or "We'll consider that." Only when you hear the customer say the words that validate your meeting's outcome have you actually achieved it.

The most important difference between you and your competitors is not your products, your company, or the services and support you offer. It's you and your ability to build a deeper relationship with prospective customers. The proof of a successful sales call comes when the customer speaks the confidential language with you and shares the unedited thoughts of his internal dialogue.

Exercise: Prior to every sales call, think about the exact words you would like the customer to say that proves he respects you. What would he say to show he trusts you more than the competition? What commitments would he make to you at the close of the meeting? Most importantly, how would he communicate the sales call was a success and he likes you and wants to see you again?

Chapter 51. How Strangers Meet

Meeting new people is stressful. If you watch strangers meet at a party, you'll notice that they are on guard. We typically don't have to worry that someone is physically threatening; we have to worry if they are a psychological threat. Therefore, we try to ascertain whether a stranger is in a dominant, equal, or submissive position in comparison to our position. Next, we try to find out what we have in common by discovering intersecting activities. Finally, we try to classify the relationship into a familiar pattern so we can decide how we should behave and whether we should invest more time with the person. The sequence is shown in figure 51.1.

The instinctual comparison of situational dominance tends to occur quickly when people meet. Just as packs of animals instinctively establish a hierarchy so that the group can function more efficiently, people are naturally inclined to seek structure in group environments. Therefore, they create mental pecking orders to understand their place in complex social settings such as parties and sales calls.

But what makes someone situationally dominant? Situational dominance can be the result of a diverse set of attributes. When two people talk at a party, one person may be better looking, more intelligent, funnier, wealthier, or better respected or have a quality that the other person lacks, such as kindness, generosity, humility, aggressiveness, assertiveness, or selfishness. Even a trait that is generally perceived as negative by society can make someone dominant.

When meeting someone new, people experience varying amounts and types of stress depending on whether they perceive themselves to be dominant, equal, or submissive. A person who feels inferior to someone else is under much more stress than a person who feels dominant. The stress manifests itself in different ways. How differently would you feel about meeting Jeff Bezos versus meeting the counterperson who serves you coffee? Most likely, you would be far more nervous when meeting one of the richest

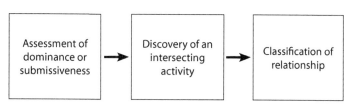

Figure 51.1 The process of meeting a stranger

men in the world. However, if you have a secret crush on the counterperson, your behavior would be quite different than if you had little interest. You likely would be in the submissive position because you'd want to be liked.

While some dominant people will surround themselves with submissive people, most dominants want to associate with people whom they perceive as equals. Equals converse with relative ease. This is a critical point. One of your most important goals when meeting with a customer is establishing yourself as an equal at least, and ideally as dominant. That's one of the main reasons why you need to speak the technical specification language, the business operations language, and the confidential language described in chapters 53–55.

The natural course of conversations is for the strangers to try to find out what they have in common. Through intersecting activities, people display their personal interests, character, and temperament and express their value systems. Intersecting activities create shared bonds and reduce the level of stress involved in meeting someone new. Intersecting activities play an equally important role in sales calls. Regardless of whether the salesperson or the customer initiated the meeting, the first intersecting activity is the sales call itself. It is the first point in common between the salesperson and the customer.

The strategy is to use the first intersecting activity (the sales call) to find *personal* intersecting activities. By doing so, you develop rapport and begin the process of building a personal friendship. In essence, you try to relieve the stress caused by the typical dominant-submissive meeting between a customer

and a vendor by turning it into a conversation between equals.

The intersecting activities salespeople talk about can be quite diverse—the local professional sports team, cars, movies, or any hobby. Usually, these first conversations are on "safe" topics, with little risk that someone's revelations will create controversy, because the goal is to reduce stress, not create more of it. In sales calls, dominance is always initially on the customer's side since he has the ultimate say over whether any relationship will be created.

However, this dominance is based upon the situation, not personal attributes. In a different social setting, the salesperson might be truly dominant because he is more charismatic, athletic, witty, and so on.

Exercise: Customers are personally evaluating you during the first few minutes of a sales call and making an initial judgment about whether they like you or not. They'll spend the remainder of the call validating whether their preliminary decision was correct. Think about how you can use the process of how strangers meet to your advantage. What intersecting activities do you like to talk about with customers, and how would they classify their relationships with you?

Once the strangers establish who is dominant and they have searched for what they have in common, then each person tries to characterize the relationship by placing it into one of the categories of familial relationships he or she is familiar with, such as a relationship with a father figure, big sister, best friend, or son.

We all have many different types of personal relationships. We have friends, family, coworkers, and neighbors. When we meet someone new at a party, we decide if we like the person and whether he or she might become a friend or is more likely to remain a distant acquaintance.

This classification also happens on sales calls. However, each customer may have an entirely different perception of your character. For example, you may be characterized as a friend by one customer and an acquaintance by another. You could be a little brother to an older customer or a big brother to a younger one. You could be thought of as a father, lover, uncle, cousin, or even an enemy.

Exercise: Let's do another exercise. Take a moment and think of the last three accounts you won. Write down the characterization that best describes your relationship with your main contact at each account. Most likely, your relationship can be described in close family terms. Here are some possible characterizations:

Acquaintance	Employee	Lover
Aunt	Father figure	Mentor
Best friend	Friend	Mother figure
Big brother	Girlfriend	Nephew
Big sister	Godparent	Neighbor
Boss	Grandchild	Niece
Boyfriend	Grandfather	Son
Buddy	Grandmother	Soul mate
Childhood friend	Husband	Stepchild
Cousin	In-law	Stepparent
Coworker	Little brother	Stranger
Daughter	Little sister	Uncle
Deadbeat	Loser	Wife

Now try the same exercise for the last three accounts you lost. You'll probably

find quite a difference in the way you characterize the relationships.

When I ask salespeople what role they take in sales calls, the majority say, "Consultant." Unfortunately, every salesperson competing for a deal is trying to be a consultant. You need to establish a stronger relationship. Some may consider this advice counterintuitive and risky. However, as part of your planning for a meeting, I recommend that you actually identify the familial relationship you wish to achieve with that person ahead of time.

Depending upon your background, you may want to be the trusted father figure, the up-and-coming son, or the soul mate the customer is searching for. Whatever it is, don't be solely a consultant. It is human nature for all customers to categorize you into a familial or friendship relationship. Knowing whether you are a customer's submissive little brother or a dominant mother figure and when to act like a buddy or be a mentor plays an important role in the sales call. When customers treat you like they would a loved one, that's a great sign that you will win the deal. Conversely, you are in big trouble if everyone in the account treats you like the weird uncle.

While it's perfectly normal to act conservatively in accounts where you are far ahead of the competition, playing it safe when you're behind is a mistake. You must take chances when you meet with customers in accounts where you think you are losing. A primary objective should be to establish a stronger personal relationship (as a son, father figure, wife, etc.) that supersedes the relationship the customer has with the salesperson of the leading vendor. Besides, since you have nothing to lose, why water down your own unique selling style and your effervescent personality?

Chapter 52. The Intersecting Activity Language

All people have outside interests, hobbies, and personal pursuits by which they display their personalities, beliefs, and values. Think about all the potential nonbusiness-related subjects you can discuss with your customers: smartphones, cars, movies, wine, college, dieting, music, pets, investments, marriage, horse racing, golf, books, firearms, professional sports, child rearing, and cigars.

Each intersecting activity also has a unique content layer language. In order to have a meaningful conversation about an intersecting activity, you need to understand its language. For example, a conversation about horse racing requires an understanding of terms such as "exacta," "furlong," and "maiden race." If you are talking with someone about wine, being able to discuss the difference between varietal and Meritage wines makes your participation in the conversation credible. Through the use and understanding of these common terms, rapport is established.

Always engage the customer in a personal conversation about the intersecting activities you have in common. By doing so, you develop rapport with the *entire* person, not just the *business* person—building the foundation of a personal friendship that sets you apart from the competition.

Exercise: You can easily identify intersecting activities of customers by observing how they have decorated their cubicles or offices. Pictures of family vacations, mementos, awards, degrees, and other personal artifacts convey their interests and the attributes of their personality. Make a mental note of all the items you see on your next sales call. Compare your list to other teammates who attend the call.

Chapter 53. Understand the Technical Specification Language

Every industry has developed its own language to facilitate mutual understanding of terminology and an exact meaning of the words used throughout the business. The technical specification language consists of these abbreviations, acronyms, business nomenclature, and specialized terms. Since it is one of the primary languages your customers speak, you must be able to speak it fluently. For example a semiconductor salesperson might tell a design engineer that his "1575.42 MHz SAW filter has a usable bandwidth of 35 MHz."

Technical specification languages have three major characteristics. First, unlike normal day-to-day language, words within a technical specification language have very narrow meanings. The language is precise and exact. For example, "100 Mbps" means "100 megabits per second," not 99 or 101. Second, the meaning of general words can be completely changed by the addition of operators (see ch. 81). Third, the language is completely androgynous. In general, no reference is made to feminine or masculine characteristics. The technical specification language is also nonpersonal. After all, it's composed of specifications, measurements, and statistics that are not typically used in regular conversations.

> *I don't have the time to educate salespeople. I expect them to walk in the door knowing everything that I do.*
>
> —Director of Information Technology

Unfortunately for salespeople, the technical specification language usually is adopted by customers as the default standard for all of their communication. This presents salespeople with a significant problem. They are trying to create a personal relationship with the buyer. However, the buyer is communicating in an androgynous, nonpersonal, technical language. More importantly, given the use of this unusual language, salespeople must somehow decipher the underlying meaning and intent of the customer's words.

In addition, the technical content of the language is the yardstick by which a customer's technical peer group (the team selecting a product) measures a person's relevant knowledge. Outside of formal titles, it's another way members of the peer group will establish a hierarchy. It's also how they will validate the sales team's value to them. Conversely, it is how the sales team members will present their product's features and the technical reasons for selecting their product.

> *When you are speaking to a pure technologist, you have to be a pure technologist. Every sentence becomes a cat and mouse game where they are testing what you know.*
>
> —Top Salesperson

It's the language C-level executives use to communicate with their subordinates and instruct them what to do. For example, the CIO may instruct the vice president of infrastructure that he would like to "replicate the SAP IBM server data in New York to the NOC in Los Angeles." Obviously, a computer salesperson who doesn't understand these terms will have a difficult time winning the company's business.

The technical specification language is one of the primary languages that is used during sales calls. Therefore, you must know the technical specification language of your products and industry. You cannot expect to conduct successful sales calls and drive account strategy if you don't understand one of the fundamental languages your customers speak.

You must internalize the technical specification language and speak it fluently. Role-playing with your company's technical experts can help you practice and test your knowledge. Stay on top of the latest industry news. Start your own blog to demonstrate to prospective customers that you know their industry. Include the blog's URL on your business cards and in the signature line of every email you send.

Most importantly, there are some sales calls where the customer's depth of knowledge is much greater than yours. Meeting by yourself with the customer and his team may end up frustrating them as their detailed questions aren't being

: SALES CALL STRATEGY

answered with the same level of precision. In this situation, it is critical to bring along your product experts such as sales engineers and other subject-matter experts. Remember, on sales calls there is safety in numbers. By having a larger reservoir of expertise to draw upon, you statistically reduce the likelihood of a bad event.

Chapter 54. Speak the Business Operations Language with C-Level Executives

The business operations language is the language C-level executives and managers use to run their organizations. Some salespeople have the misconception that you must have an advanced degree in order to speak effectively with a C-level executive. For instance, you require a master's of business administration before a CFO will value your opinion. You need an engineering degree to hold a truly meaningful conversation with a vice president of engineering because of his advanced technical background. In reality, you only need to understand their business orientation and the state of their business, what they are worried about and want to control, and the plans they want to create to improve their business as shown in figure 54.1.

While having a deep domain-area expertise is the ideal situation, in reality, all C-level executives, midlevel managers, and lower-level managers perform the same basic duties associated with running a company. They are

either creating something new and providing business innovation or controlling an ongoing process in order to control costs. These duties fall into "create" and "control" categories. The business operations language consists of these create and control descriptions:

CEO:
Creates corporate direction through top-level business goals.
Controls which departmental initiatives will be undertaken to accomplish these goals.

CFO:
Creates the financial plans to run the business.
Controls money through budgets, accounting practices, and company policies.

The orientation of the business operations language varies by the level of the organization you are selling to. First, the higher levels of the organization are responsible for short- and long-term organizational planning. Next, the lower levels of the organization are responsible for

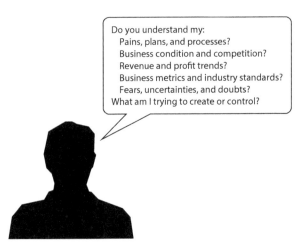

Do you understand my:
  Pains, plans, and processes?
  Business condition and competition?
  Revenue and profit trends?
  Business metrics and industry standards?
  Fears, uncertainties, and doubts?
What am I trying to create or control?

Figure 54.1 Understanding the customer's business orientation

the execution of the plan as defined by management.

Finally, the higher levels of the organization are responsible for the measurement of the execution of the plan by the lower levels as well as the plan's overall success. As a result, the create and control languages are spoken differently. People in the lower levels will tend to talk about their specific jobs and what they are trying to create, while people in the higher levels will speak about department goals. Successful customer communication is based upon providing relevant information, and the language you use to send your message must be tailored to the person's organizational role and responsibility. Figure 54.2 illustrates these differences.

Think about the senior-most executive you met during a very important recent sales call. Check each of the following create and control functions that are applicable to that person's role in the organization.

Create

☐ Prepare and present the fiscal budget.

☐ Provide forecasts.

☐ Implement new programs and policies, and provide their general administrative direction.

☐ Develop and execute departmental best practices.

☐ Sign financial agreements and long-term contractual agreements.

☐ Provide justification for all recommendations and decisions on capital expenditures.

☐ Conduct new business development activities to promote growth or decrease costs.

☐ Foster departmental and company communication.

☐ Build positive relationships with customers, the press, trade associations, and industry organizations.

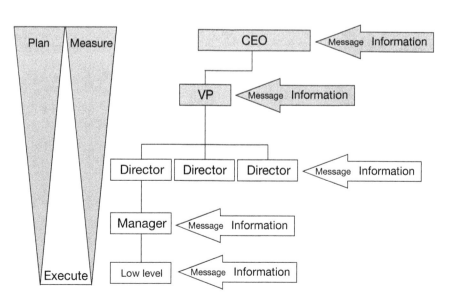

Figure 54.2 Business operations language differences by organization level

☐ Develop and maintain relations with employees, customers, and the community.

☐ Maintain responsibility for the selection, appointment, and retention of key management personnel.

Control

☐ Administer the management of daily operations.

☐ Analyze operating results versus established objectives.

☐ Take appropriate steps to reverse unsatisfactory results.

☐ Work closely with other departmental executives to ensure the company is functioning smoothly.

☐ Supervise budget performance throughout the year.

☐ Ensure that the growth of the company is in accordance with identified goals.

☐ Maintain the desired quality of products, customer service, and professionalism.

☐ Ensure that the company is in compliance with federal laws and local regulations.

☐ Operate the organization in a profitable manner.

☐ Provide oversight of and make recommendations for business initiatives.

☐ Resolve all departmental business and human relations problems.

☐ Ensure that the company's policies are uniformly understood and administered by subordinates.

☐ Establish standards for managerial performance.

☐ Recommend staffing and compensation changes within the organization.

☐ Approve all personnel promotions and staff reductions, and oversee hiring and firing processes.

☐ Conduct periodic performance and salary reviews of personnel.

Let's assume that you sell network performance management software and are meeting with the chief information officer at a new account you are trying to close. Before the call, you write down five create and control attributes of your solution that you plan to discuss using the business operations language.

Create

1. Improve the perception of the information technology organization within the company.

2. Improve responsiveness to the company's changing business needs.

3. Improve systems uptime and availability.

4. Maximize the existing infrastructure's life span.

5. Use staff more effectively, focusing on highly visible company projects.

Control

1. Reduce departmental staffing costs.

2. Control unexpected capital outlays.

3. Eliminate crisis situations that defocus daily operations.

4. Reduce IT project delays.

5. Control the demands of remote device support (smartphones and tablets) on IT.

Ideally, you should prepare solution positioning statements (see ch. 60) for each of the create and control points above. The product positioning statements explain how you accomplish the create or control objective using meaningful terms, specific benefits, and proof points.

Since a sales call is based upon the exchange of information, it is critical to tailor your message and deliver it according to the person's level in the organization. Let's assume you are meeting with a low-level network engineer at the same account as the CIO above. The create and control points you discuss will be focused on the engineer's ability to better execute his daily job duties:

Create

1. Improve daily effectiveness by quickly identifying the source of performance issues.

2. Make troubleshooting of network problems easier.

3. Proactively test and audit network performance.

4. Create network readiness prior to new technology deployment.

5. Increase the speed of network performance and throughput.

Control

1. Reduce network downtime.

2. Reduce the number of open support tickets.

3. Reduce escalations.

4. Reduce travel time to remote sites.

5. Reduce the number of network analysis tools used.

The create and control discussion will vary depending upon the industry and organizational level of the person you are speaking with. People in higher levels will be more interested in planning and measurement, while people in the lower levels will focus on tactical execution. Certain features and functions of your solution are associated with create and control tasks. Be sure to adjust your message and the manner in which you speak to mirror the business operations language of the customer you are meeting with. For example, here are the create and control points you would cover if you had a meeting with a chief medical officer who is responsible for a large network of hospitals.

Create

1. Improve clinical outcomes and patient safety.

2. Maximize resource utilization.

3. Improve coordination, collaboration, and communication among doctors, nurses, other caregivers, and patients.

4. Establish direct business-clinical connection: pay-for-performance, pay-for-outcomes.

5. Develop best practices and meaningful measures of result.

Control

1. Implement cost reduction strategies.

2. Curtail declining reimbursements.

3. Reduce patient length of stay.

4. Manage day-to-day issues of quality, safety, and customer service.

5. Plan for uncertainties surrounding healthcare reform and regulations.

Let's say you were meeting with a vice president of sales for an early stage technology company.

Create

1. Predictably grow revenue at a high rate.
2. Increase average deal size.
3. Elevate the selling level of the organization to call on senior executives.
4. Penetrate Fortune 1000 accounts through sales structure changes.
5. Build an international sales organization and worldwide presence.

Control

1. Standardize how the company and products are described.
2. Establish deal structure and discounting disciplines.
3. Reduce customer churn through retention programs.
4. Monitor hiring talent levels to reduce new hire ramp-up times.
5. Maintain cost of sales at acceptable levels.

Imagine you have a meeting with the chief marketing officer of a Fortune 1000 company.

Create

1. Create differentiated branding and offerings for the company.
2. Identify and reach new audiences and the next generation of customers.
3. Build and evangelize next-generation marketing tactics for today's digital environment.

4. Devise new models of collaboration across the team and with agencies.
5. Foster an environment that attracts and retains key marketing talent.

Control

1. Control the internal perception of marketing effectiveness and return on investment.
2. Manage a shrinking marketing budget for staff and advertising.
3. Protect the company's brand in the event of a public crisis.
4. Manage the complexity of relationships with agencies, media buying, and public relations firms across divisions.
5. Supervise budget allocation across brands, divisions, and products and the internal debate of who should get more money.

Pretend you're preparing to meet with the social media manager who works for the CMO in the preceding example.

Create

1. Create great content that performs well and resonates with my audience.
2. Initiate planning and scheduling that keeps all the stakeholders across the organization happy.
3. Develop insights that win over internal customers and power brokers and prove my value.
4. Create brand affinity and true love within my social community.
5. Produce effective social media customer care programs and response levels.

Control

1. Control inappropriate messaging across brand handles.

2. Monitor for prescheduled messaging that may inadvertently inflame a public crisis and ruin our reputation.

3. Improve influencer care and avoid missing the fact that the actress with 10 million followers is mad at us.

4. Manage the company's perception of our social media program and that what I do for a living provides an ROI to the company.

5. Direct the perception our users have of our social media management tools.

One way to determine customers' create and control functions is to study the job descriptions of their positions. They show what customers are responsible for and how they are measured. For example, the CEO's job description (see ch. 66) includes create functions such as analyzing trends and developing ideas for all areas of the business, strategizing on new ways to improve operations, and setting the company's strategic direction.

Another great way to truly understand what prospective customers are trying to create and control is to analyze your company's customer success stories. Specifically, analyze the comments customers have made and highlight what they are trying to create or control. Here's an example of a success story for a computer-aided-design tools company with the vice president of engineering's create and control comments indicated:

Our goal was to increase revenue and profits [create] through faster new product development cycles [create]. This requires having the right tools to minimize design times [control]. Now we have the ability to collaborate simultaneously [create] and effectively allocate resources on the fly [control].

—Vice President of Engineering

You can assume with a high degree of certainty that these create and control functions also apply to other vice presidents of engineering because they typically apply to similarly titled employees at other companies.

Tell Customer Stories and Position Your Value

Once you understand the prospective customer's create and control functions, you explain how your company has helped other organizations by telling stories about similar situations. An effective method of structuring customer success stories is to break them into four parts: situation, challenge, action, and results. This is known as the SCAR format (see ch. 64). Fight the natural tendency to explain how your product works and what it does using the technical specification language. Senior executives won't connect with what you're saying. Instead, position the strategic, operational, political, and psychological value of your solution as explained in chapter 65. Don't recite features and functions of your products. Instead, use solution positioning statements and be sure to "squish the bug" as described in chapter 60 whereby you invite the senior executive to speak or visit the customer you mentioned.

Finally, one of the biggest differences between you and your prospective

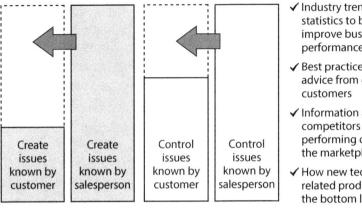

| Create issues known by customer | Create issues known by salesperson | Control issues known by customer | Control issues known by salesperson |

✓ Industry trends, metrics, and statistics to benchmark and improve business performance

✓ Best practices and practical advice from current customers

✓ Information about direct competitors and top-performing companies in the marketplace

✓ How new technologies and related products will impact the bottom line

Figure 54.3 Expanding create and control issues

customer is perspective. While the average B2B buyer will work at fewer than ten different companies over the course of a career, you are probably exposed to several times that amount of companies in any given year. Therefore, you have the opportunity to share your knowledge and expand the buyer's scope of create and control functions as shown in figure 54.3.

Exercise: Now it's time for you to conduct a very important exercise. Take a look at your customer success stories and study the comments your customers have made. Write down the title of the person you typically meet with on sales calls. Then list five create and control points the person would find important. Go ahead and write in the book, or list your ideas on a piece of paper.

Job Title:

Create	Control
1. _____	1. _____
2. _____	2. _____
3. _____	3. _____
4. _____	4. _____
5. _____	5. _____

Congratulations. If you completed the exercise, you now officially know how to speak the business operations language. The create and control discussion will vary depending upon the organizational level of the person you are speaking with. People in higher levels will be more interested in planning and measurement, while people in the lower levels will focus on tactical execution. Certain features and functions of your solution are associated with create and control tasks. Be sure to adjust your message and the in manner in which you speak to mirror the business operations language of the customer you are meeting with.

Chapter 55. The Confidential Language

The most important language spoken during sales calls is the confidential language. While the business operations language (see ch. 54) is a process-based language about what customers do on a daily basis, the confidential language is a personal language based upon what they want to do in the future. It's the language associated with the human nature of self-promotion and leading a group of people to accomplish a specific objective.

The confidential language is the most significant language spoken on sales calls. It's the language of strategic planning because it provides the customer's personal motivations for pursuing a project, the internal politics of the organization, and the unedited truth about the customer's real goals.

The confidential language has two variations, and sometimes it's easy to confuse the two. Companies and the executives who run them have a natural need to protect their images. The "public" confidential language is spoken when the customer is toeing the company line about why he is doing what he is doing. This is the official version for public consumption versus the off-the-record truth. When he's speaking the public confidential language, he is telling you the same thing he is saying to your competitors.

The "true" confidential language is spoken when the customer treats you like a confidant and shares his personal reasons why he is initiating a project and what he hopes to personally gain when it succeeds. Like a close friend, he discusses his private matters and problems with you. However, he will speak the true confidential language to only one of the salespeople competing for his business. He doesn't want to run the risk of having his true motives publicly known.

Quite often, salespeople mistake the public language for the true confidential language. See if you can determine whether each statement below is the public or true confidential language:

1. "Let me be honest with you: if this project doesn't succeed, we'll probably have to cut two thousand jobs at our Dallas operation."

2. "The strategic goal of this project is to improve our workforce efficiency during the next twelve months."

3. "Our win rate is decreasing and the CEO keeps pointing his finger at me, telling me to fix it now."

4. "Our goal is to increase sales by 10 percent, and this will require great changes to the company."

5. "Our employees act like they work for the post office. Our new CEO and I are on a mission to change this antiquated monolithic organization into a state-of-the-art customer driven company."

The odd-numbered sentences are examples of the true confidential language. They are personal revelations that would not typically be shared with someone who wasn't trusted. They reveal the customer's off-the-record opinion, personal dilemma, and ulterior motives, as well as the stress he is under. They aren't statements that would be made in public for everyone to hear. They would be said only to a salesperson who was trusted. The even-numbered sentences are examples of the public confidential language. They're generic statements that could have been said to all the salespeople because they aren't personally revealing.

In order to achieve your ultimate goal of speaking the true confidential language, you must be able to speak in each of the seven different sales call languages summarized in figure 49.3. By doing so, you will establish credibility and trust and use common languages that are at the foundation of meaningful communication. When the buyer speaks the true confidential language with you, it is direct proof that you have attained situational dominance. The buyer respects you, searches out your advice, and internalizes and acts on your recommendations.

Always keep the following principles in mind regarding the confidential language. First, you must be able to distinguish the true confidential language from the public version. Otherwise, your sales strategy will be based upon false information.

Second, customers will speak the true confidential language to only one of the salespeople they are selecting from. Therefore, you should always assume they are speaking it with one of your competitors if they are not speaking it with you. Finally, confidentiality is not freely granted by customers. It is earned through multiple interactions over time. This requires you to speak in all seven of the sales calls languages and prove you can be trusted.

Chapter 56. Sales Call Themes

The objective of every sales call is to build deal momentum. You should always be gaining momentum with the account and obtaining tangible evidence that the deal is moving in your direction. Evidence of this movement includes the elimination of other vendors, meetings with upper management or people involved in procurement, and other buying signs such

as contract reviews. The three underlying sales call themes that enable you to build deal momentum are your personal demeanor, your communication style, and the messages you deliver as shown in figure 56.1.

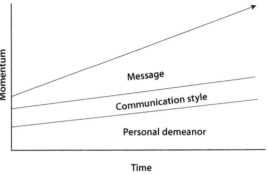

Figure 56.1 The three underlying sales call themes

You can think of personal demeanor as your physical presence. For example, some salespeople have such a lighthearted presence that customers will buy almost anything to keep them around—they're attracted to a humorous type of presence. Other customers want to associate with someone better than themselves, a person who has a character trait they feel they lack. For example, they may want to be around someone more outgoing, confident, charming, attractive, or worldly.

Our communication styles vary, depending upon whom we are presenting our arguments to. Giving long orations about your product will not win over the customer's heart and mind, whereas speaking passionately and knowledgeably will. Honest enthusiasm for your company and its products will permeate your customer's mind. The most persuasive salespeople are passionate about the company they work for and what they do for a living.

Through your communication style you establish situational dominance and customers are influenced to follow your recommendations.

Depending upon whom you are meeting, there are situations that require challenging them, while with others, aligning to their thoughts is the best course of action. Tailor your message to individuals rather than using a one-size-fits-all approach, reciting the same pitch to every prospect. Instead, you want everyone you meet with to take away his own personal message from your presentation. You want each person to have a positive feeling about your solution and how it will impact his role in the company.

Exercise: Regardless of how long you have been in sales and how accomplished you believe you are, you need to regularly evaluate your personal demeanor, your communication style, and the messages you are sending during sales calls. Therefore, I strongly suggest you make a video of yourself giving a fictitious sales presentation. In addition, use your smartphone to record your side of the conversation for the next five phone calls you make. Then while watching your video and listening to your calls, ask yourself this important question: If I were the customer, would I buy from myself?

Chapter 57. Sales Call Structure

From a sales linguistic perspective, each of the underlying sales call themes (personal demeanor, communication style, and message) has three stages, and each stage requires different linguistic strategies. The opening stage comprises the few minutes at the beginning of the call, the main stage is the longest period of interaction between the salesperson and customer, and the closing stage is the time at the end of the call. Each of the stages has different linguistic components, as shown in figure 57.1.

Your personal demeanor should vary at each stage, moving from approachability (not overfriendliness) in the opening stage and then to establishing situational dominance when interacting with the customer in the main stage. At the closing stage of the call you want to exude confidence.

Your initial communication style should be cordial initially (courteous and genuine). The main stage of the call is where a provocation or alignment strategy is employed. In some sales situations it

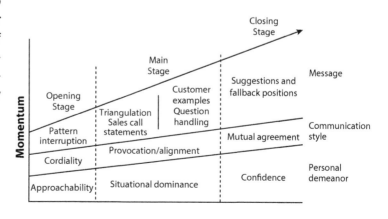

Figure 57.1 The stages and linguistic components of a sales call

is absolutely necessary to be aligned with the customer's thought process in order to win. In other circumstances the customer's thought process must be transformed and gently shaped over the course of the sales cycle. Finally, it may be necessary to divert and separate the customer from his existing thought process and change his way of thinking to stand out from the competition. This can require a subtle or radical realignment of his beliefs through provocation and challenging his preconceived ideas, biases, or methodology.

The opening message you deliver at every sales call should be a pattern interruption, which differentiates you from the competition. The main stage consists of discovery and triangulation to ensure you are receiving accurate information, sales call statements, customer examples specifically selected for the customer, and an individualized question-handling strategy. This is when you present ideas that are tailored to the customer's needs. Your "reaction read" is how you gauge the verbal and nonverbal reactions (acceptance, rejection, or indifference) the customer transmits after hearing your call statements. It's also your overall opinion of the customer participants in the meeting. Who is for you? Who is against you? And who can be swayed? The closing stage communication style is based upon mutual agreement where both the customer and salesperson agree on the next steps going forward.

During the closing, offer the customer suggestions and have prepared fallback positions in case your suggestions are rejected. We'll cover each of these linguistic components in more detail in the following chapters.

Finally, what's the appropriate time to contact a buyer following an initial call? How many days should a salesperson wait, so the prospect doesn't think he's too aggressive or downright desperate? According to my research, you should wait three days on average before you contact the buyer. However, it varies by industry with healthcare being one day; banking two days; and computers, government, and manufacturing three days. Finally, real estate is the longest period at seven days.

Chapter 58. Triangulation, Qualification, and Discovery

While most salespeople operate in a world of incomplete or incorrect customer information, Heavy Hitters (top salespeople) have a different strategy, called "triangulation." Triangulation is the process of identifying your position by using three or more data points. Heavy Hitters constantly try to triangulate their position by answering these questions: Is there a deal? Am I winning? Whom do I have to watch out for, and what can ruin this deal?

> *My top priority is to qualify whether the opportunity is winnable. The worst mistake is wasting precious time.*
>
> —Top Salesperson

The following discussion shows how you can carry out the triangulation process. It is based on the metaphor of a baseball diamond, shown in figure 58.1. (After all, Heavy Hitters are trying to score a home run.)

First Base

On the triangulation diamond, first base is the "what" base. What are the content-level words being spoken by the prospects? What specifically do these words mean? You are trying to determine as specifically as possible what the customers mean when they speak. Questions asked on first base include the following:

- Specifically, what are you trying to accomplish?
- Specifically, what business problem are you trying to solve?
- Specifically, what technical problem are you trying to solve?

As the customers answer these questions, you're trying to decipher their high-level requirements in order to target their needs. For example, let's say you sell a financial application and are meeting with prospects who are unhappy with their company's accounting system. You need to help them define exactly what is making them unhappy. Is it functionality, performance, ease of use, support, or flexibility? Suppose it's functionality. Is it accounts payable, accounts receivable, human resources, or integration? Suppose it's accounts receivable. Is it customer creation, payment application, or delinquent accounts reporting?

Second Base

Second base is the "how" base. Use second base to understand how the customers will take action. Again, try to determine in as much detail as possible how the sales process will happen by asking specifically how the customers will accomplish a task. Questions asked on second base include the following:

- Specifically, how will you make a decision?
- Specifically, how will you implement the solution?
- Specifically, how will you determine if it is successful?

You will want to know the prospects' evaluation criteria, the steps of the evaluation, and how they will determine if the evaluation is successful. Members of your triangulation team will gather this information from their respective contacts. Together, they will compile and assimilate the results. From this exercise, you will identify areas of product strength, weakness, and information you don't know. Once again, don't assume anything. Rather, you want the customer to provide clear verbal answers to your questions.

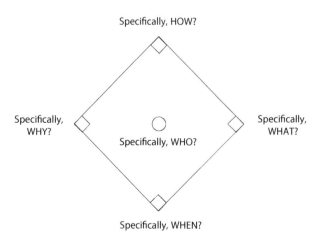

Figure 58.1 The triangulation diamond

Third Base

Now that you know specifically what customers are planning and how they intend to accomplish their goal, you need to understand why. Third base is the "why" base where you want to understand the following from the company's perspective:

- Specifically, why is the company evaluating a new financial system?
- Specifically, why is our product a better fit than our competitor's?
- Specifically, why would the company select our product?

The second element of "why" is the personal agendas of those involved with the initiative. Items on these agendas are called "benefactions," personal benefits that come from taking a particular action. The definition of "benefaction" is "an advantage that contributes to one's well-being, such as happiness, esteem, power, or wealth, and that results in influencing the way the person behaves during the sales cycle." At the personal level, ask the following questions about each participant in the customer's selection process:

- Specifically, why is this particular person on the evaluation team?
- Specifically, why would this person endorse our product?
- Specifically, why would this person oppose our product?

Home Plate

After rounding third base, you are headed for home plate. Home is the "when" base. Even if you reach third base every time you hit the ball, you don't score until you reach home. All the work the Heavy Hitter has done on the account is moot if the customer doesn't have a time frame to evaluate, decide, and purchase. On home plate, the questions include the following:

- Specifically, when will the evaluation start and finish?
- Specifically, when will a decision be made?
- Specifically, when will the customer buy?

The Pitcher's Mound

In baseball, the pitcher can throw the ball to any base at any time. The pitcher's position represents "who." "Who" can be applied to each base to determine who decided on the criteria, who will perform the evaluation, who will make the decision, and who will buy.

If you are a senior salesperson, you've probably participated in thousands of sales calls. After so many customer interactions, the mind tends to generalize the experience. Many times, you are actually going through the motions of account qualification. You assume information that isn't true, ignore important details, and misinterpret critical facts. Occasionally, you will be jolted back to reality when you are blindsided by a surprising loss. A quick review of the triangulation diamond before important sales calls will remind you that you must never take any sales situation for granted and that discovering reality is a main objective.

Chapter 59. Questions to Discover the Truth

One of the most important parts of the sales call is at the beginning of the main stage when you have the opportunity to ask questions. This is your "discovery" part of the sales call. The questions you ask also provide the opportunity to demonstrate your technical proficiency and show the customer that you understand how his business operates. Successful discovery is the first step toward building a foundation of trust and respect.

Suppose you sell enterprise software to banks and you have your first meeting with the CFO of Acme Bank, one of the world's largest banks. You are competing against Archrival Software. You assemble your sales team and make a list of all the possible questions you can ask the CFO. The five types of questions to ask customers are based upon the triangulation diamond (figure 58.1) and asking what, how, why, when, and who. Here are some of the questions you can ask:

What would you say the top five most significant challenges are?

What has prevented you from addressing these business challenges in the past?

What metrics does your CEO tend to be most interested in?

What is the toughest part of your job?

What are the three most important qualities you look for in a business partner?

Why are you looking for new software?

Why are these problems getting attention now?

Why is your budget $10 million for this project?

Why are you in charge of this decision, as opposed to the CIO or COO?

How long have you worked at Acme and where did you work before?

How familiar are you with us and the solutions that we offer?

How do projects get prioritized, and where is this project in the priority?

How do we stack up against the competition?

When will the contract approval process start, and how long would it take to get the project approved?

When can we show you a demonstration and who do you think should attend?

Who prioritizes projects like this and how are they prioritized?

Whom else are you looking at right now?

Who will be part of the evaluation team and why have they been selected?

Whom should we work with in each step of the evaluation process?

Are you aware that Big World Bank is now moving to our solution because of our superior service and track record?

What are the most important questions to ask? It depends. Aside from qualification questions, the best questions to ask are called "hypothetical questions" and "leading questions." Hypothetical questions enable you to gauge the strength of your personal relationship and include questions like those below:

Would you like to meet with our president next Thursday when he is in town?

We usually partner very closely with our customer executives and have regular advisory council meetings. Would you like to attend one?

Would you like to make site visits to other financial institutions that are using our solution?

Would you like to attend the Super Bowl with me next weekend?

Leading questions are planned in advance so that the customer's answer guides the discussion to your product's unique strategic and operational value. For example, you could ask, "What metrics does your CEO tend to be most interested in?" in order to provide the opportunity to explain the unique metrics your executive dashboard provides.

Obviously, you won't be able to ask a hundred questions during a brief sales call. Therefore, you must prioritize your list beforehand to ensure it includes your top ten most important qualification and leading questions. Even though you may have asked the same questions many times of low-level and midlevel personnel, you need to ascertain reality according to the C-level executive in charge. The C-level executive's perception of the pain, problem, and future plans may be vastly different than the reality that has been presented to you by his staff.

Exercise: Write down five leading questions you could ask on your next sales call.

Chapter 60. Solution Positioning Statements

After the salesperson has been allotted a certain amount of time by the customer to ask introductory questions, the natural flow of the sale call shifts to the salesperson making statements about his company, solutions, and customer success stories. All salespeople typically make generic claims about their products such as we reduce costs or make money. However, little meaning is derived from standard product claims. A better way to talk about your products is through solution positioning statements that utilize operators. "Operators" are specific proof points that validate a general claim (see ch. 81). Here's how to incorporate operators into solution positioning statements. Start with a high-level statement and then continue to define the statement into meaningful terms, specific benefits, and proof points:

We
  help save you money
  increase your revenues
  provide better technology
  offer a more comprehensive solution
  provide better functionality or ease of use

Because of our
  superior technology or functionality
  quality, people, customer service, or support
  ease of use or breakthrough paradigm

In comparison to
  the way you conduct business today
  how the competitor's product operates
  how your existing process functions

As a benefit, you will
  increase revenues by 30 percent
  save 25 percent
  improve your output by 3,000 units
  achieve 45 percent improvement

For example,

ABC Company implemented our solution and has saved $750,000 in the first six months

DEF Company increased revenues by $10 million in the first year

XYZ Company improved production by 400 units per day

Final proof point

I would be delighted to introduce you to John Smith at ABC Company.

If you like, I could arrange a visit to DEF Company.

Here's the case study on XYZ Company for further reading.

Squish the Bug

In baseball, all home run hitters know that the power of their swing is dependent upon their rotating the back foot, on the ground during the turn, as if they were squishing a bug. Similarly, the final proof point is how the solution positioning statement builds power whereby you prove what you're saying is absolutely true by inviting the customer to investigate it themselves. For example, inviting the prospect to speak with or visit the customer you mentioned.

Use solution positioning statements to clearly articulate your competitive differences. The demeanor and communication style you use to deliver them should be based on confidence, not arrogance, and perhaps a sense of urgency. Using product positioning statements is a more sophisticated strategy for talking to your customer's mind. They structure your arguments in a logical way using a story line that builds momentum while you deliver it.

Exercise: Take a moment to create a solution positioning statement for the most important product you sell.

Chapter 61. Handling Tough Questions

One of the hardest things to do in all of sales is to handle tough questions from skeptical prospective customers. After interviewing more than a thousand prospective buyers, I can tell you with certainty that answering customer questions successfully is often the difference between winning and losing. Here are six points to consider when answering questions:

- *Clarify the question first.* Customers ask two basic types of questions. Some are very specific questions about a feature or issue, while others are more general about a broad topic or your opinion. In both instances, make sure you understand the question before answering it. Either rephrase the question in your own mind with your own words and repeat it to the questioner aloud or ask the questioner to further explain what he meant before answering. Many times, salespeople are too eager to give an answer to a question that wasn't even asked.

- *Show your domain expertise.* If you intimately know your industry, company, and products and how they compare against the competition, you need not fear even the toughest question.

- *Make sure everyone understands.* Since most sales calls are conducted with groups of people, you should give a little background information with your answers to ensure everyone understands the topic of conversation. Don't assume everyone understands your company's buzzwords or nomenclature.

- *Provide an expert point of view.* Never forget, your customer would rather do business with a trusted consultant who has intimate knowledge of the industry than an ordinary salesperson who simply understands how the product works.

- *Remember: demeanor speaks volumes.* The most powerful response to the most difficult question isn't solely the answer you give. It's also how you say it! Regardless of the question, keep a calm and confident demeanor. Most of all, do not get defensive. Stay positive. This is a critical lesson. When confronted by someone who disagrees with your opinion, it's okay to disagree without being disagreeable.

- *Redirect inane and unfair questions.* Don't get flustered when you are asked an inappropriate question. Simply redirect the question by saying something such as, "The question you really should be asking is . . ."

Behind every question customers ask is an ulterior motive. They may want to validate a bias or throw you off track. That's why you shouldn't be too eager to answer or say yes to every question you are asked. The first step is to quickly theorize why the question was asked. Then formulate your response strategy to demonstrate your industry and

business expertise in order to command respect. Sometimes, it is best to address inappropriate questions by providing an answer that guides the customer to a different topic. Most importantly, maintain your composure at all times.

Chapter 62. Selection Pressure and Lying

When a customer asks you a question, you will provide either an instantaneous answer from your short-term memory or a calculated answer that involves your long-term memory. The instantaneous answer is available immediately since it involves the recall of a logical fact or the recollection of a flashbulb episode. Logical facts include details committed to rote memory, such as product specifications, features, and performance details. Flashbulb episodes are emotional, physical, or cerebral experiences that were so overpowering that they are permanently imprinted in short-term memory. For example, when someone says "9/11" you might immediately think of the twin towers of the World Trade Center. Both logical facts and flashbulb episodes reside in your short-term memory, which is accessed faster than your long-term memory.

Giving a calculated answer is akin to solving a mathematical equation in your mind by searching for and selecting the right answer or creating an appropriate answer based upon a set of rules learned from prior experiences residing in your long-term memory.

Three types of calculated answers are constructed in long-term memory. The first type uses a key access to search previous experiences. An example of a key access search during a sales call would be recalling previous meetings with CEOs in order to help you answer a question being asked by a CEO.

The second type, pattern recognition, requires a more complex calculation involving multiple attributes. Let's say you were asked by a skeptical, detail-oriented COO how your product is different from your major competitor's. The creation of your answer is based on previous encounters with this particular circumstance. Pattern recognition can be thought of as trying to find the what-when-where response—*what* you should do *when* you are in this circumstance *where* you need to respond to a question or execute a sales-related action.

Finally, sometimes you are presented with situations you have never encountered before and you have to use your imagination to create an answer. Making a best-guess answer requires a pattern recognition search to find closely resembling experiences plus additional hypothetical reasoning to create a new model. Obviously, this process takes the most time and my research on this subject shows that it can take up to 30 percent longer to imagine and answer rather than recall one from memory.

Customers expect you to respond to their questions within a certain time frame. When you are face to face, this time is measured in seconds, and there is a penalty for delay. If the expected length of time is exceeded, customers will perceive that you don't command the

facts, or worse yet, that your answer is untruthful. When this occurs, it is difficult to establish that you are their equal because you have lost their trust. As a result, they will not speak the confidential language with you. Figure 62.1 illustrates the impact of selection pressure during the sales call.

The main point of this discussion is that you need to anticipate the questions customers will ask and have answers prepared and internalized in advance. Create a list of all the toughest questions you could be asked and then rehearse your answers out loud until they are smoothly and quickly delivered. The answers should not be more than forty-five seconds long and should succinctly answer, not evade, the question. Referring to the example from chapter 59 where we are selling enterprise software to banks and meeting with the CFO of Acme Bank, here are some of the tough questions we should be prepared for:

Why should we do business with you?
What makes you different?
Why are you so expensive?
Why aren't you a publicly traded company (or why is your stock so low)?

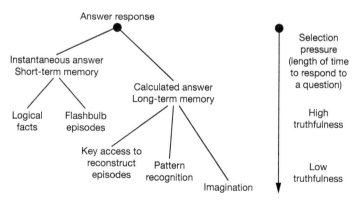

Figure 62.1 Question handling and selection pressure

Your ROI is way too high. Are you sure
it's right?

Who is your unhappiest customer and
why?

Why did ABC Bank switch from your solution to Archrival Software Company's?

What's the biggest deficiency in your
solution?

Why is your market share smaller than
Archrival Software Company's?

Tell me about yourself?

The selection pressure on salespeople forces them to produce answers
promptly. Quite often, when salespeople lie to a customer, it is more likely
because of the pressure to produce an
instantaneous answer rather than a conscious decision to mislead. In any case,
the customer will determine if your statements are true or false depending upon
your congruence. Congruence can be
thought of as "truth in communication,"
while incongruence suggests a person
is not telling the entire truth. Be forewarned, the customer will always spot
lies. Whether he calls you on them publicly depends upon how he perceives
himself and the role he takes during the
decision-making process. We will discuss buyer personas in detail later in
chapters 72–78.

Exercise: When you have a private
moment immediately following every
sales call, write down the toughest questions you can remember being asked.
Then grade your response to the customer from A to F based upon the customer's reaction. Typically, the hardest
questions require long-term memory.
Your answers to these are the ones you
probably graded lowest. By repetitively
practicing these answers aloud seven

to ten times, you will effectively improve
your believability and persuasiveness.

Chapter 63. Talking Point Format Answers

Many times salespeople are asked under-
handed questions by customers. This
questioning is disguised as information gathering but in reality only serves
the selfish motivations of the interroga-
tors. Unfortunately, novice salespeople
fall into the trap and try to respond to
questions to which there are no correct
answers. Anything that is said is used
against them.

Talking point format answers are
specifically structured responses to the
toughest questions customers ask. You
create them by writing two to four high-
level talking points followed by a short
written script. Since it's common to be
nervous on important sales calls, talking points serve as mental tags to help
you remember your script. Here's an
example of one of my talking point format answers that I use with prospective
customers and reporters.

*"Steve, there are thousands of books
about sales. Why is your book any different?"* Here are three talking points followed by the conclusion:

- It is the only book that truly explains
how to master sales linguistics.

- It is based on extensive research and
thousands of interviews.

- It provides advanced real-world
strategies.

- Conclusion: it helps salespeople influence the politics of decision-making.

Here's the written script:

I think there are three major differences. First, it is the only book that truly explains how to master sales linguistics, the new field of study of how the customer's mind uses and interprets language during the selection process. Second, it is based upon extensive win-loss research and thousands of interviews with decision-makers and top salespeople. Finally, it is written for senior salespeople and provides advanced real-world strategies that can be used immediately to close more business. The goal of the book is to help salespeople influence the hidden organizational politics that impact every purchase.

The demeanor and communication style used to deliver defensive call statements is calm, collected, and matter-of-fact. However, you want to build momentum as you make the statement and finish on a high note. This is called a "buildup." When you speak to a customer, you want to confidently peak during the final sentence of your paragraph. You don't want your voice to trail off, signaling uncertainty or lack of conviction.

A critical aspect of the sales call is not necessarily what you have planned to say. Rather, it is how you handle the tough questions the customer asks you. Your question-handling ability is what separates you from the pack. Prepare talking point statements in advance to protect yourself as you answer uncomfortable questions about your products, company, customer, and competitors.

Chapter 64. SCAR Format Answers and Customer Success Stories

Salespeople love to tell stories. Of all the stories we tell, none are more important than the examples about the customers who are successfully using our products and services. The most impactful way to structure customer success stories is using the SCAR (situation, challenge, action, result) format.

The personal connection between a customer example and its relevancy to the prospect's experiences will also determine to what extent the salesperson's claims are accepted. Therefore, the pertinence of the example chosen is very important. Presenting a company that closely mirrors the prospect's business or technical environment will make the statements more powerful. Presenting a company that the prospect doesn't recognize will have less impact. In reality, it may actually hinder the argument because the prospect might think the product is not pervasive or popular.

At the lowest level of relevance, the example used could be a well-known organization, such as Coca-Cola or Shell Oil. Certainly, these are companies that would be known by the customer. The level of relevance improves when the example company is known for its past innovations, such as FedEx or Intel, or is well respected for its quality and brand, such as Mercedes-Benz or Nordstrom. By providing examples of customers that have a dominant position in an unrelated business, such as Google, Amazon, or Starbucks, you also receive implicit approval since it is highly likely the prospect has successfully used the services or products of these companies person-ally. Therefore, the prospect makes the logical assumption that the salesper-son's product works successfully.

The company example could also include a technical environment similar to the customer's. In this case, the com-pany's name or business is de-empha-sized while its technical environment is highlighted. Let's assume the prospect is using Hewlett-Packard computers and Cisco network equipment. By provid-ing a customer example that identically matches this combination, the sales-person is able to validate his techni-cal claims that his product works in the prospect's exact technical environment.

Geographic proximity is a very com-pelling attribute of a reference. If the cus-tomer's company is based in New York, a reference to a company that is based in Los Angeles is not nearly as strong as a reference to one that is based in New York.

The ideal reference is a customer's direct competitor. This example provides the highest level of relevance and the most persuasive argument to use the salesperson's product. The best cus-tomer reference of all is a company in the same business, in close geographic proximity, and with the same business initiatives.

> Gartner and AMR are important to us for validating vendors. Much more important than trade rags. But the most important is peers in our industry. We want to talk to some-one like ourself. If you don't have someone like us, then you're prob-ably not going to get the sale.

—General Manager

Whenever you have an initial sales call, whether it is over the phone or in person, review your entire list of cus-tomers beforehand. Select five to ten customers from your list who share simi-lar characteristics as the potential cus-tomer. The potential customer may be in the same industry, a user of these com-panies' products, or a direct competitor.

The power of customer success metaphors lies in their individual inter-pretation. While the conscious mind is listening to the content of the surface-level story, the subconscious mind is deciphering its own message. On the surface, explaining how a customer is successfully using a product is a story the conscious mind will follow logically. Underneath this story, a message can be sent to the customer's subconscious mind that it is in his personal interest to select your product.

Here's how to apply the SCAR for-mat to create effective customer stories. Below, you will find an example of each part and descriptions of ideally what message should be sent to the con-scious mind and the connection to the subconscious.

Part 1 Situation—describes the history and situation.

- *Conscious message.* Describe the busi-ness problem or condition the cus-tomer was trying to solve or improve and the situation that created it.

- *Subconscious connection.* Specifi-cally identify the people involved in the selection process, including their names, titles, and backgrounds. These are people the customer can iden-tify with. When you provide these names, you are also offering them as references. Therefore, your examples should always be based upon happy, referable customers.

- *Example.* "I would like to take a moment to tell you about one of our most difficult customers, ABC Company. Their requirements were so complex that they were unsure whether any off-the-shelf product would work for them. Frankly, we had never seen a business that processed so many transactions. Their CIO, Bob Smith, was also one of the most meticulous and demanding customers I have ever met."

Part 2 Challenge—presents the challenge the customer was facing.

- *Conscious message.* Describe the different products or methods that could have solved the problem or improved the customer's situation.
- *Subconscious connection.* Explain the impact of these circumstances in terms of the decision-maker's job, career, or emotional state of being.
- *Example.* "Bob decided to bring in the top two products, ours and XYZ's, for intensive evaluations, even though he honestly believed that neither product would handle their requirements."

Part 3 Action—delineates the action that was taken.

- *Conscious message.* Outline the process the customer undertook to determine the best solution.
- *Subconscious connection.* Describe the personality, preferences, and motivations of the evaluation team members.

- *Example.* "Bob tested every aspect of the solutions: installation, ease of use, performance, and technical support. One month into the pilot test, Bob stopped testing XYZ's product because it just wouldn't scale. He spent another two months verifying every feature of our product. He wanted to make sure everything worked precisely as advertised."

Part 4 Results—describes the decision, reason, and results including metrics as proof points.

- *Conscious message.* Describe the final selection and its impact on the decision-maker or company. Always include relevant metrics that prove your accomplishments.
- *Subconscious connection.* Translate the outcome into personal terms.
- *Example.* "After two months of testing our product with their real-world transaction loads, there were absolutely zero performance lag times. Only when Bob was completely sure of his decision did he purchase our solution. Today, there are over 100,000 users worldwide accessing 10 petabytes of data. Our big data analytics tools have helped generate over $20 million of incremental revenues from their existing client base. The project has also reduced IT infrastructure spending by over $1 million in the first year alone. ABC Company is one of our happiest customers, and their project has been a complete success in their own words. I am sure Bob would be happy to host a site visit if you would like to tour his operation."

Chapter 65. Positioning Value When Meeting with C-Level Executives

Here's an important mantra to always keep in the back of your mind when meeting C-level executives: the purpose of the sales call is to talk about *their* problems, not *your* products. A successful sales call is not based upon how much product propaganda you impart. Rather, it is about the quality of the information you collect about the customer's problems and then how you prescribe your cure to improve and correct the situation in terms the customer understands. It is an outcome-based conversation fixated on achieving mutual agreement on a course of action to move forward. Let's examine how to structure a typical C-level sales call.

- *Five-minute opening stage.* The opening stage (see ch. 57), which usually lasts about five minutes or so, is where introductory questions and comments are made. While it might seem like idle chitchat, it is an important moment where executives qualify salespeople and determine their standing. Ideally, you want to control the opening stage by taking the lead and asking the questions or directing the conversation. (This is a type of pattern interruption as described in chapter 82.) The goal is to quickly show you are prepared and professional. Based upon your premeeting research, you can discuss trending industry topics or something of personal interest to the executive. For example, you might ask a question about how a competitor's recent

acquisition might impact the executive's business or discuss an interview the executive gave.

However, the executive controls the opening stage in many situations and you should be prepared for four different scenarios:

- *Poke, prod, test.* The executive will ask two or three questions to test the salesperson's knowledge and measure his business acumen.

- *"Tell me about."* The executive opens the meeting by pointedly asking the salesperson for an explanation or opinion about a business topic. This is another business acumen test.

- *"I understand."* These words are a direct signal that the executive wants to dive right into the main topic of conversation.

- *"Why are you here?"* Most meetings are put on executives' calendars by assistants at the request of subordinates, so executives can show up without any real idea of what a meeting is about. Sometimes they'll come right out and ask the purpose for meeting, and other times they might say, "How can I help you?" Calmly answer business acumen test questions. Give honest answers when asked for your opinion. Avoid small talk and jump right into business when the executive directs you. Provide background information and summarize how the meeting came about when asked the meeting's purpose.

- *20-minute main stage.* The C-level meeting conversation will be conducted mainly using the business operations language (see ch. 54). The bulk of the meeting time is spent in the main stage, which has two parts. You will spend the first third of the main stage conducting discovery by asking questions. The remaining time is spent describing how your solution solves the executive's problem and positioning its associated value. These two parts are discussed in more detail below.

- *5-minute closing stage.* The closing stage is based on achieving mutual agreement about a clearly defined course of action and the follow-up steps that will occur, who will carry them out, and the time frame for them to be completed. A target date should also be set for the next meeting. Another important goal is to establish the reconnect process by which you will remain in contact with the executive and update him on the progress of the action items. The first reconnect should be an email sent within three days of the meeting that reviews the course of action.

Main Stage—Conducting Discovery

The first phase of the main stage is your discovery of the problem: understanding the customer's specific problem, its cause, the goal that will be realized when the problem is solved, the possible options and vendors being considered to solve the problem, and the employees who will assist in solving it. The five purposes of discovery for meeting with

C-level executives are listed in order of priority below.

1. *Selling style selection.* In every account you have an important choice to make: whether you will use provocation, alignment, or transformation (see ch. 25). Will you provoke and challenge the customer to think differently about how he does business or uses products and technology? Will you try to align yourself to his current thought process and show him how you can solve his problem in the manner he prefers? Will you transform the customer's thought process over time? Will you remain adaptable and selectively challenge or align yourself depending upon individual topics of conversation?

2. *Personal demeanor.* The manner in which the customer responds to your questions will help you determine the personal demeanor and communication style you will use to achieve situational dominance. The communication style should vary, depending upon the individual you are selling to. The quality of your questions and the way in which they are asked will enable you to establish trust (see ch. 50).

3. *Business fit.* A key stage in the buyer's journey (see ch. 30) is when the business buyer assesses which vendors offer the best business value and are a philosophical fit for the business. One goal of discovery is for you to ascertain how well the cultures of the two companies match before the buyer enters this stage in order to position your company accurately.

4. *Triangulation.* Triangulation is the process of identifying your position through deal qualification (see ch. 58) and understanding the politics of decision-making. Is there a deal? Can I win? Does the customer have the need, necessary budget, time frame, and motivation to take action? When meeting with lower-level personnel, do they have the authority to make the purchase?

5. *Solution fit.* Of all the aspects of discovery, ascertaining the solution fit is probably the easiest. The criteria to determine if the account is technically qualified are developed either by product management, marketing, or within the sales organization. Through informal questioning or the completion of pre-implementation checklists or technical questionnaires, the sales team determines if the product meets the customer's technical requirements and fits the use case. The salesperson decides which features to emphasize and which to de-emphasize and how to position his company's story with the customer's technical needs in mind. Usually, solution fit is verified by meetings with lower-level personnel before you meet with executive level leaders. However, overall fit should be validated by the C-level leader.

After you conduct your discovery, you will reach a critical decision point in formulating your sales strategy. You can be in alignment with the customer's thought process on how he will solve the problem in order to achieve the goal. By building rapport and earning the customer's trust you can gradually transform his thought process over time. Or you can completely change the game by changing the customer's thought process.

Main Stage—Positioning Value

The second phase is the positioning of your solution's value and the customer's discovery of your solution. Once you have decided on your strategy, you will then define how you might solve the problem by explaining how you have helped companies in similar situations. You accomplish this by providing real-world examples that equate your solution to the four different types of product value we reviewed in chapter 40. While these examples straightforwardly explain the strategic and operational values, the political and psychological values are suggestions that are inferred by the customer when listening to the stories. Finally, you will describe the unique features and functions by which your solution achieves the customer's strategic and operational values.

Here's an example to help you understand and apply this concept. Let's assume you work for a software company that provides workforce productivity software—the Laborsaver 3000—and you are meeting with the COO of a large food-processing company.

The sales call starts with your asking questions to discover the COO's problem. In this case, the CEO has mandated that all departments cut their budgets by 20 percent. The COO will comply with this request by cutting raw material, labor, and shipping costs. He determines that half of the cost savings will have to come from reduced labor costs. However, he dreads laying off people and wants to avoid across-the-board pay cuts and employee reassignments. He would rather drive the labor cost savings through less-intrusive methods that don't hurt employee morale.

Once you have understood his problem, you decide to employ provocation using a high level of situational dominance. You specifically prescribe your solution using examples of other large food-processor customers using the SCAR format (situation, challenge, action, results) as explained in chapter 64, pointing out that Dole Food Company and Kraft Foods have reduced labor costs 10 percent through more-efficient and more-accurate scheduling of skilled employees against actual demand. The customer examples are important and should be chosen with care. These stories show the COO how he can accomplish his reduction goals and achieve strategic value (he can tell the CEO he's cut labor costs 10 percent) and operational value by improving his department's efficiency. Politically, he has satisfied the powerbroker CEO, and psychologically, he has gained the approval of his employees for preserving their livelihoods. Refer to chapter 40 for a detailed review of strategic, operational, political, and psychological value.

As the conversation progresses, the executive wants more details about how the solution works and is implemented. You then describe the relevant features and functions of the Laborsaver 3000 software that specifically explain how the strategic and operational values are achieved. The structure of the main stage of the sales call is represented in figure 65.1.

Know your strategy decision options ahead of time and answer questions in the business operations language. Even the most experienced salespeople have a tendency to recite product features and specifications when nervous. A good rule of thumb is to only speak the technical specification language when the customer does.

Chapter 66. Speaking with C-Level Executives

Keep the six Cs of selling to the C-level in mind when meeting with senior executives: confidence, control, conversation, customers, close, and confidential.

Problem	Cause	Goal	Possible options	Strategy decision	Applicable solution	Strategic and operational value	Political and psychological value	Product
I have to reduce department costs that consist of raw materials, labor, and shipping	Sales are down and the CEO mandates 20% budget cuts	Realize a 10% labor cost savings with minimal impact on my employees' lives	1. More efficient workforce 2. Employee reassignment 3. Pay decreases 4. Layoffs	**Provocation** Challenge the customer's thinking and prescribe recommendation **Adaptability** Decide to provoke or align based upon specific topic **Alignment** Dovetail to customer's thought process	Improved workforce planning and labor budgeting	A 10% labor reduction at Dole and Kraft	Satisfying CEO while maintaining department morale	Laborsaver 3000 features and functions that create the labor cost savings benefits

Executive converses in business operations language

Salesperson discovery: asking questions

Decision point The degree to which prospective customer's existing thought process, business model, or technical environment is challenged

Salesperson converses in business operations language

Executive discovery: asking questions

Figure 65.1 Sales call main stage phases and strategy decision point

- *Confidence.* Exude confidence and establish situational dominance (see ch. 99).

- *Control.* Control the interaction by planning your opening, main, and closing stages beforehand (see ch. 65).

- *Conversation.* Speak in the business operations language, not the technical specification language unless required (see chs. 53–54).

- *Customers.* Focus on outcomes by telling customer stories using the SCAR format (see ch. 64).

- *Close.* Close the meeting with a clearly defined course of follow-up actions and reconnect strategy (see ch. 65).

- *Confidential.* Listen for the true confidential language spoken by the executive.

Reaching the True Confidential Language

In the example from chapter 65 about the sales call with the COO, the conversation may have never reached the confidential language, but the call still could have been deemed successful. The executive thought your solution would solve his problem and you felt great about your performance. Everyone left the meeting excited about the prospects of doing business together, with you being the most excited of all.

However, the sales call had four major problems. First, the CEO is the emperor, while the COO is the bully with the juice (see ch. 36). The CEO will ultimately approve the method the COO uses to reduce costs. Even though the COO may decide to go with the Laborsaver 3000, the CEO might not want to spend the

time or money implementing it. He wants layoffs instead. So even though you met with the highest-ranking departmental C-level executive, you might not have a deal here after all.

Second, one of your competitors might outflank you and reach the CEO first. When the COO presents his recommendation about how he intends to cut costs and the vendor he intends to use, he'll be overruled. The third problem is that the COO has several meetings with other competitors scheduled in the days ahead and could easily change his mind.

The biggest problem with the sales call with the COO was that the true confidential language wasn't spoken. The true confidential language is a personal language a customer uses to explain what he wants to do and why (see ch. 55). The language is based on accomplishing a future objective to increase power or controlling behavior to retain power. The sales call conversation stayed at the business operations level and never approached confidentially, where the COO's true motivations would be revealed.

An example of the true confidential language would be if the COO had said, "Our CEO is a really mean guy, and he told me that it would be my job if I didn't cut costs 20 percent." Furthermore, the COO did not enlist you to help him execute his strategy of avoiding layoffs. The COO could have confided to you, "This will be a tough sell to my CEO. Is there any way we could arrange a meeting between him and the CEO of Kraft to talk about how they are saving money during these difficult times?" So even though plenty of enthusiasm was exhibited by both sides, real trust wasn't established.

How do you establish the level of trust necessary to get to the confidential language? The answer isn't simple. You know you must understand your products, the industry, and the operations of the customer's business. Three additional factors greatly determine your ability to establish trust. They are your question-handling ability, the congruence of your communication, and your personal presence and its impact on the customer's conscious and subconscious minds. In other words, you have to be respected and considered to be an equal in terms of your stature and self-confidence. This is the definition of situational dominance (see ch. 99).

Everyone has a confidence "muscle" that strengthens when it is used and atrophies when it isn't. Meeting with C-level executives requires you to flex your confidence muscle the most. The best way to build up a muscle is through repetitive motion, and the only way to build your confidence muscle is through continual meetings with people who may make you the most nervous. The easiest way to start is by speaking with the senior leaders of your company.

We have discussed how you should understand your strategic, operational, political, and psychological value to the customer. However, in reality, you and your competitors will make very similar statements about how much money the customer will save and how departmental efficiencies will be improved. The key to reaching the true confidential language is communicating your political and psychological value to the customer. Think about the different things you can say to make the customer feel more powerful and all the examples that show how your products guarantee career success. In order to truly understand the customer's orientation, you need to put yourself

in his position and understand what he or she does on a daily basis. Read the C-level executive job description below, which illustrates the attributes and the human nature of leading a group:

C-Level Executive Officer Job Description

The individual must be a visionary leader who has the ability, skills, and knowledge to take the business into the future. He must instill in the staff a passion and understanding of the business philosophies as they relate to serving customers and the company. This individual will have expertise in the areas of leadership, communication, team development, and coaching, as well as situation assessment skills. He must possess the ability to motivate or influence others as a material part of the job, requiring a significant level of diplomacy and trust. The individual will be an innovative, proactive leader who can analyze trends and develop ideas for all areas of the business and for process improvement. This individual will assess the present business and after evaluating the findings will strategize on new ways to improve operations. He must be able to develop, recommend, and set business related goals for the company's strategic direction.

When you truly understand what the customer is responsible for and how he is measured, then you understand his personal motivations for pursuing a project, the internal politics of the organization, and how buying your product will help him and the organization achieve their true goals.

Chapter 67. Questions to Ask Your Coach

A successful sales call depends on your understanding the complete environment and the interactions between the audience members. The optimum way to conduct a sales call is through holistic interactionism, a person-centered approach that combines concrete thought processes (facts, features, and functions) with abstract thought processes (politics, environment, feelings, and benefactions).

The holistic view of personal behavior acknowledges the interaction between people (their thoughts, emotions, and personalities) and the world that surrounds them at the same time. The situational nature of this theory helps explain why some customers don't want to disappoint salespeople during the sales call so they tell the salespeople what they want to hear. Meanwhile, other customers seek to avoid face-to-face confrontations so they tend to keep their objections to themselves.

The process of holistic interactionism starts with an investigation before the call to ascertain what the meeting environment will be like. Will you be interrogated Spanish Inquisition style or attend a symbiotic love fest? While it is easy to find out who is attending and what their official titles are, understanding the internal machinations of the customer's decision process requires a coach. Only a coach can tell you who is for, against, or ambivalent to your solution. Only a coach can prepare you for the various objections that will be raised during your sales presentation, objections that could throw you off track. Involving your coach in the creation of the presentation

topics, finding out what points to cover and what to avoid, is critical. Previewing the presentation with your coach is ideal.

Let's assume Mitch is your coach during this selection process. He's been providing you with accurate, proprietary information about the decision-making process and has actually told you he wants you to win. He is guiding you through the sales process and has arranged a meeting with his boss, Bob, the C-level executive who is the emperor. Mitch is a great source of information about what you can expect from Bob during your upcoming meeting, and you want to ask him questions that will help you prepare for the meeting in advance, such as the following:

What is Bob's background and what different positions has he held in the company?
What's it like to work for him?
Is he outgoing with a sense of humor or is he more serious?
Is he big picture or detail oriented?
What kind of work hours does he keep?
What are his personal hobbies?
What projects has he promoted and were they successful?
Is he well liked by the other company leaders?
What are his perceptions about my company and me?
How does he typically treat salespeople, and what should I watch out for?

These are just a few of the many questions you could ask your coach to understand the C-level executive's conscientiousness, gregariousness, and clout within the company.

Knowledge is power. You must secure proprietary knowledge about the accounts you are trying to close to obtain the power you seek. You must have a coach (see ch. 37) to win a deal. Without one, you will never know the true nature of the organization and who has the real power to make the decision. Ideally, you want to develop your coach into a guide because the most effective method of meeting senior executives is for mid- and lower-level personnel to introduce you to them. And the best coach is always the senior-most executive of the account you are trying to close.

Chapter 68. Structuring the Sales Presentation

After evaluating hundreds of corporate sales presentations, I can honestly say that they all are basically the same. You could take slides from one company's presentation and insert them in another's and no one would notice. They are all fact-based infomercials with no discernable differences.

It's not enough to say that to stand out you have to be different. Rather, you need a more sophisticated, indirect approach that differentiates your solution in the minds of customers. You can't *tell* customers you're unique, different, and one of a kind. You must *demonstrate* it to them, starting with the psychological and linguistic framework of the corporate presentation.

Honestly, they didn't present well. Their sales engineer was great and I really liked their sales guy. But in front of our leadership, he tends not to read the room well and this didn't play well. He was too
informal and way too casual. His competitor positioned themselves as much more peer-to-peer with our executives.

—Director of Technology

Traditional corporate sales presentations are typically organized into six sections: my company, my products, how they work, their benefits, our customers, and a call to action. Your presentation should be divided into four sections. It should start with a pattern interruption, move on to customer metaphors, be followed by explanations, and close with suggestions. This way of presenting is distinctly different from the presentations of your competitors. Let's examine each section of the presentation in detail.

Section 1—The Pattern Interruption

The first goal of your presentation should be to perform a pattern interruption to break the customer's mode of thinking that you are like other salespeople and to make you stand out from the competition. The pattern interruption starts the process of building rapport, engages the audience, and provokes open-mindedness. Your pattern interruption will consist of an attention-grabbing cowcatcher (see ch. 82) such as a strategy slide or money slide. Even an agenda slide can become a pattern interruption when topics are positioned pithier. For example, instead of "About XYZ Company" you could use "The Three Most Important Facts You Should Know about Doing Business with XYZ Company."

Unfortunately, the first few slides of most corporate presentations have little panache. The obligatory introduction states some facts about the company's financial position, how long it has been in business, and its office locations.

Section 2—Customer Metaphors

One of the biggest problems that most salespeople have on sales calls is that they are too eager to tell the customer about their products. The same is true for a corporate presentation, and when this happens, the presentation does not build a story line that piques interest. Instead of launching into slides about the product line and technical aspects of the products, the second section of the corporate presentation should focus on customers.

Following the pattern interruption, you need a hook. Now that the listeners' interest is piqued, you need to hook them on why they should use your product. Your best hook is to tell them stories about your customers. Most corporate presentations include an obligatory slide that shows twenty or so logos of the major companies that use the salesperson's products. That's not what I am referring to here. The second section should include six to eight slides of how specific customers are using the products, the operational results that have been improved, and the financial impact on the bottom line. In addition, it should include a quote from a customer whose name and title the audience can identify with psychologically. For example, include a quote from a customer's CFO when presenting to a financial department.

Finally, this section should have some eye-catching graphics that tie the whole story together. These could be pictures of your product at work, the person who provided the quote, or an example of the end result.

As we discussed in chapter 64, the pertinence of the customer examples is very important. Presenting examples from companies that closely mirror the prospect's business objectives will make the statements more powerful. Presenting examples from companies that the prospects don't recognize will have less impact.

Section 3—Explanations

The third section of the presentation is based upon an intellectual and logical appeal to the customer's conscious mind. Here the goal is to continue to build credibility by methodically explaining background information and facts behind the customer metaphor slides.

For example, let's say you are selling manufacturing-shop-floor equipment and one of your customer metaphor slides is about how General Electric saved $20 million in the first year of using your product. In this section you would drill down through the critical features of your product that streamlined operations. You could explain in detail how these features work technically and how they compare to other methods of accomplishing the same tasks.

The explanations section is typically the largest of the presentation. Keep in mind that smartphones, television, and the internet have changed people's attention spans and the way they want information presented to them. The best presentations deliver information in small chunks. I recommend that no single slide should take more than two minutes to cover. If it lasts longer than that, you may lose the audience's attention. Therefore, if a slide takes four minutes to explain, split it into two slides to keep the presentation moving. In fact, I will typically present anywhere from forty-five to sixty slides in an hour-long presentation yet the audience won't realize there were that many (see ch. 69).

Since most salespeople are well versed in the logic of selling, it doesn't make sense to reiterate here what you already know. Instead, let's emphasize some steps you can take to make an intellectual appeal more compelling:

- Provide independent confirmation of your facts wherever possible.

- Provide quotes from authorities (customers, analysts, and the press).

- Quantify beneficial claims with specific numbers.

- Use real-world examples, which are more powerful than hypothetical statements.

- Arrange your arguments from strongest to weakest.

- Keep it simple. Remember Occam's razor: the simpler explanation is always preferred.

- Be prepared for contradictory facts from other vendors and have factual responses ready.

- Quantify results from adverse consequences (for example, loss of revenue due to equipment downtime).

- Present the extremes and worst-case scenarios to make the other options to solve the problem look worse than they really are.

- Use alliterations—repetition of the same letter or sound of adjacent words—so that concepts are more easily remembered (for example, "durability, dependability, and adaptability").

- Include mnemonics where initial letters of words spell out a tangible word (for example, ACRONYM equals "a clever reword nudges your memory").

- Use the rule of three: whenever you make a claim, support it with three different facts.

- Create your own euphemisms that reflect the importance of your product or a particular feature. For example, a rubber band could be called a "multipurpose business instrument."

- Understand that it is all right to draw big conclusions from small statistics. Sometimes the biggest points can be made from the smallest samples.

- Brighten up the facts with interesting graphics that represent them pictorially.

- Become a storyteller, not a human dictionary. Use metaphors to explain concepts. Instead of saying "A poll showed customers prefer us three to one," say "Harris Poll surveyed four thousand buyers from across the country and found that three thousand, or 75 percent, thought our solution was far superior."

Logical arguments alone, no matter how well you present them, will not change skeptics into believers. Finessing customers to change their opinions requires an appeal to their human nature. *Finally, you must be able to defend everything you present!*

Section 4—Suggestions

The typical close to a corporate presentation is a one-slide summary of the major topics that were covered. The salesperson basically says "I hope we passed the audition." A better way to end a presentation is with very specific action items that are based upon the goal you wanted the presentation to accomplish. For example, if the goal of the presentation was to make the customer's short list, an appropriate close would be to explain the seven reasons why you believe you should be on the short list. If you are further along in the sales cycle and your goal was to close the deal, walking the customer through the implementation process or explaining your pricing methodology is an appropriate close.

These action items should be worded in the form of foreground and background suggestions. Examples of foreground suggestions include "I spoke to my contacts at General Electric yesterday and told them I was presenting to you today. They extended an invitation to come to their operation for a site visit" and "All of the analyst firms strongly encourage that customers benchmark all of the products they are considering."

Background suggestions are indirect. Showing your pricing model is a background suggestion to negotiate price. If earlier in your presentation you described how the customers at General Electric made their decision, what products they evaluated, and why they selected your solution, walking the customer through their implementation process is a background suggestion to make the customer think about implementation. Another example of a background suggestion is "The regional vice president for Archrival Software just joined our company because he was tired of dealing with continual product support problems." This background suggestion triggers a more profound emotional reaction as the customers will want you to tell them why.

The Strategy and Money Slides

Two very important slides that should be included in your presentation are called the "strategy slide" and the "money slide." The strategy slide clearly defines the business problem that needs to be solved (or the opportunity that can be created), the cause of the problem (or reason for the opportunity), the goal realized when the problem is solved (or when the opportunity is realized), and all the possible options that could be utilized to solve the problem or achieve the opportunity. The strategy slide is based upon defining the first four boxes of the main stage in figure 65.1: problem, cause, goal, and possible options.

The strategy slide is not vendor specific. Rather, it presents the customer's situation from an unbiased third-party point of view. You know you have created the perfect strategy slide when the customer asks for a copy of it so that he can post it on his office wall. Conversely, the money slide shows how your specific solution solves the problem from the strategic, operational, and, most importantly, financial perspectives. This slide summarizes the strategic value of your solution including all costs, ROI, and payback assumptions. It also shows the operational value of your solution that results from its unique features and functions. This slide summarizes why the customer should select your solution over all the others.

The strategy slide and the money slide can be used at the very beginning of your presentation as the pattern interruption. Or they can be placed at the end and incorporated into a background or foreground suggestion. In reality, your entire presentation boils down to these two slides. Do you understand the customer's problem and have you developed the credibility to recommend a solution? Have you demonstrated that you can solve the problem better than the competition?

In win-loss interviews, the sales presentation was the most frequently cited turning point during the entire sales cycle. It's the moment when you either gain momentum on your way to winning or lose momentum that you will never recover. Therefore, structure your presentation into sections (pattern interruption, customer metaphors, explanations, and suggestions) for greater impact. Be sure to include a strategy slide and a money slide.

Chapter 69. Creating Better Presentations

The standard rule of thumb is to allocate 2 minutes to present 1 PowerPoint slide (known as the 2:1 presentation ratio). Using this methodology, a 30-minute presentation would consist of 15 slides. However, I think this is outdated thinking and flat-out wrong today because we live in a nonstop digital age where audience member attention spans are shorter than ever. I firmly believe that the purpose of the presentation is not only to transmit important content, but, equally important, to serve as a visual backdrop that is dynamic and engaging because it is frequently changing.

The presentation strategy I recommend is to present 1 slide for every presentation minute (a 1:1 presentation ratio). Using this methodology, a 30-minute presentation would consist of 30 slides. I know this seems like a lot of slides, so let me explain how this works. First, there are four types of slides. Transition slides introduce a section or a new topic and are shown for just a few seconds. Short slides are typically shown for about 30 seconds, medium slides for about a minute, and long slides for around 2 minutes. Therefore, the structure of your presentation is faster moving because it is shown in smaller chunks.

Here are the fascinating results from using this strategy—the audience will think you're presenting fewer slides than you actually are. I've used this methodology for years and the overwhelming majority of the audience thinks they've seen half the sides I've presented. For example, I surveyed a forty-six-member audience following a 70-minute presentation where I showed 68 slides. Seventy-four percent of the audience thought they saw 40 slides or less while only 12 percent thought they had seen over 61 slides as shown in figure 69.1. At another meeting I presented 128 slides in 150

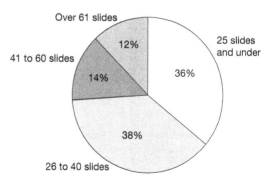

Figure 69.1 Audience members' perceptions of slides shown

minutes (two and a half hours), and when I asked how many slides I had shown the average response was 65 slides.

Let's finish the discussion about presentations we started in the previous chapter by considering the look and feel of your slides. What colors are used in your corporate presentations? I like to use two basic color schemes in my slides, red and blue. Red signifies change, aids memorization, and subconsciously tells people to slow down and pay attention—like a stop sign. Blue encourages creativity, and people associate it with explorative feelings and a sense of wonder—like the sky.

How well your presentation is received will vary depending on whether it was created by a Visual, Auditory, or Kinesthetic and who is in the audience (see chs. 110–114). Visual people predominantly rely on their sight and prefer the visual channel of information, auditory people prefer sound, and kinesthetic people are sensory-based and rely on their feelings and tactile senses (touch, taste, and smell). Slide after slide after slide of bullet points will torment Visuals. A sterile look and feel turns off Kinesthetics. Auditories like to read the verbiage on slides, so don't use too many slides that consist of a single picture. Ideally, you want your slides to match the word catalog makeup of your audience. I'd recommend you assume a general audience is composed of 45 percent Visuals, 40 percent Auditories, and 15 percent Kinesthetics.

The typical sales presentation is made to a group of people, many of whom you have never met before and who probably have different word catalog wirings. In this situation, another strategy is to present all of your ideas and thoughts in neutral wording without any reference to word catalogs. Neutral wording enables listeners to apply the catalog of their choice to gain meaning. Here are some examples of word catalog usage (the first phrase in each pair) and the corresponding neutral wording usage (the second phrase):

- Instead of "I see what you mean," use "I agree with you."

- Instead of "I hear you," use "I understand."

- Instead of "Looks good," use "I think it will work."

The direction in which your audience reads influences how they receive information, and the layout of your slides should reflect this. English, for example is written left to right. A "heat map" is a representation of where the eyes look first and gravitate toward next when initially viewing a website page, PowerPoint slide, letter, or email. See chapter 88 for a heat map example.

When you take into account word catalogs, your sales presentation will connect much better with your audience and be more influential with their subconscious minds. Provide Auditories slides they can read to themselves, engage Visuals with eye-catching graphics, and give examples that cause Kinesthetics to emote. You can use neutral wording when you don't have any idea of the audience's word catalogs. Finally, be conscious of the heat maps of the PowerPoint slides, letters, and emails you create.

There's one final point to make about your slides. The most important person your slides are designed for is you. I have identified three basic types of presenters.

Some people are completely comfortable and at ease presenting in front of groups. They have what I call a "big" presentation persona. Since their slides serve as backdrop to their talk track, they can get by with fewer bullet points and verbiage on their slides. In essence, the bullet points and verbiage on slides are a "crutch" that the presenters use to remind them of what to say next. While those with a "medium" presentation persona are good at presenting familiar information, they can get nervous depending on whom they're presenting to. The bullet points and verbiage serve as the crutch that helps them feel comfortable under duress. Finally, presenters with a "small" presentation persona are the least comfortable presenting. They require structured bullet points, verbiage, and structured animation builds to lead the presenter to the next topic. In their case, they use the crutches to help successfully carry them through the presentation.

Chapter 70. Closing Strategies

Remember the last time you were being pressured into doing something you didn't want to do? Whether the pressure came from a boss, colleague, spouse, or child, your natural response was to resist and push back. It's human nature to resist high-pressure tactics. So, how should the closing of the sales call be structured? The answer is to create a primary closing strategy, utilize fallback positions, and select an appropriate delivery technique as represented in figure 70.1.

Your primary closing strategy should be based upon securing the main objective for the meeting. The objective could be to be granted a follow-on meeting, have the customer start a product evaluation, receive approval to conduct a site survey, or negotiate final purchase terms. You also need fallback positions, alternatives you prepare ahead of time to present should the customer reject your primary closing strategy.

Your primary closing strategy and fallback positions are based on choosing to issue a command or present foreground and background suggestions. A command is an instructional statement that creates a binary type of yes or no response from the recipient. It is typically associated with a hard close and "take it or leave it" mentality. Foreground suggestions (medium close) are explicit, but they deflect the source of the request from the demander. Background suggestions (soft close) lead recipients to believe they are acting of their free will

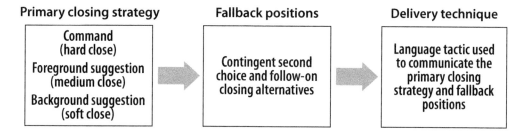

Figure 70.1 Sales call closing strategies

when in fact they have been directed to follow a message.

Let's pretend I am a passenger in your car and I feel you are driving too fast. A command would be "Slow down!" A foreground suggestion would be "You know the speed limit is forty-five miles per hour and police ticket a lot of speeders here." A background suggestion would be "A speeder was in a horrible accident last week in this exact spot." While the background suggestion may be more subtle in its delivery, it can trigger a more profound reaction.

In a sales situation, a command might be "We always recommend you benchmark the products you are evaluating." A foreground suggestion might be "*Consumer Reports* gave our product the highest rating and recommended it as the best buy." An example of a background suggestion is "One of my customers tried the other company's product and recently switched to ours."

After you have determined your primary closing strategy and fallback positions, select the delivery technique to be used during the meeting. Here are some examples, assuming the main sales call objective is to close the business deal:

- *Time-based technique.* This technique incorporates a time-based deadline.
  - *Command (hard close).* "This is the last time we'll be able to extend this offer and we need your answer now."
  - *Foreground suggestion (medium close).* "My boss told me that this pricing expires December 31 at midnight."

  - *Background suggestion (soft close).* "Think it over tonight and I will call you at 10 o'clock tomorrow morning."

- *Linkage.* This technique connects different events, subjects, or ideas.
  - *Command (hard close).* "If we give you those terms, then you must have our contract signed by the end of our quarter."
  - *Foreground suggestion (medium close).* "I'll talk with my boss and if he okays the terms, could we have the purchase order by month end?"
  - *Background suggestion (soft close).* "Our implementation team will be fully booked starting in September, so to complete your project by year end, we'll need to have the contract signed in the next couple of weeks."

- *Power of print.* This technique leverages a document or printed company policy.
  - *Command (hard close).* "Our new price list is coming out in thirty days, and I can't hold these current prices for you after that."
  - *Foreground suggestion (medium close).* "Here's our volume discount schedule. If you spend another $100,000, you'll receive an additional 10 percent off the entire order."
  - *Background suggestion (soft close).* "Should I send you a formal quotation that details the purchase price and terms?"

Maintain control of the sales call so you can employ your primary closing strategy and be prepared with fallback positions should your primary closing strategy fail. You can sequence your primary closing strategy and fallback positions with commands (hard close), foreground suggestions (medium close), and background suggestions (soft close). For example, your primary closing strategy might be based upon a hard close; first fallback position, a medium close; and final fallback position, a soft close. Or, your strategy could be completely opposite depending upon the circumstances and the type of person you are meeting with.

A study of B2B buyers shows which closing strategies are most effective from their point of view. Read the following scenario and then see how B2B buyers rated each closing strategy in figure 70.2.

You have been evaluating solutions from different vendors for the past three months. Based on your evaluation, you have a favorite solution but have not specifically told the salesperson who represents that product he is the winner. However, the salesperson knows his company is in a good position to win the business. It's approaching the end of the year, and that salesperson would like to close the deal. Please rate how effective each of the following statements would be on a scale of 1 (not effective) to 10 (very effective) in persuading you to buy from that salesperson.

A command or a hard close (statements 5, 6, 9) creates a binary type of yes or no response from the recipient. It is typically associated with a "take it or leave it" mentality. Foreground suggestions or a medium close (statements 1, 4, 8) are explicit, but they deflect the source of the request away from the demander. A background suggestion or a soft close (statements 2, 3, 7) lead buyers to believe they are acting of their free will when in fact they have been directed to follow a message.

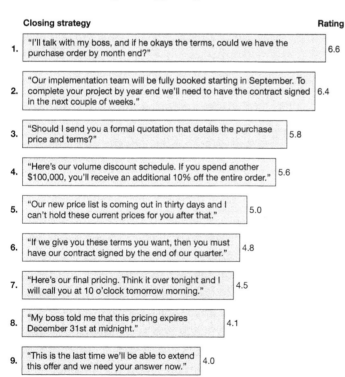

Closing strategy   **Rating**

1. "I'll talk with my boss, and if he okays the terms, could we have the purchase order by month end?"   6.6

2. "Our implementation team will be fully booked starting in September. To complete your project by year end we'll need to have the contract signed in the next couple of weeks."   6.4

3. "Should I send you a formal quotation that details the purchase price and terms?"   5.8

4. "Here's our volume discount schedule. If you spend another $100,000, you'll receive an additional 10% off the entire order."   5.6

5. "Our new price list is coming out in thirty days and I can't hold these current prices for you after that."   5.0

6. "If we give you these terms you want, then you must have our contract signed by the end of our quarter."   4.8

7. "Here's our final pricing. Think it over tonight and I will call you at 10 o'clock tomorrow morning."   4.5

8. "My boss told me that this pricing expires December 31st at midnight."   4.1

9. "This is the last time we'll be able to extend this offer and we need your answer now."   4.0

Figure. 70.2 Buyers rate closing strategy effectiveness

Chapter 71. Measuring Sales Call Success

Customers will have one of five different reactions to everything you say during a sales call. They will either reject your statements and ideas outright, ignore what you say, acknowledge they've heard you, accept what you say but do nothing, or internalize your recommendations and take action.

The reaction you receive is influenced by the level of rapport you have established with the prospective customer. Customers can experience many different types of receptive states with salespeople ranging from fear and hate to love and trust. A successful sales call is dependent upon establishing four different receptive states of rapport:

- *Personal receptive state.* The first priority is to build a personal receptive state with each individual. To accomplish this, perform a pattern interruption (see ch. 82), search for intersecting activities you might have in common (see ch. 52), and speak the customer's unique languages (see ch. 49).

- *Technical receptive state.* Take great care to build a technical receptive state through understanding the customer's problem. Qualify the customer's technical fit to the solution you offer. Provide the logical arguments that your solution can solve the customer's technical problem (see ch. 53).

- *Business receptive state.* As you demonstrate that your primary interest is in the customer's success, you begin to build a business receptive state. At this point, the customer starts to consider you as more than a vendor. You have proven your value as a business partner (see ch. 54) who has the expertise to solve the customer's problem.

- *Political receptive state.* You enjoy a political advantage over the competition when the customer believes that only your solution will help him fulfill his fantasies (see ch. 103) and achieve his personal benefactions (see ch. 101). You know you have established the political receptive state when the customer speaks the confidential language with you. The confidential language is the most powerful trust-based language by which the customer explains his personal needs, desires, and plans along with the strategy by which he hopes to fulfill them.

Complete rapport exists when these four receptive states are established. For example, synergistic sales calls are typically based upon complete rapport, whereas friendly sales calls may have only a personal or technical receptive state established.

Preplan how you will create a personal receptive state at the beginning of the sales call. As the sales call progresses, continuously monitor the level of rapport of each attendee and ask yourself if you are creating the four different receptive states: personal, technical, business, and political. These receptive states provide the positive environment that will enable your recommendations to be accepted and acted upon. Finally, be sure to prepare your colleagues who will join you on

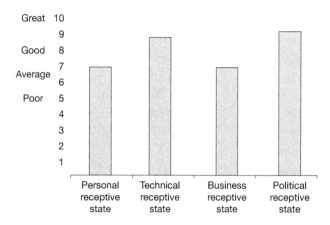

Figure 71.1 Rating sales call rapport

the sales call by helping them understand what type of sales call to expect (combative, contentious, unemotional, friendly, or synergistic).

After the sales call, rate how well you achieved each receptive state on a scale of 1 (low) to 10 (high). Graph the scores as shown in figure 71.1 (form available on www.stevewmartin.com /salesstrategyplaybookforms).

Exercise: Think about an important sales call you made recently and graph how well you achieved the personal, technical, business, and political receptive states. Now share your graph with your colleagues who attended the call with you to see if they have the same ratings.

Chapter 72. Buyer Personas Impact Decision-Making

The marketing and sales operations departments of many companies create buyer personas for the various titles of the buyers their salespeople must call on. Buyer personas provide practical messaging and information on how the salespeople should interact with the different people they meet with. Using the Laborsaver 3000 example from chapter 65, there might be buyer personas created for each executive level decision-maker (CEO, COO, CIO, CFO, and vice president of human resources), midlevel managers (director of operations, IT, finance, and HR), and lower-level technical evaluators such as HR analysts and IT project managers. The buyer persona is usually a single page or two in length and includes the following types of information:

- Elevator pitch to this type of person
- Challenges in engaging this type of person
- Industry pain
- Cause of pain
- Questions to ask
- Key messages
- Solution to propose
- Possible objections
- Business decision-maker benefit
- Technical decision-maker benefit
- Competitive differentiators
- Expected financial/operational results
- Customer successes
- Industry analyst proof points

Unfortunately, these buyer personas typically don't address the biases, personality tendencies, and political group dynamics that influence the final decision. Individuals will jockey for position to ensure their favorite vendor is selected, align themselves with more powerful coworkers for political gain, or stay out of the fray and refuse to take part in the decision. Buyer personas can be further detailed based upon the decision-makers' attributes and their different roles within the organization. This segmentation will help you formulate your sales cycle strategy and better understand where you win and why you lose. Equally important, it provides a blueprint for sales call execution.

> *The deals we win have certain similarities. You can spot them by the different types of people who are on the evaluation team.*
>
> — Top Salesperson

Tension, drama, and conflict are normal parts of group dynamics because typically any decision on what to do is not unanimous. Selection team members always feel an underlying tension because they are never 100 percent certain they are picking the right solution. Drama builds as the salespeople make their arguments and provide conflicting information to refute their competitors' claims. Interpersonal conflict between group members, as evidenced by disparaging remarks and criticisms, occurs whenever there is intense competition for a highly sought-after prize.

Beyond their formal titles and their positions on organization charts, people take on specific roles when they are part of a selection committee. Some assume roles they believe will enable them to take control of the group and steer the decision toward their preference. Others adopt new behavioral roles to deal with the tension, drama,

and conflict. You may not have realized it, but even your presence as a salesperson influences how customers act.

Selection committee members, ranging from the CEO to the lowest-level evaluator, will adopt four different decision-making roles during sales calls and sales presentations. These buyer persona roles are based upon information, character, authority, and company:

- *Information roles.* Information roles are based on the type of information people believe they should gather and the unique way in which they process and transmit information.

- *Character roles.* Character roles are based on the way people feel they should behave when they are part of a decision-making group.

- *Authority roles.* Authority roles are based on people's degree of command and their ability to dominate the group.

- *Company roles.* Company roles are based on the political power people wield and their personal disposition toward their company.

Figure 72.1 summarizes the four different categories of roles that prospects adopt during sales calls and presentations.

Information Roles	Character Roles	Authority Roles	Company Roles
Analytical	Comedian	Bureaucrat	Complainer
Believer	Dreamer	Dictator	Hired gun
Intellectual	Hothead	Empty suit	Integrator
Slacker	Maven	Old pro	Politician
Summary seeker	Optimist	Proctor	Pollyanna
	Schadenfreuder	Pundit	Revolutionary
	Straight shooter	Soldier	Vigilante

Figure 72.1 The four group buyer persona roles

In chapters 73–76, we'll introduce each of these roles. While it makes sense to determine the role of every person during sales calls, it is crucial to understand the roles of the key decision-makers. Ideally, you want to anticipate their behavior beforehand so you can use the right demeanor, create the right messages, and then deliver those messages in the way that they will be best received and understood.

In addition, you probably aren't going to attend all your sales calls alone. You might bring along your sales manager, vice president of sales, product marketing manager, professional services director, and even your CEO. Therefore, you need a common terminology to describe the customer to others. Segmenting sales calls by these roles will help you communicate your sales call strategy to colleagues and prepare them for the type of customer they are going to meet.

I work with people; I do not work with companies. Everything I do is individually tailored to that unique person who is sitting across the table from me.

—Top Salesperson

Chapter 73. Information Buyer Persona Roles

Every evaluator involved in the selection process has the responsibility to assess vendor information for accuracy and provide an opinion as to which solution is best. However, evaluators assume this duty with different levels of due diligence, ranging from focusing on minutiae to being big-picture oriented. They are classified as analytical, believer, intellectual, slacker, and summary seeker. Figure 73.1 shows research results on how evaluators classified their

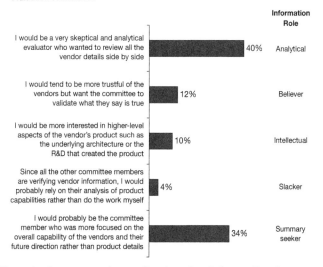

Let's say you are part of an evaluation committee that is selecting between vendors for a $2,500,000 purchase that will enable a very important company initiative. There are six different members on the committee from across different departments of the company. Therefore, this is a very political decision as committee members have vastly different points on which vendor should be selected. Thinking back about all the different decision-making teams you have been a part of, which role do you think you would take if you were on this evaluation committee?

	Information Role
I would be a very skeptical and analytical evaluator who wanted to review all the vendor details side by side	40% Analytical
I would tend to be more trustful of the vendors but want the committee to validate what they say is true	12% Believer
I would be more interested in higher-level aspects of the vendor's product such as the underlying architecture or the R&D that created the product	10% Intellectual
Since all the other committee members are verifying vendor information, I would probably rely on their analysis of product capabilities rather than do the work myself	4% Slacker
I would probably be the committee member who was more focused on the overall capability of the vendors and their future direction rather than product details	34% Summary seeker

Figure 73.1 B2B evaluator research results showing information buyer persona roles

information assessment style when part of a complex decision-making committee. It provides a guideline of what to expect the composition of an evaluation committee to be.

Analytical

Analyticals are full of doubt and have the highest levels of skepticism. They verify every statement made by a salesperson, and they want to validate every piece of information. Therefore, analyticals immerse themselves in features, functions, and specifications. They take their role as information gatherer very seriously and do not want to be embarrassed by missed details.

Customers with advanced degrees in the sciences (computers, mathematics, engineering, etc.) are more likely to be analyticals. This should not be a surprise since they've had years of systematic education followed by a business career that was heavily focused on scientific methods and data analysis.

When meeting with an analytical, do not go on the call without someone on your side who has commensurate technical or industry knowledge. You have only one chance to make a great first impression, and being unable to satisfy the customer's analytical mind will be the death knell of the meeting.

However, your overriding objective should not be to let technology talk or deep discussions about minutiae dominate the entire meeting. Rather, you must keep the meeting on track and drive the agenda to reach your desired outcome for the call. Never let your own technical team hijack the meeting and take control. They should know in advance that they are there under your direction.

Believer

You will meet some believers who unquestioningly accept your information at face value. In some cases, this is because it requires a vendor's product to make the project that the person is so emotionally committed to become a reality. The project might be his brainchild or a determining factor in his career progression (or whether or not he keeps his job). Therefore, there is a tendency to believe vendors and promote them internally.

In other cases a customer is a believer because he is not well versed in working with salespeople or buying products. It might be early in his career, or he might be new to the management role or the company. Believers don't know what questions to ask or how to make a major procurement within their own company. If this is the case, you must adopt a different familial role with them than when working with an analytical. You need to mentor them through the process like a father explaining to his adult son how to fill out his tax forms or an older brother explaining to his younger sibling the criteria that should be used when selecting a college.

Believers have the propensity to be found in certain departments. For example, the vice president of human resources, chief talent officer, or chief learning officer are wired quite differently than the CFO, CEO, and CIO. They're usually not as adept at dealing with salespeople. Since they might not wield much organizational power, they often don't know how to make large purchases happen. When the senior-most leader in the deal is a believer, there is a higher likelihood that no purchase will ever be made. Therefore, the sales strategy has to take this into account and you must "help" the believer sell internally.

Intellectual

When it comes to details, an intellectual is the opposite of an analytical. Intellectuals are more interested in the general, theoretical, and philosophical aspects of products. Intellectuals approach the gathering of information in a cerebral, professorial way. They are open to learning and seek personal enlightenment. For example, an analytical might want a side-by-side checklist comparison of a product's features, whereas an intellectual would be more interested in the product's underlying architecture and why it was made in the first place.

Be forewarned about intellectuals. You're going to think a meeting with them went great because the topic of conversation was at the 30,000-foot level. Usually, meetings with intellectuals end on a positive note and with everyone involved feeling good. That's the style of intellectuals. They're not typically going to confront you and devalue your solution in person. For them, every meeting is a learning experience.

Later, intellectuals will let their department members sift through the details. You should anticipate that this team will find technical objections and a variety of other reasons why your solution won't work for them. Therefore, you must continually be selling at all levels of the organization if you suspect the C-level executive is an intellectual. Solely executing a top-down sales strategy will most likely fail.

Slacker

Slacker customers tend to conduct a low level of due diligence and a cursory verification of the information that is presented to them. They are generalists who aren't fixated on details like analyticals nor are they all that concerned with them in some cases. Slackers don't know, don't care about, or will mistakenly ignore important information. In addition, they will deny that they know anything when asked tough questions by salespeople.

Slackers are typically found in very large companies with immense bureaucracies where one department has no clue what another is doing. While slackers are rare, you might run into one in federal, state, and local government accounts or monolithic industries such as automobile and insurance. The single most important question to ask yourself when you meet a slacker is, Does this decision-maker have the wherewithal to make a purchase? Nine times out of ten the answer will be no.

Summary Seeker

A summary seeker is a curious person who is more concerned with the big picture than small details. Summary seekers quickly grasp complex subjects and tend to make snap decisions about the relevance of information. They are typically more trusting than analyticals but less patient than intellectuals. Heavy Hitter salespeople love to sell to summary seekers.

It's not surprising that the majority of C-level executives are summary seekers because they are extremely busy. The nature of running a department or company means they have to manage down to employees, out to customers, and up to even more important executives and the board. Therefore, they don't have the time or mental bandwidth to process tons of detailed information. That's why important facts, risk assessments, value judgments, and the rewards of moving forward with the purchase should be summarized and presented to them in a succinct manner that is easily understood.

Identifying information roles helps you understand whether to present a high-level summary to a summary seeker or be prepared to dive into the details with an analytical. If the latter is the case, you know that you must bring along your colleagues who have a commensurate industry background and technical expertise. The types of information gatherers you call on vary by industry.

Analyticals are more common in the semiconductor business because of the technical nature of designing and manufacturing computer chips. There are far more summary seekers in the advertising industry, and this makes sense because people tend to make quick decisions on ads based upon first impressions. Over time, your goal should be to develop the specific breakdown of information role types for customers you call on for the industry you're in. For example, you should know that 55 percent of your sales calls are with analyticals, 25 percent with summary seekers, and 20 percent with intellectuals.

Chapter 74. Character Buyer Persona Roles

Just as people change their behavior whenever they are in groups, evaluators adopt new character traits depending upon which of their colleagues are participating with them on the sales call. They will behave quite differently in front of fellow employees than when they are alone with you. Here are the most common character roles that evaluators assume. They are classified as comedian, dreamer, hothead, maven, optimist, schadenfreuder, and straight shooter. Figure 74.1 shows research results on how evaluators classified their character traits when part of a complex decision-making committee. It provides a guideline of what to expect the composition of an evaluation committee to be.

Comedian

Comedian customers thrive on being the center of attention and always seem to have a smart remark or joke handy. While a psychiatrist might say the comedian's disruptions are driven by thoughts of inadequacy, this character role serves an important selection-process function: the comedian's silliness releases the evaluation team's pent-up stress.

Be careful when you meet with comedians. Since they are so friendly and jovial, it is easy to be lulled into a false sense of security and take their word at face value. Moreover, when evaluators become comedians, they are attempting to remove themselves from the stressful position of being the final selector and dissociate themselves from the decision.

Dreamer

Whether they have a momentary daydream about a vacation to a tropical destination or a fantasy about marriage that has been fostered since childhood, people love to dream about the future. Some dreamers are fixated on one goal, while others long for just about everything.

During sales calls and the selection process, dreamers tend to fall in love quickly with a particular salesperson or the solution they believe will help them realize their fantasy soonest. However, they are impulsive buyers who suffer from immense mood swings, which can cause them to second-guess their initial selection and frequently change their minds.

As opposed to the comedian, dreamers are salespeople's dreams come true. Their main motivation is usually based upon satisfying their ego, and that's a powerful purchase driver. In a perfect world you want your dreamer to also be a powerful customer—someone who can make the grand initiative happen because he is the bully with the juice or the emperor (see ch. 36). However, you should be extremely skeptical of dreamers because they will talk the big talk but in reality are frequently duds.

Hothead

You definitely know when you meet with hotheads. They are impatient people with very short tempers. Sometimes hotheads explode during the sales call and publicly berate their own employees and colleagues. Worse is when they are

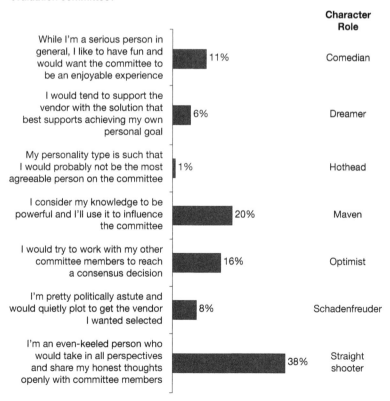

Let's say you are part of an evaluation committee that is selecting between vendors for a $2,500,000 purchase that will enable a very important company initiative. There are six different members on the committee from across different departments of the company. Therefore, this is a very political decision as committee members have vastly different points on which vendor should be selected. Thinking back about all the different decision-making teams you have been a part of, which role do you think you would take if you were on this evaluation committee?

Statement	Percent	Character Role
While I'm a serious person in general, I like to have fun and would want the committee to be an enjoyable experience	11%	Comedian
I would tend to support the vendor with the solution that best supports achieving my own personal goal	6%	Dreamer
My personality type is such that I would probably not be the most agreeable person on the committee	1%	Hothead
I consider my knowledge to be powerful and I'll use it to influence the committee	20%	Maven
I would try to work with my other committee members to reach a consensus decision	16%	Optimist
I'm pretty politically astute and would quietly plot to get the vendor I wanted selected	8%	Schadenfreuder
I'm an even-keeled person who would take in all perspectives and share my honest thoughts openly with committee members	38%	Straight shooter

Figure 74.1 B2B evaluator research results showing character buyer persona roles

combative and condescending to you. Hotheads don't like to meet with salespeople, so they verbally abuse them in front of their staffs! The best way to handle this intentional act of humiliation is to maintain your composure as best you can and not take the attack personally. I have found that many company founders happen to be hotheads. They are used to barking orders and getting their way through domination.

Maven

The goal of maven customers is to use the selection process to demonstrate their knowledge and intelligence to others. They're smart and they know it. Quite often, mavens are fascinated by electronic gadgets and own the latest technologies. They may adorn their bodies with these precious objects in an expression of prowess. They typically won't listen to the opinions of others or accept personal criticism because they already know exactly what's best. Therefore, you won't win arguments with mavens. Selling to them requires an indirect psychological sales strategy as they will not be swayed by any vendor's logic or reason.

You must sell to a maven's ego. At every opportunity elicit his feedback, not so much for its own merits but so your maven can hear himself talk about your solution. Bring the specialists within your company to your meeting—technical gurus, product managers, and various members of the executive staff. Invite mavens to participate on customer advisory boards or provide feedback on internal product specification reviews. If you treat the maven with the respect he deserves, you'll find out he isn't such a tough person to sell to after all.

Optimist

Some evaluators feel compelled to befriend everybody, including all the salespeople from the various companies who are calling on the account. Optimists dislike confrontation and feel very uncomfortable knowing that someone is at odds with them. Therefore, the information they provide must always be discounted because it is being given for the sole purpose of pleasing the questioner and may not be the actual truth. Optimists will be amenable to any decision because they always go along with the group.

Personally, I don't like to sell to optimists. I want to know where I stand in an account. I want to know the answer to the most important question in all of sales: "Will I win the deal?" Tell me the truth as soon as possible so I don't waste my precious time. I don't want prospective customers to tell me what they think I want to hear. I want the truth, and so should you.

Schadenfreuder

Some people take delight in the failure and misfortune of others. This delight is called "schadenfreude." While a hothead wears his emotions on his sleeve and might explode in rage, a schadenfreuder plots quietly behind the scenes. While a hothead is searching for the best solution and actually plans on buying something, quite often the schadenfreuder never intended to buy from you in the first place. It is all a game to him and he delights in tormenting salespeople. The most extreme schadenfreuders are misanthropes—they hate people.

Schadenfreuders can be truly evil, and at the end of your encounter you will have psychological scars to prove it. Sometimes they present just enough optimistic information to keep you engaged when they really have no intention of buying your product. They'll entice you with claims of big purchases that are just off in the horizon. I remember attending a meeting with one of my salespeople who called on a schadenfreuder CTO. At one point the CTO asked the junior salesperson how he was going to spend all the commission he was going to make off the sale, but the CTO never intended to buy. It was an obnoxious trick question that infuriated me. You must exercise self-respect and walk away from the schadenfreuder's account.

Straight Shooter

Straight shooters have a strong sense of honor and integrity. They are not alarmists but usually even-keeled evaluators who will listen to what each salesperson has to say. Heavy Hitters love selling to straight shooters. Straight shooters are sincerely interested in finding the best solution for the people who will implement and use it. They work together with their colleagues toward a common goal and vision. They are open-minded, they listen to others' opinions, and they take pride that they are part of the team.

The best way to sell to a straight shooter is to become one yourself. While an aggressive, high-energy strategy might be appropriate in certain sales situations, mirroring the straight shooter's behavior is an equally effective strategy. Every communication with him should be

structured and well documented. Don't fudge on the truth; give definitive truthful answers to his questions.

Consciously slow down your speech, breathing, and mannerisms from your normal hyperactive pace. The straight shooter's orientation is long-term, and you will probably not be able to accelerate the selection process. The evaluation process will be well thought out and lengthy. The winner will be the last vendor standing, the one who exhibited the attributes necessary to satisfy the straight shooter. In essence, the sales cycle is a miniature dry run of the long-term relationship.

Knowing the character roles informs you how to act in their presence. You adopt a "tell it like it is" demeanor with a straight shooter, carefully select your words with a hothead, and foster the fantasies of dreamers. You should not believe the schadenfreuder's claim that there is a big deal to be won, and you should expect the optimist to give your competition the same compliments that were given to you. Mavens and comedians narcissistically believe themselves to be uniquely special, so treat them as the center of attention.

Chapter 75. Authority Buyer Persona Roles

People's authority does not always correlate to how long they have worked for their company or have been employed in their profession. In reality, selection committee members adopt authority roles in order to influence their colleagues and the decision outcome. They are classified as bureaucrat, dictator, empty suit, old pro, proctor, pundit, and soldier. Figure 75.1 shows research results on how evaluators classified their information authority when part of a complex decision-making committee. It provides a guideline of what to expect the composition of an evaluation committee to be.

Bureaucrat

Bureaucrats are focused on selection processes and procedures. However, they will use the selection processes for their selfish gain or to exercise their political power. Many bureaucrats are consumed with maintaining the status quo. Most frequently, the best way to prevent change is to stop the purchase process entirely, so that is what bureaucrat customers often try to do.

A sales call with a bureaucrat can be extremely frustrating for two reasons. First, he may use a variety of tactics to dominate you. For instance, he knows that salespeople tend to lack patience and attention to detail and don't like forms and paperwork. He'll purposely exploit these weaknesses to protect himself and his company.

The second reason has to do with how the bureaucrat behaves during the meeting with you. The meeting with the bureaucrat may have been arranged by an underling (midlevel or low-level

Let's say you are part of an evaluation committee that is selecting between vendors for a $2,500,000 purchase that will enable a very important company initiative. There are six different members on the committee from across different departments of the company. Therefore, this is a very political decision as committee members have vastly different points on which vendor should be selected. Thinking back about all the different decision-making teams you have been a part of, which role do you think you would take if you were on this evaluation committee?

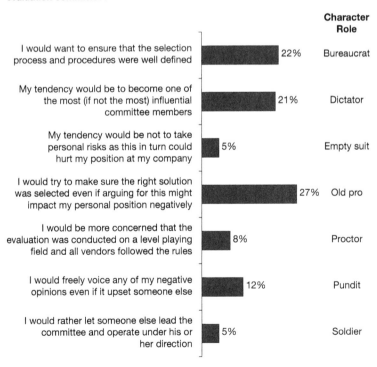

	Character Role
I would want to ensure that the selection process and procedures were well defined	22% Bureaucrat
My tendency would be to become one of the most (if not the most) influential committee members	21% Dictator
My tendency would be not to take personal risks as this in turn could hurt my position at my company	5% Empty suit
I would try to make sure the right solution was selected even if arguing for this might impact my personal position negatively	27% Old pro
I would be more concerned that the evaluation was conducted on a level playing field and all vendors followed the rules	8% Proctor
I would freely voice any of my negative opinions even if it upset someone else	12% Pundit
I would rather let someone else lead the committee and operate under his or her direction	5% Soldier

Figure 75.1 B2B evaluator research results showing authority buyer persona roles

person) who enthusiastically supports you and your solution. Because he has been championing your cause internally, you are optimistic about your chances of winning the business. However, when you meet the bureaucrat you quickly realize that a purchase will never happen or that the bureaucrat has other ideas about whom the company should do business with. After months of time and effort, all the hopes you had to win the account are gone. This is why you must meet with C-level decision-makers early in the sales cycle.

Dictator

Dictator customers are focused on decreeing the company's direction. Whereas a comedian uses humor to keep himself in the spotlight, dictators use unrelenting power to maintain their prominence. These domineering taskmasters are usually interested only in immediate results, what your solution has to offer here and now.

Even if an evaluation team has been assembled under the guise of making an impartial selection, the dictator rules its members through oppression, intimidation, or fear. Most dictators are narcissists (preoccupied admirers of themselves). However, they are typically very polished executives. They don't necessarily broadcast their power or goose-step around the office like a fascist ruler, but they rule their obedient masses with the same ruthlessness. When you shake the hand of a dictator, you are usually shaking the hand of the bully with the juice.

Empty Suit

If you are unsure whether or not the customer you are working with actually

has the ability to make a purchase, you are probably selling to an empty suit. He may not have the political clout or authority to buy. Therefore, you have to make a calculated decision on whether or not to pursue the business and always try to spread yourself out and meet others within the organization.

Worse yet is when someone says he has buying authority but he doesn't. In extremely large organizations, empty-suit customers protect themselves by hiding behind inflated job titles that are not justified by their experience, knowledge, or ability to lead. While empty suits may be charming and gregarious individuals, they have misconceptions about their own strengths and how the organization views them.

Empty suits are mainly preoccupied with keeping their jobs, and this can result in two different behaviors. They can be motivated to find a vendor partner to help them gain power, or they can be extremely hesitant to move a purchase forward or to ruffle the feathers of others within the organization. An empty suit will typically make a great impression on the first sales call. However, each subsequent meeting becomes more frustrating if you realize you are wasting your time.

Old Pro

Old pro customers are case-hardened evaluators who have years of experience working with vendors. They are experts at managing the selection process, they know what to expect from the vendors, and they command respect. You don't exaggerate to an old pro because you'll be called on it every time. Even though the old pro's demeanor may be gruff and cantankerous or seem unapproachable, deep inside is an individual who seeks friendships. Heavy Hitters love to sell to old pros. The key is finding an intersecting activity you have in common and selling yourself to them by establishing a trusting familial relationship.

Proctor

In the academic world, proctors oversee the administration of tests to ensure that none of the students cheat. The business world has proctors whose sole purpose, so it seems, is to ensure that the selection process is followed to the letter.

Whereas a bureaucrat is motivated to stop the purchase decision, a proctor seems more concerned about following the rules of the selection process than the actual selection itself. For example, a purchasing manager who is a proctor will punish vendors who violate the selection process. This obviously creates a challenge because your goal is to implement a strategy that changes the selection process to your benefit. Therefore, you must either be in the account first and attempt to set the rules with the proctor or develop rapport with another higher-level executive, an old pro for instance, so that he can override the proctor.

Pundit

Every group has a pundit—a person who feels compelled to continually parade his or her opinions. On selection committees, these constant critics are the equivalent of a backseat driver. They assail other committee members, find fault with the direction they are taking, and attack vendors with a barrage of criticism.

Pundits will authoritatively pass judgment on you and your solution in your

presence to throw you off track. They'll say things right in front of you like "That will never work for us" or "Your competition is better." These assaults are pundits' self-defense mechanism for avoiding a relationship with you (because they favor another competitor) or dissociating themselves from their decision-making responsibilities. Never forget, one of a customer's most prized possessions is his opinion.

Soldier

Corporate soldiers are paid to perform their jobs without question. Soldier customers have the lowest level of power and will dutifully follow orders passed down the chain of command. The soldier's mantra is "Ours is not to question why; ours is but to do or die."

When the CIO tells the IT director what company to do business with, the IT director becomes a soldier who has just received his marching orders. This is why you should always sell at the highest possible level in every account because you want to meet the person issuing the orders, not executing them.

Recognizing the authority roles will provide insight into sales calls during the decision-making process. Is the customer a dictator who will bully the selection committee? Is he a proctor who is more concerned about the rules of the selection than the selection itself? Is he an empty suit who lacks the wherewithal to make any decision at all? Customers' words and actions during sales calls will reveal who they are and what action you should take next.

Chapter 76. Company Buyer Persona Roles

People's titles tell only part of the story about their role within a company. In the business world, selection-committee members take on additional company roles beyond their position on the organization chart. These roles show their true political power and their personal disposition toward their company. They are classified as complainer, hired gun, integrator, politician, Pollyanna, revolutionary, and vigilante. Figure 76.1 shows research results on how evaluators classified their company role when part of a complex decision-making committee. It provides a guideline of what to expect

the composition of an evaluation committee to be.

Complainer

Complainers are rebels who are dissatisfied with their personal predicament inside the company. Because of this, they might clandestinely plan to undermine the decision-making process. In the business world, complainers feel cheated by their company in some way. They might believe they are not receiving the recognition and respect they deserve.

Frequently, complainers are out to prove themselves better than someone else at their company or to prove that their department is the best in the company. They'll purchase products not only

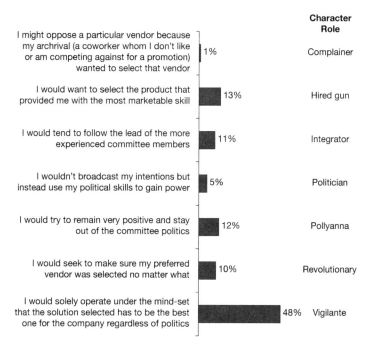

Let's say you are part of an evaluation committee that is selecting between vendors for a $2,500,000 purchase that will enable a very important company initiative. There are six different members on the committee from across different departments of the company. Therefore, this is a very political decision as committee members have vastly different points on which vendor should be selected. Thinking back about all the different decision-making teams you have been a part of, which role do you think you would take if you were on this evaluation committee?

Character Role

I might oppose a particular vendor because my archrival (a coworker whom I don't like or am competing against for a promotion) wanted to select that vendor	1%	Complainer
I would want to select the product that provided me with the most marketable skill	13%	Hired gun
I would tend to follow the lead of the more experienced committee members	11%	Integrator
I wouldn't broadcast my intentions but instead use my political skills to gain power	5%	Politician
I would try to remain very positive and stay out of the committee politics	12%	Pollyanna
I would seek to make sure my preferred vendor was selected no matter what	10%	Revolutionary
I would solely operate under the mind-set that the solution selected has to be the best one for the company regardless of politics	48%	Vigilante

Figure 76.1 B2B evaluator research results showing company buyer persona roles

to further their cause but to undermine the success, power, and authority of others inside the company. During the sales cycle, they will frequently identify with and relate to a salesperson more than to their own coworkers. It is actually best to meet with a complainer alone so that he will share his secret plans with you.

Hired Gun

Hired guns are corporate expatriates. They are not emotionally invested in their jobs or completely committed to the company they work for. They tend to select products they believe will help them get their next job. The motto of a hired gun is "There is no such thing as a bad product if it helps you get your next job." Hired guns are market-share sensitive. They like to do business with gorillas, the dominant players in the market. Therefore, if you sell for a chimp-sized company, you are in an extremely dangerous position when the bully with the juice is a hired gun.

Integrator

Integrators are collaboration-oriented people who are ingrained within their organization. These knowledgeable corporate citizens listen to and respect authority. Therefore, they tend to "play by the rules." They have an understanding and appreciation for how their department fits within the company. They're up to date on the latest company and organizational announcements and news. Usually, they've worked at their company for some time but can be new employees as well.

They are problem solvers who work well in group settings. These team players are very supportive of their company's purpose. They do tend to avoid conflict and don't engage in win-or-lose interactions with coworkers. As a result, they have good internal relationships and will informally mediate disputes when they arise between coworkers. That's not to say they don't have their own opinions on how things should be done, they just moderate themselves to conform to their environment.

Politician

Politicians in a company are smooth schemers who opportunistically maneuver to hold onto or gain power within the organization. They speak with carefully selected words and try to display a professional demeanor at all times. It's not surprising that most higher-level executives are politicians because it requires political acumen to make it to the top.

Politicians are the influential statesmen of companies. They are experienced in dealing with company issues, know how to make things happen, and get their way in the process. They're more polished than complainers. They hold their cards close to their chest and won't broadcast their intentions until you have proven that it is in their political interest to do so.

Pollyanna

Pollyannas believe the company they work for is the best, whether it is or not. Usually, they absolutely love their jobs and find good in everyone and everything. Typically, these overly optimistic customers are hard workers and may have spent their entire careers at one or two companies.

Pollyannas have a tendency to ignore ugly facts and underestimate the complexity of the solutions they purchase. They are genuinely excited about the upcoming purchase, and Heavy Hitters are grateful for their naiveté. Obviously, it makes sense for salespeople to mirror their excitement and enthusiasm.

Revolutionary

Revolutionaries are out to create upheaval in their organization. They are agents of change who seek to remake the company's culture, its mind-set, or the way it does business.

As opposed to complainers, revolutionaries have sincere motives and want the company to succeed. For example, they might be trying to change a technology-driven company to a customer-focused one, to reinvigorate company morale, or to enter new markets. They seek solutions that will help them accomplish their revolution. Whenever a new executive joins a company, he becomes a revolutionary who seeks to consolidate his power by creating grand initiatives. That's why you should always keep track of executives on the move and be the first salesperson to meet with them in their new job.

Vigilante

Company vigilantes are skeptical buyers who want to protect their company from the claims of vendors. At the extreme, they are eternal naysayers, out to prove that none of the vendors' proposed solutions will work for their company. Vigilantes see their right to voice their opinion as a sacred trust. They take the

decision-making process very seriously and vote for the product they believe adds the most value to the company's day-to-day operations and long-term strategy.

Vigilantes do not trust salespeople. Their trust has to be earned. They'll make every vendor respond to immense RFPs and complete laborious spreadsheets—each product feature and operation has to be fully documented to prove it exists. They'll require meticulous hands-on evaluations of each product and painstakingly documented findings. They won't buy until they are completely satisfied, and when they meet with salespeople, they can be cross-examiners as opposed to collaborators who are trying to make the relationship work out.

Who's the Most Influential Committee Member?

A key objective of the buyer persona research was to understand who would take a vocal role in arguing for their preferred outcome and their ability to sway the final decision of the committee. Based on the results, the most vocal member of the committee (revolutionary) is one of the least influential in the ability to sway the final decision as shown in figure 76.2. Conversely, the most influential member

	Vocal role and argue for their outcome	Ability to sway committee decision	Overall Ranking
I would be upset with the individuals on the committee who were promoting a decision that impacted me negatively	6. 52%	6. 47%	6. Complainer
I would want the committee to make a decision that made performing my role easier	7. 44%	7. 40%	7. Hired Gun
I would listen to the recommendations of the more senior committee members	2. 77%	2. 71%	2. Integrator
I would use my political skills to make sure the decision I wanted was selected	4. 62%	3. 63%	3. Politician
I would maintain a positive outlook and participate in the decision-making process	5. 53%	5. 49%	5. Pollyanna
I would seek to make sure my preferred outcome was selected no matter what	1. 81%	4. 50%	4. Revolutionary
I would put my personal situation aside and make sure the decision made was best for the company	3. 74%	1. 74%	1. Vigilante

Figure 76.2 Most influential evaluators

(vigilante) is the least self-centered. He would put his personal situation aside to make sure the best decision was made for the company. This unbiased person is trying to find the right solution.

The least influential and vocal committee members (complainer and hired gun) are the ones who are fixated on themselves. It's interesting that the second most influential member (integrator) would listen to the more senior committee members. Based on these results, the most influential committee members will operate in the best interest of their company, listen to and respect authority, and use their political skills to influence outcomes.

Identify company roles so you can understand how much influence each evaluator has and what his buying motivations are. A hired gun wants to be reassured that selecting your solution will selfishly help his career, while a revolutionary wants to know that you are equally committed to the cause he is fighting for. Don't be misled by the Pollyanna's optimism or discouraged by the vigilante's pessimism. Expect the complainer to quickly open up to you and complain about his personal situation, while a politician will not confide in you until he feels it's safe.

Chapter 77. Applying Buyer Persona Roles

During sales calls and the selection process as a whole, the role each team member adopts will depend on the roles other members of the decision process occupy. For example, there typically can be only one dictator at a time. Selection team members have to assume other roles once these roles are taken. Conversely, a team can have multiple pundits, schadenfreuders, and analyticals. People assuming these roles actually encourage other selection team members to join them.

The roles people take on during the sales cycle determine how you will communicate with them. Most interestingly, these roles can vary from purchase to purchase. For example, a CIO who has a vested interest in the internet provider his company uses to run its business might be an analytical during the selection process. Conversely, he's a slacker when it comes to the purchase of toner cartridges because he doesn't care.

Perhaps the most important aspect of customer role-playing to remember is that customers do not play the same role with each vendor. For example, an evaluator might present himself as a schadenfreuder and vigilante to you while being a straight shooter and politician with your competitor. Under these circumstances, you will not win this deal. Therefore, you must evaluate not only how selection-team members are relating to you but, equally important, theorize how they are relating to your competitors.

How do you communicate with a person you have never met before? How do you best present your story, and what demeanor should you use to persuade him to speak in confidence with you? These roles help us understand evaluators' dispositions and motivations and the granularity of the information you should present. Why should you segment sales calls by the different customer decision-making roles? Because it will help you strategize, plan, and execute

Information role	Helps determine how you will present information and who should attend the customer sales call
Character role	Prepares your colleagues for the unique group dynamics of the customer's meeting
Authority role	Provides insight into the customer's decision-making process
Company role	Explains the customer's ulterior motives, how he perceives himself, and his power within the company

Figure 77.1 Purpose of determining customer decision-making roles

your sales call. Figure 77.1 summarizes the purpose of each buyer persona role.

Some group decision-making combinations are dangerous and unpredictable. Be extremely cautious when meeting customers who are hothead dictators, schadenfreuder bureaucrats, and proctor vigilantes. One bad move during sales calls with these customers and the account is lost. Conversely, believer optimists and empty-suit Pollyannas are extremely bad combinations for another reason. The likelihood that these customers can make a major purchase happen is infinitesimal.

For the purposes of applying group decision-making roles, let's pretend we are part of the sales team working on the Acme account, a Fortune 1000 company that is making a million-dollar purchase of state-of-the-art business software to replace its existing antiquated mainframe software. The Acme decision-making team is composed of Bob Adams, chief information officer; Nancy Smith, director of information technology; Mitch Jackson, project leader;

and Mortimer Jones, vice president of purchasing. They are evaluating different enterprise software solutions.

Since the initiative to replace the mainframe software was championed by Bob, we surmise he is the emperor. Therefore, our sales strategy must include sales calls with Bob. This is also a persuasion sales cycle type (see ch. 16) because it has a well-defined selection process and has issued an RFP, and we know we are competing against our two archrivals. We know there is a 30 percent chance the team already has a favored vendor who will win the deal. Therefore, we need to determine if biases exist and build relationships at all levels as soon as possible in order to develop a coach.

Next, we make our assessment and categorize buyer persona roles of the Acme evaluators as represented in figure 77.2.

Bob's a seasoned executive with the business skills and political acumen to lead the organization. Nancy has worked

	Information Role	Character Role	Authority Role	Company Role
Bob Adams CIO	Summary seeker	Straight shooter	Old pro	Politician
Nancy Smith IT Director	Intellectual	Maven	Soldier	Pollyanna
Mitch Jackson Project Leader	Analytical	Maven	Pundit	Hired gun
Mortimer Jones VP of Purchasing	Analytical	Hothead	Bureaucrat	Vigilante

Figure 77.2 Buyer persona decision-making roles for Acme's evaluation team members

for Bob for seven years and is a maven who understands the details of the daily operations of the department. She's an optimistic soldier who marches to Bob's orders. Mitch is an accomplished technical expert. He's a cocky pundit who has little loyalty to the company. Mortimer is a hard-to-get-along-with numbers guy.

We theorize and prioritize the kinds of stress each person is under. Bob is mainly under corporate citizenship stress. He's worried about cutting costs during tough economic times. Nancy is under pressure from Bob. Bob has mandated that she cut her budget by 30 percent this year. She's worried about how Bob perceives her. Mitch is an analytical who wants to understand every technical detail, so he makes sure they are selecting the product with the best functionality. He suffers from informational stress. Mortimer is consumed with corporate citizenship stress. He's an analytical who wants all aspects of the business relationship documented in the contract. He believes he is the company's fiscal watchdog.

All of the evaluators have different motivations based upon their company roles. As a result, their perceptions of our solution's strategic, operational, political, and psychological value (see ch. 40) will be different. Here are the different values we provide Bob:

- Our strategic value is that we are the most cost-effective solution and provide the best return on investment.

- Our operational value has many aspects: we automate a number of functions that employees currently do by hand, our system is faster so they will be able to process orders

faster, and the software has more functionality so user satisfaction will increase.

- From a political standpoint, our state-of-the-art graphical user interface will help improve the image of the IT department within the company.

- From a psychological standpoint, Bob's been worried about the old system for years, ever fearful that it will crash at critical times of the month and year. Our system will bring him much-needed peace of mind.

Buyer personas enable you to theorize about the people you will be meeting so you can plan your sales call accordingly. You should also adapt your strategy and selling style to match the information, character, authority, and company roles of the person you are meeting with. Prepare yourself with facts and specifications in anticipation of meeting the analytical. Massage the maven's ego during the call. Tell it like it is and don't fudge the truth when meeting with an old pro. Support the revolutionary's goal to become the organization's change agent.

Every sale is different because there is always a different cast of characters. I map out everyone in the account. I want to know how they think and what they think about me, my competition, and each other. The technology guys can love you and the business guys hate you or vice versa. The most difficult part of the sale is understanding what motivates someone and building all the different relationships so you can manage the account.

—Top Salesperson

Chapter 78. Negotiation Strategy

Most salespeople learn how to negotiate through the school of hard knocks by trial and error. However, the negotia-

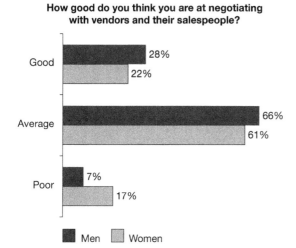

How good do you think you are at negotiating with vendors and their salespeople?

Figure 78.1 Buyers rate their negotiation skills

tion session is one of the most complex and least understood types of customer meetings. While it's a good idea to prepare as if the person you'll be negotiating with is an experienced expert, the reality is that only about one in four buyers consider themselves to be good negotiators as shown in figure 78.1. Therefore, don't always assume the buyer has better skills and more knowledge because their negotiation strategy is based on the illusion of control.

Negotiation Classifications

While every negotiation is unique, negotiations can be classified by the demeanor of the participants as combative, contentious, unemotional, friendly,

and synergistic as shown in figure 78.2. Combative negotiations are antagonistic interactions with nonexistent rapport. Usually, this type of negotiation occurs when the evaluators hand over the negotiation duties to procurement or legal personnel who don't have any personal attachments to the evaluation process. In general, purchasing agents and lawyers have pre-existing biases against salespeople and vendors, and this influences their negotiation style. Furthermore, there's quite a difference between how procurement, sourcing, and supply chain personnel negotiators think of vendors. While all are measured by the money they save their company, sourcing and supply chain think in terms of win-win vendor relationships (see ch. 28).

Contentious negotiations may begin congenially but are characterized by controversy or a dispute on a major topic that leads to bad feelings by the end of the meeting. In this situation, the deal is at extreme risk and in jeopardy. Unemotional negotiations lack outward displays

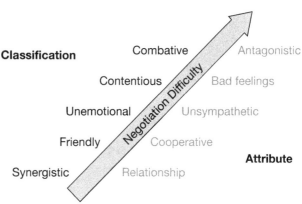

Figure 78.2 Negotiation classifications and attributes

of emotion, and even though the meeting could last an hour, the negotiator remains aloof and unsympathetically distant. This is also one of the characteristics of smaller point-specific deals where the buyer is going through the motions in one sense because it's just another day in the office.

Negotiators classified as friendly are generally receptive, cooperative, and open to your ideas. In synergistic negotiations, there is a genuine excitement to move forward on the part of both parties, and the negotiation serves to deepen the relationship between companies. This is frequently the case with many large enterprise purchases. Synergistic and combative sales calls are at the extreme ends of the scale of mutual trust and receptive states (see ch. 71).

Negotiation Variables, Timing, and Order

Negotiation variables include price, terms of purchase, and the contract language that will govern the relationship. Each of these variables is interrelated with the others. For example, you may wish to drop your price in exchange for quicker payment terms or using your contract instead of the customer's. You may change the terms of purchase, such as the deposit and milestone payments, depending upon the price the customer will pay.

Because legal terminology is such a highly specialized form of technical specification language, it's generally outside the salesperson's scope of negotiations. However, it's very important that salespeople understand the most frequently cited objections to their company's

contract, such as acceptance clauses, the definition of users, or uptime guarantees. It's the salesperson's responsibility to position these topics early in the sales cycle in order to find out if legal issues will prevent the deal from closing.

Determining the right time to negotiate can be a complex decision. Here's some general rules of thumb. With persuasion sales cycles (RFP types of evaluations as described in chapter 16), you want to postpone the negotiation and provide your final price as late as possible, after the final winner has been publicly announced. With creation sales cycles (hypothesis-based "we can help you" deals as described in chapter 16), the opposite is true. You want to pull forward the negotiation and final pricing as far as possible so this unplanned budgetary expense is budgeted and there is adequate time for it to be approved.

The customer will have his or her agenda and list of demands and objections. Some issues will be minor and easily resolved, while others will be major and hard to settle. You should enter the negotiation with the full expectation that you will reach an agreement and the

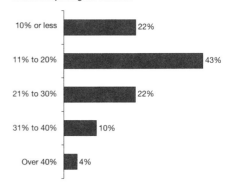

Figure 78.3 Price increase sensitivity of buyers

prospect will become a customer shortly. Therefore, it's usually best to work through the issues starting from easiest to most difficult. Furthermore, if you get stuck on one of the minor issues, push it off to the end. Keep your momentum.

What's the Right Discount?

Deciding on how much to discount your product can be a tricky proposition because buyers have different sensitivities about the price they are willing to pay. For example, a study of buyers found that they fall into different price-increase categories as shown in figure 78.3. Twenty-two percent would switch to another product when maintenance and support fees increased up to 10 percent, 43 percent would switch if fees increased between 11 to 20 percent, and 22 percent if fees increased 21 to 30 percent. It would require more than a 30 percent increase to cause 14 percent of buyers to switch.

What percentage discount do buyers expect? Study results indicate the answer depends upon the personal attributes of the buyers involved. For example, women expected deeper discounting than men when asked what they would pay for a $300,000 purchase as shown in figure 78.4. It should also be noted that 84 percent of buyers expected a discount of 20 percent or less in this scenario. Based on the study of price increase and discounts, it seems buyers fixate on the 10 to 20 percent range.

Psychological versus Absolute Discounts

There are two main types of discounts: psychological and absolute. A psychological discount is one that is extended to placate buyers and make them feel that they have been fairly treated and not taken advantage of. If this discount isn't in line with what they perceive others have received, they will hesitate to move forward with the purchase. Since the buyer is committed and has already made the purchase mentally, the discount has to be only enough to reaffirm

Let's say you are in charge of negotiating an important $300,000 technology purchase that will enable a business initiative that will save your company $1 million. Realistically, what price do you expact to pay after negotiations?

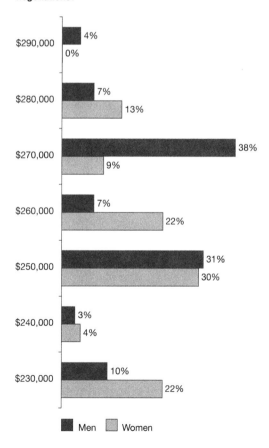

Figure 78.4 Discount sensitivity of buyers

mutual trust and remove the fear of buyer's remorse (see ch. 128).

Conversely, an absolute discount is a deep discount that is presented to customers only out of absolute necessity to close the deal. These buyers will not move forward until their specific discount demands are met. In this situation, every attempt should be made to re-emphasize the value and ROI payback of the purchase.

Twenty Negotiation Tips and Tactics

Here are twenty tips and tactics to review prior to your next negotiation.

1. *Don't do it alone.* There's safety in numbers so take along your manager and other savvy negotiators from within your company. Getting the win is more important than risking the deal because you want to be the hero who did it all by himself. Plus, it will be easier to get the deal approved internally if your senior leaders were part of the process.

2. *Plan ahead.* Meet with your team ahead of time to plan your primary negotiating strategy and secondary fallback positions in the event your primary position fails (see ch. 70). Assign the roles each teammate will play (moderator, main negotiator, final decision-maker, and good cop/bad cop). Three planning elements need to be thought through: how the deal should be structured and the negotiation issues and limits from your company's position, the anticipated issues from the customer's perspective, and the outcomes you

personally need to make your quota or compensation goals.

3. *Qualify and start the negotiation process early.* Ascertain the customer's procurement and legal processes as early as possible during the sales cycle with the same diligence you devote to understanding the customer's selection process. Ideally, the negotiation process will start during the first sales call with a prospective client. As early as possible during the sales cycle, you should preview difficult contract issues and educate the prospect on why your company takes a certain position—for example, the manner in which payments have to be structured in order to meet revenue recognition guidelines. Explain how the deal is of no value to your company if the contract cannot be recognized as a revenue recorded accounting event. This will help soften the customer's viewpoint on the issue and eliminate surprises later. Moreover, this may help develop an internal champion who will fight for your position internally.

4. *Expect three negotiations.* Regardless of what the buyer says, expect an initial negotiation, an iterative round, and a best-and-final negotiation. You may even deal with a different person at each round, so always ask, "Who is the best-and-final negotiator?"

5. *Adopt a PET (positive/emotional/tough) demeanor.* Maintain a positive demeanor even when pushing back—for example, explaining that the discount the customer is asking for isn't in his best long-term interest because without any profits your

company would be unable to build new products, offer product support, and some day be out of business. Appeal to the person's emotional character and sense of fairness. It's easy to be a tough negotiator if you truly respect the value of your products, your company, and yourself. Stay tough and calm, and be comfortable with silence so you don't yield to selection pressure (see ch. 62) and give in first.

6. *Negotiate in the presence of someone who cares present.* Make sure your coaches and the bully with the juice are at the negotiation to keep their procurement and legal teams in check.

7. *Do it in person.* People are far more collaborative and less confrontational in person than over the phone. Plus, you can't read others over the phone like you can in person.

8. *Remember that history repeats itself.* Play back past negotiations in your mind. What were the sticking points and who gave in first?

9. *Know the players' personas.* Use LinkedIn to research each person you will be negotiating with. You might have a mutual contact whom you can learn more about the person from. Are the players "old school" negotiators who aggressively go after a win-lose relationship with vendors? Better yet, ask your coach about their negotiation style. In chapter 76, we review company buyer persona roles based on people's political power and their personal disposition toward their company. These roles influence negotiating skills as well. For example, vigilantes and politicians

consider themselves to be the best negotiators while the Pollyannas and integrators rated themselves worst.

10. *Establish situational dominance from the start.* Specify the time, location, and attendees for the negotiation. Define and publish the agenda.

11. *Keep a concession list.* At the beginning of the negotiation, list all the issues that need to be resolved from both sides. As the negotiation progresses, track what concessions were made by both parties. Refer to this list when needed to keep the concessions from becoming lopsided.

12. *Clarify meaning with questions.* Don't assume you know the meaning of the terms the customer says. Equally important, don't stereotype definitions based on past negotiations. For example, the customer's definition of "acceptance clause" might be very different from other clients.

13. *Enforce time.* Every offer should have a deadline. Every deadline should be enforced.

14. *Use the power of print.* Bring along printed copies of your price book, discount schedules, policies, and program details so the customer feels comfortable he's getting a fair deal. Refer to them when the customer tries to negotiate further.

15. *"Doubt the other product is as good as yours."* There's an important reason why you're sitting in the chair and the competition isn't. You won the evaluation, so take the negotiator's comments with a grain of salt.

16. *Leverage past success.* When negotiating with existing clients, be sure to review metrics and milestones that

show how well you've performed and prove you're worth the extra money. Don't flinch when new prospective clients say, "We don't have the money" or "It's all comes down to price" or "We don't have to do this right now." Tell them about the payback your customers are experiencing.

17. *Always expect one more thing.* Be forewarned, expect a last demand even after you think everything has been finalized.

18. *Qualify what happens next.* Congratulations, you've made it through the best-and-final negotiations. However, you should still be paranoid. Qualify the process to get the final paperwork signed and money paid. Triangulate (see ch. 58) with coaches and internal contacts to confirm everything is on track.

19. *Build your internal relationships.* Schmooze your legal, contract, and sales operations teams. Make sure they have a positive impression of you as a team player and not a rogue salesperson.

20. *Know when to hold and fold on an issue.* Members of another exotic profession share some of the same qualities as salespeople—professional poker players. Like sales, their profession is about formulating strategy, knowing human nature, and winning. Poker players have acquired an uncanny ability to read their opponents' unintentional mannerisms and predict the cards they are holding. When playing poker or conducting a negotiation, you cannot emit the scent of weakness.

Meanwhile, professional poker players are masters of their own emotions who are as comfortable matching the bet on a bluff as they are when they hold four aces. Poker players know that any novice can have a lucky streak. However, it's the serious players who make money in the long run. They study the game and constantly seek to improve their skills. Seasoned gamblers have encountered every card combination. They always remember which cards have been dealt and measure their bets carefully in accordance with their odds of winning. Similarly, during a negotiation, you need to know when to hold your ground on an issue or fold so you can collect your winnings in the end.

Chapter 79. Sales Call Preparation Checklist

The diligence with which you prepare yourself and your colleagues for a sales call will directly influence the success of your meeting. However, it's an imperfect world and you will never have 100 percent of the information you would like about the customer you will be meeting. In this case, you need to theorize about the missing pieces of information based upon your past customer meetings and summon your sales intuition. Use the following checklist to help you prepare for your next meeting. [Source chapters are referenced in brackets.]

What is our goal and my personal outcome for the meeting? [50]
How will I obtain trusted advisor status? [50]
What interesting intersecting activities can I talk about with the prospect? [51, 52]

What familial relationship role should I assume during the sales call? [51]

Am I prepared to speak the customer's technical specification language or do I need to bring along product specialists and other SMEs? [53]

What is the cause of the customer's problem and our solution to solve the problem, worded in the business operations language? [54]

Has the customer spoken the confidential language with me in the past and what did he confide? [55, 66]

What pattern interruption and cowcatcher will I employ at the opening stage of the meeting? [57, 68]

What is my triangulation and qualification strategy? [58, 59]

What solution positioning statements will I use? [60]

What are the most difficult questions I expect the customer to ask and how will I handle them? [61, 62]

What customer success stories do I plan to share? [64]

Will my sales call strategy be based on alignment, transformation, or provocation? [65]

What leading questions do I plan to ask? [59]

How will I structure my presentation? [68, 69]

What are my primary closing strategy and fallback positions? [70]

How will I measure sales call success? [71]

What is the customer's informational decision-making role? [73]

What is the customer's character decision-making role? [74]

What is the customer's authority decision-making role? [75]

What is the customer's company decision-making role? [76]

What is my negotiation strategy? [82]

NEW ACCOUNT PENETRATION STRATEGY

Chapter 80. Don't Use Dead Words

We connect with people through the words we speak, the way in which we say them, and the congruence of the words to our demeanor. However, the words we use are complex objects that don't mean the same to everyone. To understand this, let's do a word association exercise. What is the first thought that comes to mind when you read the words "dog," "sports," "church," "marriage," and "children"?

If you have a dog, you probably thought of your dog. A picture of your dog may have come to mind, and you may have said your dog's name to yourself. The word "sports" may have caused you to think about the sport you played in school because words are anchored to our memories. The word "church" could elicit many different responses, ranging from a sense of purpose to a resistance to authority, depending upon your orientation. Meanwhile, marriage is to some a blessing; to others, a dream; and to the unlucky, a nightmare. So your reaction to the word "marriage" is likely based on your experience.

All of these words have something in common. In order to be understood, they must be interpreted into something meaningful: familiar thoughts and terms. This process occurs in three steps: determining the lexical meaning of a word, translating the word into personal meaning, and finally, forming a psychological impression determined by how the word is cataloged. The first step is comprehension, checking whether or not the word can be found in the personal dictionary you keep inside your mind. Your lexical dictionary determines your word comprehension. The average person's dictionary contains about fifty thousand words.

After your lexical dictionary has defined a word, personal meaning is associated with it. For example, your lexical definition of the word "children" might be "kids between two and twelve." In your mind, children are not teenagers or babies. Your mind then tries to derive personal meaning from the word "children." If you have children, you might immediately think of your son, your daughter, or all your children. You might think of a child playing or even a schoolroom. Thus, another level of personal interpretation occurs. The deepest level of meaning occurs inside the mind's word catalog, where the word is associated with psychological meaning. While your lexical dictionary defines the basic meaning of words, your word catalog links that meaning to your past experiences. For example, you may have felt a sense of pride when you thought about your children and a specific memory, such as a school graduation ceremony or a sporting event they competed in.

New words are continually introduced into the English language. They pass through periods of introduction, adoption, and then widespread use when they are universally known. Then they are subject to "linguistic inflation" from overuse. For example, the word "green" as it refers to environmental friendliness is in a period of linguistic hyperinflation and is quickly losing its value. At the end of an overused word's life cycle, its meaning is deadened from the word's excessive use. This is what has happened to the words "powerful," "reliable," and "scalable." Overused words that have lost impactful meaning are called "dead words."

Sometimes the terms your marketing department believes are so important and persuasive actually detract from your credibility. I have reviewed hundreds of corporate PowerPoint presentations. Not only do they all look the same, but they all use the same general words to describe their company's unique advantages. Open your corporate presentation and see how many of these terms and phrases you can find:

World leader	Greater productivity
Market leader	Improve customer satisfaction
Best-in-class	
Best-of-breed	Better visibility
Cost effective	Scalable
End-to-end solution	Manageable
Increase revenues	Reliable
Reduce costs	Powerful
Competitive advantage	Easy to use
	Dynamic

These dead words have been so overused that they actually have a negative impact or no impact at all. As opposed to dead words, "rich words" evoke a deeper personal meaning, importance, and even cachet. For example, a "salesperson" can also be called a "solution specialist." Rich words can be used to describe product qualities like "intelligently" designed, "straightforward" operation, or "ingenious" craftsmanship.

Whether you are trying to connect with a CEO or a computer programmer, the first step of communication is to check comprehension—whether or not your spoken words can be found in the personal dictionary that is kept inside the customer's mind. Don't assume he understands the lexical meaning of the words you're using just because everyone in your own company does. Avoid using dead words that detract from your credibility and actually decrease rapport. Instead, use distinguishing rich words that impart significance.

Chapter 81. General Words Require Operators

Suppose I go to a McDonald's restaurant and order a cheeseburger. Regardless of the way I enunciate the word "cheeseburger," whether enthusiastically, soberly, or abruptly, I will still be served a cheeseburger, not a Big Mac or a Quarter Pounder. In this example, "cheeseburger" has a specific meaning.

Let's say you go to a pizza parlor and when you are asked for your order, you say, "pizza." The server will give you a blank stare. Do you want small, medium, or large? Do you want toppings? Unless the restaurant has only one pizza on the menu, "pizza" is a general word. A general word requires the use of additional words for the message to be received accurately. These additional words, called "operators," are used in conjunction with the general word to change the meaning. For example, adding the words "large," "deep-dish," and "pepperoni" add meaning to the word "pizza."

If you tell a customer your solution is "fast and reliable," what have you communicated? It's through the use of operators that specific meanings are added and meaningful communication is completed. If you tell a customer your solution is "fast and reliable, will print two hundred pages per minute, and has a 99.99 percent uptime rate," you have communicated something meaningful. It's important to recognize the difference between general and specific words. In sales, general words are used predominantly to describe and market product advantages. Probably three of the most regularly used terms are "performance," "reliability," and "scalability."

The phrases below were taken from the website home pages of three prominent companies:

- "ABC Company enables organizations to exceed performance and reliability expectations."

- "DEF Company combines power and scalability to meet your business needs."

- "XYZ Solutions automatically and intelligently delivers the best possible performance and availability."

These statements are known as "truisms" where their marketing departments have made a claim that they believe to be true. However, from their customer's point of view the claims are met with skepticism. Other popular truism terms include "new and improved," "increased flexibility," and "price performance."

Little meaning can be derived from these claims unless operators are added. Here's the point: when speaking with buyers, always validate the general claims about your products with specific features or specific examples to give credence and meaning to your statements.

Not all words are equally persuasive. General words such as "performance," "reliability," and "quality" by themselves are not influential. Operator words, words that improve the persuasiveness of general words, must be added to influence a customer's mind. Adding "nine hundred pages per hour" to define "performance" adds a comparison-point meaning. Adding "one hundred thousand hours mean time between failures" to specify "reliability" helps makes the general word more convincing. Believability is improved when "lifetime guaranteed replacement" is associated with "quality."

Chapter 82. Always Use a Pattern Interruption

Put yourself in the position of the customer for a moment. You've met hundreds of salespeople and have found many of them to be friendly, courteous, and professional. Each of them also wants to build a personal relationship with you. You can't let this happen. You aren't going to build a friendship with everyone when you know you are going to select only one person to do business with. That wouldn't be practical or comfortable. Therefore, you are reserved and on guard and you keep your distance.

You also have met your share of salespeople who were pushy, arrogant, or just plain incompetent. Some salespeople lied straight to your face and broke their promises. They overcommitted what their products could do and misled you about what they couldn't. As a result, you initially treat every salesperson you meet with extreme wariness.

Now if you're the salesperson meeting this customer, the first step of your call should be to perform a pattern interruption to break the customer's mode of thinking and stand out from the competition. A pattern interruption consists of a cowcatcher and a hook. Let me explain with the following analogy. A smartphone can store thousands of songs. If you thumb a playlist, each song has just a few seconds to capture your attention. If the introduction isn't interesting, different, or exciting, you move on to the next song. The term I use to describe this critical lead-in is "cowcatcher." The catchy part of the song is called the "hook." It can be the melody, a phrase, or the chorus that you remember and in some cases, can't get out of your mind.

Most people associate the term "cowcatcher" with the metal grill on the front of a locomotive. However, "cowcatcher" had an entirely different meaning in the early days of the entertainment industry. It was a radio or television show's opening moments in which the performers tried to grab your attention and caused you to stop and look.

A great cowcatcher engages the mind, appeals to the imagination, and helps the presenter gain credibility. One technology company I worked for was the top-rated NASDAQ stock for a period of five years. In fact, during one two-year time frame, $32,000 worth of this company's stock grew to be worth

$1,000,000. I always opened my presentations with a chart of the stock price as the cowcatcher and then explained the facts behind the stock's appreciation as the hook. Prospective customers would be more than intrigued; they were downright fascinated and eager to learn more. Many would even buy my company's stock.

Customers are not only skeptical, they're nervous. Meeting someone new is a stressful experience, and the customer's internal dialogue is on high alert. One of the biggest challenges you face is establishing a sufficient level of customer rapport to ensure your message is received in an open and honest manner. This is why you must interrupt customers' patterns of negative thinking and lower their natural defenses. From this point forward, think how you can begin every telephone call, sales call, and presentation with a pattern interruption.

Chapter 83. The Perfect Elevator Pitch

Even senior salespeople may find this exercise to be very challenging. What makes it difficult is that you already think you can do it easily. The exercise requires you to time yourself because it must be completed in no more than forty-five seconds. Ideally, you want to be in a private place where you can say your answer aloud.

Exercise: I would like you to pretend that you are in an elevator at one of your industry's trade shows. You are heading down to the lobby when the doors open on the thirtieth floor. You instantly recognize the executive who walks in and quickly glance at his name badge to confirm he is the CEO of the most important account you would like to start working with. You have never met him before nor have you been able to generate any interest from his organization. You have forty-five seconds to introduce yourself, explain what your company does in a way the CEO would find interesting and applicable, and motivate him to take the action you suggest. Ready? Go!

So, how did you do? You are to be commended for completing this exercise. Even the most successful salespeople find this pressure-packed exercise difficult. At sales training workshops, I will ask salespeople to perform this exercise with me in front of their peers. Many times they become flustered or quit halfway through and they ask me if they can start over again. My answer is always no because you have only one chance to make a great first impression.

Here are the six most common mistakes salespeople make with their elevator pitch:

- *They use truisms.* They believe their company's own marketing pitch, which makes claims that are not considered entirely true by the listener. As a result, they instantly lose credibility.

- *They describe themselves using buzzwords.* They repeat industry buzzwords or, worse yet, use technical buzzwords that are known only within their company.

- *They use fillers.* They make too much small talk or ask frivolous questions

that reduce their stature and make them even more submissive to the customer.

- *They demean themselves or the listener.* Their statements make them into mere salespeople, not business problem solvers. They unintentionally demean the listener by asking impertinent questions or assuming the listener knows exactly what they are talking about.

- *They present an unreasonable close.* They don't take into account that they are talking to a senior company leader and use a close that is unrealistic or demands too much of the customer.

- *They are incongruent.* Their tone, pitch, and tempo of speech don't match. They speak too fast and their quivering tone broadcasts that they're nervous and submissive.

Here's an example of a poor elevator pitch. The problems are identified in brackets. Luke Skywalker, a salesperson for XYZ Technologies, is attending a trade show and happens to be in the elevator with Norman Bates, chief information officer at Wonderful Telecommunications.

Hello, Norman. How are you today [filler]? Do you have a moment to talk [filler]? My name is Luke Skywalker and I work for [demeans salesperson] XYZ Technologies. Have you heard of XYZ Technologies [demeans listener]? Umm . . . [filler] Well, we are the leading provider [truism] of business transformational outsourcing [industry buzzword]. We have a unique extended-hybrid implementation methodology [technical buzzword]. Do you have time for me to buy you a cup of coffee and hear more about it [unreasonable close]?

A successful elevator pitch will incorporate the following linguistic structures:

- *Softeners.* A softener eases listeners into the next thought or is used to set expectations. When you say, "I'm sorry to bother you," you are using the preapologizing softener technique.
- *Facts.* A fact is the undisputed truth. Facts are recognized instantaneously.
- *Logic.* Logic is inferred by the listener to be true. Two main types of logic are used in sales situations: linear and geometric. The formula for linear logic is A plus B equals C, meaning when A and B are true statements, then the C statement or idea is also true. For example, "Our solution is 10 percent faster" and "We are 25 percent cheaper"; therefore, "We are the better solution." The formula for geometric logic is if X is true, and X equals Y, then any statement that is true for X also applies to Y. For example, "We are helping Allstate Insurance reduce costs 10 percent" and "You are an insurance company like Allstate Insurance"; therefore, "We can help you reduce your costs 10 percent."
- *Metaphors.* Metaphors are educational, personal, and action-based stories. The purpose of each of these metaphors is to tell, teach, and enlighten the listener, with the ultimate goal of changing his or her opinion or behavior. While educational metaphors

appeal to the conscious intellect, personal and action-based metaphors can be tailored to the subconscious mind. Also, all three types can be connected, interwoven, and mixed together in any combination.

- *Suggestions.* Foreground suggestions are direct and explicit ("*Consumer Reports* gave our product the highest rating"). Background suggestions are indirect and their meaning is inferred ("One of their customers recently switched to our product").
- *Fallback position.* Every customer conversation is actually a negotiation between verbal dominance and submissive silence. Instead of giving ultimatums that force the customer to accept or reject your close, provide options from which customers can select. Always have alternate suggestions prepared in advance.
- *Silence.* Silence is an important and useful linguistic structure. It indicates you are listening and waiting for a response. Silence can actually be used to gain dominance during conversations.

Here's an elevator pitch that incorporates these linguistic structures:

Norman, hi, I'm Luke Skywalker with XYZ Technologies [fact]. It's a pleasure to meet you [softener]. I'm not sure if you are familiar with us [softener], but we work with AT&T [fact]. They've had to reduce their IT costs during these tough times [geometric logic]. I'm here because James Bond, the CIO of AT&T, is presenting a case study on how he cut his IT costs by 20 percent using our outsourcing solution [metaphor, background suggestion]. There'll be CIOs from some of our other customers, including General Electric and Johnson & Johnson, speaking as well [fact, background suggestion]. The session is tomorrow at 1:00 p.m. if you can make it [foreground suggestion, softener]. [Pause—silence, waiting for response.] That's too bad [softener]. I'd be delighted to send you his presentation [fallback position, foreground suggestion]. Great. Just to confirm your email address, that's Norman.bates @wonderful.com. Is there anyone else I should send it to [fallback position]? [Pause—silence]. Okay, that's Ferris Bueller, your vice president of infrastructure. Thanks, Norman. You'll be hearing from me shortly.

The most important linguistic structures used in this elevator pitch are the metaphors. Ideally, a metaphor will cause the mind to immediately recognize the importance of the information, accept the message, and follow the suggestion. The proof of a metaphor's success is evidenced by a change in the verbal and physical language the listener emits. This could range from an enthusiastic verbal response to a subtle readjustment to an open posture indicating the person is receptive to your ideas.

Your words are your most important competitive weapons. In this regard, your ability to deliver a compelling elevator pitch is your biggest and most reliable armament. There are many sales situations where you have only a minute or two to conduct an entire sales call.

For example, you could be walking down the customer's hallway and bump into the CEO or meeting with a lower-level contact when the vice president drops in. You must be able to deliver a compelling and memorable message during this pressure-packed time-sensitive encounter. Write down your elevator pitch and analyze its structure for the use of buzzwords, fillers, and truisms.

Chapter 84. Using Investigative Research

Before you attempt to send an email or letter or make a cold call to penetrate a new account, you need to research the business and the person whom you are trying to gain an initial meeting with. Old-fashioned detective work is still vitally important today. Fortunately, the internet makes information more readily available than ever. Study every page of information on the customer's website as though your life depended on it. Read the annual report, press releases, and product information, and scan all the various financial documents. From these documents you can derive your initial thoughts about your product's strategic, operational, political, and psychological value (see ch. 40).

Another type of investigative research has a profound impact on whether or not your efforts will be successful: you must find the "right" people to contact within the account. You can find out who's who in any company in several ways. First, the company's website probably has an "about the company" page that may list senior executives. If the company is public, senior executives will be listed in the financial reports that can be found on its "investor relations" page. You can also search financial websites such as Yahoo! Finance (http://finance.yahoo.com) and the Securities and Exchange Commission (http://www.sec.gov) for financial filings.

However, this information is far from complete for the purpose of penetrating the account. Ideally, you want to collect four critical pieces of information. First, knowing the date the company's fiscal year ends will help you coordinate your efforts to penetrate new accounts. Three to six months before the fiscal year ends, C-level executives will start thinking about their next year's goals along with the initiatives to accomplish them and the budget associated with each initiative. This is a crucial time to be gaining "mindshare." Budgets begin to be shaped through an iterative process with the CEO, CFO, or entire executive team. They become set in stone after the budget has been approved by the board of directors, usually before ninety days into the new fiscal year.

Remember, there are certain points in the year when a strategic conversation is academic and other times when it's relevant. Second, you want contact information about employees at all levels of the organization (midlevel managers and lower-level project people along with all the executive-level leaders). For example, if you were selling security software, you would like contact information for the chief information officer, chief technical officer, chief security officer, and vice president in charge of networking or infrastructure. You also want contact information for midlevel managers (director of information technology, director of security, manager of global networks) and key lower-level personnel (senior firewall administrator, IT security specialist, and lead network engineer). There are many different providers of this detailed information, including LinkedIn,

DiscoverOrg, Salesforce.com's Data.com, and many more.

Third, you need each person's precise title. There's a big difference between finding out that someone is the "vice president of global manufacturing applications" versus knowing someone who goes by the more nebulous title "vice president of information technology." Knowing the more detailed title will help you send better targeted messages.

Finally, you need accurate and complete contact information. You need the correct spelling of each person's name and his or her personal usage (whether someone goes by Charles or Chuck, for example), as well as the person's mailing address, direct phone number, and, of course, the all-important email address.

It can be well argued that the first sales call with a prospective customer is the most important. Before you pick up the phone to make a cold call, fire off a letter, or press the button to send an email, research the company and the employees within it that you are trying to contact. This is the first step toward creating a tailored message that will elicit a positive response.

Chapter 85. Cold Calls, Letters, LinkedIn, Drop-Ins, and Email

There are five basic communication vehicles at your disposal to reach new customers: cold calls, letters, LinkedIn, drop-ins, and email. While you can use any of these communication vehicles to secure initial meetings with customers, let's take a moment to review the pluses and minuses of each method.

Cold Calls

Here are some observations about cold calling. First, the odds of connecting with the person you are trying to reach are less than 5 percent, so you will most likely go to voice mail. Most of the time salespeople talk too fast when they leave their message. In particular, the phone number at the end of a long-winded speech is said the fastest. Is someone really going to replay the voice mail three times to get your phone number right? Some salespeople assume the listener knows exactly what they do when the opposite is true. Many salespeople are either nervous, bored, or both. They ramble on in a dreary, unexciting way. Why should they expect me to have any enthusiasm for what they're selling when they don't show any?

You must be able to leave a succinct message. In no more than twenty-five seconds you must identify who you are and why the customer should call you back. Your message must be delivered in a clear, commanding, yet approachable tone. Therefore, every time you plan on making cold calls you should rehearse leaving the voice mail. I suggest that you call your own voice mail three to five times and practice leaving the message you plan to use. Listen to your voice mail, put yourself in the customer's place, and ask if you would call yourself back.

> *The number of cold calls that I get from vendors is phenomenal to the point that I don't even answer my phone.*
>
> —Director of Systems and Process

I have some more bad news to share with you regarding the effectiveness of cold calls. Almost all of the C-level executives I have spoken with have never returned a cold call. Should you cold call senior executives? Yes, cold calling does have a specific purpose during the new account penetration process: it should be used mainly as a follow-up device after an email or letter has been sent. However, I have a totally different attitude toward cold calling lower-level and midlevel personnel. I have heard so many stories over the years about large deals that started with a cold call that I can't recall them all.

> *The way we found out about them was from a cold call. Had they not called we never would have looked at them.*
>
> —Programmer

Salespeople who relentlessly cold call someone are making a mistake. I guess they think their persistence will win that person over. Conversely, these salespeople are infringing on personal time and space. They will grow to be despised. I have a very different opinion about email because it is a cafeteria-type communication channel. Voice mail is a serial communication channel. A person has to go through messages in order, one at a time. Email is different; someone can pick and choose which emails to open and do so in whatever order he or she wants. Therefore, it's not so bothersome when someone sends an occasional unsolicited email as you can block the sender if the frequency gets too intrusive.

Letters

Letters sent by snail mail must meet one important condition: the letter and associated marketing collateral that is sent to the customer must be totally unique. The material and message you send should vary according to the level of personnel in the account you are trying to penetrate. Senior executives should receive short, high-level summary information, such as press articles, one-page reviews, and short case studies about their competitors whom you are doing business with. Save the company brochure, white papers, data sheets, and other detailed information for the midlevel and lower-level personnel.

Think about all the different types of items you can send to a potential customer other than a standard letter of introduction. You can send interesting news clippings and serious-sounding industry updates that help validate your marketing claims. You can send company tchotchkes such as T-shirts, baseball caps, and mouse pads that carry your company's name and logo. Most of the time these items are taken home and given away to family and friends, and it's great advertising when Junior parades around the house wearing your company's T-shirt. Remember, whatever you send should be as unique as possible while still promoting a professional image.

LinkedIn

Over 500 million business professionals have LinkedIn profiles so they can network with colleagues. That includes approximately 133 million profiles in the United States. If we put that number into perspective, almost two out of three adults in the United States have a LinkedIn profile. Today, a quality LinkedIn profile is a mandatory part of having a successful sales career (see chapter 95 for instructions on creating a compelling profile). In fact, my study of sales professionals who enthusiastically use LinkedIn revealed that over 40 percent have generated revenue based upon their LinkedIn-related efforts. The research suggests that LinkedIn is a valuable tool to penetrate new accounts and establish wider, higher, and deeper relationships with existing clients.

Drop-Ins

B2B reps who cover large territories endure lots of windshield time as they drive from client to client. So it makes sense for them to stop by prospective client businesses along the way and drop in unannounced. The goal of drop-ins is to gain a "beachhead" entry point at the account. The focus is on getting a small initial win that would expand over time. The win could range from getting the customer to meet with you in person, see a demonstration, include your firm in the next round of competitive bids, test one of the products you provide, or order a very small amount of a product and conduct a trial.

In general, drop-ins aren't appreciated by busy customers and are considered an interruption. Moreover, you'll most likely be screened out at the front desk, and the odds of actually meeting with senior decision-makers who reside in the corner offices far away from the front desk are extremely low or nonexistent. However, drop-ins can be productive within certain types of industries and for certain types of products.

Pharmaceuticals, building-related products or services, and business consumables such as packaging and office supplies are all examples where drop-ins can lead to successful outcomes. In fact, I've heard many top salespeople recount how a multimillion-dollar account was the result of a drop-in. However, always keep these three points in mind when considering drop-ins.

1. *Leave a personal takeaway.* Don't just drop off your business card or standard company brochure at the front desk like every other rep. Leave something that creates a personal association. It could be a letter explaining why you stopped by and how you can help the company based on how you've helped hundreds of others. Or, you could create a blog-like article that provides an interesting perspective on the industry and information the customer would consider personally helpful. Include your picture and background information about yourself in the byline. Whether it be a company T-shirt, gourmet cookies, or a book about Six Sigma that you inscribed, leave something unique that separates you from the pack.

2. *Don't break character or demean yourself.* A customer I was interviewing told me, "The market leader never does drop-ins; only the B and C players do." While people generally admire someone who is persistent, drop-ins aren't usually appreciated. As a result, you'll probably be challenged by junior front-desk employees who make you feel unimportant. Even though you're under duress, maintain your composure and don't break character. Breaking character (see ch. 44) occurs when the salesperson doesn't exhibit a professional, respectful, and self-assured composure. Don't be fooled when someone with half your industry knowledge chastises you because you had the audacity to try to help the company. Instead, put yourself in his or her position and formulate a strategy to win the person over. The most basic element of selling is making the inconsequential feel important and the underappreciated feel respected.

3. *Watch for negative cues.* It's important to recognize that there are different perceptions of drop-ins that are company specific. Someone who works for a company that is one hundred miles from the nearest major city would probably be more receptive to drop-ins and appreciate a salesperson who went far out of his way to try to meet him or her. Another person who has twenty different salespeople dropping in during the week probably considers them a nuisance. In this case, use another method to connect.

Email

One of the first lessons every new salesperson learns is to "call high," to try to reach the most senior-level executive. Therefore, it's not surprising that senior-level executives are continually harassed by salespeople. When you try to call the CEO or vice president of a company, you face a monumental challenge because the entire organization is designed to protect him from you. Most likely, you will be screened by an assistant or directed to an underling. The letters you send to executives tend to suffer the same fate. Given this reality, the preferred vehicle of communication is email.

> *I received an email. I usually never bother with them. But this one caught my attention and I actually read the entire email. I forwarded it to one of my managers and asked him to bring them in for a meeting.*
>
> —Vice President of Engineering

The subject line is the single most important part of the email. Its sole purpose is to catch someone's attention and motivate the person to open the email. The best emails start with a great cowcatcher (see ch. 82). Here are some actual examples of bad subject lines from emails I have received.

- *Subject: Increase Revenues 1000 percent! This overpromising subject line means the email will immediately be considered spam and deleted before it has a chance to be read.*

- *Subject: Business Proposal Information. This subject line incorrectly sets readers' expectations. They'll feel deceived when they open the email and see it is from a stranger trying to sell them something.*

- *Would you be interested in XYZ Product? The answer is no when the question is presented this way.*

The hook is the catchy part of the email. It's the first few sentences that deliver a punch and motivate you to keep reading. The cowcatcher and the hook work together synergistically. Great emails have an interesting cowcatcher and a provocative hook.

Here's an example of a terrible email *exactly as I received it* with my critique immediately following.

Subject: Please advise

The pressure is on to grow revenue faster. How will you adapt business to reach goals? XXXX can help you gain a strong competitive edge. Let me show you can use XXXX to:

- Drive better results.
- Increase customer satisfaction and loyalty
- Expand your market share.

Do you have time this week or next for a brief discussion about your business needs? Please reply with the best time for me to contact you.

Best regards,
XXX XXXXXX

This email has the wrong subject line. It is titled "Please advise," which gives the reader the impression it is from someone the reader knows about a business issue the sender needs advice on. When the reader opens the email and sees that it is spam, it creates a "negative receptive state" because the reader feels deceived. If this email was intended for a vice president of sales, a better title would have been "Increase revenues by increasing sales calls." If intended for a CFO, "Five tips to decrease your cost of operations" could have been used. These titles set the readers' expectations and create a "positive receptive state."

The email suggests the sender is a simpleton. It also has typos and grammatical mistakes. We'll discuss the roles

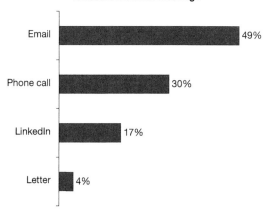

Since salespeople are trying to develop a relationship with you all the time, what is the best way to secure an initial meeting?

Figure 85.1 B2B buyers' contact preferences to secure an initial meeting

of dominance and submission during communication in chapter 99. This submissive email is written at the level of a fifth grader when scored by the Flesch-Kincaid test. Is a senior-level executive really going to want to meet with an elementary school student?

The email is also too generic to grab the reader's attention. It uses strategic terms like "grow revenue," "competitive edge," and "increase customer satisfaction" generically without any explanation. These terms are so over-used by everyone in sales that they are "dead words"—they have no meaningful impact. The sender didn't conduct any background research so that he could craft a message that would appeal to the recipient. The best way to tap into these values is by tailoring your message directly to the intended recipient based upon the person's role within the company. A one-size-fits-all email is less effective because the vice presidents of marketing, sales, and finance face very different day-to-day challenges.

Which Communication Vehicle Do Buyers Prefer?

What's the best communication vehicle to secure an initial meeting? A study of B2B buyers reveals that 49 percent prefer email, 30 percent prefer a phone call, 17 percent prefer LinkedIn, and only 4 percent prefer a letter as shown in figure 85.1. Be forewarned, these percentages vary by gender, and 63 percent of women prefer salespeople to contact them via email (see ch. 130).

Should you send a video introductory email? As of this writing, the results are very mixed. While it is a unique way to get a prospect's attention, it can turn off prospective clients. Think about it from your perspective: would you rather quickly scan an email to see if it is of interest or watch a video from a stranger? My recommendation would be to test it with a few prospects first and be sure to have colleagues review and critique the video beforehand.

The internet has fundamentally changed the way people communicate. You must master how to use email to penetrate new accounts. Your success will increasingly depend upon it in the future. You'll never get an initial face-to-face meeting if your introductory message doesn't connect with its intended target.

Chapter 86. When Should You Contact Prospects?

The toughest task in all of sales is penetrating new accounts and securing meetings with busy prospective buyers. Think about it: the same people you are trying to reach are also continually being hounded by your competitors and dozens of other salespeople.

Salespeople who were over 100 percent of their annual quota prefer to prospect on different days of the week depending on their gender. In order of most to least preferred day of the week, salesmen chose Tuesday, Monday, Wednesday, Friday, and Thursday; saleswomen prefer to prospect on Wednesday, Thursday, Tuesday, Monday, and Friday.

But the most important question to ask to settle the prospecting question is, "What day of the week do prospective buyers think is the best day to contact them?" The best day of the week is Tuesday, which 50 percent prefer, and the worst day is Monday, which was only selected by 7 percent. The second-best day is Thursday, which was selected by 17 percent, and the third-best day is Friday with 15 percent as shown in figure 86.1.

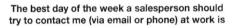

The best day of the week a salesperson should try to contact me (via email or phone) at work is

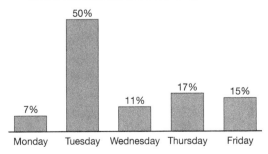

Figure 86.1 B2B buyers rate the best day of the week to contact them

Chapter 87. The "1, 2, 3, Rest, Repeat" Account-Based Marketing Campaign

The strategy to penetrate new accounts is called the "1, 2, 3, Rest, Repeat" Account-Based Marketing (ABM) campaign. It requires adopting a new philosophy about contacting senior executives and other employees within organizations based upon four principles.

First, an Account-Based Marketing campaign is a structured methodology to penetrate new accounts. As opposed to a shotgun approach where one-size-fits-all generic messages are blasted out to the multitudes, ABM is a customized approach that takes into account the specific orientation of targeted potential buyers. Whereas the response rate for a generic email blast will be .5 percent, the response rate for ABM campaigns is a tenfold increase and averages 5 percent.

Because of the time it takes to create and manage the customized campaign, an ABM campaign is typically targeted for sweet-spot and near-sweet-spot accounts (see ch. 15). At these accounts you have a close solution fit or past vertical industry experience.

Second, you must believe that every company will become a customer of yours because you honestly believe that you can help the business. Essentially, it's just a matter of time before you connect and work together. You must believe in what you're doing. Your efforts cannot be based upon half-hearted motivations. You must have a conviction that you, your products, and your company are the only true solution for the customer. When you have this mind-set, it is impossible to consider yourself an obnoxious telemarketer or discourteous email spammer. Rather, you are on an urgent mission to save the customer from making an ill-advised decision that will create a less-than-perfect workplace.

Third, your attempts to contact a customer will take time. In essence, you are running a political campaign that will take several months and in many cases over a year. While you obviously want to generate immediate interest, you need to set your own expectations so you don't get frustrated by a lack of results and stop campaigning. The campaign ends only when the customer buys your solution or specifically tells you to stop contacting him.

Fourth, the reason why the customer doesn't respond to your message is not that he's disinterested or too busy. Rather, consider it your fault because you didn't send him the right message. While you didn't get the message right this time, you should also know that you will get it right over time. Therefore, you should never be bashful about contacting the customer again.

Campaign Cadence

The 1, 2, 3, Rest, Repeat ABM campaign is based upon sending a series of three unique messages that have different structures and intentions. These actions are followed by a period when you go quiet and do not make any attempts whatsoever to contact the customer. Once this time frame is over, you start another campaign with a series of different messages.

It's very important to understand this Here's how this cadence works:

Step 1—Send an initial credibility or custom message. This introductory message identifies in an interesting way who you are and what you do, while the custom message focuses on specific problems that the prospect is most likely experiencing.

Step 2—Send a tactical offer message or custom message. The tactical offer message is centered upon a business problem, industry theme, or an applicable offer such as research papers or an invitation to a webinar. Or, you can send the custom message.

Step 3—Send a final message. This message is the culmination of the campaign.

Step 4—Rest. During this period, you do not contact the customer.

Step 5—Repeat. After the rest period has ended, you start another campaign with a series of three entirely new messages.

Most companies and salespeople make two critical mistakes when they try to reach customers. They either contact them once and stop if they don't get a response or contact them way too much. They mistakenly believe they are gaining mind share and acceptance by sending a newsletter or announcement every other week or once a month. The exact opposite is true. They are devaluing and diluting their message.

> They're too aggressive in their sales tactics, and this is upsetting. Big organizations like us have a process you must go through. It's good they don't take an initial no for an answer,

but they're kind of relentless in contacting us. Once they reach the ultimate decision-maker who says "not at this time," they are looking for different people and angles to work. But it eventually goes from "not at this time" to "I don't want to work with those guys!"

— General Manager

Your strategy to penetrate a new account should not be a one-time action. Instead, it requires an ongoing campaign that can utilize all four communication vehicles at your disposal: email, telephone cold calls, LinkedIn, and letters (direct mail). Ideally, you should coordinate the order in which you send the communiqués. For example, you could send a letter in step 1, follow up with an email in step 2, and phone the customer a few days later in step 3. Or, you could make a phone call followed by an email and LinkedIn connection request.

Typically, the time frame to accomplish the first three steps should be between sixty and ninety days. If you try to shorten the contact period, your messages will run the risk of being considered a nuisance. The rest period should be at least two to three times the time it takes to execute steps 1 through 3. For example, if you are messaging to someone on a once-a-month basis over a three-month time frame, the rest period should be six to nine months.

However, this does not mean you go completely dark and stop prospecting with the account. This is because you want to have several different campaigns that are targeted at specific individuals over the course of the years. In essence, you are always in front of the account because you are messaging to different people at different levels of the organization across different departments. For example, you could have four different ABM campaigns for one company where each campaign is executed at different times of the year as shown in figure 87.1.

What is your philosophy to penetrate new accounts? If you're like most salespeople you probably don't have one. Rather, you reflexively increase your prospecting activity when your pipeline is empty. The 1, 2, 3, Rest, Repeat ABM campaign leverages sales linguistics to secure initial meetings. Follow the steps explicitly and you will achieve even greater sales success.

Structuring Messages for the 1, 2, 3, Rest, Repeat ABM Campaign

Because people have different motivations, they have different perceptions of a product's value. The perceived value depends on the psychological, political, operational, and strategic value it provides the evaluator (see ch. 40).

Psychological value is one of the most important values in terms of motivating purchasing action. At the root of every decision is a desire to fulfill one of four deep-seated psychological needs: satisfying the ego, being accepted as part of a group, avoiding pain, and ensuring survival. Therefore, you should understand your product's psychological value and how it applies to the person you are trying to reach.

Political value involves organizational power. Your product can make someone more powerful outright, or it can provide much-needed visibility that enables a person to be in contact with the company's powerbrokers.

People's success in an organization is dependent upon the success of their department's operations. You can think of operational power in terms of how your solution impacts a person's résumé. Finally, strategic value is the reason evaluators give to others in the company as to why they are purchasing a product. Strategic value includes gaining a competitive advantage, increasing revenues, decreasing costs, increasing productivity, improving customer satisfaction, improving quality, and standardizing operations.

The message you send to customers should be based upon these four product values. You must communicate to potential buyers that you can help them solve critical department problems and help them become experts and an internal source of knowledge, thereby making them powerful. To see how this can be done, let's look at an example of a generic email for a marketing campaign targeted at senior executives in the automobile industry.

Subject: Increase Profitability and Maintain Dealer Partnership Loyalty!

Dear Mr. Smith,

My name is John Johnson from XYZ Corporation. We are the leader in

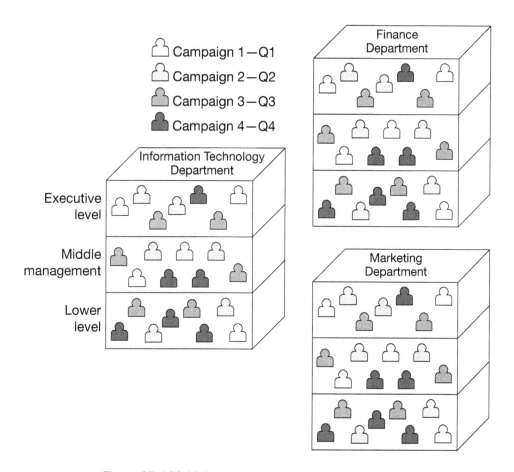

Figure 87.1 Multiple campaigns coordinated at different times to a targeted account

providing solutions that help accelerate time to market and improve customer communications. We're helping customers such as Ford, Toyota, and Honda automate their relationships with their distributors, dealers, and parts suppliers. In a recent strategic implementation, we were able to deliver Ford a robust solution that allowed them to communicate more effectively with their worldwide dealer distribution channel, drastically increasing customer service and loyalty. XYZ Corporation can help you

- Improve communications with critical partners
- Speed time to market and increase dealer retention
- Implement a "best practices" approach for all enterprise communications

For a free evaluation of our robust solutions, please call or email me at your earliest convenience.

Best regards,
John Johnson

Here's another version of the same email. While the main message isn't changed significantly, the goal is to employ a better cowcatcher and hook and to tap into all the different types of customer value.

Subject: How Toyota Maintains Critical Dealer Relationships

Mark,

Q. How do Toyota, Ford, and Honda maintain near-perfect dealer relationships?

A. XYZ Corporation has helped them automate and streamline all aspects of partner communications.

For example, Toyota distributes thousands of unique messages and memorandums to its worldwide dealer distribution channel on a daily basis. Toyota has drastically reduced turnaround times while increasing customer service using XYZ's solution. As a result, they have cut costs and accelerated time to market.

If you would like to learn how you can improve relationships with all your important business partners, contact me at your earliest convenience. Finally, please expect my call on March 2nd to discuss our free dealer communication analysis program.

Thank you,

John Johnson
(123) 456-7890
John.johnson@XYZcorporation.com
www.xyzcorporation.com

The most important aspect of the email is not the bullet points of benefits; rather, it is the psychological impression it creates on the reader. When salespeople try to penetrate a new account, they are considered enemies, so they are met with disdain and fear. Salespeople must turn negative resisters into positive accomplices. In the above example, I was trying to make the email recipient become psychologically attached to the sender.

One recipient might envision starting a grand project like Toyota's for his own personal gain. Another might want more information so he could impress others with his expertise. Someone else might have criticized his company's dealer communications in the past and thought, "If it is good enough for Toyota, it should work for us." He just wants this painful problem solved.

Before you attempt to send an email or letter or make a cold call to penetrate a new account, you need to research the business and the person whom you are trying to gain an initial meeting with. The purpose of your investigative research is to enable you to tailor your subject line so the reader feels compelled to open it. Another key reason for conducting research is to help you determine the different values your solution offers. Reading the CEO's letter to the stockholders in the company's annual report will help you understand the state of the business and the major initiatives planned for the new year. Reviewing the 10-K financial report will provide you with details about the business challenges the company faces. Press releases announce new programs and company crusades that are being undertaken. Meanwhile, industry analyst reports explain how the company is faring compared to the competition. Notice how the email doesn't recite a list of product features and benefits. It explains real-world results in a plain-spoken way without buzzwords.

Take a look at the last sentence of the closing paragraph, "Finally, please expect my call on March 2nd to discuss our free dealer communication analysis program." This sentence employs two linguistic strategies. First, the sender *grants* himself permission to contact the recipient next week. Let's examine the email from the recipient's perspective to understand this concept. This email was written respectfully. It created a positive receptive state when the reader opened it, provided valuable information, and at 125 total words didn't take too much of the reader's time. It also established credibility via customer metaphors and employed an interesting cowcatcher and hook. It was well written from a grammatical perspective, which confirmed the sender's professionalism. As a result, the recipient would probably not be offended if the sender followed up next week with an introductory phone call. However, the call must be made. If not, the momentum and credibility of the email established are lost.

The second linguistic strategy is to purposely use general words. What is a "dealer communication analysis program"? Frankly, the prospective customer wouldn't know what it is, and that's the idea. We spoke about general words and their interpretation in chapter 81. In this instance, the email is building credibility, momentum, and rapport. The original email was self-centered and closed with "For a free evaluation of our robust solutions." In the revised version we are purposely using a general word structure (dealer communication analysis program) because we want the customer to interpret these terms in the way that is most important to the customer and relevant to his problems and aspirations. One final point: while this example is of an email, this message structure applies to letters as well.

Finally, timing can be everything. While emergency and interrupt-driven purchases (see ch. 27) can be made at any time during the fiscal year, planned spending occurs in the fourth quarter when budgets are approved. Therefore, it is imperative to introduce your solution to new prospects no later than the third

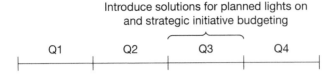

Figure 87.2 When to contact the customer for planned spending in the next fiscal year

quarter time frame, as shown in figure 87.2.

The following comment shows the importance of timing.

> There is a delicate balance in trying to contact me because you don't want to waste my time, but it is good to check in with me once in a while. If someone is continually hounding me, they get turned off pretty quickly. Let's say once a week for three weeks. We go through an annual budgeting process and capital expenditure request. The first step in the process is a real rough benefit cost analysis. My submission process has got to be completed around September. Usually, around June, July, and August I start putting my ducks in a row and coming up with cost justifications. From my point of view, if you don't let me know about your product until January or February then you have missed my cycle. It really behooves you around June or July to remind me of your product.

—Director of eCommerce

Put yourself in the customer's position and theorize on the psychological, political, operational, and strategic value you and your solutions provide. Control your destiny. Don't send emails that are mini-infomercials that give away the power of responding solely to the customer. Study the message structure and fight the urge to explain too much. Instead, structure the email so the customer finds it enticing and awaits your follow-up action with anticipation.

Chapter 88. Step 1— Send a Credibility or Custom Message

The purpose of the first message of the 1, 2, 3, Rest, Repeat ABM campaign is to establish credibility and develop some level of recognition with the customer you are trying to reach. The first message you send to a prospective customer is a critical communication event. Therefore, you want to carefully select the message type and format you will use. While I recommend sending a credibility or custom message in step 1, it's important to note the tactical offer message described in step 2 below can be used in step 1 as well. In fact, the credibility, custom, and tactical offer messages can be used interchangeably depending upon the situation.

Credibility Message

In the credibility message example below, Michael Corleone, a salesperson for Acme Advertising Solutions, is trying to reach Vincent Vega, the chief marketing officer of ABC Technology Company, a multibillion-dollar technology giant. Pay particular attention to the tone of the email. It's not too personal. Since the two men have never met, the message is intentionally more formal. However, Michael doesn't want to be overly formal with the use of language and the saluta-tion, or the recipient will discount the let-ter as a sales pitch.

To: Vincent Vega, CMO@ABC Company
From: Michael Corleone@Acme
Advertising
Subject: Vincent, Marketing Campaign
Ideas for ABC Company

Hello Vincent,

Acme Advertising Solutions has pro-vided online marketing solutions for many leading technology companies including:

Apple	IBM	NEC
Cisco	Intel	Oracle
EMC	McAfee	SAP
Hewlett-Packard	Microsoft	Symantec

Our clients have cost-effectively improved their brand recognition while increasing new sales opportunities.

"Acme Advertising's targeted online marketing campaign increased our lead generation activities by 300 percent."

—Jack Sparrow, CMO, Oracle Corporation

"Acme's 'One World, One System' commercial series has improved our name recognition across all our key market segments."

—James T. Davis, CMO, Hewlett-Packard Corporation

"We were thrilled to win the presti-gious Zippy Award for our innova-tive online advertising campaigns."

—David Bowman, CMO, Intel Corporation

I'd be delighted to meet with you and share some thoughts and ideas we have for ABC Technology Company. Please expect my introductory call on Tuesday the 21st at 3:00 pm.

I look forward to speaking with you,

Michael Corleone
(123) 456-7890
Michael.corleone@acme.com
www.acme.com

The subject line is the cowcatcher, solely intended to encourage Vincent to open the email. His name is part of the subject, so the inference is that the mes-sage is from a real person asking for a meeting, not from an automated spam-bot. As he opens the email, the first thing his eyes will focus on is the list of recog-nizable company names. This is due to the email's "heat map."

A heat map is a representation of where the eyes look first and gravitate toward next when initially viewing a website page, PowerPoint slide, letter, or email. Figure 88.1 shows an example of a heat map for a PowerPoint slide of someone who reads left to right. Areas are colored

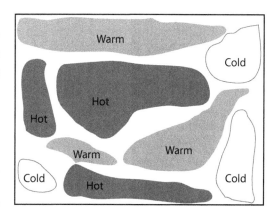

Figure 88.1 Sample heat map for a PowerPoint slide

according to the instinctual tendency to look at them from hot (high) to cold (low).

This hook makes him go back and read the entire message. Notice how this email avoids making outrageous claims such as "Acme is the world's leading advertising firm." Rather, it is completely factual: these are our clients, and this is what they have to say about us. Nor does the email go into a detailed explanation of what Acme Advertising does.

The subject line uses the term "marketing campaign." To a CMO like Vincent, the term can mean a wide variety of things: advertising campaigns, lead-generation programs, online marketing, customer research, competitive research, brand development, and so on. Intentionally, the email does not point out what it's referring to. This is an example of a broadcast-unicast messaging technique. It's intended to let the recipient derive his own personal meaning from an ambiguous term.

While researching the business, Michael found out that ABC Technology's sales are down from last year. Therefore, he theorizes that the sales department is haranguing marketing about needing more qualified leads. If this is the case, Vincent might interpret the email from the standpoint of lead generation, and Michael has a higher likelihood of securing a meeting. The first customer quote reinforces this interpretation. This is an example of a background suggestion.

The list of companies provided in this email is extremely important. Examples of customers that are successfully using a company's products and services are the most important metaphors a salesperson can use. The personal connection between a customer example and its relevancy to the prospect's experiences will determine to what extent the salesperson's claims are accepted. Therefore, the pertinence of the examples chosen is critical. Presenting a company that closely mirrors the prospect's business environment will make the salesperson's statements more powerful.

Specific customer quotes were selected for this email. Since Michael has never met Vincent, he really doesn't know what's on the CMO's mind. He doesn't know if he thinks his job is in jeopardy or he's next in line to become the president of the company. So Michael wants quotes that will connect to the different psychological benefits. The first customer quote focuses upon pain avoidance.

Based upon Michael's past experience working with CMOs, he knows that lead generation is always a source of pain. Maybe Vincent feels inferior to his peers at the other companies listed in the email. He might hire Acme so he can be part of the group. This is self-preservation. Or since he's worked with his current ad agency for seven straight years, he might feel it's time for a refreshing change. This is related to mental and emotional well-being. The third quote is based upon self-gratification and the ego. What CMO wouldn't want to win a prestigious Zippy Award and prominently display the award in his office?

There are a lot of buzzwords out there. Pull me in with some business benefits and let me know about your customers.

—Senior Vice President Product Management

How Long Should the Email Be?

Emails should be designed for both desktop and smartphone reading. Therefore, it's very important that you preview them on a smartphone to ensure they are formatted correctly. While a general rule of thumb is to keep your emails relatively short, if you employ a cowcatcher and heat map strategy, you don't have to be overly concerned with the email length because the smartphone reader will most likely save the email for desktop viewing later. Here's an example of the credibility email above shortened specifically for smartphone viewing in figure 88.2.

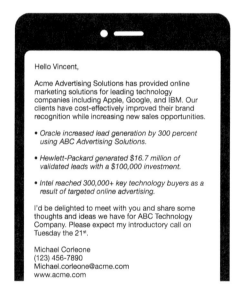

Figure 88.2 Credibility message on a smartphone

In this example, the three longer customer quotes are replaced with case-use examples. They are examples showing how customers are using the products and the benefits they are receiving. The three bullet-point examples below replaced the comments:

- Oracle increased lead generation by 300 percent using ABC Advertising Solutions.

- Hewlett Packard generated $16.7 million of validated leads with a $100,000 investment.

- Intel reached 300,000+ key technology buyers as a result of targeted online advertising.

The Custom Message

While the credibility message shows how current clients have benefited from your solution, the custom message focuses on specific problems that the prospect is most likely experiencing. For example, let's assume that Vincent Vega is now in charge of his company's online product sales and the salesperson provides a solution that enables companies to sell online more efficiently. Based upon the salesperson's knowledge of the industry, a custom message sent to Vincent would focus on the three problem areas he's most likely concerned about and struggling with as shown in figure 88.3.

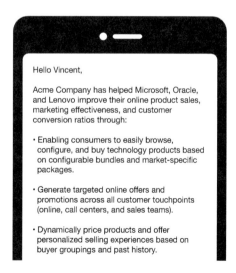

Figure 88.3 Custom message focused on specific problem the customer experiences

Exercise: Creating a message that earns you an initial meeting is both an art and a science. I have reviewed hundreds of credibility messages, and more than three quarters of them actually do more harm than good. Now it is time to conduct a very important exercise. I would like you to close this book and review the standard introduction email or letter you send to customers. Put yourself in their position. How would you respond to it? It's always tough to find out why someone is talking to you. Why would I schedule an hour or two with my staff? Sometimes you can be too smart and you have to dumb your message down. Tell me what your product does and how it is going to help me in a simplistic way.

Chapter 89. Step 2—Send a Tactical Offer or Custom Message

Assuming the customer didn't respond to your first email, you send him a second, tactical offer or custom message (see ch. 88) email. The tactical offer message is centered upon a business problem or industry theme and presents an applicable offer such as best practices, research, or an invitation to a webinar, event, or training session. The goal of the tactical offer message is to bolster the sender's status as a trusted advisor who provides added value to the prospect. In the example below, Luke Skywalker, a salesperson for XYZ Technologies, is trying to secure a meeting with Norman Bates, chief information officer at Wonderful Telecommunications.

To: Norman Bates, CIO@Wonderful Telecommunications
From: Luke Skywalker@XYZ Technologies
Subject: Norman, Outsourcing Strategies for CIOs

Norman,

During today's hypercompetitive times, IT organizations are required to maintain round-the-clock uptime with smaller budgets and fewer resources than ever. Below, you will find links to articles that address this critical issue.

7 CIO Strategies to Maintain Application Availability with Fewer Resources

Gartner Group Study of the Recession's Impact on Long-Term IT Planning

How to Reduce Operational IT Costs by Outsourcing

When and Where IT Outsourcing Makes Sense

XYZ Technologies has helped hundreds of CIOs maximize their IT budgets through application outsourcing.

"We were surprised by the cost savings. It has been 20 percent more than we expected."

—Charles Foster Kane, CIO, AT&T

"We started small by outsourcing non-mission-critical applications three years ago. Today, 70 percent of our applications are outsourced."

—Forrest Gump, CIO, Johnson & Johnson

"We've achieved our primary goal of reducing costs while maintaining

our service levels. Now we've freed up valuable resources to work on critical new business projects."

—Stanley Kowalski, CIO, General Electric

Norman, please let me know if you are interested in our complimentary outsourcing cost-savings analysis. The complimentary study takes approximately two days to complete and will provide you with a detailed savings assessment, key risk factors, and completion timelines. I will follow up with you on April 21st to answer any questions you may have about our analysis program.

Luke Skywalker
(123) 456-7890
Luke.skywalker@xyz.com
www.xyz.com

Based upon Luke's research and experience, he knows that one of the main challenges CIOs face during tough economic times is providing high levels of service with less money and fewer resources. "Norman, Outsourcing Strategies for CIOs" is a topical cowcatcher. It's quite different from "Norman, Meeting Request." The subject line also indicates that the email is not from a salesperson asking for a meeting but from an important source of independent information that could potentially help the CIO.

Obviously, Luke wants to secure a meeting so that he can begin the cost-savings study. However, any forward progress in starting a relationship with the CIO should be considered positive. For instance, if Norman clicks on a link to one of the articles, this is a positive step and the email was a success.

This email has three major parts. The first part is the offer. This fulfills the email's requirement that it provide independent information. Four links are provided to articles that most CIOs would find relevant and interesting. Although they may have been written by XYZ Technologies, they are informational as opposed to vendor-centric promotional collateral. (It's important to note that emails with attached documents are more likely to be caught by spam filters.) The articles are the email's hook.

The second part is composed of customer metaphors, stories from customers confirming the salesperson's solution or company. Since most CIOs are extremely risk averse, all of the quotes are intended to make Norman feel more comfortable that outsourcing is mainstream. Included are quotes from CIOs of another telecommunications company and traditionally conservative companies General Electric and Johnson & Johnson.

These customer quotes are also examples of the simulation persuasion technique. Simulation is structuring language to provoke a particular emotional or physical response. For example, salespeople want the customer to simulate the benefits and feelings of owning their products during a sales cycle. Car salespeople are experts at using simulation. The test drive is a way to get the buyer to simulate the fantasy of owning the car. They want the test driver to enjoy the smoothness of the ride, experience the "new car" aroma, and feel the power of the acceleration. They know that a person who successfully simulates ownership during the test drive is a good prospect for a sale.

The same principle applies to the CIO. If Luke can get Norman to envision

Hello Norman,

Cybersecurity is the number one concern of CIOs according to a recent survey by *CIO Magazine*. The latest data breach at Equifax is an example of how vulnerable even the most secure-minded companies are today. I would like to invite you and your staff to attend an online webinar on March 31ˢᵗ.

Seven Steps Every CIO Should Take to Secure Their IT Operation

Featuring Obi-Wan Kenobi, Chief Information Security Officer and Founder of ABC Technology

Figure 89.1 The tactical message example showing an invitation to an event

being a happy customer while reading the email, he is well on the road to securing a meeting. Simulation exercises the senses and engages the personality. Luke wants Norman to ask himself, Why aren't we outsourcing?

The third part of the email is the tactic to get the initial meeting. This is the call to action. In the email Luke is asking Norman to participate in a cost-savings analysis project. A tactical email needs to have a much stronger closing statement than a credibility email because you are specifically asking the executive to take action to fulfill one of his fantasies. Therefore, an operator is added that explains what the analysis entails.

All sales involve selling a fantasy. The fantasy is that the product you are selling is going to make the customer's life easier, make the customer more powerful, save money, mitigate risk, or enable the customer to make more money. The feature set of your product validates the fantasy elements of your story. The tactical offer message can also be an invitation to a webinar, relevant event, demonstration, or training session. The event's appeal is that it helps the customer fulfill

one of his fantasies in some way. The example in figure 89.1 shows a tactical offer message, sent to Norman from an IT security salesperson, in the form of an invitation to a webinar.

Chapter 90. Step 3—The Final Message

At this point, you may have attempted to contact the customer twice without success. You can either send another credibility message, a follow-up tactical-offer message, or the "final" message of the campaign. In the example below, Willy Loman, a salesperson for Interstar Networks, is trying to reach John Blutarsky, the chief technology officer of Freedom Financial Investments. Through his research, Willy knows that Freedom Financial Investments is using his archrival's product, Slowmo Networks. Please note that it is more important to pay attention to the more aggressive tone and structure of the language in this example than to understand the technical terms being used.

To: John Blutarsky, CTO@Freedom Financial Investments
From: Willy Loman@Interstar Networks
Subject: John, Slowmo Networks Performance Comparison

John,

I've sent you emails to explain Interstar Networks' advantage over Slowmo Networks. We offer superior performance because our architecture is based upon virtual processes. This is more efficient than Slowmo Networks' architecture, which uses a single-machine address. While the single-machine address solution redundantly broadcasts all messages, our solution sends specific information packets to the applicable computer. This results in up to 75 percent less network traffic.

For example, Goldman Sachs recently switched from Slowmo Networks and improved its network performance by over 60 percent. I would be delighted to set up a conference call for you to talk with John Smith, CTO at Goldman Sachs. Could we schedule a time?

Willy Loman
(123) 456-7890
Willy.Loman@Interstarnetworks.com
www.interstarnetworks.com

The above email shows several examples of how operators can be used. Operators are required to take the generic claims and translate them into proof points the customer understands and believes (see ch. 81). For example, in the email to the CTO, the general word "performance" is being operated on by the descriptor "architecture is based upon virtual processes." The term "more efficient than" is being operated on by the phrase "uses a single-machine address." The salesperson then details the differentiation between the two architectures, which is less traffic and faster performance.

To further validate his argument, Willy offers a specific customer example to illustrate his claims. Equally important, to have his claim accepted as the truth, he offers to introduce the prospect to the existing customer. In other words, he says, "Don't take only my word on this; talk to my customers."

Here's another example of the final message that is structured from a business perspective using client proof points as opposed to the previous technical example. Notice the reference to the financial investment firms in the subject line and throughout the email to entice the CTO to open the email and read it.

To: John Blutarsky, CTO@Freedom Financial Investments
From: Willy Loman@Interstar Networks
Subject: John, Goldman Sachs & Schwab Network Advantage

John,

I sent you a couple of emails because I wanted to share with you how leading investment companies including Goldman Sachs, Schwab, Morgan Stanley, and JP Morgan are solving their toughest network performance issues. For example, Goldman Sachs will have more than 250,000 online users on an average day with zero network latency using Interstar Networks. Could we schedule a meeting to discuss how Interstar Networks can help you resolve your most difficult network challenges?

Willy Loman
(123) 456-7890\Willy.Loman@Interstarnetworks.com
www.interstarnetworks.com

The last in the series of messages of the 1, 2, 3, Rest, Repeat ABM campaign is called the "final message." After sending this message you will not contact the customer for weeks or even months in some cases. Therefore, you need to structure the final message more aggressively than the credibility and tactical messages. The final message should have a harder close than the credibility and tactical messages. Penetrating new accounts requires a concerted and concentrated campaign that is conducted within a psychologically compelling linguistic framework such as the 1, 2, 3, Rest, Repeat ABM campaign.

Chapter 91. How Top Salespeople Use LinkedIn

A study I conducted reveals how top salespeople use LinkedIn to research accounts, prospect for leads, and generate sales. All of the study participants sold technology-based products to mid- to large-size companies. The study included three types of salespeople: 33 percent were inside salespeople who sold exclusively over the phone, 41 percent were outside field reps responsible for acquiring new accounts, and 26 percent were outside field reps who managed existing client accounts. The results suggest there are four basic LinkedIn user classifications:

- *Enthusiast.* Twenty-five percent of the study participants were classified as enthusiast users. Enthusiasts have fully developed LinkedIn accounts and use LinkedIn continuously during the day. They believe it is an important tool for generating product interest and promoting their company to potential customers. Enthusiasts were more likely to be outside salespeople responsible for acquiring new accounts.

- *Casual user.* Forty percent of participants were classified as casual users

who access their account on a regular basis. They consider LinkedIn a useful tool to research and learn more about prospective clients.

- *Personal user.* Fifteen percent of participants would be classified as personal users. Their LinkedIn accounts have ample information about their job history and past accomplishments. Their main purpose for having a LinkedIn account is for job related networking, and they rarely use LinkedIn for work-related purposes.

- *Nonparticipant.* Twenty percent are nonparticipants. Nonparticipants don't have a LinkedIn account or their profile contains very little personal information and fewer than twenty contacts. They don't consider LinkedIn a priority and seldom access their account. These salespeople were more likely to be older than enthusiasts, and the majority worked in the same position or at the same company for many years.

Contact Types

The composition of contacts varied greatly between enthusiasts and casual users. Over 85 percent of enthusiasts indicated they use their LinkedIn account to engage prospective customers during the sales process, while only 20 percent of casual users did. Twenty percent of enthusiasts' contacts were prospective customers, whereas it was less than 4 percent for casual users. Business partners (resellers, consultants, industry influencers, and so on) who affect customer purchasing decisions account for about 28 percent of contacts for enthusiasts and roughly 17 percent of casual users.

Customer Research

Every enthusiast and nearly half of casual users use LinkedIn to find out whom they should contact in order to secure customer meetings. Over 90 percent of enthusiasts and 65 percent of casual users use LinkedIn prior to customer meetings to find out more about the people they will meet. Specifically, they are interested in where the customers have worked in the past and whom they might know in common. Both groups also use LinkedIn extensively to verify a person's title. About 55 percent of enthusiasts and 10 percent of casual users use LinkedIn to research their competition. In addition, enthusiasts mentioned they will monitor a prospective customer's connections to find out which competitors and salespeople are working on the account. Overall, LinkedIn was rated as a research tool (on a scale of 1 to 5, with 5 being highest) by enthusiasts at 4.1 and 2.5 by casual users. Over 85 percent of enthusiasts and 50 percent of casual users indicated they would use LinkedIn to ensure they were contacting the right person but make first contact via email.

Use of Groups

On average, enthusiasts belong to twelve groups and casual users to four. Both enthusiasts and casual users indicated their main purposes for joining groups were to follow companies of interest, improve industry-related knowledge or sales skills, and keep in touch with colleagues they had worked with in the past. About 60 percent of enthusiasts and less than 20 percent of casual users responded that they belonged to groups their prospective customers were part of.

Existing Client Communication

Seventy percent of enthusiasts reported they used LinkedIn to keep existing customers informed about their company's offerings. Those who did used LinkedIn to send short messages that contained links to press releases, white papers, analyst reports, product announcements, and company produced videos.

LinkedIn-Generated Revenue

Over 40 percent of enthusiasts indicated they have successfully generated revenue based upon LinkedIn-related efforts. Less than 20 percent of casual users successfully generated revenue directly attributed to LinkedIn. Overall, 18 percent of all survey respondents indicated they have generated additional sales as a direct result of their LinkedIn activities. However, this number is deceiving. In order to truly measure LinkedIn's effectiveness, you must take into account how many salespeople are enthusiasts, casual users, personal users, or nonparticipants.

The Power of the LinkedIn Network

The networking power of LinkedIn is determined by the number of contacts that are called first-degree connections—people you are directly connected to. Your first-degree connections are connected directly to their first-degree connections. These are your second-degree connections. Your second-degree connections are connected to their first-degree connections. These are your third-degree connections. For example, you are connected to a manager (first-degree connection), who is connected to the director (second-degree connection), who is then connected to the vice president (third-degree connection).

LinkedIn Social Networking Strategy

LinkedIn is a fantastic networking platform you can use to help you get higher and wider in your accounts by establishing relationships through your first-degree connections. Therefore, you should adopt the following LinkedIn networking strategy.

1. *Build your online brand with a meaningful LinkedIn profile persona.* Establish yourself as a knowledge leader or thought leader as described in chapter 95.

2. *Connect with all your customer contacts at existing and past companies.* Send them a personalized invitation to connect if they are not part of your network today.

3. *Share articles, announcements, and interesting product information with your network and all the groups you belong to on a regular basis.* Post articles about your company and products on your profile as viewers will see them when they check your profile.

4. *Don't search anonymously.* I've heard many stories about sales that started when the prospect connected with a salesperson who viewed his profile

5. *Within existing clients, reach out to new contacts who work in other areas of the company.* Send them a personalized invitation that explains your role.

6. *Send a personalized LinkedIn invitation whenever you meet someone new who might be of value to your network.* This includes new contacts, business partners, salespeople, and consultants you meet on a daily basis. Follow LinkedIn etiquette and never send someone you don't know an outright solicitation for business after he or she connects with you. Post articles and important announcements in order for them to become familiar with you first.

7. *Accept connection requests from people who should be part of your network.* Be careful not to diminish your personal brand and online persona (see ch. 95).

8. *Join groups that are relevant to you.* There are tens of thousands of different LinkedIn groups. Join between eleven to seventeen different groups that will help you stay on top of your industry and allow you to extend the reach of your company's marketing efforts by sharing information with them.

9. *Be careful of posting "selfie" type videos.* Most of the self-shot videos that users post on LinkedIn do more harm to the person's brand and online persona than good.

10. *Become a social listener.* While social listening is most commonly associated with companies that monitor social media conversations about their products, it can be applied to prospecting as well. It is the process of following prospects on LinkedIn (and Twitter) and monitoring the conversations they participate in, their comments, and the posts they make. The salesperson then participates in the conversation by providing

insightful complimentary comments, liking the posts, and sharing them with their own network. Social listening is a less intrusive and more subtle prospecting method than sending an email or cold calling the prospect.

Sixty-six percent of buyers will visit your LinkedIn profile before an important vendor meeting, while 59 percent will visit after the meeting. Structure your profile to win over your next client as described in chapter 95. A deficient LinkedIn profile breaks your character (see ch. 44) and sends a negative image to the prospective customer.

PART V

PERSONAL SALES STRATEGY

Chapter 92. Take the Top Sales Professionals Test

I conducted an extensive study of more than one thousand salespeople and sales management leaders to determine the attributes of top sales professionals—those who achieved more than 125 percent of their assigned quota last year. This is a very select group as only 15 percent of the study participants met the criterion. Conversely, 16 percent of participants were under 75 percent of their quota, and the majority (69 percent) achieved 75 percent to 125 percent of their annual quota.

The top sales professionals have been in sales an average of sixteen years and achieved the annual quota assigned to them 88 percent of the time during their careers. This is 22 percent higher than the average of study participants who achieved less than 75 percent of their quota last year.

Participants completed an extensive survey on subjects that included sales strategy preferences and past sales performance and answered a wide variety of questions to better understand their values and personal beliefs. This chapter contains a cross section of the questions the study participants were asked to complete.

Except where noted, I'm not suggesting that these attributes are exclusive to overachievers. Indeed, top, average, and underperforming salespeople share many of the same traits. Nor am I claiming that sales success is dependent upon one particular behavior or another. Rather, this chapter provides an overview of the attitudes of top sales professionals and serves as a reference to compare yourself. Specifically, the results are divided into five key areas: (1) focus and motivation, (2) career orientation, (3) customer interaction strategy, (4) attitude, and (5) self-perception.

1. Focus and Motivation

Money is extremely important to me and how I measure my personal success

- ☐ Very true
- ☐ True
- ☐ Neutral
- ☐ Untrue
- ☐ Very untrue

Are you money motivated? It's not surprising to find that top sales professionals are money motivated. Twenty-three percent thought the statement was very true and 43 percent selected true. Twenty-four percent selected neutral, while only 10 percent disagreed with the statement.

But there is another way to think about money motivation—that's in terms of its association with greed. We normally associate greed negatively with a miserly scrooge or a corrupt character. While this may be society's definition, in sales, the greed instinct takes on an entirely different meaning. In sales, greed and self-respect are closely intertwined. Greed can be thought of as the desire to be fairly paid for one's time.

You have probably worked with many different types of salespeople, and you may have noticed that some gravitate toward working on "big deals," while others "nickel-and-dime" their way to their quota working smaller deals. The greed instinct is actually a key influencer in the way sales professionals work their territory, and this is linked to how money motivated they are. For example, 71 percent of the sales professionals who were under 75 percent of their annual quota indicated they would rather pursue a medium-size deal that has a higher probability of closing than a large deal that has a lower chance of closing. In comparison, only 47 percent of top performers would pursue a medium-size deal over a larger deal.

Obviously, the absence of greed can impact sales performance. Nearly half of sales professionals who were under 75 percent of their quota lack the greed instinct. They selected very untrue, untrue, or neutral when asked about being money motivated; this indicates that they aren't nearly as money motivated as top sales professionals. In addition, twice as many top sales professionals thought the statement was very true compared to salespeople under 75 percent of quota.

Being respected and recognized as one of the best by my peers at my company is very important to me.

- ☐ Very true
- ☐ True
- ☐ Neutral
- ☐ Untrue
- ☐ Very untrue

Top sales professionals aren't solely motivated by money. I theorize that one of the reasons for the intense preoccupation with money is that it serves as undisputed validation that the salesperson is an expert who deserves respect. The study results also provide proof that top sales professionals are highly motivated by status and recognition. A staggering 84 percent of top salespeople indicated that being respected and recognized as one of the best by peers at their company is very important to them as shown in figure 92.1.

Top sales professionals feel their opinion matters and always want to be heard. They truly believe they are experts in the field of sales and know exactly how

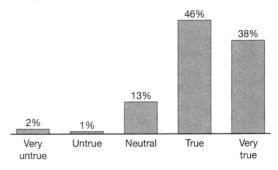

Being respected and recognized as one of the best by peers at my company is very important to me

Figure 92.1 Top salespeople rate the importance of being respected

sales should be done. They naturally seek to achieve the alpha (or dominant) position within their group to ensure they are heard. Whether formally or informally, they desire to see their actions emulated by other team members, and the only way to achieve the alpha position is by becoming a top salesperson.

The leadership position top sales professionals seek is not necessarily reflected in their title—it is a position of prominence based upon their knowledge and the recognition that comes along with being thought of as an expert.

Which statement best describes you?

- ☐ I am very dependable and good at prioritizing my time.
- ☐ I am a likable person who makes customers feel comfortable.
- ☐ I believe my knowledge is powerful.

When asked to select the statement that best described their personal focus, 42 percent of top sales professionals said they are a likable person who makes customers feel comfortable. At the foundation of all sales is a relationship between people. Great salespeople have an innate talent to build these relationships by creating rapport. Their presence has an appeal that makes the customer feel at ease. They build personal alliances based upon understanding individual wants and needs. The customer trusts them.

Thirty-two percent of top sales professionals consider themselves very dependable and good at prioritizing their time. These sales professionals are oriented differently than the group who selected likability. When asked to select

three words that they would use to describe themselves, the most frequent selections were "confident," "productive," and "responsible." In separate personality testing I have done in the past, 85 percent of top salespeople had high levels of conscientiousness. They are classified as having a strong sense of duty and being responsible and reliable. These salespeople take their jobs very seriously and feel deeply responsible for their results.

Twenty-six percent of top sales professionals believe that their knowledge is their most powerful attribute, and this group had the highest average quota attainment last year at 170 percent. These salespeople are masters of language. They are accomplished communicators who know what to say and, equally important, how to say it. Through their domain expertise and the knowledge of their industry, products, technology, or business, they have developed the ability to persuade skeptics to buy.

2. Career Orientation

I am the type of person who

- ☐ Lives my life one day at a time
- ☐ Has a written or mental list of tasks I want to accomplish
- ☐ Is frequently thinking what my future will be like in five, ten, or more years

Top sales professionals think about work a lot. In fact, the results from another study question indicate they find themselves thinking about their job over half of their free time on weeknights and weekends. I would argue this statistic proves that sales requires a higher level of job fixation than most careers. In addition, top salespeople are goal and outcome focused. Fifty percent said they were the type of person who keeps a written or mental list of goals they want to accomplish as shown in figure 92.2.

While you might associate this with someone who prefers order and structure, this is not the case, as 81 percent of participants who selected this response indicated they prefer a wide variety of activities as opposed to repetitive daily routines. I surmise the list provides a reinforcing visual representation of forward progress and milestones of accomplishment as completed items are crossed off and also serves as a practical reminder.

Thirty-seven percent of top salespeople indicated they're frequently thinking about what the future will be like in five, ten, or more years. Only 13 percent described themselves as the type of person who lives life one day at a time. These sales professionals employ less structure to their sales methodology when compared to those who maintain lists or are constantly thinking about the future.

The salespeople in these three groups not only have different types of personalities but also work on deals in completely different ways. More list

maintainers said they focus on situations where they were more likely to win when working on deals. More future thinkers indicated they follow their instincts, while more one-day-at-a-timers said they take calculated risks when working on deals.

The fundamental reason I'm in sales is

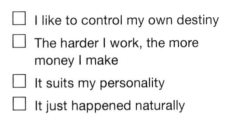

What is the fundamental reason you're in sales? The responses from top sales professionals about the fundamental reason they went into sales were fairly evenly split as shown in figure 92.3.

One way to analyze these answers is by grouping them into two distinct categories. Controlling your destiny and working harder represent the "sales as a career" category. This is a group of confident, like-minded individuals who share many traits and characteristics. They answered most of the survey questions similarly, and their answers tended to show more conformity to the expected norms of sales behavior.

The second category is "sales as a lifestyle." The diverse nature of the answers indicate this group is composed of more independent thinkers who are more outgoing and gregarious. They think differently than the first group. For example, the members of each group were asked if they agreed or disagreed with the

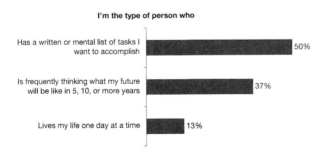

Figure 92.2 Top salespeople describe the type of person they are

The fundamental reason I'm in sales is

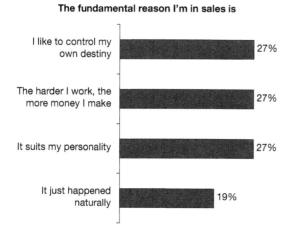

I like to control my own destiny	27%
The harder I work, the more money I make	27%
It suits my personality	27%
It just happened naturally	19%

Figure 92.3 Top salespeople describe the reason they are in sales

following statement: "I like to win but cannot stand to lose because the pain of losing is greater than the joy of winning." Twice as many top sales professionals in the "sales as a career" category thought the statement was very true. Conversely, twice as many "sales as a lifestyle" category thought the statement was very untrue.

3. Customer Interaction Strategy

Rank the following sales strategies in order of effectiveness:

___ Asking questions that show your expertise

___ Driving the topics of conversation

___ Getting the customer to emotionally connect with you

___ Showing the value and benefits of your solution

___ Tailoring your sales pitch to the customer's needs

The top sales professionals ranked five different sales strategies based on their effectiveness. The top-ranked strategies were "Getting customers to emotionally connect with you" followed by "Tailoring your sales pitch to the customer's needs" and then "Asking questions that show your expertise." The two lowest ranked strategies were "Showing the value and benefits of your solution" and "Driving the topics of conversation."

The ranking of the answers may surprise, or even upset, the sales enablement and sales training professionals who are reading this report. You see, most training programs are predicated on showing the value and benefit of solutions. They share the same fundamental flaw. They think of customers as rational decision-makers who use logic and reason exclusively. Meanwhile, successful salespeople understand and appeal to the emotional, political, and subconscious decision-maker. They have to build a trusted relationship and personal friendship in a short period of time.

I tend to

☐ Feel personally responsible and dedicate myself to ensure my clients' success

☐ Have cordial relationships with my clients because we are both busy

☐ Keep a general pulse on what's happening with customers after the sale

☐ Develop very close personal friendships with my clients

What type of relationship do you have with customers following the sale? Contrary to what many people think of as a requirement for sales success, only 16 percent develop very close personal friendships with their clients. Rather, 36 percent of top sales professionals indicated they feel personally responsible and dedicate themselves to ensuring the client's success. Twenty-six percent indicated they have cordial relationships, and 22 percent keep a general pulse on what's happening with the customer after the sale.

What's the best sales strategy? While it's hard to pick the outright winner, the evidence suggests the worst sales strategy is to keep a general pulse on customers. Figure 92.4 shows some results associated with each of the answers so you can make your own decision.

4. Attitude

Let's do a word association. Write down the first word that comes to your mind when you read the following:

Sales manager   _____

Sales process   _____

The study participants were asked to complete word associations to allow a better understanding of their workplace attitudes. The written answers were then categorized as having a positive connotation, a negative connotation, or a neutral connotation that was neither bad nor good. For example, 53 percent of the associations to the term "sales manager" were positive, and the top three answers were "coach," "leader," and "mentor." Twenty-seven percent of the answers were negative, and the two most frequently mentioned were "pain" and "overhead." Twenty percent were neutral,

	Over the course of my sales career, I estimate I have attained the quota I was assigned ___ percent of the time	I would rate my career-advancement success last year on a scale of 1 (low) to 10 (high) as	Percentage who graded their overall career as an A or A+
Feel personally responsible and dedicate myself to ensuring my client's success	90%	7.78	44%
Have a cordial relationship with my client because we are both very busy	90%	7.87	33%
Keep a general pulse on what's happening with the customer after a sale	84%	7.03	32%
Develop a very close personal friendship with my client	87%	7.40	48%

Figure 92.4 Metrics associated with customer relationship strategy

and the most frequently cited words were "management" and "forecast."

Forty-two percent of the answers for "sales process" were positive associations, with the most frequently mentioned terms being "important" and "necessary." Thirty-seven percent were neutral words, and the top answers were "methodology" and "structure," while 21 percent were negative, with the top-mentioned words being "long" and "convoluted."

The words you say to yourself are the most important words you use all day. Do you continually question yourself or say positive reinforcements throughout the day? Do you tell yourself "It's just a job," or are you excited about what you do for a living? Your internal mantra, whether positive or negative, will influence your career success. For example, top sales professionals who described their sales manager as a "coach" or "leader" rated their career-advancement success last year at an average of 8.6 on a scale of 1 (low) to 10 (high) on average. Those who used "pain" or "overhead" rated theirs at 7.2 on average.

5. Self-Perception

Please pick the top two qualities you think prospective customers admire the most about you:

- ☐ Athleticism
- ☐ Attractiveness
- ☐ Charisma
- ☐ Creativity
- ☐ Eloquence
- ☐ Enthusiasm
- ☐ Follow-through
- ☐ Industry experience
- ☐ Product knowledge
- ☐ Professionalism
- ☐ Sales acumen
- ☐ Technical aptitude
- ☐ Trustworthiness

When top sales professionals selected from a list of qualities they thought prospective customers admired most about them, the top responses were (1) trustworthiness, (2) professionalism, (3) follow-through, (4) product knowledge, and (5) enthusiasm. However, the definition of "trustworthiness" seems to be individually determined, based upon the responses to the following question.

Which statement do you agree with most when working with prospective customers?

- ☐ If the customer's best interest is served by slightly obscuring information, that's okay
- ☐ Subtle information manipulation is reasonable, so long as the truth is served.
- ☐ Sometimes you have to do whatever you must to get the important evaluators to back you.
- ☐ You don't have to point out every blemish of your product offering.
- ☐ Nothing but the whole truth is acceptable.

Salespeople expect deception from competitors. However, the most damaging deceptions actually come from customers. Customers will lie to you for a variety of reasons: to protect themselves, to make you feel better about yourself, and to help your competitors.

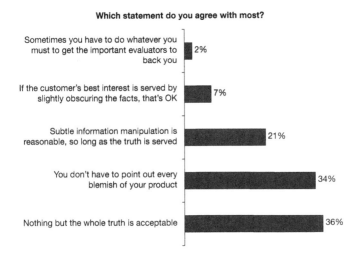

Which statement do you agree with most?

Sometimes you have to do whatever you must to get the important evaluators to back you — 2%

If the customer's best interest is served by slightly obscuring the facts, that's OK — 7%

Subtle information manipulation is reasonable, so long as the truth is served — 21%

You don't have to point out every blemish of your product — 34%

Nothing but the whole truth is acceptable — 36%

Figure 92.5 Top salespeople's attitudes about truthfulness

As a result, customers will say things they don't mean and mean things they don't say (see ch. 104).

Conversely, do salespeople lie? Society in general thinks they do. I've arranged the study participants' answers in terms of their general perception of truthfulness from low to high in figure 92.5. Based upon my personal experience interviewing and studying thousands of salespeople, I'll argue that the overwhelming majority of business-to-business salespeople (95 percent) consistently tell the truth. And the study results validate this in my mind.

To better understand why I believe this, we need to refer to the psychological theory of "holistic interactionism." This is the notion that behavior is not based solely on personality but is ultimately influenced by a person's situational interaction with the environment. For example, a boisterous extrovert is quiet and reserved while in a library. A soft-spoken introvert might turn into a screaming maniac while rooting for his or her favorite team at a football game.

Now, you probably consider yourself to be an honest person. Think about the last time you interviewed for a job. Did you voluntarily point out all your flaws? Of course not. Rather, you may have overemphasized some of your positive points, and that doesn't necessarily make you a liar. The same logic applies to the context of a sales call.

How would you describe yourself? Select the three words from the list below that describe you best.

- ☐ Charming
- ☐ Cheerful
- ☐ Confident
- ☐ Empathetic
- ☐ Frank
- ☐ Funny
- ☐ Humble
- ☐ Likable
- ☐ Productive
- ☐ Proud
- ☐ Quick-witted
- ☐ Responsible
- ☐ Shrewd
- ☐ Smart
- ☐ Tough
- ☐ Wise
- ☐ X-factor (a combination of all the traits listed)

Perhaps the most interesting part of the study is the perception of top sales professionals and how they described themselves when compared with those who achieved less than 75 percent of their quota. When presented with the same list of seventeen choices, the most frequently selected answers for those under 75 percent of their quota were responsible, likable, confident, empathetic, smart, and humble. Describing themselves as being likable, empathetic, and humble suggest they have a submissive selling style. The answers for top sales professionals (over 125 percent of their quota) were confident, X-factor (a combination of all the traits listed), quick-witted, likable, responsible, and productive. These selections suggest that top sales professionals have a higher level of self-confidence, stronger belief in their verbal acuity, and higher opinion about their ability to produce results. This self-assured, egocentric view suggest a more dominant selling style.

Perhaps the most important difference between the two groups can be found in the concept of the X-factor. I specifically created the term for this study in order to quantify an interesting aspect of behavior I have personally witnessed in interviews with salespeople. In general, underperforming salespeople are less likely to think out of the box and more likely to behave in the traditional manner that would be expected of a salesperson. Conversely, top salespeople not only think outside the box but also have a tendency to question the norm and create their own rules. This requires the highest level of confidence and a quick-witted personality that is on constant alert for both opportunities and dangers. Equally important, it requires the core belief that all of their personal attributes and sales skills are truly their competitive difference.

Chapter 93. The Seven Personality Traits of Top Salespeople

Over the past decade, I have had the privilege of interviewing thousands of top business-to-business salespeople who sell for some of the world's leading companies. I never grow tired hearing their stories of how they win extremely competitive six- and seven-figure deals. I've also administered personality tests to them. My goal was to measure their five main personality traits (openness, conscientiousness, extraversion, agreeableness, and negative emotionality) to better understand the characteristics that separate them from their peers.

The test results from top performers were then compared against average and below average performers. The findings indicate that key personality traits directly influence top performers' selling style and ultimately their success. Below, you will find the main key personality attributes of top salespeople and the impact of the trait on their selling style.

1. *Achievement orientation.* Eighty-four percent of the top performers tested scored very high in achievement orientation. They are fixated on achieving goals and continuously measure their performance in comparison to their goals.
   Selling style impact: political orientation. During sales cycles, top sales performers seek to understand the politics of customer decision-making.

Their goal orientation instinctively drives them to meet with key decision-makers. Therefore, they strategize about the people they are selling to and how the products they're selling fit into the organization instead of focusing on the functionality of the products themselves.

2. *Curiosity.* Curiosity can be described as a person's hunger for knowledge and information. Eighty-two percent of top salespeople scored extremely high curiosity levels. Top salespeople are naturally more curious than their lesser-performing counterparts.

   Selling style impact: inquisitiveness. A high level of inquisitiveness correlates to an active presence during sales calls. An active presence drives the salesperson to ask customers difficult and uncomfortable questions in order to close gaps in information. Top salespeople want to know if they can win the business, and they want to know the truth as soon as possible.

3. *Modesty.* Contrary to conventional stereotypes that successful salespeople are pushy and egotistical, 91 percent of top salespeople had medium to high scores of modesty and humility. Furthermore, the results suggest that ostentatious salespeople who are full of bravado alienate far more customers than they win over.

   Selling style impact: team orientation. As opposed to establishing themselves as the focal point of the purchase decision, top salespeople position the team (presales technical engineers, consulting, and management) that will help them win the account as the centerpiece.

4. *Lack of gregariousness.* One of the most surprising differences between top salespeople and those ranking in the bottom one-third of performance is their level of gregariousness (preference for company and friendliness). Overall, top performers averaged 30 percent lower gregariousness than below average performers.

   Selling style impact: situational dominance. Dominance is the ability to gain the willing obedience of customers such that the salesperson's recommendations and advice are followed. The results indicate that overly friendly salespeople are too close to their customers and have difficulty establishing dominance.

5. *Lack of discouragement.* Less than 10 percent of top salespeople were classified as having high levels of discouragement and being frequently overwhelmed with sadness. Conversely, 90 percent were categorized as experiencing infrequent or occasional sadness.

   Selling style impact: competitiveness. In casual surveys I have conducted throughout the years, I have found that 90 percent of top performers played organized sports in high school. There seems to be a direct correlation between sports and sales success as top performers are able to handle emotional disappointments, bounce back from losses, and mentally prepare themselves for the next opportunity to compete.

6. *Lack of self-consciousness.* Self-consciousness is the measurement of how easily someone is embarrassed. The by-product of a high

level of self-consciousness is bashfulness and inhibition. Less than 5 percent of top performers had high levels of self-consciousness.

Selling style impact: aggressiveness. Top salespeople are comfortable fighting for their cause and not afraid of rankling customers in the process. They are action oriented and unafraid to "call high" in their accounts or courageously cold call new prospects.

7. *Conscientiousness.* Eighty-five percent of top salespeople had high levels of conscientiousness, whereby they could be described as having a strong sense of duty and being responsible and reliable. These salespeople take their jobs very seriously and feel deeply responsible for the results.

Selling style impact: account control. The worst position for salespeople to be in is to have relinquished account control and to be operating at the direction of the customer, or worse yet, a competitor. Conversely, top salespeople take command of the sales cycle process in order to control their own destiny.

Not all salespeople are successful. Given the same sales tools, level of education, and propensity to work, why do some salespeople succeed where others fail? Is one better suited to sell the product because of his or her background? Is one more charming or just luckier? The evidence suggests that the personalities of these Heavy Hitters play a critical role in determining their success.

Chapter 94. Are Top Salespeople Born or Made?

Are top salespeople born or made? In other words, must top salespeople be born with the prerequisite sales instincts, or can someone learn to become successful in sales without them?

Based upon my research, experience, and observations, I estimate over 70 percent of top salespeople are born with "natural" instincts that play a critical role in determining their sales success. Conversely, less than 30 percent of top salespeople are self-made—meaning, they have had to learn how to become top salespeople without the benefit of these natural abilities. In addition, for every one hundred people who enter sales without natural sales traits, 40 percent will fail or quit, 40 percent will perform at or near average, and only 20 percent will be above average (these figures vary by industry and the complexity of products sold).

Based on the figures above, the real question that should be asked is, What determines whether or not a self-made salesperson will become successful? While it's easy to recite a laundry list of general reasons for success (hard work, persistence, intelligence, integrity, empathy, etc.), my experience in the field and the research I've conducted indicates four key factors that determine the self-made salesperson's destiny. They are language specialization, "modeling" of experiences, political acumen, and greed.

Language Specialization

The first differentiating factor between the success or failure of the self-made salesperson is language specialization. While all competent salespeople can recite their product's features and business benefits, very few are mavens who can conduct intelligent conversations about the details of daily business operations. Every industry also has developed its own technical language to facilitate mutual understanding of terminology and an exact meaning of the words used throughout a business. The technical language consists of abbreviations, acronyms, business nomenclature, and specialized terms (for example, RAM, CPU, and flash drive in the computer industry).

Successful self-made salespeople possess domain-area expertise and speak the corresponding business operations language, or have deep knowledge of the industry's technical language. These languages are the yardstick by which customers measure a salesperson's true value and greatly influence their purchase decisions. Lesser-performing self-made salespeople are not as fluent in these languages, so they tend to focus on likability and friendliness with prospective customers.

Modeling of Experiences

Modeling is the mind's ability to link like experiences and similar data into predictable patterns. Salespeople continually learn through the ongoing accumulation and consolidation of information from their sales calls and interactions with customers. From this knowledge base, salespeople can predict what will happen and what they should do in light of what they have done in the past.

Modeling can be thought of as the engine that drives sales intuition. For example, let's say a salesperson is asked by a skeptical, analytical, financial-oriented prospective customer how his product is different from his major competitor's. His answer would be based on previous experiences with similar circumstances. Modeling can be thought of as trying to find the what, when, where response—what you should do when you are in a particular circumstance where you have to act.

Successful self-made salespeople have an effective methodology to store and retrieve all the verbal, nonverbal, factual, and intuitive information that occurs during sales calls and sales cycles. This results in a greater proficiency to win business than less-successful self-made salespeople who do not learn from their past mistakes and instead repeat them.

Political Acumen

Unfortunately, many underperforming self-made salespeople take a textbook-type approach to sales and concentrate solely on the procedural aspects of the sales cycle. They don't take into account the human nature of sales and how people and politics determine the outcome.

Politics are based upon self-interests. Therefore, customers do not readily reveal the internal machinations of their decision-making. Political acumen is the ability to correctly map out each decision-maker's influence and motivations. Successful self-made salespeople consider this their top priority. Political acumen drives winning account strategy whereas strategic planning without political acumen is a losing proposition.

Greed

We normally associate greed with a corrupt character or miserly scrooge. While this may be society's definition, in sales, "greed" takes on an entirely different meaning. In sales, greed and self-respect are closely intertwined. Greed can be thought of as the desire to be fairly paid for one's time. Time is a salesperson's enemy because time is finite. Time is the governor that determines how many deals can be worked and where effort should be focused. Salespeople are on a mission to learn the ultimate truth, "Will I win the deal?" Greed compels successful self-made salespeople to push themselves beyond their comfort zone and ask difficult qualifying questions while continually pushing for the close. Conversely, lesser successful self-made salespeople do not possess this inward drive.

Chapter 95. Creating Your Brand and LinkedIn Online Persona

Who are you and what makes you unique? I've asked that question of hundreds of salespeople and I'm always surprised by how many responders of every age have difficulty answering it. The reason why is that they haven't taken the time to formalize their own brand. Over the years, I have observed that the best salespeople know who they are and are true to themselves. As a result, they can articulately describe their brand.

One methodology for describing yourself is to create a "brand statement." The brand statement consists of a short one- to three-word description of who you are, a ten-word description, and a fifty-word description. Each statement must support the others. Here's my brand description, for example; notice that each of the longer statements supports the preceding shorter one.

My brand in one to three words:
Respected sales expert

My brand in ten words or less:
Accomplished sales author, sales effectiveness trainer and noted sales researcher

My brand in fifty words or less:
Author of the Heavy Hitter series of books on the human nature of complex sales. My corporate training has helped over 150,000 salespeople become top revenue producers at companies including IBM, Google, and PayPal. I'm a regular research contributor to the *Harvard Business Review* and teach at USC's MBA program.

Here's a brand statement example for a B2B salesperson.

Brand in three words or less: Strategic accounts closer

Brand in ten words or less:
Politically astute problem solver who closes strategic accounts

Brand in fifty words or less:
My diverse business, finance, and operations background enables me to creatively solve clients' critical problems, thereby aligning myself with their decision-making process. Because of my insights-based account control

strategy, I have closed three of the top five revenue accounts in my company's history and received the President's Award each year.

Exercise: Now it's time for a very important exercise. Create your own brand statement consisting of three-word, ten-word, and fifty-word brand statements.

An Important Question You Should Be Prepared to Answer

Perhaps the most important question a customer can ask you is, "Tell me about yourself." Unfortunately, it's easy to be caught off guard and flub the answer, thereby missing a key opportunity to differentiate yourself from your competitors. The secret to nailing this question is to have two types of answers prepared in advance. These answers are an intrinsic part of your brand and the talk track (preplanned scripted message) that describes who you are.

The first type is based on your personal life and called a "character answer." This answer focuses on a specific character trait and tells a personal story that explains what type of person you are. It provides the listener with a background story that demonstrates your personal qualities, attributes, and temperament. Here's an example of a character answer that focuses on the person's competitive nature character trait.

I consider myself to be a very competitive person. I think it's partly because I was the youngest of four children and I always had to compete with three very talented siblings. For example, my brother was an all-star football player, and that motivated me to start playing football. I went on to earn a college scholarship and was team captain. I'm in sales because I like the competitive nature of it. I'm the kind of person who likes to measure how I'm doing. In sales, you know when you are winning or losing, and I like to win.

The second type of answer is based on your professional life and is called a "progression answer." This answer recounts past career successes along with your progression and accomplishments. It logically explains what you're doing today and why you're doing it. Here's an example of a progression answer.

I've always been fascinated with technology and graduated from college with a computer science degree. I joined IBM as a consultant in its retail practice and worked on big data-warehouse projects for Walmart and Costco. I was then selected to take on a sales role in the newly formed big data practice. Without any sales experience to speak of, I became one of the top salespeople within IBM, winning the President's Award several times. I then joined ABC Company, which was a Silicon Valley start-up at the time. Over a two-year period, our revenues grew from $7 million to $75 million. Now I have the privilege to manage key client relationships, including Amazon and Uber.

When do you use the character and progression answers? It depends upon whom you are talking with. As a general rule, senior-level executives want to know what type of person you are, so the character answer is better. After all, their lower-level staff members have met with you and vetted your background. The progression answer is appropriate for mid- and lower-level personnel along with those who are more technically inclined. However, it's always best to select the answer that you think will have the most impact.

Creating a Compelling LinkedIn Profile

Grab your smartphone and Google your full name along with the name of the company you work for. If you're like 95 percent of salespeople, the first result Google returns will be your LinkedIn profile. Similarly, if you conduct the same search on Google images, the first result will be your LinkedIn profile picture. After trillions of these types of searches, Google's heuristic engine has learned that searchers want to access LinkedIn profiles first. Go ahead and take a moment right now to Google yourself if you haven't yet.

We can classify salespeople's LinkedIn personal profiles into two categories. LinkedIn 1.0 profiles are those where the subjects describe how wonderful they are and list all of their accomplishments. Their profile's main purpose is to help these salespeople find their next job; they're basically a copy of their resume online. LinkedIn 2.0 profiles are different. They're more sophisticated and their purpose is to help these salespeople find their next customer, not their next job. Specifically, the goal of a LinkedIn 2.0 profile is to

- Present a professional image of who you are
- Present a story about your brand in an impactful way
- Show your history to prove you're qualified
- Reinforce your reputation as demonstrated by customer recommendations and what connections say about you and endorse you for
- Provide a public history of your productivity and results
- Establish your online persona as a knowledge leader or thought leader

You have a very important decision to make about your brand and how you present your online persona via LinkedIn. You can position yourself as a valuable *employee* who works for your company. You can position yourself as a *knowledge leader* who shares industry updates, business information, and articles written by others with your network of connections. Or you can position yourself as a *thought leader* who writes articles and provides personal thoughts, opinions, and business advice with your network. A LinkedIn 2.0 profile positions the person as a knowledge or thought leader, not solely an employee.

A LinkedIn profile has many elements, which can be confusing. So I like to use the metaphor of a lion to explain them. Specifically, I group elements by importance into the head, body, and tail as shown in figure 95.1. The head is the most attention-getting part of the lion, with the mouth being how you roar your brand to the marketplace. It contains the most important branding elements of your profile. The body contains elements that show you're qualified and respected. The elements of the tail show what you're professionally interested in.

LinkedIn Profile Guidelines

Below are guidelines for creating a 2.0 profile. It should be noted that LinkedIn makes changes to the platform continuously. Furthermore, with LinkedIn's acquisition by Microsoft, you can expect all of their tools (Outlook, Word, Excel, etc.) to be integrated with LinkedIn over time.

- *Personalized LinkedIn URL.* Edit the standard URL that is assigned to your profile and remove the mishmash of characters and numbers that follow your name. For example, change www.linkedin.com/in /bob-Johnson-60345b to www.linked in.com/in/bobjohnson.

- *Background/banner picture.* The background picture is the banner at the top of your profile. Use one that is provided by your company, or ensure the one you select on your own has the correct resolution. Your background picture should reinforce your personal brand.

- *Head-shot photo.* This is the single most important element of your profile. Your picture should be of high quality, exude professionalism and likability, and encourage someone to want to meet with you. Don't use pictures that include your children, spouse, or possessions or were taken in a social setting (wedding, restaurant, etc.) and include someone's partially cropped head, arm, or shoulder.

- *Headline.* Your profile is not your résumé, and the headline doesn't have

Head
Personalized URL
Background/banner picture
Head-shot photo
Headline
Number of connections
Summary
Media
Articles and activity

Body
Work experience
Projects
Publications
Endorsements
Recommendations
Education, awards, and certifications
Personal details and interests

Tail
Groups
Companies following
Influencers following

Figure 95.1 The elements of a LinkedIn profile grouped by importance

to be your job title. Use a headline that shows how you help customers, such as "Changing the Way Companies Store Information" or "Supply Chain Optimization Specialist."

- *Number of connections.* At a minimum, you need to have a critical mass of over five hundred connections to show you're a legitimate LinkedIn user.

- *Summary.* Your summary is a very valuable piece of online real estate. Take time to craft a summary that explains who you are and promotes your brand. I also recommend to my clients that their marketing department provide a standard summary about the company and why it is unique that all employees can use.

- *Media.* Add videos and PDFs about your company, customer success stories, and products to your profile.

- *Articles and activity.* You need to actively participate on LinkedIn in order to be considered a knowledge or thought leader. Post interesting articles about your company and customers. Write articles about topics you think prospective clients are interested in. Add media to your profile such as company videos, brochures, and data sheets.

- *Work experience.* Don't recite your job description; rather, explain how you help your customers become more successful.

- *Projects.* Share stories and examples about the successful customers you've helped.

- *Publications.* List important white papers and research reports you or your company has written.

- *Endorsements.* The lack of endorsements can be considered a red flag by potential buyers, and you should have at least forty endorsements for the four skills that show up on the top of your profile. Think about it for a moment. If no one cares to endorse you, then you might not be a knowledge or thought leader.

- *Recommendations.* You need a minimum of four high-quality recommendations written by your clients.

- *Education, awards, and certifications.* Share your college degree, relevant awards you've received, and certifications you have attained. College students and recent graduates should provide a detailed list of coursework and business-related extracurricular activities.

- *Personal details and interests.* I recommend keeping your profile very professional and strictly focused on business. No one really needs to know that your birthday is in March or that you like yoga.

- *Groups, companies, and influencers.* You should belong to at least eleven groups whereby you can follow your industry and companies that reinforce your brand. Regarding influencers, my recommendation is not to follow anyone who could possibly be considered offensive by someone else. For example, if you follow a particular politician, you risk alienating others who don't support that person.

Exercise: If you have a poor LinkedIn profile, then you're breaking character (see ch. 44) before you meet the customer. This is because 66 percent of customers will view a salesperson's LinkedIn profile before an important meeting. Evaluate your LinkedIn profile using the guidelines above. Is it a 1.0 profile? How does it compare, and what elements need to be improved?

Chapter 96. You Are a Walking, Talking Metaphor for Your Brand

Your most important metaphor is you. You are a walking, talking metaphor. The way you dress, present yourself, and represent your product provides important symbolism to the customer. Your customer has standards and certain expectations about the way you will act, look, and speak. These standards vary greatly among customers, companies, industries, and places. Selling drilling equipment in Texas is different from selling computer chips in Silicon Valley or hotel supplies in Hawaii. Each requires a salesperson to use a different presence and demeanor to build credibility and gain rapport.

Presence and demeanor will greatly influence the customer's decision. For example, would you hire a personal trainer who was extremely out of shape? An interior designer who dressed sloppily or out of style? Would you visit a dentist who had terrible teeth and who used dilapidated equipment? Physical presence projects an important message to the customer.

Buyers have innate personal biases. In fact, 91 percent of B2B buyers agree with the statement that better-looking salespeople have an advantage. Figure 96.1 shows how buyers prefer the salespeople they meet to dress.

It makes sense to dress like your customers and express yourself in a manner they are comfortable with. The way you dress should show that your first concern is the customer's success, not your own self-interests. While we want to communicate success, we don't want the customer thinking he's being overcharged.

That's why I frown on elaborate adornments and expensive jewelry such as gold cufflinks and watches. Leave them at home unless the customer is wearing them too. Remember, a salesperson's dress and demeanor and how he treats the customer serve as a metaphor for their future relationship. The clothes you wear should represent your personal brand, so don't overdo any particular aspect of the way you present yourself.

All salespeople are friendly, helpful, and attentive during the sales cycle because they know the customer is constantly evaluating them. It's after the sale is made and the commission paid when true service begins. A salesperson's humility is in fact a metaphor for service and selflessness. An ostentatious salesperson who is full of bravado

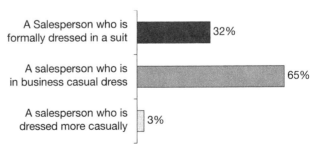

Figure 96.1 B2B buyer dress preferences

will alienate far more customers than he wins over. The customer doesn't expect to see him once the deal closes. Meanwhile, the unpretentious salesperson naturally builds rapport. People expect he'll stay around after the deal closes.

If you scored high in dominance in the personality test in chapter 99, you should carefully select what you wear based upon the customer you're meeting with. You do not want your physical presence to cause you to be perceived as arrogant. On the other hand, no one wants to associate with a vagabond who looks like he slept in his clothes. Find a point between the two extremes, where the clothes you wear communicate your professionalism without alienating the customer.

Finally, people naturally want to be around positive people. Conversely, salespeople who constantly criticize the competition are less likely to win over customers. Think about yourself for a moment: do you like to be around people who are negative and demeaning?

Chapter 97. The Principles of Customer Communication Using Sales Linguistics

Without language, you really wouldn't exist. You wouldn't be able to share your ideas, display your personality, and express yourself to the world. You couldn't communicate your needs and desires to others, and the never-ending dialogue within your mind would stop. The words we speak truly define who we are. However, since we are talking all the time, we underestimate the complexity of communication and take the process for granted.

The conversations salespeople have with customers are quite complex. They consist of verbal and nonverbal messages that are sent consciously and subconsciously. Successful customer communications are the foundation of all sales, and Heavy Hitters naturally speak in the language of their customers. The question is, What do they say?

Language is studied in many well-established fields. Sociolinguistics is the study of language use in society and social networks. Psycholinguistics is the study of how the mind acquires, uses, and represents language. Neurolinguistics is the study of how brain structures process language. Today, an exciting new area of study called "sales linguistics" applies aspects from these fields to the conversations salespeople have with customers. The goal of sales linguistics is to understand how salespeople and their prospective customers use and interpret language during the decision-making process.

The principles of sales linguistics are these: every customer speaks in his or her own unique language, salespeople build rapport through harmonious communication, the customer will always lie, persuasion requires a personal connection, buyer personas determine the language that should be used, sales intuition is language based, and establishing situational dominance is the ultimate goal.

Customers Speak Unique Languages

Each person on this planet speaks his or her own unique language. All the mundane and traumatic experiences of your life have determined the language you use. Just as no one else has had your exact life experiences, no one else speaks your precise language. Therefore, the language two people use to describe the same situation may be very different. Unfortunately, most companies arm their salespeople with a "one-size fits-all" company sales pitch.

The first principle of sales linguistics is that every customer speaks in his or her own language. It is based upon understanding the customer's interpretation of your message and its associated psychological impact. For example, reading the word "snake" might cause you to visualize a rattlesnake, a python, or a cobra. While these are all specific interpretations of the word, they all may naturally evoke fear and negative emotions. Conversely, if you raised a pet snake as a child, you probably have a positive mental association. Since the personal meanings of words can vary greatly, you may even have thought of an unscrupulous businessperson when you first read the word "snake."

Rapport Is Harmonious Communication

Unfortunately, when most salespeople meet with prospective customers, they talk in only their own language about their product's features, functions, and benefits. When Heavy Hitter salespeople meet with customers, they talk about their problems, plans, and personal aspirations. They speak their customers' language in order to build rapport.

Rapport is a special relationship between two individuals based upon harmonious communication. However, human communication occurs in several different forms and on several different

levels. An immense amount of information is conveyed verbally, phonetically, physically, consciously, and subconsciously. Heavy Hitters naturally adapt their mental wiring and language to mirror the customers'.

Whether Inadvertently or On Purpose, the Customer Will Always Lie

Salespeople expect deception from competitors. However, the most damaging deceptions actually come from customers. Salespeople are on a mission to learn the ultimate truth, "Will I win the deal?" And they want to find the truth about winning an account as early as possible.

Customers will lie to you for a variety of reasons: to protect themselves, to make you feel better about yourself, and to help your competitors. As a result, customers will say things they don't mean and mean things they don't say. When you ask at the end of your sales presentation, "Does everyone believe we are the best solution?" even though everyone nods, the audience may include objectors who will try to sabotage your deal later on (see ch. 104).

Persuasion Requires a Personal Connection

Salespeople are paid to persuade. But what makes them persuasive? Is it their command of the facts and their ability to recite a litany of reasons why customers should buy? In reality, the most product-knowledgeable salesperson is not necessarily the most persuasive one because it takes more than logic and reason to change buyers' opinions. A personal connection must be established.

Persuasion is the process of projecting your entire set of beliefs and convictions onto another human being. It's not about getting others to acknowledge your arguments or agree with your business case; it's about making them internalize your message because they believe that it is in their best interests. Ultimately, persuasion is the ability to tap into someone's emotions and reach the deeper subconscious decision-maker within that person.

Sales Intuition Is Language Based

The mind does not treat all information equally. Some information is ignored, some information is misinterpreted, and some information is generalized based upon past experiences. Unfortunately, many salespeople edit information to support their pre-existing beliefs. Salespeople with "happy ears" tend to believe what they are told by the customer. Others view the world through rose-colored glasses and will always interpret information emanating from the customer in a favorable light. Such ambiguities and delusions are disastrous.

Conversely, top salespeople accurately interpret information using their sales intuition. They are continually cataloging their successes and failures based upon all the different types of verbal and nonverbal languages the customer is communicating. They store patterns of individual and group meeting behavior. Through their sales intuition, they are able to integrate their spoken words with the sales situation based upon their experiences with similar types of people and past sales cycles.

Buyer Personas Determine the Language That Should Be Used

Buyer personas are a method of categorizing customer behavior based upon the psychological motives behind the customer's use of language. Customers participating in sales calls can be classified into different decision-making roles depending upon how they process information, how they behave as part of a selection team, their political power, and their personal disposition toward their company (see chs. 72–77).

The segmentation strategy provides a predictive framework to anticipate customer behavior. Since the salesperson has a deeper insight into customer behavior based upon past interactions, he is able to create more compelling presentations and conduct more persuasive sales calls. This strategy also serves as a communication methodology to educate and prepare the colleagues who will attend the sales call with the salesperson.

Situational Dominance Is the Ultimate Goal

We typically equate persuasion solely with satisfying the analytical mind. However, we are not as objective and analytical as we think, and even the most well-thought-out decision is ultimately determined by emotional and subconscious influences. Selling requires capturing the hearts and minds of customers based upon a strategy that takes into account the emotions of the decision-maker as well as the logical reasons to buy. Customers aren't completely logical decision-makers in the real world. The decision-making process is a blend of human nature and logical rationalization. At the foundation of all sales is a relationship between people. The interaction between these people, the intangible part of the sales process, is ultimately responsible for the decision being made. Logic and reason play secondary roles.

Customers' inertia, the drive to "do nothing," far outweighs the logical reasons you espouse for buying your product. You can recite a litany of reasons and a laundry list of benefits, and customers still won't buy your product. You need to package these ideas in a format that leaves an impression and creates a call to action that customers understand and that persuades them both mentally and emotionally to proceed. This requires you to establish "situational dominance" during sales calls and gain the willing obedience of customers. From the perspective of sales linguistics, *situational dominance* is when the customer listens to your opinions and advice, internalizes your recommendations and agrees with them, and then follows your course of action.

Heavy Hitter salespeople are accomplished communicators who know what to say and, equally important, how to say it. Through their mastery of language, they are able to convey and decipher deep underlying messages that less-successful salespeople miss. While using the same language as most salespeople, they have developed an uncanny ability to influence nonbelievers to trust them and persuade complete strangers to follow their advice. Through sales linguistics, you can learn how they turn skeptics into believers and persuade prospective customers to buy.

Chapter 98. Personal Connection Languages

Who taught you how to become persuasive? You probably learned much of what you know by trial and error. Or you might have known a naturally persuasive coworker, friend, or colleague and tried to emulate your mentor's methods, honing your skills through informal interactions.

You may have taken debate, public speaking, and communications classes while in school. However, they most likely focused on hard skills such as the memorization and presentation of structured arguments. Anyone can recite facts, and two people can say the exact same words with entirely different results. Mastering the soft skills—understanding how to build rapport with skeptics, how people process and interpret information, and how to dovetail your ideas into a person's personal desires—is what ultimately makes someone influential.

The purpose of sales linguistics is to understand how salespeople and their prospective customers use and interpret different languages during the decision-making process. Specifically, the objective is to provide salespeople a framework that enables them to gain a trusted advisor relationship with customers. A trusted advisor is a salesperson whose opinions and advice on business and personal matters are sought out and followed. The seven different types of sales languages are listed below:

1. *Word catalog language.* The mind's method for receiving and interpreting information based upon the three sensory channels—visual, auditory, and kinesthetic (see chs. 110-113).

2. *Internal dialogue language.* The never-ending stream of communication inside the mind that represents honest, unedited, and deep feelings (see ch. 107).

3. *Physical language.* Also known as body language, the nonverbal communication that is constantly being emitted by the customer's body posture (see chs. 106, 123–124).

4. *Intersecting activity language.* Interests, hobbies, and personal pursuits by which the executive displays his personality, beliefs, and values (see ch. 52).

5. *Technical specification language.* The androgynous, nonpersonal, and technical communication that is based upon the nomenclature and technical terms of the executive's industry (see ch. 53).

6. *Business operations language.* The language that is specific to the daily running of the executive's business and his role in the organization (see ch. 54).

7. *Confidential language.* The most powerful trust-based language by which the customer explains his personal needs, desires, and plans along with the strategy by which he hopes to fulfill them (see ch. 55).

These languages can be divided into two categories. The lower-level languages are responsible for the personal connection between people and consist of the word catalog language, internal dialogue language, and physical language. The higher-level languages are logic and psychological appeal languages. They consist of the intersecting activity language, technical specification language, business operations language, and confidential language. Figure 98.1 represents these languages and their associated conversational themes.

Although we will discuss each of the personal connection languages in this section in detail, it's important to mention the different types of dialects now. When most people think of the word "language," the first association that comes to mind is English, French, Spanish, Japanese, and so on. However, these are only local dialects by which words are delivered. Accordingly, the fundamental principles and concepts of sales linguistics are focused on how the human mind communicates, creates words, and interprets information.

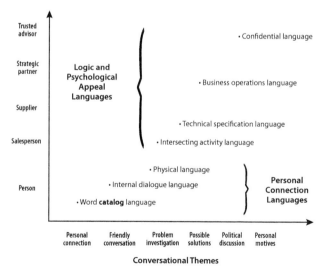

Figure 98.1 Ideal progression of languages during sales calls

Therefore, the concepts are applicable to any dialect of language regardless of its origination.

When you strike up a conversation with customers you probably believe that everyone is speaking a common language. However, no universal language exists because everyone's mind is so distinct. People actually talk in many diverse languages. Therefore, if you want to communicate more persuasively and learn how to make lasting impressions, you should learn to speak each of the different sales linguistics languages.

Persuasion is not solely the recital of logical arguments or factual information to a listener. Instead, it is the process of projecting your entire set of beliefs and convictions onto another human being. It's not about getting others to acknowledge your arguments or agree with your business case; it's about making them internalize your message because they believe that's the only way to create real change. In order to accomplish this goal during sales calls, you should understand and be able to fluently speak the four different content layer languages with your customers (see chs. 52–55).

Chapter 99. Situational Dominance Is Your Ultimate Goal

The concept of situational dominance has three distinct sales applications. First, it is core to the personal communication strategy used during customer interactions. Second, it plays a key role in formulating sales cycle strategy as it relates to when provocation or alignment is used. Third, it is used to drive

sales team strategy and manage internal resources. In other words, situational dominance can be applied to sales calls, sales cycles, and how you direct the sales team. Finally and most importantly, it is a requirement to obtain trusted advisor relationship status (see ch. 50).

Customers can think of a salesperson as someone who is trying to sell something, a supplier with whom they do business, a strategic partner who is of significant importance to their business, or a trusted advisor whose advice is followed. Obviously, a trusted advisor enjoys significant advantages over the competing salespeople. However, just 18 percent of the salespeople buyers met over the past year would be classified as trusted advisors whom they respect.

Customer Interaction Strategy

In every customer conversation you will find yourself in one of three places. You can be in a submissive position, where you are not respected and the customer rejects or ignores what you say. When you are in this position, the prospective customer thinks of you solely as a salesperson who is trying to sell him something. You can be in an equal position, where the customer respects you and is interested in hearing what you have to say. Or you can be in a dominant position, where the customer accepts your arguments, internalizes them, and then acts on them. Figure 99.1 illustrates the three situational dominance positions.

A successful customer conversation starts by recognizing that a quick personal connection occurs between people based mainly on nonverbal communication and physical appearance. How long is it before a prospective customer

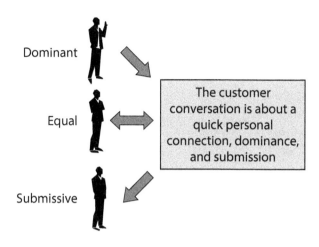

Dominant

Equal

Submissive

The customer conversation is about a quick personal connection, dominance, and submission

Figure 99.1 Situational dominance positions

makes an initial assessment of whether or not he likes you during your first sales call? While most people say it is almost instantaneous, the answer is between 15 and 180 seconds, according to my research. Then, he'll spend the next 11 to 18 minutes of the meeting validating whether his preliminary decision was correct.

Situational dominance can be thought of as gaining the willing obedience of the customer. The customer listens to your opinions and advice, internalizes your recommendations and agrees with them, and follows your course of action. This is based on the lasting impression the customer has of you.

A salesperson's goal is to gain dominance over a willingly submissive customer. While dominance is commonly associated with brute force, this is not the case in sales. It's simply how people judge others. People are continually sensing whether their position is superior to yours, relatively equal, or inferior in some way. In turn, this impacts what they say during conversations and how they behave. A relaxed dominant salesperson speaks freely and guides the conversation as he confidently shares

his knowledge and opinions. He is in control. An anxious submissive salesperson is forced into reactive behavior and his tendency is to operate under the direction of the customer, never being in control of the account.

While some dominant people will surround themselves with submissive people, most dominants want to associate with people whom they perceive as equals. Equals converse with relative ease. One of your most important goals when meeting with a customer is establishing yourself as an equal at a minimum. That's why you need to master the technical specification language and the business operations language of your industry described in chapters 53–54. Only by knowing the customer's company goals, business problems, technical frustrations, and personal aspirations will you be able to explain how you can address them.

If all the solutions we are evaluating have the same payback, it becomes a sales job as to who can sell best to our upper management. What you say and how you say it is truly what sets you apart.

—Chief Financial Officer

Obviously, a salesperson who can employ a wider range of dominant traits can sell to a wider range of customers. Knowing which trait to draw upon is determined by your sales intuition. For instance, in one account you might display an optimistic attitude to instill optimism when the evaluators are nervous and scared. In another account you might display outward skepticism, forcing the customer to explain why he believes his company will actually make a purchase. In both circumstances you have established dominance.

You probably have used a wide range of attributes to establish your dominance, depending on the customers you have met with. That's a fundamental trait of Heavy Hitters. They behave in a way that makes them dominant, even if that means they must behave submissively.

Every account has an equilibrium point of dominance versus arrogance. It's the point where the customer respects your conviction and is not offended by your demeanor. Even though you promote your agenda with determination, you are not considered pushy or overbearing.

Direct and Indirect Approaches

However, at times you have to confront the customer directly—in some situations you have to challenge the customer's beliefs, process, and decisions for his own good. This takes courage and conviction as the quotes below show. However, you have to be sure the scenario requires provocation and not alignment with the customer's thought process (see ch. 25). Furthermore, you have to become comfortable with very uncomfortable situations.

The RFP came out and it was geared for our competitor. We declined the RFP twice. They thought I was being rude, but I had to change their process for them to see our value. We said, "We want your business, but we have to do it this way." The main contact that worked with us was not our biggest fan, and the CIO slapped our hand and said, "If you work this way, we don't want to work

with you." It was a very risky strategy. We endured months of demos and antagonistic meetings. But if it wasn't for this strategy, we would have never closed this account.

—Top Salesperson

We basically told them that their "baby was ugly" and their system was a mess. They were shocked and protested. I thought we were done, but three weeks later they called us back.

—Top Salesperson

You have to address the elephant in the room. I confronted them point blank: "Why aren't you talking to us anymore?"

—Top Salesperson

You can use two basic approaches to establish dominance during sales calls. The direct approach is based upon personal prowess, while the indirect approach is based upon finesse. The approach you should use depends upon attributes of your personality. Now it's time to measure your situational dominance. Read the following questions and select the answer that suits you best.

Let's pretend you are having a hallway conversation with three colleagues. Do you usually

(A) remain silent the majority of the time, letting others speak;
(B) speak for an equal share of the conversation; or
(C) find yourself talking the majority of the time?

Using the hallway example above, if someone said something you disagreed with, would you typically

(A) remain silent;
(B) challenge the person to explain himself; or
(C) confront the person directly?

When speaking with colleagues, are you someone who

(A) carefully edits your words;
(B) tactfully speaks your mind; or
(C) is completely open and honest with all your thoughts?

When you are part of a group, are you someone who

(A) is fine letting someone else lead the group
(B) occasionally leads the group
(C) usually leads the group?

Your number of A, B, and C answers represents your situational dominance from low to high. If you answered all Cs, that would indicate a naturally high level of situational dominance. Conversely, all As would be associated with a low level and Bs a medium level.

If you have a naturally high level of situational dominance, you are typically well suited to use a direct approach. This approach is based upon first establishing yourself as the focal point of the purchase. In essence, the customer is buying into your credibility, your personal experiences, and your ability to help him accomplish his goals. Be careful; when most buyers meet with salespeople who have high levels of situational dominance

there is an immediate reaction: they love them or hate them.

If you have a naturally low level of situational dominance, you are probably better suited to use an indirect approach. This approach is based on establishing the capabilities of your company and products as the focal point to move yourself to the position of being an equal. For example, a salesperson with low dominance who transitioned his career from a technical position into sales can have an equally dominant presence as a seasoned sales veteran. However, he has to use a different approach. Instead of projecting a powerful presence in person, his deep-rooted technical understanding of his product draws customers to follow him and makes him dominant.

Collaborative Ambition

One of the underlying principles of situational dominance is that it is based on the concept of "collaborative ambition." Regardless of whether the direct or indirect approach is used, the customer must believe that the salesperson is acting in his best interest even though he or she realizes the salesperson's ultimate goal is to make a sale. Collaborative ambition unites these two vastly different people. While they have different motivations, both parties serve as instruments for the other to achieve the personal goals each wants to fulfill. Collaborative ambition is key to becoming a trusted advisor (see ch. 50).

Sales Cycle Strategy

In chapter 25 we reviewed the three paths for working on an account. You can be in alignment and agree with how the customer intends to solve his problem or achieve his goal. In this case, you sub-missively *follow* the customer's lead. You can gradually transform his thought process over time till he considers you an equal who is operating in his best interest. Or you can use *provocation* to dominate the customer and completely change the customer's selection crite-ria or sales process. Remember, "domi-nant" is not a negative term. It simply refers to someone following your advice and recommendations.

Team Selling Strategy

The concept of situational dominance also applies to how the salesperson manages the presales resources that are involved in a sales cycle. The sales-person should control and coordinate all meetings, presentations, and techni-cal evaluations. He is in charge of the company resources that are assembled to win the account, regardless of their departmental origin, including manage-ment, engineering, support, consulting, marketing, and product management. The salesperson should be the prospec-tive customer's main point of contact for all customer communication. In essence, the salesperson has to establish domi-nance internally within his own company.

The salesperson is responsible for defining the products that will be pro-posed and ensuring they match the cus-tomer's needs. As the team leader, he confirms to the rest of the project team that the customer is qualified from a busi-ness and technical perspective, moti-vates the team, and takes responsibility for the overall relationship with the cus-tomer and ongoing account satisfaction.

The presales engineer (or other prod-uct specialist) is mainly responsible for

understanding the customer's technical profile and presenting the company's technical solution. The system engineer conducts the process that determines the level of technical fit between the ven-dor's product and the customer's tech-nical environment. The system engineer is also responsible for solution design, product evaluation, and implementa-tion of the project. Members from other departments, such as consulting or sup-port, may also perform certain tasks at the system engineer's direction. Most importantly, the system engineer is responsible for the technical relationship with the customer and the ongoing tech-nical satisfaction with the product. In this role of a customer advocate, the system engineer represents the customer and facilitates meetings with the techni-cal support department. Here are some interesting customer quotes to consider.

> *I'm going to say this bluntly. Tell the sales engineer to shut up and let the salesperson do his job. The engineer hijacked the discussion. I'm glad he was enthusiastic about his product, but there was no room for discussion about our needs.*

—IT Manager

> *Their salesperson was a typical sales guy who wanted to make a sale. The engineer knew what he was talking about and could answer questions. Since I come from an electrical engineering background, I asked technical questions and the engineer gave answers I liked. I didn't really like the salesperson.*

—Director of IT

Vendor A's sales team was best. It was evident the sales rep and engineer had worked together for a long time. There was a synergy between them that gave us the confidence to buy their products.

— Chief Technology Officer

Chapter 100. Communication and the Mind

Upon your birth, your brain was a tiny malleable computer. Even though all the circuitry was in place, the software had yet to be installed, so its functions were extremely limited. As you experienced the world, your senses began gathering more information and turning on all the software switches inside your mind.

During the first five years of your life, 90 percent of your brain's growth and development occurred.[1] Your mind evolved as it interacted with the world around you and recorded strange and exciting new experiences. You learned to speak by mimicking the people around you, and by the time you were five years old, your vocabulary was about twenty-five hundred words.[2] Today, your mind knows the meaning of about fifty thousand different words.[3]

Your brain has an incredible capacity to sort, prioritize, and process. As you read this book, your lungs are breathing and your heart is pumping blood to all parts of your body without your having to think about it. Meanwhile, you are consciously moving your eyes to the next word to be read and saying that word to yourself. When you reach the bottom of the page, your hand and arm will automatically execute a complex series of muscle movements in response to commands from the brain to turn the page.

Your brain has three major parts: the cerebrum, cerebellum, and brainstem. From a sales perspective, we are most interested in what is happening within the cerebrum. The cerebrum controls our voluntary functions, such as body sensations, learning, emotions, and language.

Most of the recent advances in understanding the inner workings of the mind have come from brain scans and neuro-imaging techniques such as PET (positron emission tomography) and FMRI (functional magnetic resonance imaging), which make it possible to observe the human brain at work. These images reveal changes in activity of the various brain regions depending on physiological activities. For example, while a person is seeing, hearing, smelling, tasting, or touching something, certain areas of the brain light up on the scan.

While neuroscientists have named the parts of the brain and know their overall functions, the three-pound pale gray organ still remains a mystery. No one truly knows how the mind works. Somewhere deep inside you is you. You are surrounded by your conscious, or "controllable," and subconscious, or "uncontrollable," minds, which in turn are surrounded by your internal dialogue. Your internal dialogue is the never-ending conversation you have with yourself. It's repeating the words of this sentence to you now. It is very dominating. It's always on, always engaged, and always talking to you. It drives the language you speak to prospective customers during sales calls as well as your actions. Your customer's internal dialogue is equally active.

The conscious mind, subconscious mind, and internal dialogue affect your external communication: the words you speak, and your voluntary (planned) and involuntary (unplanned and inadvertent) body movements. Figure 100.1 represents the interaction between external communication and the mind.

It's helpful to think of this diagram when meeting with customers. Usually, the subconscious mind is busy managing all the systems of the body (nervous, muscular, respiratory, digestive, and circulatory) without much effort, and it is working independently of the conscious mind most of the time. However, during a sales call, the spoken words and actions of the participants can have an immense effect on the subconscious mind, resulting in changes to the body. These involuntary body movements provide important customer feedback when analyzed in conjunction with the customers' verbal conversation. It is extremely important to monitor all of the sales call participants for these bodily changes. Are they tense or relaxed? Are they breathing faster or slower?

The subconscious mind retains information that the conscious mind doesn't. Storing everything in your conscious mind simply isn't efficient. Remember the last time you misplaced an important item (your keys, wallet, or glasses)? At first, you employed a conscious strategy to find it. You may have thought about where you had recently been and gone back to those locations. If you didn't find the item, hours, days, or weeks may have gone by. Then suddenly, without specifically thinking about it, you knew exactly where the items was. Your subconscious mind found it.

In the same way, when your prospective customers say, "Let me sleep on it" or "I will get back to you," they are actually saying, "Let me see if my subconscious mind has any objections since it has some additional information that I don't have right now."

During the sales call, your words and actions have an immense effect on the conscious and subconscious minds of the prospective customer. One of your top priorities is to recognize and correctly interpret all the different types of verbal and nonverbal information the customer is communicating to you. The most important part of a sales call is not your product pitch. Instead, it is the customer's reaction to what you say. In other words, always think about people first and products second during sales calls.

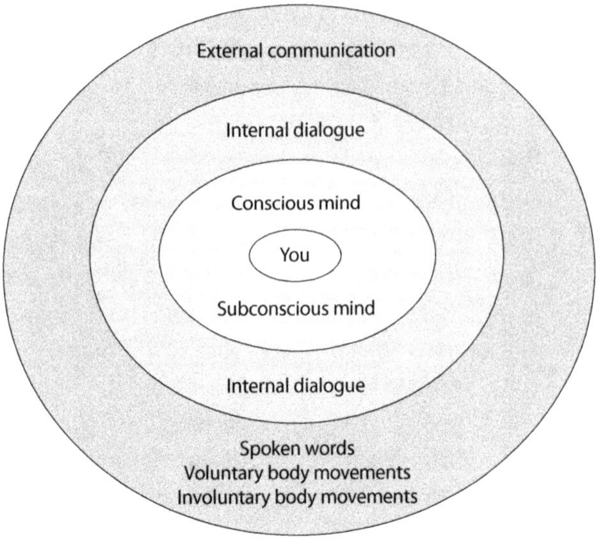

Figure 100.1 External communication and the mind

Chapter 101. Understanding Customer Benefactions

The grand strategy behind a successful sales call is based upon selling to human nature. Customers purchase products that increase their happiness, esteem, power, or wealth. They rationalize these psychological decisions with logic and facts. For example, a vice president of a manufacturing company may explain that he wants to buy a new conveyor system because it will save a million dollars a year when, in reality, he is making the purchase to show the CEO that he is a prudent, fiscally conservative businessman. The desire to impress the CEO (the benefit) drives the conveyor system purchase (the action). The term "benefaction" refers to the psychological benefits that determine a person's actions.

Four core psychological drives determine selection behavior. These four benefactions are well-being, pain avoidance, self-preservation, and self-gratification. Physical well-being, the will to survive, is one of our strongest desires. It weighs heavily in the minds of both customers and competitors. Making customers feel their jobs are safe in your hands is a top priority during sales calls. Ideally, you would like them to believe (whether it is true or not) that the competitive solutions are actually threats to their livelihood. Customers are equally concerned with maintaining their mental and emotional well-being.

When something is hurting you badly, the desire to eliminate the source of pain can be all-consuming. Pain is one of the best purchase motivators because customers are forced to act quickly and decisively to eliminate it.

Companies experience different kinds of pain all the time. Nuisances can create dull aching pains in every department, such as a temperamental copy machine. Throbbing pains may reappear occasionally, like internet service providers that go down momentarily every few months. And stabbing pains require immediate attention, for example, when the order-entry system is down and products can't be shipped and sales cannot be made. Companies can live with dull aches and cope with throbbing pains as necessary. But the stabbing pains receive immediate attention and dictate budgeting.

Self-preservation, the third core psychological drive, is the desire to be recognized for our unique talents while still belonging to a group. Customers and salespeople alike naturally seek the approval of others. Customers purchase items that they believe will enhance their stature and protect their group position. They not only want to be respected by their peers but also want to become group leaders. Naturally, salespeople want to be pack leaders too.

Self-gratification is the desire to put our own needs before everyone else's. Customers will go to great lengths to purchase something that makes them feel better about themselves and superior to others. Egos drive the business world.

Unfortunately, most salespeople are taught to sell solutions solely based upon customer pain. In fact, well-being, ego, and self-preservation are the real motivators behind most sales. The list below reveals the true reasons why customers buy your product.

Consider these customer statements:

- I have big career ambitions.
- I want to be more powerful.
- I'm risk-averse.
- I want my team to be happy.
- I'm naturally skeptical of vendors.
- I like to be part of a group.
- I want the security of a marketable skill.
- I want that promotion.
- I want to keep my job.
- I like new challenges.
- I want to please others.
- I want to be important.
- I like you!

It's not solely your product's performance, ease of use, or efficiency that customers are in love with. It's you. Therefore, your priorities should be to earn customers' love and trust by understanding their personal needs, desires, and fantasies. You must know if they are just trying to hold on to a job, prop up their importance, or bring about a long-awaited promotion. Once you understand these desires, you become part of the customers' political landscape, aligned with the decision-making process.

The conscious mind is obsessed with achieving four benefactions: physical and mental well-being, pain avoidance, self-preservation, and self-gratification. People buy products they believe will help them fulfill deep-seated psychological needs: satisfying the ego, being accepted as part of a group, avoiding pain, and ensuring survival.

You want customers to view you as the only person who can address their personal needs, solve their painful business problems, and help them achieve their career hopes and life's desires. You want them to sincerely believe that you are the only salesperson who is truly acting in their best interests.

Chapter 102. The Better Salesperson Syndrome

At the root of situational dominance is the "Better Salesperson Syndrome," which is based on the theory that people will naturally gravitate toward people they feel are better than themselves in some way. In this respect, the Better Salesperson Syndrome helps explain the old saying that opposites attract. For example, my wife has many qualities that I admire. She is far more patient and kind than I'll ever be. I am attracted to these qualities.

The theory also applies to sales. When customers are choosing between two similar products, they will not always buy the better product. Rather, their tendency is to buy from the salesperson they believe is the better person. So while one salesperson may have a slightly better product and be more proficient in explaining its features and functionality, in the end the customer will buy from the person who has the personal attributes the customer most admires. (Obviously, if one product is light years ahead of another, then the Better Salesperson Syndrome is neutralized.)

Some customers will gravitate to a friendly and responsive salesperson. They admire and respect these qualities. Others might enjoy being around an aristocratic salesperson in cufflinks and a monogrammed dress shirt. Perhaps these customers behave and dress in a similar way and have some deep-seated desire to be like him. Because people admire different qualities in other people, every sales call is unique.

Your situational dominance in any setting is dependent upon the submissiveness of the person you are talking with. It is not a measure of how easily you overpower the person. Rather, it depends on the traits that the other person respects, admires, or does not possess. For example, a customer may be submissive to a salesperson's industry expertise, technical aptitude, or product knowledge.

Many people become submissive when they perceive a salesperson to be better looking, more charismatic, or more enthusiastic than they are. For instance, I know several vice presidents of sales who will hire a good-looking salesperson with average sales skills over a great salesperson who is not so attractive.

Most customers tend to gravitate to salespeople who are similar to themselves. They want to be surrounded by competent, successful people. However, opposites attract as well. For example, very meticulous, no-nonsense customers sometimes bond with lackadaisical, carefree salespeople who are their exact opposites. These customers seem to be hypnotized into a submissive position.

One of the best salespeople I ever knew was the most unorganized, lackadaisical, smart-mouthed goof-off I ever met. However, a certain cross section of executives absolutely adored him because he always said exactly what was on his mind in the most politically incorrect way. Surprisingly, the executives he bonded with were usually straight-laced, button-down CFOs and CIOs. I think they found his uniqueness intoxicating

compared to the personalities of the staff members they had to deal with daily.

Exercise: Now it's time to do a quick exercise to help you discover what makes you dominant in customer meetings. The list below includes just a few of the wide range of dominant traits that people respond to submissively. As you read the list, think about when you used one of these attributes to put yourself in a dominant position over your main contact (who was probably a midlevel management or lower-level person) at a recent account you won. Recall not only the account but the specific person who responded to you submissively and followed your lead.

Athleticism	Open-mindedness
Attractiveness	Optimism
Business knowledge	Organization
Charisma	Passion
Cleverness	Persistence
Compassion	Pessimism
Curiosity	Product knowledge
Eloquence	Professionalism
Empathy	Sales acumen
Enthusiasm	Sense of humor
Friendliness	Seriousness
Honesty	Straightforwardness
Humor	Technical aptitude
Hyperactivity	Thoroughness
Industry expertise	Thoughtfulness
Integrity	Tolerance
Lackadaisicalness	Trustworthiness
Negotiation skills	Wholesomeness

Now repeat the same exercise while thinking of the senior-most executive you met with at the same account. Were you able to establish dominance? If so, was there a difference in your dominance and the attribute you used when compared to your meetings with the lower-level person? Remember, even a trait that is typically associated with weakness can be used to establish dominance.

Your sales intuition guides your behavior and the way that will make you dominant, even if that means you must behave submissively. For example, empathetically listening to a customer describe his problems is submissive behavior, but it will enable you to establish a dominant position with him later. Only by knowing his goals, objectives, frustrations, and fantasies will you be able to explain how you can address them with your solution. In reality, you will be in a dominant position because you will control his happiness. Now all you have to do is use the right linguistic strategy to convince him or her of it.

For instance, in one account you might display an optimistic attitude in order to instill optimism when the evaluators are nervous and scared. You might say to them, "I've worked with many other customers with the identical problem. They have been able to solve the problem within a couple of months of implementing our project."

In this example, the salesperson has become a dominant source of hope to someone in pain. In another account you might display outward skepticism and say, "I am not sure you have the wherewithal to implement our solution," forcing the customer to explain why he believes he can implement the solution successfully. In both circumstances you have established dominance.

Chapter 103. Utilizing Customer Fantasies

People connect with others very quickly, and first impressions can have a long-term impact. Customers tend to make snap judgments early in the sales process based upon whom they like and respect. By demonstrating your competence, you expose your competitors' incompetence.

Knowing the details of how your product works and being able to answer customers' questions about your company are obviously vital parts of sales. However, the real questions to answer honestly are, Compared to the salespeople I am competing with, how well do I know my solution? and Is my industry expertise an advantage, or is my weakness a disadvantage? If you don't know the answer to either of these questions, your fear of being outpositioned and blocked from the account by your competitors may come true.

Those who are feared are hated. You want customers to realize that your competitors are riskier than you, uncaring, deceitful, and unable to fulfill the customers' fantasies. However, you need to understand what fantasies are. Most people think that fantasies have to be really big, such as "One day I will be on the cover of *Fortune* magazine." In fact, fantasies can be very small. Some people think of fantasies mainly in a sexual context, when in reality most fantasies are quite mundane.

Fantasies are just unfulfilled wishes. For example, you might wish to finish this book quickly. Until it's fulfilled, this wish is one of your many fantasies. You also might want to make $500,000 next year. That's a bigger, longer-term fantasy.

Customer fantasies can be big or small, specific or general. For example, the CEO might wish to leave work on time today in order to be home for an important family dinner. The vice president of North American sales might want to become the vice president of worldwide sales. The CFO might want to become the president and chairman of the board someday. Each of these fantasies has a different scope and duration.

When you have built relationships, demonstrated competence, and proved that you can fulfill fantasies, you will naturally dovetail with the internal politics of the decision-making process. Most importantly, using the strategy of selling to the human nature of customers forces your competitors to use a strategy based solely upon the products they sell. Because your strategy is stronger, you put your competitors in a position of weakness. Never forget, your sales call strategy is to dehumanize the enemy by differentiating yourself personally, as figure 103.1 shows.

All salespeople want their customers to like them. But it requires a linguistic strategy to establish the personal connection to become a trusted advisor who is respected by the customer (see ch. 50). Proving you are more trustworthy than the competition is based upon truthful communication, and the customer will fear your competitors when you speak the customer's unique languages and your rivals can't.

Regardless of the complexity of your product or the sophistication of your customers, the final decision-maker is always human nature. To validate this statement, all you have to do is think back to the deals you have lost when your product and price were best. You probably came in second place because you had third-rate relationships.

Before a sales call starts, silently remind yourself that one of your objectives is to determine the fantasies of all the participants. Try to theorize what their short- and long-term fantasies are. Go ahead and make a deep psychological diagnosis about what is driving each person's fantasy. A person who wants a

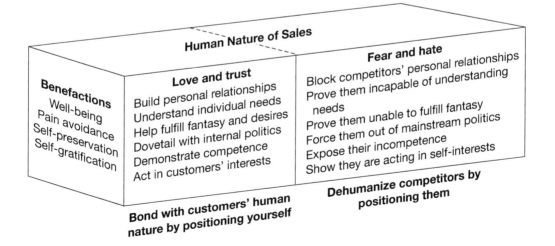

Figure 103.1 Human nature of sales calls

promotion to vice president to gain more power is quite different from someone who is seeking the promotion for personal validation or a bigger paycheck.

Customers have many different types of fantasies, and quite often they need help from vendors to fulfill them. Therefore, ignoring customers' fantasies is a big mistake. You must tap into them before your competitors do. However, customers will not usually broadcast their fantasies. It's up to you to figure them out and convince the customers that only through your solution can their fantasies be realized.

Exercise: Now think about the most important deal you are currently working on. Theorize what type of fantasy each of the key evaluators has and how you could position your solution to help them achieve it.

Chapter 104. All Buyers Are Liars

All buyers are liars. Now this may seem like a harsh statement; therefore, it requires further explanation. First, we need to define the different types of lies customers tell because some are more destructive than others. Of course, customers tell fibs and falsehoods that contradict the truth. Other times, they'll simply withhold important information from you, which in itself is a lie because they haven't told you the entire truth. Worst is when they are giving a competing salesperson proprietary, privileged information that they are not sharing with you.

Lying often occurs subtly, for example, when customers overemphasize the importance of a certain feature or present an irrelevant step in the decision-making process as a red herring to throw you off the scent of the truth. Sometimes, customers will strictly adhere to their selection-process guidelines, never giving any more information to you than they say they're allowed to give. Usually, each of these types of lies is intended to hide their personal bias toward another competitor.

However, sometimes customers lie out of benevolence—they will lie to protect a salesperson's feelings. Most people don't enjoy hurting or humiliating others. In addition, you were taught at the earliest age "If you don't have something nice to say, don't say anything at all." It's also human nature to avoid confrontation. So when a sales call ends and the salesperson asks, "Will we win the business?" most customers will give an optimistic answer. They don't want to let down or embarrass the salesperson, so they'll tell a lie for momentary relief. However, the truth will be revealed later—usually when the customer avoids the salesperson's follow-up calls.

Prospective customers will like some salespeople and dislike others. To protect themselves, they will instinctively try to keep any conversations with the disliked salespeople at a nonpersonal business level. They'll rebuff the attempts of the disliked salespeople to befriend them. Meanwhile, they will reveal much more about themselves to their favorite salesperson. One of the most important questions to ask yourself about the prospect you are meeting with during the sales call is, Are you lying to me? If the answer is yes you must find out why.

Chapter 105. Understanding the Process of Communication

A sales call is a scheduled communication event. Salespeople create long-term relationships between companies based upon the process of communication between the people who work for these companies. This process is very complex. However, since we are communicating all the time, we may underestimate the complexity of communication and take the process for granted. We tend to ignore the subtleties and, for the most part, become preoccupied with our side of a conversation.

It's important to recognize that people communicate in layers. These layers are very flexible and can be combined in many different ways. Layers can be entirely eliminated or they can be fused together to form entirely new meanings. The layers of the human communication model are shown in figure 105.1.

The human communication process is also very efficient. We have the flexibility to send the same message structure with distinctly different meanings. Take the following example:

- Mary, could you please send the report.

- Mary, could you *please* send the report.

- MARY, COULD YOU PLEASE SEND THE REPORT.

All these sentences use the same words but result in very different interpretations. When Mary reads the first sentence, she will feel a low sense of urgency and receive no indication of any unhappiness that the report has not been sent. The other sentences imply a different sense of urgency and even discontent that the report hasn't been sent.

The human communication model layers are like piano keys. Different sounds, or meanings, are created by pressing particular keys together in patterns or repetitions. Piano keys may be depressed forcefully or softly, just as communication may be explicit or subtle. The combination of keys may result in a soothing melody or just noise.

With or without conscious effort, you most likely have mastered each of the layers of the human communication model. However, the *interaction* between the layers is of particular interest to salespeople. When people speak, the layers are totally interactive. Any layer can communicate with any other

Content	The actual words spoken
Phonetic	The enunciation of the words you are speaking
Purpose	The reason or point you are communicating
Representational System	The system used to interpret and present those words
Internal Dialogue	The never-ending dialogue inside your mind
Physical	The impact the words you are receiving or sending have on your body

Figure 105.1 The human communication model

layer as shown in figure 105.2. The layers can also be combined to form complex statements that can convey additional or different meanings to content-layer words.

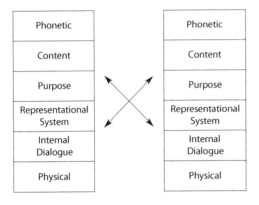

Figure 105.2 How the layers of Human Communication Interact

Here's an illustration of how the various layers can be combined, using the example of asking Mary for a report. Suppose I see Mary coming to my desk to give me the report. Following are some of the ways I could respond to her:

- *Physical.* I could give her a big smile and a high-five. She would obviously interpret this to mean I was pleased. My communication is congruent because my facial expression and hand slapping are communicating the same message.

- *Content plus phonetic plus physical.* I could say "Thanks" in my normal tone of voice but present a very forced, fake smile. My communication is incongruent. Mary would have to do some internal assessment as to what I was trying to communicate.

- *Physical plus content plus phonetic.* Holding my arms over my head, I could say at the top of my voice,

"I see I *finally* have my report!" This congruent communication would definitely get the point across about my unhappiness the report was late.

The content layer, the actual words being spoken aloud, represents only a fraction of the total communication spectrum that is being presented during any conversation. Additional layers can be added on top of each other to convey even greater meaning. The layers can be used selectively to abbreviate our thoughts and speed up communication while still preserving the original message. For example, we shrug our shoulders instead of saying, "I don't know."

The layers can be aligned to create holistic, congruent communication. Your sales intuition naturally interprets congruent messages as being honest and true. However, if the layers are at odds with each other, or incongruent, you know further investigation is required.

Each of the communication layers can also communicate both consciously and subconsciously between themselves. For example, when a person lies, the subconscious mind will affect the phonetic and physical layers of communication. The pitch, tone, and volume of the voice may change along with the person's posture, demeanor, and skin tone.

Finally, to further complicate the process, human communication is always occurring in several different forms and on several different levels. An immense amount of information is being conveyed phonetically, verbally, physically, consciously, and subconsciously. The dark continent of the human communication model is the subconscious mind. It has the ability to permeate each layer. As it seeps through, it sends out signals about a speaker's honest intent.

Whether the customer is speaking or listening to you, you need to evaluate each layer of the human communication model and determine its message and meaning. You should develop the ability to listen and sense all of the information a customer is projecting, regardless of whether it is being delivered consciously or subconsciously. Another term for this ability is "sales intuition."

Exercise: Many struggling salespeople fixate on the content layer and the words from customers' conscious minds. They miss the critical information that would enable them to predict if they will win or lose the deal. Make a conscious effort to pay attention to all the layers of human communication at your next sales call because it is an opportunity to add information and experiences to your sales intuition.

Chapter 106. The Physical Layer of Language (Body Language)

Everyone is well aware of the physical layer of the human communication model at the bottom of the figure in the previous chapter. You were introduced to this layer when you were a baby. When you were two days old, you were able to distinguish a happy face from a sad face. Soon thereafter, you naturally understood that a smile, hug, or kiss is to be interpreted as something very good.

The physical layer is also known as "body language." Unfortunately, this term has been sensationalized over the years in books on everything from dating to cosmetic surgery. However, since it is the more widely recognized term, I use it interchangeably with the "physical layer." Body language can be very subtle or more powerful than the actual words being spoken. Body language is unique in that it is a three-dimensional language. Heavy Hitters are masters at reading body language and using their own bodies to communicate. When considered in conjunction with the other layers of the human communication model, the physical layer plays an important role.

When people are discussing issues they are passionate about, their hearts pump more blood and their skin flushes. The volume of their voices may rise and their speech quicken. Conversely, people who are bored or apathetic will fidget or become lethargic. People who are worried may feel sick to their stomachs, and their bodies will broadcast this. Consequently, you should stay astutely aware of the physical communication of the body. Here are four key reasons why you should understand the physical layer:

- The key to developing long-term successful relationships is rapport. Just as you develop rapport by using the customer's spoken language, you also develop rapport at the physical layer. In other words, you want rapport with the customer's body as well as his mind.

- During sales calls, you are continuously searching for feedback on the prospect's receptivity to your solution, and the physical layer provides important nonverbal reactions to your statements. It provides another visible checkpoint that can be used to ensure everyone participating in the meeting understands and agrees with you and your sales pitch.

- You want to be able to "perceptively persuade." Perceptive persuasion involves leading the customer to buy your product. The physical layer provides another channel by which you can communicate with customers and influence them to buy. Here's another way to explain this: the words you say and the words other people say to you affect your entire body. As a result, the body is continuously influencing your mental state.

- It could be argued that what's important isn't what customers say during the sales call; it's what they don't say. A survey conducted by UCLA made some startling statements about persuasion. When respondents were asked to judge various speakers' performances, 7 percent said the words they used were most important, 38 percent said it was the quality of their voices, and 55 percent said it was their nonverbal communication.[1] These results suggest that more meaning is derived from the nonverbal communication than from the actual words being said.

Heavy Hitters want to communicate with a customer's physical layer in order to develop rapport. They are aware of a customer's body language and analyze it to ensure they are communicating effectively. They also try to understand any communication from the customer's subconscious that may be revealed physically. These unintentional

messages will help them determine their chance of closing the deal.

Most salespeople recognize the obvious information presented to them by a customer during a sales call, such as written technical requirements and formal decision milestones. However, customers will say things they don't mean and mean things they don't say. Your ability to correctly recognize and interpret misleading, subtle information will enable you to create the correct account strategy. Search for false or contradictory information from the physical layer that signals the true intentions of the customer.

Chapter 107. Reading the Customer's Internal Dialogue Layer

Every waking hour, a stream of communication is going on inside your mind. You are always talking to yourself. This conversation is an unedited, honest discussion that represents your deepest feelings. This is the second layer of the human communication model (fig. 105.1)—the internal dialogue layer or simply the "internal dialogue."

Usually these internal conversations remain internal. Occasionally, they'll slip out. We are all familiar with the term "Freudian slip." A Freudian slip happens when you say one thing but mean another. Freudian slips often occur because you are having two simultaneous dialogues—the words you are speaking externally to others (content layer language) and the internal dialogue within your mind. Sometimes you accidentally substitute a word from your

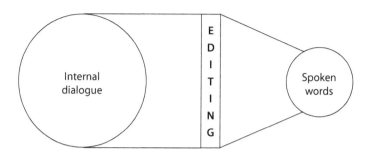

Figure 107.1 Spoken words as a subset of the internal dialogue

internal dialogue into your external dialogue. In other cases, you get confused between the two. For example, you may create a new word that is a combination of the first syllable of your content word and the last syllable of your internal dialogue word. In either case, these slips can be very embarrassing.

Usually, the words being spoken externally are a subset of the internal dialogue. In between is an editing process to filter the precise statement. This is particularly true on sales calls. Customers will heavily edit their honest thoughts, as represented by figure 107.1.

When people are being totally honest, they repeat their internal voice word for word without editing. People also abandon the editing process during times of great emotions: when they're very sad, extremely mad, or ecstatic or experiencing any other intense feelings. When people are consumed with their emotions, they don't have the wherewithal to plan what they are going to say. The words are spoken in the same instant that they are created within the mind.

During the sales call, your internal dialogue is at its loudest. It is constantly communicating, telling you what to say next and how to respond to questions. It also monitors the rapport being established with participants. You can't turn off your internal dialogue. It's always there, always working consciously. It's also being affected by your subconscious memories of past experiences.

When you make a sales call, you are not talking to people. You are actually talking to their internal dialogues. Understanding this will help you conduct successful sales calls because your main concern is a customer's state of mind. Remember that the words customers actually say represent only a fraction of their true feelings.

Exercise: Think about the new client sales calls you've conducted over the past month. What percentage of the people did you connect with? In other words, how many did you feel truly liked you, believed in your message, and wanted to see you again? Most likely, the percentage was lower than 50 percent. One of the reasons is that the human communication model is unique to each of the people you met. The point is, if you say the same thing in the same way on every sales call, you're making a mistake because each person communicates differently.

Chapter 108. Recognizing the Purpose Layer

Words are assembled to communicate an idea or experience. Every sentence of every conversation between salespeople and customers is purpose driven. One way to think of this is that customers have an ulterior motive for everything they say. Of course, you and I have been communicating with selfish interests all of our lives.

Salespeople and customers are self-centered in their communications. Each is constantly trying to extract information from the other. Salespeople will collect this information to create their account strategy, the long-term plan to win a deal. They are trying to uncover technical, political, and personal information in order to assess their current position and continually refine their strategy. To implement the strategy, they will determine a tactical plan and the daily tasks that are required.

Meanwhile, customers are trying to obtain information about the salesperson's company, products, and customers. Their main goal is information assessment. Whether formally or informally, they have developed and prioritized their needs. They need information in order to measure the fit of the salesperson's solution.

Three types of information are presented by customers during sales calls: obvious, interpretative, and calculated. Obvious information is a validated fact or a tangible object that can be seen and touched. An example of obvious information is a prospect's business card, which shows the person's title and contact information. Interpretative information requires the observer to make a personal judgment to determine its meaning. For example, someone might refer to a color as "tan" while another person may call it "light brown" or "beige."

Calculated information is based upon the combination of obvious and interpretative information. For example, when a customer spends an hour more than allotted to meet with you (obvious information) and after the call you felt it went well (interpretative information), you would calculate that the odds of winning the business are very high. Whereas obvious information is concrete and definite, the meaning of calculated and interpretative information is more subtle and subjective to personal judgment.

Exercise: During your next sales call, try to pay attention to why something is said and how it is said, rather than what is actually said. In essence, you want to understand the story behind the story and theorize what is truly on the customer's mind. Therefore, you need to study the purpose, content, and structure of the language the customer uses. Try to discern obvious information from interpretative and calculated information. Don't let your personal biases and opinions influence an honest assessment of the success of the sales call.

Chapter 109. Mark Your Words

The phonetic layer of the human communication model (fig. 105.1) is the enunciation of the actual words strung together in the form of a sentence. This layer can alter the meaning of the sentence to convey a completely new or sometimes opposite meaning. For example, let's say I tell my wife, "Your hair looks great," but my voice trails off at the end of the sentence. She would immediately be concerned that her hair does not look good. This incongruence would then cause her to ask what I actually meant. Congruence can be thought of as "truth in communication." If I say to her, "Your hair looks great!" and emphasize the word "great," my sentence is aligned (congruent) with the content of the words.

If the customer says to you, "We'll find some time to schedule a product evaluation" in a sullen tone with a lack of enthusiasm, you know you probably won't be invited back. Conversely, if the sentence is said with excitement and conviction, the customer is far more serious about moving forward.

Phonetics can be consciously applied to spoken words to create greater impact or to clarify the meaning. Telling a customer, "Yeah, we have the feature too" is different from exclaiming to a customer, "Yes! We have that feature!" The last statement exudes confidence and excitement and is said with a different purpose. This is known as "marking."

Marking words calls the listener's internal dialogue to pay attention. Marking has two purposes: it alerts the listener's conscious mind to highlight a specific thought, and it tells the subconscious mind to remember what might otherwise have been ignored.

Words can be marked by varying their pronunciation with inflection, volume, pitch, speed, or accent. The most common way to mark is to increase the volume. However, decreasing volume, even whispering, is just as effective in business meetings. In addition, words and phrases can be used to mark other words. If I say, "Listen up!" "Here comes the important part," or "If you're wondering what's next," your awareness and anticipation are heightened.

You can even use all aspects of body language, including hand gestures, facial expressions, posture, and movements, to mark words. You can point at the audience, raise your hands above your head, shrug your shoulders, move to the right or left, or make other body movements to distinguish certain ideas. Regardless of how you mark words, the listener's internal dialogue hears them and processes the information in the conscious mind immediately. Meanwhile, his subconscious mind recognizes the specific words that were marked.

The manner in which customers pronounce words provides vitally important information about their honesty and intent. Truthful communication occurs when all layers of the human communication model are in agreement—for example, when spoken words match the way in which they are said. Incongruence is misleading communication where layers of the human communication model contradict each other—for example, when the customer's enunciation contradicts the words being said.

Exercise: During a sales call, you can highlight your important thoughts by "marking" your words with different enunciations. The volume and tone of your voice can be used as cues to capture the attention of the customer's internal dialogue. Try this on your next sales call. Slow down your tempo of speech by half when you are covering the most important reasons why the customer should do business with you and watch the customer's reaction. Does he or she lean slightly forward toward you? Touch his face with a hand? Appear more introspective? If so, you have successfully marked and subconsciously distinguished these thoughts.

Chapter 110. Recognize Visual, Auditory, and Kinesthetic Wiring

The toolset you use during sales calls is language. The words you speak are a collection of symbols ordered to express your reality. The words you speak truly define who you are. We mistakenly assume other people speak in our language, but they really don't. We incorrectly believe that their words are based upon the same symbolizations as ours. In reality, words are linguistic labels for very complex personal experiences. For example, words like "childhood," "marriage," and "success" can evoke very complicated feelings and memories. The representational system layer of the human communication model (fig. 105.1) is responsible for the interpretation and meaningful association of words.

Words are not the flat, black-and-white letters depicted in the dictionary. They are three-dimensional objects that contain feelings, sounds, and pictures when they are said or read. Even the shortest words can trigger small dramas within the mind because words are tightly intertwined with memories.

The conversations you and your customers have together are quite complex because the languages you both use come from different worlds. Ultimately, conversations are streams of information that are transmitted and received in completely different formats.

Unfortunately, when many salespeople meet with prospective customers, they talk in only their own language and only about themselves. The subject of the conversation is me, me, me: my company, my product's benefits, and my product's features and functions. Because the meeting is so important and they're nervous, many salespeople understandably fall back on reciting their canned marketing pitch. When you meet with customers, talk about them, them, them: their problems, their values, and their plans and desires. Most importantly, speak the customers' language by adapting your language to match their word catalog.

Your word catalog is more than the dictionary inside your mind that determines a word's meaning. It is also the methodology by which you ascertain correct interpretations of a message and associate complex psychological meanings.

All of the experiences of your life have determined the language you use—the surroundings where you grew up, the language used by your loved ones, where you went to school, your friends, your career, the amount of money at your disposal, and even your spirituality. Just as no one else on this planet has had these experiences, no one else speaks your precise language. Therefore, the language two people use to describe the same situation may be very different. You and the customer have accumulated unique sets of memories.

These experiences, both good and bad, have shaped your perception of the world. Through your senses, you are constantly adding to your cumulative knowledge of how your world

Reality	Sensors	Influences	My Reality
As it is	Sight, sound, touch, taste, smell	Family, money, work, friends, schooling, spirituality	Experiences catalogued

Figure 110.1 Cataloging reality

functions. As you accumulate new experiences, they are edited and influenced by your history. As a result, it is accurate to say every person functions in his or her own unique world. Your world is your own personal reality. You use your "word catalogs" to catalog your experiences and describe your world to others, as shown in figure 110.1.

Through language, we represent our thoughts and experiences. We use words to represent the sensory experiences of sight, sound, touch, taste, and smell. The map we use to describe and interpret an experience is based upon one of three word catalogs—visual, auditory, and kinesthetic. "Visual" refers to pictures and imagery, "auditory" to sounds, and "kinesthetic" refers to touch and internal feelings.

Most people use one word catalog more frequently than the others. This word catalog has become their default, or "primary," mode of communication. You can identify someone's primary word catalog by listening to the adjectives, adverbs, and nouns he or she uses in conversation.

People whose primary word catalog is based on sight will describe their experiences in visual terms. They are likely to say, "I see what you mean," "Looks good to me," or "Show me what to do." People with a primary word catalog based on sound will say, "Sounds great," "Talk to you later," or "Tell me what to do." People with a primary word catalog based on feeling might say, "I've got it handled," "We'll touch base later," or "I don't grasp what you mean."

An additional level of psychological meaning also derives from the word catalog. The word catalog attaches a psychological interpretation to words. Let's think about fire for a moment. We easily recognize the difference between the flames from a burner on a stove and a raging fire consuming a high-rise building. Although they are both fires, they each create different mental and emotional interpretations. When we think of a stovetop fire, we might picture warming a can of soup or creating a culinary feast for friends. When we think about a terrifying high-rise fire, the impact on our emotional state is quite different. Your word catalog not only created the mind's-eye picture of both fires but also pulled forward the psychological meaning associated with each usage.

You have had a completely unique set of experiences in your life. And you have kept a record of your past existence by cataloging pictures, sounds, and feelings. As you make your way through your daily life, you are interacting with the outside world by repeatedly sending and receiving messages based upon your word catalog. Never forget, each customer's background is very different from yours so each speaks a unique language.

Great benefits in communication and persuasion are gained if you understand your customers' primary word catalog and adjust your communication to fit their worlds. Recognizing this concept is extremely important for senior salespeople to recognize. The customers you are successful selling to are probably wired like you. Your goal is to be able to successfully sell to customers of all types. Therefore, you must be able to recognize different communication types and adapt your communication style to match them.

Chapter 111. How People Receive and Transmit Information

If you are right-handed, you have a dominant left side of the brain. If you are left-handed, you have a dominant right side of the brain. Your brain is wired a certain way because two hemispheres make up the cerebrum. The right side controls the left side of the body. The left side controls the right side of the body. This cross-management occurs because the nerves connecting to the body cross the spinal cord. You were born with this wiring and you cannot easily change it. Similarly, you are wired a certain way to transmit and receive information.

In conjunction with your genetic wiring, your mind developed strategies to interpret the wide varieties of information you had to contend with. To remember what you had seen, you had to think in pictures to imagine or replay what you saw. To remember what was said, you had to recall sounds. You would repeat to yourself what you heard. To remember what you were doing, you had to form an association between your body and feelings.

Three channels of information continually bombard your brain with information: visual, auditory, and kinesthetic. You can't turn off your senses. You can't slow down your vision, turn off your sense of touch, or silence your hearing. Your mind has had to adopt a strategy to

assess and prioritize incoming information. While you were born with a tendency to prefer one stream of information over another, during your childhood you adopted the channel-processing strategy your mind uses today. Figure 111.1 represents how people receive and transmit different streams of information.

You've used your strategy for decades now. It is ingrained in your mind. The majority of the words you use in daily conversation actually reflect your strategy. You favor certain channels of information and vary the use of words according to these channels. In addition, the language you use is intimately connected with who you are.

Some people have a more dominant ear (the one you use when you talk on the telephone), a dominant leg, and even a dominant eye. To determine your dominant eye, take a sheet of paper and cut a hole about one and a half inches wide in the middle. Hold the paper out in front of you at arm's length and use both eyes to stare through the hole at an object that is at least twenty feet away. Now close one eye at a time. The object will remain in

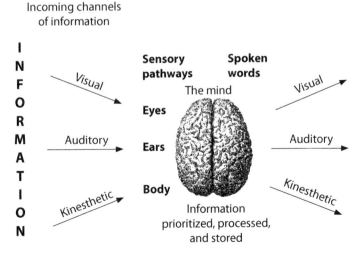

Figure 111.1 How people receive and transmit information

the middle of the hole when your dominant eye is open and will be covered by the paper when your weaker eye is open.

Similarly, people have a dominant, primary word catalog. A word catalog is the mind's method of gathering information, accumulating knowledge, and recording experiences based upon the visual, auditory, or kinesthetic senses. Your word catalog is also responsible for the association of psychological meanings to words. Your dominant word catalog might be visual, auditory, or kinesthetic. You also have a weaker, secondary catalog and, finally, a recessive catalog.

People process information with their word catalogs using pictures, feelings, or words, according to the strength of each catalog. Because spoken language is the system we use to communicate our experiences, people describe their experiences and convey their thoughts in terms that match their word catalog wiring.

However, people do not use one word catalog exclusively. Instead, they use all three word catalogs. You have a primary word catalog, which is your "default" method for accessing your catalog of experiences. It is the catalog used most often. People with a visual primary word catalog think in terms of pictures, those with a primary auditory word catalog think in terms of sounds, and those with a primary kinesthetic word catalog think in terms of feelings. Your secondary word catalog is your next strongest method for accessing your catalog. Finally, your recessive catalog is your least used and least developed access method.

You can tell what people's word catalog wiring is by noting the adjectives and verbs they use in their conversations.

An adjective is a word used to modify a noun, and a verb is an action word. However, some words can be used as either a noun, verb, or adjective, and this usage will significantly change the interpretation of the word catalog. The first sentence of each pair represents a visual, auditory, or kinesthetic usage, while those in the second sentence do not imply any particular word catalog:

Don't *glare* at me.
The *glare* of the sun was intense.

Map out your account strategy.
Please hand me the *map*.

Please *watch* your mouth.
His *watch* is broken.

Focus on the problem.
The camera has automatic *focus*.

It *sounds* difficult.
That crash made a loud *sound*.

The italicized words in the sentences above are verbs that imply a particular word catalog. Although the same words are used in the right-hand column, they are used as nouns. As you know, a noun is a word that describes a person, place, or thing. In general, nouns do not imply any particular word catalog. People with a primary visual word catalog will use visual keywords more frequently than auditory or kinesthetic words to describe their experiences. Here are some examples of visual keywords:

Beaming	Expose	Murky
Bleak	Fade	Observe
Bleary	Focus	Outlook
Blight	Frame	Perspective
Blind	Gaze	Preview
Bright	Glimpse	Reflect
Brilliant	Glance	Viewpoint
Chart	Glare	Dazzle
Clarify	Graph	Scan
Clear	Hallucinate	See
Cloudy	Hazy	Shine
Demonstrate	Highlight	Show
Diagram	Illuminate	Sight
Diffuse	Illustrate	Snapshot
Disappear	Image	Spectacle
Discern	Imagine	Spot
Display	Light	Stare
Distinguish	Look	Survey
Dreary	Magnify	View
Emit	Map	Watch

People with primary auditory word catalogs will use auditory keywords like these in their conversations:

Accent	Chord	Promise
Amplify	Crunch	Quiet
Articulate	Cry	Rave
Ask	Denounce	Recap
Assert	Dictate	Retreat
Attune	Digress	Ring
Audacious	Discuss	Say
Audible	Drone	Shout
Backfire	Edit	Slur
Back-talk	Giggle	Snap
Banter	Hum	Sound
Bark	Implore	Speak
Berate	Loud	Spell
Bicker	Noise	Talk
Blare	Note	Tell
Boast	Paraphrase	Vague
Cajole	Persuade	Yell
Call	Plead	
Chime	Profess	

People with primary kinesthetic word catalogs will use kinesthetic keywords like the following:

Ache	Feel	Push
Bash	Friction	Queasy
Bask	Gnaw	Rough
Bat	Grab	Rub
Bend	Hard	Scratch
Bind	Heart	Sense
Bit	Heavy	Sharp
Blink	Hit	Smell
Boot	Hold	Smile
Bounce	Impact	Smooth
Bow	Impress	Spit
Breathe	Irritate	Squash
Caress	Kick	Sticky
Catch	Leap	Stink
Chafe	Mark	Strike
Chew	Move	Taste
Choke	Nip	Thaw
Chop	Pique	Throw
Clinch	Plug	Touch
Cough	Post	Walk
Crawl	Press	Weigh
Draw	Pull	

Although nouns do not usually imply any particular word catalog, there are exceptions to this rule. When a person's communication is dominated by nouns that can be associated with one of the word catalogs, this is a good indication of that person's wiring.

For example, if an email has a pervasive or repetitive use of nouns such as "photograph," "picture," or "maps," this would provide additional clues that the person has a primary visual word catalog. When people continually refer to conversations they were part of, this would suggest they have a primary auditory word catalog.

This book refers to people with a sight-based primary word catalog as Visuals. Similarly, people with sound-based

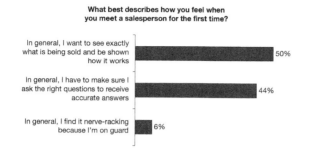

What best describes how you feel when you meet a salesperson for the first time?

In general, I want to see exactly what is being sold and be shown how it works — 50%

In general, I have to make sure I ask the right questions to receive accurate answers — 44%

In general, I find it nerve-racking because I'm on guard — 6%

Figure 111.2 B2B buyers' responses about meeting a salesperson for the first time

or feelings-based primary word catalogs will be referred to as Auditories or Kinesthetics.

Developing rapport by connecting with customers is a top priority in every conversation. Knowing which word catalogs customers prefer and speaking to them in their language will help them fall in love with you and your solution. The more stressful or tense a situation is, the more likely people will communicate in their primary word catalogs.

People also tend to lie in their secondary or recessive word catalogs. Your customers are continually telling you in which channel they would prefer you to communicate with them. For example, what do they say to you at the end of a phone call? Visuals tend to say, "See you later" or "I look forward to meeting with you again." Auditories might close with, "I'll talk to you later" or "I'll call you later." Kinesthetics might finish with, "Stay in touch" or "Keep in close contact." Equally important, what do you say to end your phone calls and emails? Take a look at the last twenty emails you have sent and examine your closing sentence. This short exercise provides the first clue to understanding how you are wired to receive and transmit information.

In a study of B2B buyers, the most interesting aspect of the question "What best describes how you feel when you meet a salesperson for the first time?" is not the actual responses; rather, it is that 50 percent of buyers selected a visual response, 44 percent selected an auditory response, and only 6 percent chose a kinesthetic response as shown in figure 111.2. Salespeople can gain great benefits in communication and persuasion when they can recognize buyers' word catalog usage and are able to adjust communication to fit the buyers' world.

Chapter 112. What Is Your Word Catalog Wiring?

What is your primary word catalog? Here's an exercise that will help you understand how you are wired. Print out the last ten business emails you sent to colleagues within your company and the last ten personal emails you sent to friends or family. Write the letters V, A, and K across the top of a piece of paper. In the left column write "Work," "Personal," and "Total." The chart should look like figure 112.1.

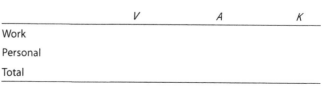

	V	A	K
Work			
Personal			
Total			

Figure 112.1 VAK keyword chart

	V	A	K
Work	III	||||| I	III
Personal	|||||	||||| |||||	||||| IIII
Total	||||| III	||||| ||||| ||||| I	||||| ||||| II

Figure 112.2 Sample results of a VAK keyword count and VAK pattern

You are now ready to perform a "VAK keyword count." Examine the emails and circle each occurrence of a visual, auditory, or kinesthetic word. Remember to circle the word only when it is used in the context of an action or description ("you *light* up my life," not "please turn the *light* on"). As you circle the words, add a tally in the appropriate column. The chart may look something like figure 112.2 when you are done.

Did you notice a difference between the tallies from your work and personal emails? Most likely, the language in your work emails is more androgynous and technical; therefore, the counts will be lower. I like to joke that this is because most communication in the business world is in fact "senseless." Were the counts evenly dispersed or clustered under one catalog? In the example above, the person's word catalog wiring is primary auditory, secondary kinesthetic, and recessive visual. You can do a similar exercise with the emails you receive to determine a sender's word catalog wiring.

Exercise: The first step to broadening your appeal to a wider audience and becoming more persuasive during sales calls is understanding how you are wired and whether you are a Visual, Auditory or Kinesthetic. Do not read further until you perform the VAK count exercise above. How are you wired? Are you a primary Visual, Auditory, or Kinesthetic? Did you notice a big difference in keyword counts between your work and personal emails?

Now conduct VAK counts based upon the emails sent to you by the key contacts for the most important deals you are trying to close. Compare their VAK counts to yours and think about whom you have the best and worst rapport with. Most likely, you share very similar wiring with individuals with whom you enjoy harmonious communication, and you're wired differently from those with whom you have tenuous relationships.

Chapter 113. Determining the Customer's Word Catalog Wiring

I have spoken at the sales meetings of hundreds of companies. In order to secure the speaking or training engagement, I have to contact and persuade one of five C-level executives to buy: the CEO, the president, the vice president of sales, the chief marketing officer, or the chief operating officer. This is my exact target market.

Before I even consider sending an email or letter, I first study the language used by the executive I am trying to reach. I'll search the web for video and magazine interviews, company videos he has appeared in, articles he wrote, entries on his blog, and letters he may have written to customers or employees. I'll analyze any language sample that will help me understand how he is wired. I will also conduct VAK counts when I speak with him in person or over the phone. I suggest you do this by bringing a notebook to your next meeting or keeping one by your phone. Whenever you meet with someone, perform a VAK count to determine the primary, secondary, and recessive word catalogs of the person you are talking with. You don't have to count for the entire meeting or conversation—just until you have a basic understanding of the person's wiring. Better yet, take along your manager or associate to a meeting and have him conduct the count so you can concentrate solely on your presentation. The manner in which your manager or colleague speaks to the customer and whether your colleague emphasizes visual, auditory, or kinesthetic words will indicate the customer's wiring to you.

Another trick is to place customers' business cards inside your notebook and write the VAK counts directly on them (in tiny print). Later, you can review the cards and refresh your memory about people's wiring. The results of your VAK counts will be fascinating. You will begin to be able to identify people's word catalogs in a very short time. You will also spot patterns and similarities between people who share the same word catalogs.

Your ultimate goal is to become aware of VAK keywords automatically without any handwritten counts. You want the process to become a natural part of listening so that, for example, when a customer is explaining his company's needs, you hear not only his content-level words but also the VAK keywords. Therefore, I suggest you

start conducting VAK counts for all customers you meet with (and even other people you meet with). Obviously, it's important to know how everyone within a prospective account is wired. Also, people tend to hire those who are similarly wired. In this regard, meeting with the director may help you better understand how the vice president he or she reports to is wired.

Exercise: Analyze the emails, letters, or communications your customers may have made on the internet to determine their word catalog wiring prior to phone conversations or in-person sales calls. Perform VAK counts during sales calls to further understand and validate their wiring.

Chapter 114. VAK Count Patterns

As you begin to perform VAK keyword counts, you will notice some patterns developing. Figure 114.1 shows VAK counts for three speakers, each of whom made a forty-five-minute presentation. Interestingly, their VAK counts were representative of the three major types of VAK count patterns: balanced, strong secondary, and dominating primary.

The president has a visual primary catalog along with strong auditory and

	Visual	Auditory	Kinesthetic
President/CEO	20	17	14
Vice President of Engineering	16	20	2
Product Manager	5	34	4

Figure 114.1 Sample VAK keyword counts

kinesthetic catalogs. This is a very balanced pattern. This wiring suits him well in his position. As president, he is responsible for the vision of the company, and it makes sense to have a Visual in that role. Other responsibilities of the president are company communication and consensus building. His well-developed auditory and kinesthetic catalogs help him naturally accomplish these two tasks with people who are not visually wired.

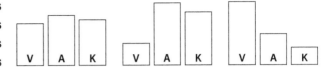

Figure 114.2 Balanced pattern, strong secondary pattern, and dominating primary pattern

The vice president of engineering has an auditory primary catalog and a strong secondary visual catalog. His kinesthetic recessive catalog is almost nonexistent. The nature of the vice president of engineering's position is both analytical and visionary. He has to be able to give specific direction to the programming teams in order to build products. Since the communication framework by which this is done is a functional specification (a detailed description of the product in the form of words), having an auditory primary catalog helps.

Meanwhile, he has to chart the product road map; therefore, having a strong visual secondary is desirable. Since the vice president of engineering is immersed in the technical specification language (the precise, androgynous, nonpersonal language that uses technical operators to modify general words, as described in chapter 53), a strong kinesthetic catalog is not necessarily needed in this position.

The product manager has a primary catalog that is so overwhelmingly dominating that the secondary and recessive catalogs are very rarely used. This pattern is called a "dominating primary." In this example, the person has a dominating auditory primary catalog. A dominating primary catalog could be visual or kinesthetic just as well.

This person's role is primarily technical. One of his main job functions is to create detailed technical collateral, such as white papers, data sheets, and technical content for the company's website. Having a strong auditory primary catalog is helpful in accomplishing these tasks. Figure 114.2 shows examples of a balanced pattern, strong secondary pattern, and dominating primary pattern. The strengths of the three catalogs in the balanced pattern are relatively close. However, the strength of the catalogs are different in the strong secondary pattern, where the visual word catalog is far weaker than the auditory and kinesthetic catalogs, and the dominating primary pattern, where the visual word catalog is strongest.

Balanced communication is a key attribute of effective persuasion. Balanced communicators create better rapport. They don't limit themselves by speaking exclusively from a single word catalog. They connect with Visuals, Auditories, and Kinesthetics equally. Therefore, a balanced speaker naturally reaches a broader audience.

People use all three word catalogs, just in different amounts and priorities. For example, a person might use visual words 60 percent of the time, kinesthetic words 25 percent of the time, and auditory words only 15 percent of the time. The strength of each of your catalogs and the order in which you use them can profoundly impact your ability to persuade during sales calls. Therefore, you must know your word catalog usage and determine whether you have a balanced, strong secondary, or dominating primary pattern. Equally important, you must be able to determine the customer's pattern and how it compares to your wiring.

Finally, people naturally gravitate to jobs that suit their word catalog wiring. On average, more Kinesthetics work in people-related positions like nursing, acting, and teaching. Auditories gravitate toward language-based professions and dominate fields that involve writing and talking. Visuals tend to work in fields such as advertising, movies, and designing.

Chapter 115. Interpreting Sayings and Clichés

Sayings and clichés may be used by people with any primary catalog. However, usually a specific phrase is used more often by people with one particular catalog. For example, "sizzling hot" is most likely to be said by Auditories. They hear the sizzling sound. Upon hearing this phrase, Visuals might picture a grill with something sizzling on it, and Kinesthetics might think of a finger actually touching the grill (particularly if they have burnt themselves in the past).

Exercise: Below is a list of sayings and clichés. After each phrase, mark a *V* for visual, *A* for auditory, or *K* for kinesthetic. If you think a phrase has multiple interpretations, write the order of what you

believe is the priority usage. Here are some examples:

"music to my ears," A
"from their perspective," V
"tough nut to crack," K, A
"that's alarming news," A

The answers follow, but don't look at them until you finish the entire list. Also, it's okay to write your answers in the book.

"keep your fingers crossed"
"armed to the teeth"
"down to the short strokes"
"iron out the problem"
"we'll keep pinging him"
"barking up the wrong tree"
"ducks in a row"
"look them in the eye"
"we'll hammer it out"
"banging the phones"
"coin rattling down the pipe"
"see how the smoke clears"
"die a slow death"
"bury the hatchet"
"level playing field"
"a little bird told me"
"hit the nail on the head"
"ear to the ground"
"bite the bullet"
"that's a new twist"
"clear as a bell"
"smoke and mirrors"
"chip on his shoulder"
"quit your bellyaching"

Based on my experience, here is the most likely usage of these phrases matched to the word catalog. Don't worry if your answers don't match exactly because your interpretation is influenced by your own wiring and my interpretation by mine.

"keep your fingers crossed," K
"armed to the teeth," K, V
"down to the short strokes," K
"iron out the problem," K
"we'll keep pinging him," A
"barking up the wrong tree," A, V
"ducks in a row," V
"look them in the eye," V
"we'll hammer it out," K, A
"banging the phones," A
"coin rattling down the pipe," A
"see how the smoke clears," V
"die a slow death," K, V
"bury the hatchet," K
"level playing field," V, K
"a little bird told me," A, V
"hit the nail on the head," K, V
"ear to the ground," A, K
"bite the bullet," K
"that's a new twist," K
"clear as a bell," A, V
"smoke and mirrors," V
"chip on his shoulder," K, V
"quit your bellyaching," K, A

In addition to the VAK keywords, catch phrases, descriptions, and clichés also reveal a speaker's word catalogs. Some individuals use an unusually high number of clichés for example. These people tend to be strong Auditories, and they actually say a cliché to themselves first before repeating it out loud. In fact, Auditories tend to spend more time listening to themselves speak than do Visuals and Kinesthetics because the volume of Auditories' internal dialogues is higher.

Exercise: The sayings and clichés used by customers during sales calls are more than just catch phrases. Pay attention to them and they will help you determine a customer's word catalog wiring and whether he is a Visual, Auditory, or Kinesthetic. Ultimately, they will help you understand and think like your customer. For example, if the customer tells you, "We'll look at the numbers and get back to you," you could reply, "Let me show you a couple of areas of cost savings that might not seem so obvious." When the customer says, "We want more bang for our buck," you might respond, "Tell me what sounds fair to you." If he comments, "We're weighing all the possibilities," you might come back with, "What can we do to tip the scale in our favor?"

Chapter 116. How VAK Sensory Information Impacts Price

The conversations salespeople have with prospective customers are quite complex. They consist of verbal and nonverbal messages that are sent via the visual, auditory, and kinesthetic channels. Can different amounts of visual, auditory and kinesthetic information influence the price customers will pay for an item? I conducted a sales linguistics experiment in order to answer this question.

Study participants were separated into three groups, and six items were presented to them in a classroom setting. All participants were business professionals and university graduates between the ages of twenty-four and fifty-seven. The groups were asked to estimate the price of each item and rank whether they had a low (one point), medium (two points), or high (three points) level of comfort with the answer they gave.

The participants were presented with an eclectic mix of items. In order, they were shown a baseball hit by famous home run hitter Manny Ramirez of the Cleveland Indians, a six-inch wooden penguin honoring Admiral Richard Byrd's expedition to the South Pole, a black plastic stapler, a copy of Rudyard Kipling's *Second Jungle Book* published in 1915, a vintage brass letter opener from Italy, and an 1886 Morgan US silver dollar.

The first group was presented only visual information consisting of a picture of the item and a brief description. (The descriptions were excerpted from websites that sell the object or provide background information.) The second group was shown the same visual information as the first group, but the description was read to them with dramatic emphasis and accentuation. The third group was shown the visual information, read the description in the same manner as for group two, and also provided the opportunity to hold and inspect the item before making their guess.

Figure 116.1 shows the average group comfort scores; you'll notice the scores increase with the addition of more sensory information by approximately 20 percent. The third group, who received the highest amount of information (all three sensory channels), also had the highest sense of comfort with their answers.

The average total overall prices for the groups varied greatly, with group two (visual and auditory information) being the highest at $325,000. In addition, 29 percent of group two members estimated all

the items cost over $250,000, whereas none did in group three. Clearly, the test results show that different amounts of visual, auditory, and kinesthetic information influence the perception of the items' prices. The experiment also provides other important lessons for sales and marketing professionals.

Customer Communication

The mind does not treat all information equally. Some information is ignored, some information is misinterpreted, and some information is generalized based upon surrounding experiences. For example, study participants assumed "This is a Major League Baseball hit by Manny Ramirez" to mean that it was a home run ball, when in fact it was only a foul ball. The reason this happened is due to how the ball was introduced, "Manny Ramirez is one of only twenty-five people to have hit over five hundred career home runs. His twenty-one career grand slams is the third most all-time behind legendary Lou Gehrig. His twenty-nine career post season home runs are the

	Group One	Group Two	Group Three
	Visual Only	Visual/ Auditory	Visual/Auditory/ Kinesthetic
Average Answer Comfort	1.6	1.9	2.3
Total of All Items	Group One	Group Two	Group Three
	Visual Only	Visual/ Auditory	Visual/Auditory/ Kinesthetic
Under $5,000	40%	32%	65%
$5,000 to $50,000	27%	23%	24%
$50,000 to $250,000	23%	16%	11%
Over $250,000	10%	29%	0
Group Average	$49,000	$325,000	$17,000

Figure 116.1 Average overall total price for each test group

most by any player in history." Listeners naturally associated the verbiage about home run facts to the baseball, proving you should never assume customers have understood what you are trying to communicate and always verify that they have received your message correctly.

Suggestion Susceptibility

The mind is quite susceptible to spoken suggestions. Group two's average total price was nearly seven times that of group one and close to twenty times the average of group three. Your tone, tempo, and demeanor can have more impact on a prospective customer than the actual words you speak. This is a particularly important point for salespeople who sell primarily over the phone because it's not only what you say, but how you say it.

Email Communication

Salespeople have increasingly grown to rely on email as their primary method of communication with prospective and existing customers. A downside to this dependence is that the persuasiveness of verbal suggestions is forfeited. Examine the last twenty-five emails you sent. Where would a phone call or in-person conversation have been better suited?

Product Demonstrations, Evaluations, and Pilot Projects

Some salespeople are in too much of a rush to demonstrate their products while others don't want to slow down the sales cycle by having the customer conduct a lengthy product evaluation or pilot project. But this study provides an entirely new reason why demonstrations, evaluations, and pilot projects should be avoided. The results suggest

that hands-on familiarity with an item can actually lower the perception of its value. For example, the average price of the brass letter opener for group three who handled the item was $100, while group two's average was nearly $10,000. Sensory triangulation is the process of verifying information using the three data points of sight, sound, and touch. The people in group three were able to create a more detailed map of each item in their minds. As a result, their estimates were far more accurate than the other groups'.

Sales Presentations and Demonstrations

The "talk track" that accompanies sales presentations and product demonstrations plays a critical role in shaping the prospective customer's perception of value. In this regard, many companies don't take the time to ensure the fluency of the members of their sales organizations by providing them compelling written scripts and testing them to ensure they are able to deliver them persuasively.

Chapter 117. Speaking Pattern Characteristics

Many salespeople pay attention only to the words a customer speaks. They don't pay attention to the person's speaking characteristics—the tone, tempo, volume, and patterns of words. In addition to VAK keywords, you can determine a customer's primary word catalog by his speaking characteristics.

Auditories are actually talking to themselves and tend to speak in repetitious patterns. The pattern could be melodic or more like Morse code. The Morse code–type pattern tends to be monotone. Certain words are enunciated in the pattern. In the following examples, all the "dot" words are enunciated in a similar way, and all the "dash" words are accented in a different way:

- We are committed to your satisfaction.
  (Dot . . . dot . . . dash . . . dot . . . dot . . . dash)

- We guarantee high performance and availability.
  (Dot . . . dash . . . dot . . . dash . . . dot . . . dash)

- Some Auditories speak in a monotone voice.
  (Dot . . . dot . . . dot . . . dot . . . dot . . . dot . . . dot)

Other Auditories have speech patterns that are more melodic. Their sentences are more wavelike; that is, the ends of their sentences will vary in pitch, tone, or even pronunciation from the beginnings.

Auditories tend to be very proficient masters of the technical specification language, the nonpersonal, androgynous, technical talk used in the customer's industry (see ch. 53). Auditories tend to not "leak" or show their word catalogs through the use of VAK keywords as much as Kinesthetics or Visuals. However, when their secondary catalog is kinesthetic, more VAK keywords will be embedded in their conversations. Auditories also tend to quote what they have been told by others. They will also quote themselves in their conversations. Here are more examples of auditory sentence structures:

- "Our meeting went great. Bob told us, 'We did a great job and everyone is excited to work with us.'"

- "The meeting was going really well and then 'boom, boom, boom,' we were asked some really tough questions."

- "And I started to ask myself, Are they still a partner of ours?"

The speech pattern of a Visual is quite different from that of an Auditory. Strong Visuals are being bombarded with pictures inside their brains. As a result, they have a difficult time keeping the pace of the words being said synchronized with the pictures being created in their minds. This condition is somewhat analogous to a computer's CPU (central processing unit) having to wait for the mechanical movements of the disk drive to be complete before it can further process any information. As a result, strong Visuals are constantly trying to speed up the mechanical process of speaking. Therefore, they usually talk faster than Auditories or Kinesthetics. Here are examples of sentence structures of strong Visuals:

- "WE ARE COMMITTED TO YOUR SATISFACTION."

- "VISUALSHAVEALOTTOSAYAND ASHORTTIMETOSAYIT."

To strong Visuals, words are an interruption of the pictures or ideas in their minds. They have to get them out of their internal dialogue as fast as possible because thoughts are constantly getting stacked up. Therefore, they speak with energy and a sense of urgency.

In presentations they tend to speak even faster. Their stream of speech may be interrupted only by the necessity to breathe. Have you ever heard someone insert "um" in every other sentence? Visuals tend to do this more than Auditories or Kinesthetics. This filler word is basically used as a checkpoint to synchronize the images in their minds with their spoken dialogue. The ums are also said at the same speed and tone as the other words.

Conversely, Kinesthetics say "um" much slower and in a deeper tone than the other words they speak. Their ums are actually synchronized with their feelings, and this takes extra time. You also may notice them looking down when they say "um." Meanwhile, the Auditories' ums are not enunciated any differently and blend in with the rest of the sentence. However, Auditories tend to use ums as a part of their editing process to ensure the words they are saying are politically correct. The um provides them additional time to choose their spoken words with more precision.

Visuals tend to talk not only faster but also louder. Visuals are painting a picture for their audience. When they are telling their story, they are trying to make the language represent all the detail and complexity of a picture. You've heard the saying "A picture is worth a thousand words." For Visuals, it's true, and they have to communicate all of the thousand words to convey the picture they are seeing. Therefore, Visuals tend to be the most talkative too!

Having to "always" communicate a thousand words at a time creates a lot of energy. When giving a presentation, Auditories will stand in one place or a small space, and Kinesthetics will shift their weight back and forth. Visuals' arm gestures are more exaggerated since they are illustrating a picture with their bodies. They'll outstretch their arms as far as they can horizontally (so that they resemble a cross) to make their point. Kinesthetics are more likely to make the same point by holding their hands vertically (with one hand over the head and one hand at the waist). Auditories hold their hands closer to their bodies and will use arm gestures sparingly.

While making a PowerPoint presentation, Visuals will point at the screen frequently and may use an index finger like a laser pointer. Kinesthetics will extend an arm, using the entire hand or palm to point. Auditories will most likely point an arm (in the locked position of a push-up) straight in front of the body or from the shoulder horizontally. You will notice that Visuals' arms are held higher on the body or over the head. Kinesthetics will cradle or hold themselves with their arms and hold their arms lower, at the waist.

Most people wrongly assume that people with a kinesthetic primary catalog are overly emotional, introverted, or extroverted. This may or may not be the case. Kinesthetics simply catalog their experiences in terms of feelings. However, people who are strongly kinesthetic will reflect this in their speech patterns, and in turn their personalities will be affected.

Kinesthetics tend to speak slower than Auditories and Visuals. Their speech is slower because they are frequently checking their feelings while they speak. Their speech pattern may also be frequently accentuated by their breathing, which is deeper than that of Visuals and Auditories. When speaking to a group, they tend to talk directly to a single person in the audience, unlike Visuals, who will constantly scan the audience. When talking about issues, Kinesthetics are more likely to associate a person with the issue or task at hand.

Strong Kinesthetics tend to be more dramatic in their speech patterns. They commonly insert pauses and use voice inflections. Unlike Auditories with their Morse code patterns, Kinesthetics are "feeling" the words they are speaking. Their tone of voice tends to be lower because they are constantly validating and comparing their feelings with what they are hearing and saying. Here are examples of sentence structures of strong Kinesthetics:

- "*We* are committed to *your* satisfaction!"

- "*I enjoyed* meeting with *you*."

Every communication with Kinesthetics is personal. The emphasis is on the words "we," "your," "I," "enjoyed," and "you" because they directly correlate with the Kinesthetics' feelings. For example, their interpretation of "we" is actually "my company and I," and their interpretation of "you" is "you and your company." These words represent very personal feelings, so their enunciation is likely to be slower or in a lower tone than the other words in the sentence. Kinesthetics' speech has other patterns. For example, Kinesthetics' voices will tend to rise at the end of sentences or fall and trail off.

The language Visuals, Auditories, and Kinesthetics use reflects the different ways they define their own reality and interact with the real world. Since company purchase decisions usually includes a cross section of Visuals, Auditories, and Kinesthetics, it's obviously important to be able to communicate in each channel. Keep in mind that people with certain word catalogs communicate better with each other than other combinations. For example, strong Visuals and strong Kinesthetics naturally communicate together better than strong Visuals and strong Auditories. Auditories naturally communicate better with Kinesthetics than with Visuals. Kinesthetics have an intrinsic communication advantage since they are always in touch with their own feelings and are sensitive about the feelings of others. This consideration is incorporated into their communication process.

If you are talking with customers who are wired exactly as you are, you are already mirroring them (see ch. 125). Most likely, these are people you naturally communicate with and who are the easiest for you to sell to. However, it takes skill and effort to communicate with someone who has a primary catalog that is the same as your recessive catalog. Ultimately, you want to become a "communication chameleon" who can adapt to any word catalog.

If you are a Visual talking to a Kinesthetic, slow down and speak in terms of feelings; this will naturally lower your voice tone and decrease your volume. If you are a Kinesthetic talking to a Visual, speed up and speak in terms of pictures; this will naturally raise your voice tone and increase your volume. Auditory salespeople face more of a challenge than Visuals or Kinesthetics in presenting their thoughts to customers. If you are an Auditory, you must make a conscious effort to watch the people you are talking to in order to make sure they are grasping what you are saying. What sounds good to you may not look good to a Visual or feel right to a Kinesthetic.

Good advice to Auditories is to stop listening to yourself talk and make sure you are hearing what the customer is saying.

Conversely, Visuals and Kinesthetics should adopt auditory speech characteristics when they are speaking. Just as a chameleon changes colors to match its surroundings, your goal is to change your speaking mannerisms to match those of the person to whom you are speaking. To establish rapport, you need to mirror the way customers communicate and enter their world, not make them enter yours.

Chapter 118. Learning-Style Exercise

When my children first entered grade school they had to complete a wide variety of examinations including hearing, eyesight, and learning-style testing. The purpose of the learning-style test was to determine if the student had visual, auditory, or tactile (also known as kinesthetic) learning preferences. Here's a quick test to help you determine your learning style. Circle the letter preceding each statement that best applies to you.

1. I like to learn about the new products my company is offering by:

    A. Viewing product information and watching presentations

    B. Listening to someone describe the product and talk it through with me

    C. Using the product or having someone demonstrate how it is used

2. To learn the features and benefits of a new product, I like to:

    A. Write them down so that I can review them in the future

    B. Repeat them and practice saying them aloud

    C. Rehearse through role-plays or pretending that I am with a prospective customer

3. At sales training sessions I:

    A. Take notes on important topics so I can look at them after the meeting

    B. Like hearing discussions about important information

    C. Like participating in exercises and role-playing

4. When making an important customer phone call:

    A. I may have prepared a list of topics or notes to remind me of what to say

    B. I tend to talk more than I listen

    C. I like to move, walk around, or doodle on a paper during the call

5. To remember what happened on a sales call:

    A. I remember how someone looked or replay what happened in my mind

    B. I remember what someone said

    C. I remember what someone did or how I felt at the moment

6. Let's say you have to take a test to prove you trained on a new product. What's the best way for you to study for the test?

    A. Read the new product guide and review the pictures, charts, and figures

B. Have someone quiz me about the topics so I can answer them out loud

C. Make index cards or notes that I can flip through and test myself

Now add up the number of As, Bs, and Cs you have circled to find your primary, secondary, and recessive learning styles. The As are visual learning style, Bs are auditory, and Cs are kinesthetic. So if you had three As, two Bs, and one C, you would be classified as a primary visual, secondary auditory, and recessive kinesthetic learner.

Every sales call provides you the opportunity to educate the customer about the benefits of doing business with your company and why your products are better than the competition's. In one sense, you are the teacher and the customer is your student. However, you've most likely been teaching to every student in the same way. That's because you're teaching using your own learning style. Understanding the customer's learning style enables you to present your information to the customer in a more impactful way. Most of the time a person's word catalog and learning styles are very closely related. Be forewarned, it can be different and I've noticed this in about one-third of people whom I have tested.

Incorporate the different learning styles into your sales call strategy. Make sure you have a PowerPoint presentation to show visual customers or be prepared to show them how your product works by drawing on a whiteboard. Auditory customers are more likely to want in-depth conversations, so be sure to bring along your colleagues who can answer all of their detailed technical questions.

Kinesthetics tend to prefer hands-on demonstrations and trial product evaluations and will become frustrated with vendors who are unable to provide them.

Chapter 119. Eye Movements and Long-Term Memory

Everyone lives in his or her own world. The world you experience is not the real world but rather your perception of the world. The way in which you perceive your world is intricately connected to the language you use and how you sense your surroundings. You use your senses to define everyday experiences for storage in your brain. Your word catalogs are the storage and retrieval mechanisms used to access these experiences. They are also responsible for the words you select to communicate your world to others.

I was first introduced to the concept that eye movements are related to long-term memory over thirty years ago. At the time, I had the good fortune to work as a computer programmer for a brilliant doctor who introduced me to neurolinguistics. He had started a medical billing company following many years practicing medicine. He originally studied neurolinguistics in order to better communicate with his patients and understand their mind-sets and behaviors. He also found the principles equally applicable in the business world. Later, when I transitioned my career into software sales, I realized that by understanding my customers' verbal and nonverbal communication, including eye movements, I could predict and influence their future behavior.

You are constantly accessing your short-term and long-term memory. However, it is much easier to access your short-term memory. Accessing your long-term memory is harder and slower. In computer terms, short-term memory is your RAM, while long-term memory is your hard drive. Much like a computer's disk drive, accessing your long-term memory requires some "mechanical" movements, and access to long-term memory can be seen. Conversely, short-term storage is accessed "electronically" and is therefore unobservable.

Amazingly, by observing people's eye movements, you can follow the mechanical movements of the brain that happen when they access their long-term memory. By watching their eyes move, you can determine if they are making pictures in their mind, listening to themselves speak, or experiencing feelings. From this information, you can determine their word catalog wiring and the primary language they use. Most importantly for salespeople, you can learn how to sequence customer questions so specific movements are triggered in order to determine a customer's truthfulness and your future likelihood of winning the deal.

Researchers at the Brain Science Institute discovered that short-term memory is transferred to a different site within the brain to become long-term memory over time, and this is directly related to eye movements. To understand eye movements and their relationship to short- and long-term memory, let's pretend you were learning how to play golf and eagerly scheduled seven daily golf lessons. The newly learned skills from your first and second golf lessons would be stored in short-term memory. As you repeat the exercises daily, these new skills would become stored in long-term memory around the fourth day along with their associated eye movements. Here's the institute's physiological explanation (in technical specification language!): "Command signals that control eye movement are transmitted to the vestibular nucleus in the medulla oblongata over two routes: one direct and the other indirect passway via the parallel fibers and Purkinje cells of the cerebellar cortex. The vestibular nucleus processes the command signals transmitted over both routes and outputs the processed signals to the motor nerves, which in turn, control the movement of the eye."[1]

So now we know that eye movements are closely linked to *establishing* long-term memories, but why are they made when *retrieving* those memories? The brain is a widely distributed neural network with information and memories stored throughout. Eye movements are believed to cause the left and right hemispheres of the brain to better interact with each other. This is known as "hemispheric interaction," and close coordination between the hemispheres is necessary to retrieve certain types of memories. For example, the right hemisphere may maintain information that the left hemisphere requires to retrieve a certain memory. Eye movements to the left activate the right hemisphere, and eye movements to the right activate the left hemisphere. Most interestingly, studies have shown that moving the eyes thirty seconds back and forth from left to right improves memory retention before an event. (Try it before your next big sales call.)[2]

Researchers believe that eye movements help activate the areas of the mind that are involved in processing visual, auditory, and kinesthetic information. For example, the left and right temporal lobes (located at the temples) are involved in the processing of auditory sensations. Scientists have recently pinpointed the parietal cortex (at the top of the head in the middle of the brain) as the area that encodes visual information (after it passes from the eyes through the lateral geniculate nucleus to the back of the brain).[3]

Brain scans of highly emotional people show increased activity in the anterior cingulate (located behind the eyes deep toward the bottom of the brain).[4] Imaging studies have also proven the anterior cingulate is directly linked to sociability and a person's ability to read and respond to social cues such as facial expressions.[5] When remembering pictures, people will move their eyes up to the right, keep their eyes straight while defocusing their pupils, or move their eyes up to the left, as illustrated in figure 119.1.

When remembering sounds, people will move their eyes straight to their right, down to their left, or straight to their left, as illustrated in figure 119.2.

People will move their eyes down to the right when remembering feelings, as illustrated in figure 119.3.

Before we go further, it is important to define the two different types of long-term memories. Some long-term memories can be recalled precisely (precise memories), and some memories are recalled by creating, constructing, and comparing images, sounds, and feelings (assembled memories). Assembled memories will usually cause a different eye movement than precise memories. For example, a Visual might move his eyes up and to the left when asked how many bridesmaids and groomsmen were in his wedding because he's mentally viewing a picture from his wedding album. But the same person may have to look up and to the right when asked to name the church where he was married. Because he couldn't precisely visualize the name, he had to construct the answer and use

Figure 119.1 Visual word catalog eye movements

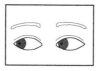  

Figure 119.2 Auditory word catalog eye movements

Figure 119.3 Kinesthetic word catalog eye movement

his imagination to picture the wedding license, the pastor, or the front of the church. Assembled memories require the use of imagination in order to fill the gaps of missing information.

Eye movements reflect the inner workings of the mind. Let's suppose people are asked, What was the best day of your life? Visuals may start searching their memories by looking for stored pictures before finally deciding on a specific day, such as the day their first child was born. To search their memory banks of pictures, their eyes would move up to the right, move up to the left, or look straight ahead with the pupils defocused. Once retrieved, the picture could then trigger the feeling they had of holding the baby for the first time. Their eyes would move down to the right to get the feeling. Finally, to recreate the entire experience, their eyes may move down to the left or straight to the right or left to actually recall the sound of the baby crying.

Have you ever tried to have conversations with people who would not look at you? Perhaps they tilted their heads down and stared at the ground during the entire discussion. Maybe they turned their heads slightly to the right or left so they seemed to be looking at something behind you. Or they could have cocked their heads back, as if they were looking at the sky. These are examples of people who have an exceptionally strong or dominant primary catalog. These people have a single catalog that is so controlling that their heads become an extension of their eye movements. If their heads tilt down and to the right, that indicates they are dominant Kinesthetics, while people who always tilt their heads up are dominant Visuals. When people tilt their heads down and to the left or laterally away from you for the majority of your conversation, you can assume they are dominant Auditories. The person you may have thought of as being

shifty-eyed or untrustworthy may actually just be an Auditory.

While some people will make very obvious eye movements, other people's eye movements are very subtle and consist of quick glances away from you. Some people have to blink to think. They have to close their eyes for a second to retrieve information. In this case, you will be able to see the bulge of their pupil and iris on the eyelid as the eye moves. The main point here is that you have to pay close attention and look for subtle movements as well as obvious eye movements.

When people search their long-term memories, they will quite often perform a "search loop." Their eyes will initially go to their primary system, then their secondary, then their recessive and repeat the pattern. Their eyes will look as if they are going around in circles. They are simply trying to find a mental tag (by sifting through different pieces of information) that will help them bring back the entire memory.

There is also a very rare group of people that I call "Masterminds." One or two out of one hundred people have the uncanny ability to instantly recall exceptionally detailed autobiographical memories and past personal experiences, even though they may have occurred decades before. I surmise that they have more neural pathways that enable their superior memory. Even though most of the Masterminds I have ever met have been Visuals, they don't seem to make any eye movements at all. Here's an interesting story about the only MBA student who has earned a perfect test score on the difficult midterm exam I administer. Her father has a photographic memory and she's a strong Visual.

The mind is an incredibly complex system, and there will be exceptions to the general rules above. For example, left-handedness impacts eye movements about 50 percent of the time based upon my observations. Since only 10 percent of the population is left-handed, this means that 5 percent of the people you meet will be wired in reverse. But this is only my guess, not a scientifically proven fact. Their kinesthetic (down to the right) and auditory (down to the left) eye movements are reversed.

A longtime salesperson once told me that people are lying when they look away from you to the left while answering questions. Unfortunately, for twenty-five years he had been misinterpreting the eye movements of Auditories. Correctly interpreted, eye movements will help you understand the prospective customer's primary word catalog, thereby enabling you to present information to him in the appropriate visual, auditory, or kinesthetic channel.

Exercise: When you first meet a customer, ask questions that require long-term memory access such as When did you start working here? What did you do before you started working here? Where did you grow up? and What was your first job here? The eye movements made while answering these questions will help you get a preliminary idea of the customer's word catalog wiring.

Chapter 120. Long-Term Memory Eye Movement Test

At this point, you may be skeptical about whether eye movements can really explain what is happening in the brain. Try the following experiment. However, before you start, you will need to find a mirror because this exercise is much more meaningful when you can watch yourself.

Below, you will find a list of questions. All of these questions are intended to make you access your long-term memory. However, some answers are actually stored in your short-term memory. Finding answers in short-term memory doesn't require any specific eye movements. For example, if I ask, When did you wake up this morning? the answer is available instantaneously without much work. However, if I ask you what time you woke up two weeks ago last Saturday, that answer may require some additional thought.

As you read each question, try to follow your eye movements. Specifically, concentrate on where your eyes move first to "search" for the answer and make a notation of it. Use *UL* to reflect upper left and *UR* for upper right. Write *SL* for straight left, *S* for straight center with no eye movement at all, *SD* for straight with defocused pupils, and *SR* for straight right. Write *DL* for down left, and *DR* for down right. Also try to pay specific attention to the exact position of your eyes when you actually "find" the answer.

1. What did you have for dinner last Friday?

2. What was the name of your third-grade teacher?

3. What was your favorite vacation?

4. What was the best job you ever had?

5. What was the best sports event you ever attended?

6. Who is your favorite music group?

7. Where were you when you received your first real kiss?

8. What was the worst sales call you ever went on?

9. What account that you closed are you most proud of?

10. What was the license plate number of your first car?

What happened? Did you have to look away from your reflection to answer a question? Where did your eyes move first? What was the last position of your eyes when you found an answer?

Let's examine the questions further. They are all date dependent and designed to access your long-term memory. However, it's possible that some of the answers were in your short-term memory. It depends on you. If you're reading this book on Saturday, it's easy to remember what you had for dinner yesterday. However, if you're reading it on Thursday, the answer may be in long-term memory. If you had Friday's dinner at your favorite restaurant or ate with a classmate you hadn't seen in ten years, then it would be more likely that the experience would be in short-term memory. If there wasn't anything particularly eventful about the meal, it was probably placed in long-term memory.

I could not tell you who my third-grade teacher was. However, I do know a person who can name each of her teachers, even though she attended school over forty years ago. Not surprisingly, she is now a counselor and has dedicated herself to helping others. Obviously, her teachers had a lasting impact on her, and this information has been stored to reflect its importance.

If it has been a long time since you took a vacation, you probably had to do a complex mental search to determine your favorite one. If you were on vacation last week, you may have recently performed this comparison, and the results are still in your short-term memory. If all of your vacations have been indistinguishable or you had a problem selecting an answer, you may have continued in a "search loop."

It's easy to spot people using their search loop. Their eyes move around in a circle, going from catalog to catalog. They'll start in the primary catalog, move to the secondary catalog, go to the recessive catalog, and then repeat the process. Someone with a particularly strong dominant primary will get stuck with his eyes in the primary word catalog position. When this happens in a sales call, you know the customer is trying to "find" the answer. Since the answer isn't immediately retrievable, the customer's answer will most likely represent his best guess and will need to be validated.

This experiment was intended to make you aware of your own eye movements. This exercise should have helped you understand and validate your own word catalog wiring. Don't be concerned if you were unable to complete every question, as it is hard to track eye movements when you can't look yourself in the eye. It's very important to note that your eye movements were probably not all the same because you might have had to use your imagination to create part of the answer in order to make a complete recollection. Remembering a precise memory and imagining an assembled memory may have required different eye movements.

For example, let's say you are an Auditory. When you answered the question about who your favorite music group is, you could have accessed your long-term memory, precisely selecting your favorite band causing your eyes to move straight to your left. Conversely, maybe you like a hot new band, but you couldn't recall its name. Using your imagination, you may have had to play your favorite song in your head before you remembered the band's name and this caused your eyes to move straight to the right. On the other hand, if you had recently attended your favorite band's concert, the answer would probably be in short-term memory, and there wouldn't have been any eye movements.

Two categories of information are kept in your long-term memory: date-dependent experiences and minutiae. Just like a computer's RAM memory, your short-term memory has a limited amount of space. In comparison to RAM, the computer's disk drive (long-term storage) has much more space available. Similarly, your long-term memory is almost infinite. Therefore, your brain is continually optimizing what is kept in short-term memory and "writing," or transferring, it to your long-term memory. As time goes by, the relevance of an event diminishes, causing the event to be reclassified into long-term memory. In addition, your brain will place small details that are considered trivial directly into long-term storage. In this case, the date of the experience has nothing to do with where the experience is stored. It is being stored based solely upon its importance.

Now, take the list of ten questions to some loved ones or friends you know very well. Without telling them why, ask them some of the questions. However, instruct them not to tell you the answers. Rather, at the instant they know the answer, have them say, "Got it!" After each question make two notations—where their

eyes went first and where their eyes were when they said, "Got it." You should get a very consistent pattern. Once again, the place their eyes consistently move to indicates their primary word catalog. Most likely, it will also be the same place they find the answer.

The key to successfully understanding the customers' physical layer (see fig. 105.1) is to first establish their baseline movements. Baseline movements are the customers' default nonverbal communication style. For example, at the beginning of a sales call you could ask nonthreatening questions that invoke long-term memory in order to establish the baseline eye movements. These questions could be about date-dependent experiences or minutiae and hard-to-remember details. For example, When did your company go public? What was the highest stock price? and How many employees worked at the company when you started?

Later during the call as you ask more intense qualifying questions about the customer's selection process and perception of competitors (see ch. 58), mentally compare the customer's eye movements to the baseline established earlier. Calibrating eye movements (see ch. 122) will help you ascertain whether or not you are being told the truth.

Chapter 121. Short-Term Memory Eye Movement Test

Now, let's do another experiment. Pay particular attention to what movements your eyes make as you repeat the questions below, or better yet, ask yourself these questions while looking at yourself in a mirror:

1. What did you have for breakfast today?
2. What color is your car?
3. What is your birthdate?
4. What is your zip code?
5. What is your social security number?

Did you notice completely different eye movements compared to those in the previous exercise or no movement at all? While the set of questions in the previous chapter required you to access your long-term memory, the above set of questions probably didn't. Most likely, the answers were already in your short-term memory because the experience happened recently or you use the information all the time. In computer terms, the answers to these questions were cached (held temporarily) in your RAM, while the answers for the long-term memory questions required you to access the hard drive.

Take a minute and complete the following eye movement exercise. Try to hold your eyes in each position for at least ten seconds. After each eye movement, make a mental note on whether the position was more comfortable than the others.

- Up and to the right
- Up and to the left
- Straight to the right
- Straight to the left
- Down and to the right
- Down and to the left

What happened? Did some movements feel strained while others were easy? Suppose that in the analysis of your emails you performed in chapter 112, your VAK count indicated that you have a visual primary, kinesthetic secondary, and auditory recessive wiring. Most likely, the auditory eye movements were noticeably more uncomfortable to make than the others. If your VAK count indicated that you are wired with an auditory primary, kinesthetic secondary, and visual recessive, then the visual movements were most likely harder to do.

When customers answer your questions, try to recognize their short- and long-term memory eye movements. This will provide important information about what is going on inside their minds. When you ask a customer different qualifying questions, you should expect the appropriate eye movements or no movements at all. For example, the answer to What is your budget? should be in short-term memory. This is a very important factual constraint, so you shouldn't see eye movements associated with imagination or long-term memory. If you do, you should assume the customer's budget is not set or it might not be approved.

Chapter 122. Reading the Customer's Mind

A polygraph machine measures the body's response (breathing, heart rate, and temperature) of a subject to determine if the person is answering questions truthfully. At the beginning of a polygraph test, the administrator asks a certain number of questions known to be true, such as the subject's name and social security number. These questions calibrate the response of known answers to the machine's measurements.

Similarly, you can calibrate eye movements of individuals by watching their responses to questions with known answers. By doing this, you can establish a baseline measurement of their truthfulness. For example, here's how you can sequence questions during a meeting with a customer to ascertain whether or not he is telling you the truth. In essence, you are reading the customer's mind. Based on your VAK count, you know he is auditory primary, kinesthetic secondary, and visual recessive.

Salesperson: How long have you been evaluating solutions?

Customer: (*Eyes left , momentary pause.*) Well, we started last . . . November.

Analysis: Since the evaluation started over ten months ago, this question was a date-dependent event stored in long-term memory.

Salesperson: When do you plan to roll out the first systems?

Customer: (*Eyes straight, not defocused, instantaneous answer.*) Our plan is to be up and running by the end of Q2.

Analysis: This is another date-dependent question. However, the answer was in short-term memory. This is probably an important project date, and it is always on his mind.

Salesperson: Where will the first system be implemented?

Customer: (*In a search loop, eyes left, down to the left, up to the right.*) Probably . . . Los Angeles.

Analysis: This question may have caused him to search for an answer. He was actually making his best guess because the decision is not final.

Salesperson: What other companies are you talking to?

Customer: (*Eyes straight, not defocused.*) We are looking at Acme, Beta Company, and ABC Company.

Analysis: The answer resided in short-term memory. He's probably talking to all the vendors on a regular basis.

Salesperson: Does one of the solutions sound better than the rest?

Customer: (*Eyes up to the right.*) No, they all sound the same.

Analysis: This answer is incongruent communication. His eyes were in the visual position as he spoke auditory words.

In the preceding example, the first four questions established the baseline measurements. The decision-maker's eyes moved to the left when he accessed his long-term memory. They were straight and centered (not defocused) when he accessed his short-term memory. Any eye movements outside these two ranges must be evaluated in context with the answer.

We can assume that the answers to the first three questions were truthful. The third answer was the customer's best guess. Based on the nonpolitical content of the question, this would be an appropriate assumption. The answer to the fourth question, about which companies he is evaluating, should be in short-term memory. If the answer "Acme, Beta Company, and ABC Company" was given extemporaneously at a quick tempo, then you could assume he was being truthful. If he went into a thirty-second search loop to produce the other vendors' names, he was editing his response, which is another form of incongruence, and this requires further investigation. If you observe very complex eye movements for seemingly simple questions or no eye movement for questions for which you would expect movement, then you need to investigate further to ensure the person is being truthful.

The fifth question is the interesting one. The five questions were purposely sequenced in this order. The salesperson wanted to know if the playing field was level or one vendor was favored. His goal was to find the truth. The first four questions established the baseline to set up the fifth question. While the first four questions provided valuable information about the sales process, they also gave the salesperson a chance to calibrate the answers to the customer's word catalog. The answer given to the fifth question was most likely a lie because it was incongruent communication.

In congruent communication, a person's words and thoughts corroborate each other, and the *entire* body is in alignment when the message is delivered. However, the customer contradicted himself while answering the fifth question. His eyes went up to the right to his visual recessive catalog. This is the first incongruence. Based on the previous questions, we would have expected that his eyes would go to either short-term memory (straight, not defocused) or long-term memory (straight left). Since his eyes went to the visual position instead, it can be assumed he was "imagining" or creating an answer. This is a very important point to emphasize about word catalog eye movements. Imagining something typically requires a different eye movement than recalling something from memory. For example, Visuals' eyes might move up and to the right when accessing long-term memory and up and to the left when using

imagination. Sometimes people will have to access an entirely different word catalog to evoke their imagination. For example, Visuals might move their eyes down and to the right, which is indicative of a kinesthetic movement, when they use their imagination.

The second incongruence is that the visual eye movements did not match the layer language used. "No, they all sound the same" is an auditory statement. However, when the customer said this, his eyes were in a visual position. The two incongruencies suggest there is mental conflict and this person is not telling the entire truth. These types of incongruence happen all the time during sales meetings.

Most salespeople rely on their intuition to tell them they are being misled. However, it can be risky to base decisions solely on gut feelings. The methodology tracking eye movements and matching these movements to customer's spoken words provides you with observable proof points to validate your intuition. Carefully sequence questions you ask customers and be on the lookout for incongruence.

Chapter 123. Word Catalog Impact on the Physical Layer (Body Language)

The physical layer of communication, also known as body language, can be very subtle or more powerful than the actual words being spoken. The physical layer is unique in that it is a three-dimensional language. In essence, the response on the outside of our bodies represents what's going on inside our minds. Our posture indicates our comfort level in any particular situation.

Understanding the nuances of body language is a tricky proposition. First, you cannot assume that each body movement means the same thing for everybody. For example, I worked with an individual who moves his right foot constantly during every meeting. This is his "rapport position," or the position he assumes when he is in a receptive state. He is very different from someone who shows impatience by moving in the identical way. Second, the way to understand the meaning of a physical movement is by observing the movement over time. The time period could be as long as an hour or as short as a few minutes. Finally, the ability to recognize and interpret a person's body language can help you validate the person's word catalog language.

For example, you can learn a lot from someone's handshake. Here are some observations. Kinesthetics tend to shake hands a little longer than Visuals and Auditories. Dominant Kinesthetics will put their other hand on top of the handshake or pat the other person on the shoulder or arm. Visuals tend to shake hands with a faster up-and-down movement. Recessive Kinesthetics tend to not make eye contact when they shake, almost as if they want to end the unpleasant process as soon as possible.

Save a mental imprint of the handshake from the beginning of the meeting and compare it with the handshake at the end of the meeting. Was it more sensual or colder? Longer or shorter? Did the amount of direct eye contact change? Was there more than one handshake? Did the person pat you on the back or touch you in some other way during the latter handshake? Handshakes provide instant feedback about how a meeting went. Like a kiss with your lover before you board a plane, the longer and more emotional, the better. From now on, be conscious of handshakes.

Hand movements will also vary based on a person's word catalog. Visuals and Kinesthetics will use hand movements while speaking much more frequently than Auditories. The position of Visuals' hands will be high in context with their bodies, usually at the chest or above. Visuals will use their hands to point to things—they want to make sure you see what they think is important. The fingers of their hands are usually straight or pointed out. They have no problem extending their arms and hands as far as they can because they want you to see the "big picture." They will use their hands as imaginary markers to help draw pictures of the content they are trying to communicate. Visuals' hand movements will be quicker because they are exploding with thoughts that must be communicated now.

Kinesthetics will make "deep" hand gestures while they communicate their feelings. That is, their gestures will be lower on their bodies in accordance with their feelings on a subject. The fingers of their hands will be in a closed or interlocked position. They will touch and hold their bodies while they speak. They may use their hands to cradle their heads or use their arms to hug their bodies. Their hand movements tend to be slower and more deliberate than Visuals' or Auditories' because formulating feelings takes more time than creating pictures or assembling words.

Auditories listen to themselves speak. This alone is a full-time job; therefore, they will use fewer hand movements. When they do use them, they tend to keep their hands closer to their bodies. Another term for this is "dinosaur hands" since their arms are being held like the arms of a *Tyrannosaurus rex*. Their hand gestures will tend to be at the middle of the body, lower than Visuals' hand gestures but higher than Kinesthetics'. Their hand movements also tend to keep time with their voice tempo.

Another aspect of the physical layer is breathing. You may not have noticed this, but people actually breathe quite differently from each other. Obviously, people breathe at a different pace depending on whether or not they are performing a physical activity. The aspect of breathing that we are interested in, however, is the changes in breathing patterns that occur while customers are in their normal state (when most business meetings take place), and these changes can be quite subtle. If a customer is wearing a suit or jacket or if glancing at the customer's chest would be considered inappropriate, breathing patterns can be observed by watching people's shoulders rise and fall as they inhale and exhale.

Different breathing paces can be observed by watching different areas of the abdomen. Some people breathe fast and some slow. Some people have a repetitive rhythm to their breathing: deep breath, pause, deep breath, pause. Some people's breaths are quick and shallow. Visuals tend to breathe shallower and higher in the chest, while Kinesthetics breathe deeper and lower in the belly. Auditories' breathing is somewhere in between. How someone breathes is really not that important. What is important

is trying to spot a change in a breathing pattern. A change is a signal that a person's internal communication state has changed and the level of rapport has fluctuated. This is valuable information to help you identify a customer's state of rapport. People experiencing rapport are relaxed and their breathing reflects this.

In the business world, people rarely express their true emotions outwardly. Facial muscles are used more to inhibit the public display of emotion rather than to show it. Therefore, a salesperson only has small variations of a customer's facial expressions to study. Pay particular attention to the following nuances of customers' facial expressions during sales calls. Are the corners of their eyes becoming tight or relaxed? Are their eyebrows rising or lowering? Is their forehead tensed up? Are their lips, chin, and jaw becoming relaxed or tight?

As we discussed earlier, the key to understanding the physical layer is to establish the customer's natural baseline movements early in the sales call and then compare them to the movements as the sales call progresses. Changes between the baseline facial expressions at the beginning of the sales call versus the expressions at the end serve as a visual checkpoint to determine whether or not you have established rapport. Customers' facial expressions will broadcast whether or not you're liked. If they are more tight-lipped and squinty-eyed than at the beginning of the call, you have probably lost.

To a lesser extent than facial expressions, skin tone can also give subtle clues to a person's emotional state. In a tense meeting, for example, you may witness the skin tone of someone who is scared or unnerved turn ashen gray. When successful sales calls conclude, the participants' skin tone may seem warmer.

How do you "read" customers during a sales call? How do you know when the sales call is going well? The physical layer provides a visible feedback mechanism that enables you to continually gauge your level of rapport with the customer. Identify the customer's rapport position and continually monitor when it changes and what topic of conversation caused the change. Pay attention to "microexpressions" as the customer answers your questions and reacts to what you are saying. Microexpressions are brief nonvoluntary facial movements that last less than a second.

Chapter 124. Observing the Physical Layer

In sales, we are interested in three main aspects of the physical layer of communication. First, we want to interpret people's state of receptiveness to our ideas as exhibited by changes in their rapport. Second, we want to observe the physical layer to help validate our assumptions about people's primary, secondary, and recessive word catalogs. And third, we want to match their body language with the content of their spoken words in order to identify congruencies or potential incongruencies.

The sales world normally uses one of three prevalent meeting positions: all the participants at a meeting are sitting, one person is making a classroom-style presentation to a group of people who are sitting, and two or more people are standing in a conversation. These positions cover the majority of sales situations and are worth studying in more detail.

Group dynamics are very complex. In group meetings, the pecking order is reflected in where a person sits. Whether at a round table or in a classroom setting, the person with the most influence will choose a dominant place to sit. For example, at a long, boardroom-style table, these people will be found at the center of the table, and a spot will be left for them there even if they are late. If the table is shorter, dominant people will sit at one of the ends, while their subordinates will cluster around them.

At a round table, the dominant position may be the seat facing the door or the one with the best view outside. In a large classroom-style setting, dominant people will sit in the front of the room or in the most visible position. This is the position that provides the best location to see the presentation and to be seen by the audience. Occasionally, dominant people will sit in the very last row so they can be in the position of leaving whenever they please. Regardless of the setting, where a person sits is of primary importance.

Now that you know where influential people will sit, let's examine their posture. Most meetings start with people in a "closed" posture versus an "open" posture. In a closed posture, the body is folded up on itself. Probably the most familiar closed posture is the arms crossed on the chest. More subtle closed positions are legs crossed, ankles crossed, hands interlocked on the table, and both hands touching the face. A person in a closed position may also face away from the focal point of the meeting or presenter.

A closed posture does not necessarily indicate a negative attitude. Rather, it is a natural position of skepticism that shifts to an open position as rapport is created. The open position represents the best environment in which to communicate your message. When people change to an open position, it may be as obvious as their uncrossing their arms and lowering them to the table. More likely, the change will be a lot more subtle. They may relax the tightness in the parts of the body that are folded: arms, hands, legs, ankles, feet, and even lips. They could also move their folded arms from their chest to their waist. Or they could switch position, such as going from legs crossed with the right leg on top to legs crossed with the left leg on top. Watch for these subtle changes and make a mental notation of when they happen. Who was speaking? What was the topic? Was there a variation in facial expression that accompanied the move?

People are continually opening and closing their positions throughout a meeting. It's important to identify a person's closed and open state and watch for patterns of reoccurrence during the meeting. Heavy Hitters know they need to investigate why they lost a person's open state and will pause to ask the person if he or she has any questions or try to solicit an opinion on the topic being discussed.

On a sales call, constantly survey all of the meeting participants to see if they are receptive to your ideas and moving from closed to open positions. The goal is to uncover any confusion and objections as early as possible. You do not want objections to remain hidden until it is too late to address them successfully. Even if someone else from your company is presenting, do not relax but carefully and continuously examine everyone's physical state. Try to be the first person to enter the meeting room

so you can take the position that affords you the best viewpoint to observe all of the meeting participants.

Chapter 125. Pacing, Mirroring, and Leading

I drive to the local mountains to vacation during the summer and winter. The trip takes several hours each way. Usually, I will drive at the pace of the car in front of me, keeping a distance between that car and mine that I feel comfortable with. I will automatically maintain this distance until the pace of the car in front of me becomes too fast or too slow. Sometimes, I will keep pace to the music on the radio and find myself speeding up to the tempo of the song. Pacing can be thought of as the natural process of adjusting your tempo to your environment.

On freeways, cars tend to cluster together instead of being evenly dispersed. It seems that the cars act together as a group and will accelerate or slow down together. This is mirroring, which can be thought of as the conscious act of modifying your behavior to fit your surroundings.

The car in front of me is also "leading" my behavior. Let's assume I have been mirroring the car in front of me for the last ten minutes. Suddenly, the driver swerves to the right. I will follow his lead and prepare to swerve to the right, even though I have not actually seen the danger. Leading is the process of influencing another person's action by yours.

Heavy Hitters use pacing, mirroring, and leading to gain rapport with their customer. They are constantly monitoring the customer's physical communication—handshakes, hand movements, breathing, facial expressions, and body posture. They know that by changing the style to match the customer's, they will create more effective communication because the customer is more comfortable, relaxes, and lowers his defensive guard.

When we watch someone else perform an action, mirror neurons in our minds fire off and respond as if we were doing it ourselves. Mirror neurons help explain why laughter is contagious, why we grimace in pain for people we don't even know, and why we feel like crying when we see others cry. However, not everyone has the same amount or strength of mirror neurons. Therefore, we need a strategy to put ourselves in the "mental shoes" of the customer and help lead him to understand the value of our company, our products, and ourselves.

Ultimately, a good salesperson wants to become a communication chameleon. Just as the chameleon changes colors to match its surroundings, your goal is to change your speaking mannerisms to match the buyers'. That includes speaking in their languages (industry, technical, and job function) and adopting their physical attributes, such as body posture, speech tempo and patterns—even how they dress. The ultimate reason you want to mirror buyers is because they want to interact with salespeople who are like them. For example, 81 percent of buyers prefer to talk with someone who has the same mannerisms they do.

Consider handshakes in the context of mirroring. You start a handshake using a medium grip and instantly react to the other person's grip. If the person's grip is firmer, you grip harder, and vice versa. The length of the handshake is also equally matched to the other's. You have instinctively been mirroring for your entire career!

Mirroring breathing styles is the first step in helping you create rapport because it makes you recreate the customer's world with your body. If someone breathes slowly, you have no choice but to slow down the pace of your speech and movements along with your breathing. If a person breathes faster than you, your actions will naturally speed up.

Mirroring body posture is accomplished by making a subtle reflection of the customer. The most obvious mirroring is a direct reflection, like the opposite image in a mirror. For example, when someone sits with legs crossed, you sit in the identical position with your legs crossed oppositely. Or you cross your arms tightly to your chest, in the exact opposite position of your counterpart during a conversation while standing.

However, this type of mirroring is too obvious and can potentially be perceived as patronizing. Rather, the mirroring we want to use is much more discreet. Instead of crossing your legs to directly mirror someone, cross your legs at the ankles or even cross your arms. Instead of standing with your arms tightly folded, cross your arms in a looser fold at the waist or stand with your legs crossed. Let's think about handshakes in the context of mirroring. Every time you shake someone's hand you instinctively mirror their grip strength.

Assuming you have been successfully mirroring your customer, now it's time to test whether you have rapport by leading. Leading can be thought of as the process of using your actions to guide another person's behavior. Let's assume that you are fifteen minutes into a meeting. You have been successfully mirroring the customer's breathing and body positions. You feel you have gained rapport and now want to test if this is true. Slowly, you start varying your breathing, and the other person follows your lead. Slowly, you change your body position, and the other person changes as well. If you are doubtful about leading, think about how contagious yawns are during meetings.

The ability to consciously develop a formalized process of pacing, mirroring, and leading can be used to influence a person's state to be more open or receptive to your message. Most likely, you don't have a formalized process to accomplish this. It comes naturally. Salespeople with strong kinesthetic catalogs do this instinctively. However, this process can be learned by anyone.

Exercise: You can perform exercises to help build the skill set necessary to pace, mirror, and lead customers during sales calls. At your next meeting, choose one person and spend the entire meeting mirroring and leading the breathing of that person. Similarly, in other meetings, pick a body position, such as the position of the person's hands or feet, and mirror it along with the person's breathing through the entire meeting. Continually add new layers of sophistication to your mirroring and leading. You can even mirror how a person speaks, including his tone, tempo, and volume.

Chapter 126. Comprehension and Your Communication Level

Poor communication is a surefire way to jeopardize any deal, damage any client relationship, and lose business to the competition. Whether in person or via email, you must make sure you are communicating at the customer's level. If you use a level that is too low, you will not be respected and will never be in a position to establish situational dominance. In addition, comprehension requires that the message be conveyed at the recipient's communication level, not too far below or above the level of the words in his or her lexical dictionary.

Any communication consists of one of three types of messages—recreational, instructional, and frustrational. A recreational message is socially enjoyable communication. Examples include talking to a friend, listening to music, and reading a novel. This type of communication has the highest level of comprehension where the meaning, nature, and importance of the words are personally understood. About 95 percent of the words are known and recognized as shown in figure 126.1.

Instructional messages are based on teaching, telling, or passing along knowledge. Instructional messages include directions, commands, advice, and even questions. When customers ask you questions, they are actually instructing you to give them the specific information they need. Instructional messages are sent during briefings, training sessions, chalk talks, and sales calls. However, they typically have a slightly lower level of comprehension than recreational communication—about 85 percent.

Frustrational messages include any type of communication that is either not understood or is considered objectionable by the recipient. Let's say you and I are having a conversation and I say that a colleague of ours is a "loquacious prevaricator." Our level of rapport would drop if you did not know that these words meant "talkative liar." Frustrational messages have the lowest level of comprehension—under 80 percent.

Frustrational messages include offending or disagreeable messages. For example, a command given by someone who does not have greater expertise or authority over the recipient is a frustrational message. The inclination is not to follow it.

Conduct this exercise to determine your communication level. Gather at least ten different samples of your writing. These could be proposals, letters, reports, or emails. Cut and paste them into one Microsoft Word document and then enable the "Show readability statistics" box. Now spell-check the entire document, and you will see your Flesch-Kincaid grade

level index. (For additional step-by-step instructions, enter "readability" in the Word Help search—instructions vary by release.) The result is a number that corresponds to the grade level at which you communicate. For example, a score of 9.0 would indicate that the text is understandable by an average student in ninth grade.

I typically write at a Flesch-Kincaid grade level score around 12. That is my natural communication level. It's also an appropriate communication level for my target audience. The majority of sales books that target business-to-consumer salespeople, who sell products such as cars, are written around the eighth-grade level. Since my target market is senior business-to-business salespeople who typically have a university degree, a level of 12 is appropriate.

Exercise: What is the communication level of the customers you sell to? If they have advanced degrees in computer science, engineering, or finance, are you communicating at their level? One way to find out is to perform Flesch-Kincaid grade level scoring on all the communications they have sent you and those you can find on the internet. Whether in person or via email, you must make sure you are communicating at their level. If you use a level that is too low, you will not be respected and will never be in a position to establish situational dominance. Conversely, if you use a level that's too high you may be misunderstood.

Recreational messages are socially enjoyable communication with the highest level of comprehension and personal meaning.

Instructional messages are based on teaching or passing along knowledge and typically have a slightly lower level of comprehension.

Frustrational messages include any type of communication that is either not understood or considered objectionable by the recipient.

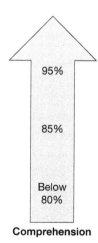

95%

85%

Below 80%

Comprehension

Figure 126.1 Effective communication and comprehension level

Chapter 127. Enunciation, Pronunciation, and Minimizing Accents

If English is your second language, you may frequently encounter a communication challenge when speaking with native language English speakers. Speaking English with a heavy accent can create a significant roadblock to building successful business relationships.

> *My tendency is to shy away from doing business with salespeople who I have a hard time understanding. I'll also change vendors if my team continually complains they are experiencing communication challenges.*
>
> —Vice President of Information Technology

Your enunciation, or clarity of speech, impacts your ability to communicate clearly with prospective clients. Can the client distinctly recognize the words you say and understand the meaning of what you are trying to express? Pronunciation is the manner in which you speak, including your tone, tempo, volume, and stressing of words. For example, I've worked with many foreign-based companies and have taught hundreds of foreign exchange students. Many EASL (English as a second language) speakers don't talk in the correct volume. Some talk too loud for normal conversation and others speak way too softly. With this in mind, here are six recommendations to minimize an accent and improve comprehension with better enunciation and pronunciation.

1. Slow Down Your Speaking Tempo 30 to 50 Percent

Probably the single most important recommendation is to speak slower. Many languages, such as Spanish and Indian languages, are generally spoken much faster than English. So when an Indian speaks English the tempo is too fast for a North American native English speaker's ear to process. When you are talking to someone over the phone, you should slow down your speech by 50 percent at a minimum. The guideline when speaking to someone in person is to slow down your speech by 30 percent. Because others can see your lips move while you speak, they can process the words you are saying more easily. Slowing down your speaking tempo will improve comprehension dramatically.

2. Use a More Monotone Speech Pattern

EASL speakers have a tendency to speak in a more melodic manner than native English speakers. Words and the syllables within them are emphasized where the native English speaker does not expect them. Because inflection patterns are different, they are not easily recognized. For example, the emphasis might be on the wrong syllable or the sentence stressed in the wrong way. A sentence may unexpectedly go up in pitch and then fade at the end quickly. Try to make a conscious effort to speak in a more monotone voice that doesn't rise and fall in pitch so every word sounds close to the same.

Figure 127.1 serves as a visual representation of the problem native English speakers face when hearing an EASL speaker with a heavy accent. Smoothly

Expected inflection

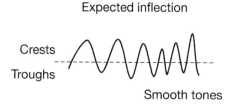

English spoken without accent

Compressed and unexpected inflection

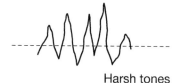

English spoken with heavy accent

Figure 127.1 Representation of the verbal impact of unexpected Inflections

spoken English is shown on the left. The listener knows when to expect syllables to be inflected. There's also gap time between the words (and even syllables), so the listener more easily processes them. The example on the right shows a faster tempo of sounds spoken in a manner that is harsher and more unpleasant to the listener's ear. The listener has difficulty processing the words because the syllabic emphasis is not where it is anticipated. Finally, the range between crests and troughs is more pronounced, making comprehension more difficult.

3. Recognize Mistaken Pronunciation Tendencies

The best way to reduce your accent and improve the comprehension of your spoken English is through practice. Therefore, it's important to determine which sounds are causing the most confusion when you speak. Mandarin Chinese speakers typically have difficulty pronouncing V as in verify, J as in justice, CH as in Chicago, and SH as in shower. Many Indian speakers substitute the S sound for a Z sound. Pronunciation exercises can be used to correct mispronunciations. For example, say the word "snake" aloud three times. Notice the S sound comes from the front of the mouth. Now say "zebra" aloud three times. Notice how the Z sound comes

from farther back in the mouth and the throat. Take a moment to analyze the words you struggle to say and ask your colleagues to point out the areas where you need to improve.

4. Pretend You're Talking to a Ten-Year-Old Child

Some nonnative English speakers will speak in an overly loud or harsh style. The stream of speech is composed of very forcefully pronounced words that can literally hurt the ears of native English speakers. For example, when I ask my MBA students from China who have this problem to speak in their native language, their voices are pleasant to listen to. My advice to them is to pretend they are speaking to a ten-year-old child. In other words, soften what you say and lower your tone of voice.

5. Have Your Written Communications Reviewed

It's always a good idea to have an important email, report, or letter written to a prospective customer or existing client reviewed by colleagues and your manager prior to sending it. For nonnative English speakers, this is even more important. Specifically, is the message structured correctly? Is it easily understood? Is it grammatically correct?

6. Become an Even More Active Listener

Everyone knows salespeople should listen intently when customers talk. But did you know there are two types of listening? Active listening is intently paying attention to what the customer is saying and how he is saying it. You are focused on understanding the meaning of his words and trying to determine his purpose for saying them. Passive listening is surface-level listening where you quickly pass judgment on the speaker's thoughts. Consequently, you are mentally fixated on your response while the person is talking. Nonnative English speakers should be even more focused on being active listeners. Listen to the other person's speaking habits (tone, tempo, and pattern) and mirror them using the techniques described in chapter 117.

Chapter 128. Buyer's Remorse and Coping Mechanisms

We naturally assume that customers will react in one of two ways to our pitch: they'll like it or they won't. However, customer behavior is far more complex. To better understand the impact of human nature on evaluators, I conducted a study of B2B buyers who were asked to recount the last time they experienced significant buyer's remorse.

Buyer's remorse occurs after the purchase is made when the buyer feels a sense of regret, guilt, or anger and second-guesses the decision. Most people mistakenly associate buyer's remorse with an impulsive, spur-of-the moment buy or assume it is caused by the pressure tactics of a salesperson. However, the research results define and prioritize ten different root causes as shown in figure 128.1. When all of these root causes are

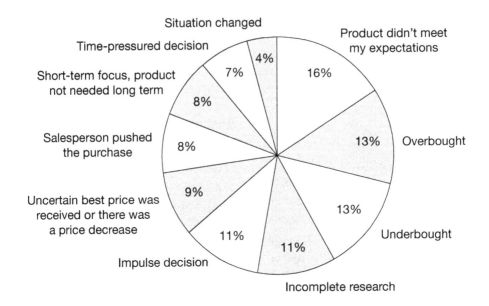

Figure 128.1 The sources of B2B buyer's remorse

totaled, about 70 percent of the time the buyer's own action caused the person to regret the purchase, not the salesperson or the product that was sold.

The collection of these negative sales experiences over evaluators' lifetimes shapes how they buy and whom they prefer to do business with. As a result, buyers experience a mental tug-of-war when deciding which product to select and confusion about whether they should make a purchase at all. Therefore, they adopt coping mechanisms when facing the stressful situation of selecting between salespeople and their solutions.

Coping mechanisms are psychological and behavioral strategies people use to manage stress and threatening situations. They are a psychological strategy for avoiding buyer's remorse. Here's a list of the common buyer coping mechanisms salespeople encounter on sales calls:

- *Attack.* Some customers categorize all salespeople as unethical evildoers. Generalizing all salespeople into a single group helps them handle the ordeal of buying, and a salesperson should not take this attack personally.

- *Avoidance.* Certain customers will seek to avoid the people and situations that cause distress. They'll keep the conversation solely at the surface level and won't answer tough questions. Confronting customers who use this coping mechanism causes them to avoid the salesperson even more.

- *Business-level conversation.* Some customers instinctively try to keep the conversation at a business level

with the nonfavored salespeople. They do this to protect themselves because they don't want to let anyone down. This is one of the more prevalent coping mechanisms buyers use to deal with salespeople.

- *Compensation.* Customers sometimes make up for a weakness in one area by overemphasizing another. For example, a prospect will fixate on a unique feature of a competitor's product even though that product is less capable overall.

- *Intellectualization.* Some customers will avoid showing any emotion and focus instead on facts and logic. However, even the most analytical and unemotional customers have a sentimental favorite that they want to win.

- *Passive-aggressiveness.* Some customers project a friendly superficial presence but are secretly plotting against the salesperson. This is one of the worst predicaments to be in.

- *Rationalization.* Certain customers use logical reasons in an illogical way to publicly validate their emotional favorite. For example, they'll say they can't use a product because it doesn't support international monetary conversions even though they don't conduct any international business.

- *Reaction formation.* Some customers take a polar opposite position to everything a salesperson says. They simply don't want to buy from that person.

- *Trivialization.* Some customers trivialize a favored vendor's major deficiency while maximizing the minor shortcomings of another. This is a sure sign that they have a favorite vendor.

One of the most prevalent coping mechanisms used by buyers is silence. Figure 128.2 shows B2B buyers' reactions when they hear a salesperson say something they disagree with.

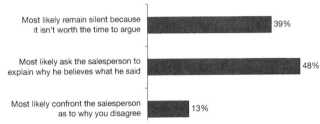

If a salesperson said something you disagreed with during a sales call, what would you do?

Most likely remain silent because it isn't worth the time to argue — 39%

Most likely ask the salesperson to explain why he believes what he said — 48%

Most likely confront the salesperson as to why you disagree — 13%

Figure 128.2 B2B buyers' coping mechanism responses

Successful salespeople also continually catalogue successes and failures. They store patterns of individual and buyer committee behavior and link them to the sales process. Their goal is to understand the core of the customer's psyche and address the hidden biases and silent objections that are always in the back of the buyer's mind.

Finally, sometimes what customers say about you really applies to them. They'll say your price is too high when, in reality, they couldn't have afforded it in the first place. They will say your solution is technically inferior when they don't have the wherewithal to implement it. In other words, the most significant and prevalent customer coping mechanism is lying.

The customer has developed a pattern of behavior for dealing with salespeople after hundreds of interactions. Since it is usually based upon negative experiences, the first goal of every sales call should be to perform a pattern interruption (see ch. 82). You want to dissociate yourself from all the other salespeople and their previous negative sales calls. One way to accomplish this is by "detaching" and doing something completely different or totally unexpected.

Perform detaching when customers resort to their favorite coping mechanism during your sales call. Detaching can be an effective tool in sales situations where you want to change behaviors quickly. For example, when a customer attacks you by saying "Your price is too high!" you might say, "I could rationalize all the reasons why we charge what we do, but those would be rational lies. Please tell me how we can find the middle ground to make this business happen."

Chapter 129. The Differences between Salesmen and Saleswomen

Do salesmen sell differently than saleswomen? Based on research involving over one thousand sales professionals, there are many differences and an equal number of similarities. A distinct difference becomes apparent when favorite school subjects are analyzed by gender (in chapter 41 we reviewed the results for all buyers). The favorite subject of women was language or composition with 32 percent selecting it, while only 8 percent of men did. Twenty-eight percent of men ranked history as their favorite subject, which was nearly double the proportion of women, at 15 percent.

What do history and language/composition classes have in common? History is associated with the rise and fall of countries, iconic military battles, and important people who shaped their time. Language and composition classes focus on the skills of reading and writing, which may be developed through reading classic books or writing essays. In one sense, both subject areas revolve around storytelling. Therefore, it should not be surprising these are the top two subjects selected because salespeople are natural-born storytellers. Based on the survey results, it could be argued that history is the more masculine form and language/composition is the more feminine form of storytelling. Both are based on telling a meaningful story in a cohesive way that leads the listener to believe.

In an effort to determine competitiveness, study participants were asked if they agreed with this thought-provoking statement: "I like to win but cannot stand to lose because the pain of losing is greater than the joy of winning." Forty-two percent of men versus 25 percent of women agreed that this statement was very true or true as shown in figure 129.1. This statement frames winning not from a standpoint of loving to win but from the point of view of hating to lose. The results suggests men are more competitive by nature.

One of the most striking differences between male and female sales professionals was how they perceive themselves. Study participants were asked to select three words from a list of seventeen that they felt best described themselves. The top answer for both men and women was "confident" with 42 percent and 41 percent of mentions, respectively. However, the second answer was quite different. Thirty-three percent of men selected "responsible," while 32 percent of women selected "empathetic." Only 19 percent of men selected "empathetic," and it was ranked in the eighth position of importance. For the third answer, 32 percent of men selected "likable," while 32 percent of women selected "smart."

When asked to select two qualities they thought customers admired the most about them, the results were nearly identical for men and women. The top three responses were "trustworthiness," with 56 percent of mentions for men and 58 percent for women; "professionalism," with 37 percent for men and 34 percent for women; and "follow-through," with 31 percent for both men and women.

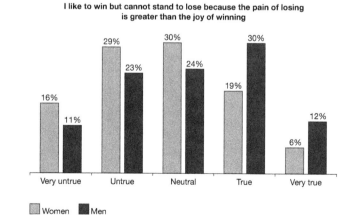

I like to win but cannot stand to lose because the pain of losing is greater than the joy of winning

Women   Men

Figure 129.1 Competitive differences between salesmen and saleswomen

The type of relationship salespeople will develop with customers is influenced by their gender. Women develop more intimate relationships and bond with their clients. For example, when asked how they work with their clients, 44 percent of women versus 34 percent of men selected "Feel personally responsible and dedicate myself to ensuring their success." Twenty-one percent of women versus 17 percent of men selected "Develop very close personal relationships with my clients." Men are more likely to have superficial relationships with clients. Twenty-nine percent of men versus 18 percent of women indicated they "Have cordial relationships with my clients because we are both very busy." Twenty percent of men compared to 17 percent of women "Keep a general pulse on what's happening with clients after the sale."

Are salesmen or saleswomen more successful? The results show that more

men made their quota than women. Fifty-three percent of men reported making their previous year's annual quota compared to 43 percent of women. Twenty-four percent of both men and women were over 125 percent of quota, while 29 percent of men and 19 percent of women were between 100 and 124 percent of quota. At the low end of performance, one out of four men and one out of three women were under 80 percent of quota. Quota attainment is also impacted by whether or not the salesperson has a mentor as discussed in chapter 11.

Are there different career motivations for men and women? The biggest difference is that for one out of three women compared to one out of five men, a career in sales came about through happenstance as shown in figure 129.2. When asked to choose the fundamental reason they're in sales, 21 percent of men and 33 percent of women selected, "It just happened naturally." Conversely, 29 percent of men and 19 percent of women selected "The harder I work, the more money I make."

Study participants were also asked, "On a grade of A+ to F, how would you rate your career overall?" Men and women ranked their careers similarly with one exception. Significantly more women graded their careers as A+ than men. Eighteen percent of women compared to 12 percent of men rated their career as A+.

But there's another important takeaway from the overall career rating. Whether you are a man or woman, sales is a truly great career choice. I do not think there are many professions where 72

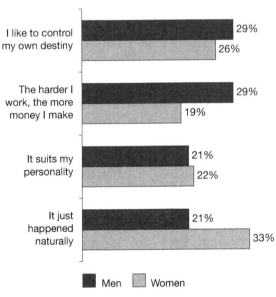

Figure 129.2 Career motivations of salesmen and saleswomen

percent of the men and 75 percent of the women in the field would grade their overall careers at B+ or higher. Based upon the thousands of sales professionals I've met, I'll argue that the decision to pursue a career in sales wasn't even theirs to make in the first place. Rather, they're simply fulfilling their life's destiny and lucky to be in a profession that is both financially rewarding and personally satisfying.

Chapter 130. The Differences between Men and Women Buyers

All salespeople know there are subtle differences between selling to men versus women, and research I conducted with over 350 buyers confirms it. In regard to salesperson selling styles, women preferred salespeople who make them feel comfortable and take care of their long-term needs. Men preferred the salespeople who understand and then match a solution to solve their specific problem as reviewed in chapter 26.

Another difference is that 61 percent of women compared to 48 percent of men think that one of the biggest mistakes a salesperson can make is to assume prospective buyers know less than they actually do. However, every sales situation is uniquely influenced by the buyer's background. For example, there are vastly different results when responses are analyzed by industry and department. Eighty percent of women in the technology industry indicated the worst mistake is for the salesperson to assume the prospective client knows less than he or she does. Conversely,

67 percent of women who work in the accounting department indicated the worse mistake is for the salesperson to assume the prospective client knows more than he or she does. A key lesson is to never assume two buyers are exactly the same, because their behavior and perceptions are greatly influenced by the industry and department they work in.

The study participants were asked to complete word associations to gain an understanding of their attitudes toward salespeople. The written answers were then categorized as having a positive connotation, a negative connotation, or a neutral connotation that was neither bad nor good. In general, men have a more positive perception of salespeople. For example, 48 percent of the associations to the term "salespeople" were positive for men, while 39 percent were positive for women. Conversely, 35 percent of the associations for women were negative versus only 21 percent for men. The top three answers for men were "money," "persuasive," and "tactics." The top answer for women was the negative word "aggressive," followed by "persuasive" and "money."

Decision-Making Behavior

Men and women buyers have different perceptions about decision-making committees as well. In general, women believe that committees are more effective, will take a more active role on them, and feel they have greater influence on the decision. However, gender influence on group decision-making dynamics is a very complex subject. Let's examine three different scenarios: decision-making among a group of friends, decision-making among colleagues at work, and finally, decision-making as part of a vendor evaluation committee.

Men and women behave quite differently when making decisions among friends as demonstrated by the example of selecting a vacation destination in figure 130.1. Forty-one percent of men would lobby for their preferred destination even if it wasn't right for their friends, while none of the women selected this response. In all, 46 percent of men selected self-centered responses such as lobbying for the location or opposing someone else's location. In comparison, 14 percent of women selected the self-centered response that they would seek to make their preferred location the destination no matter what. Overall, women are twice as likely to be more collaborative and focused on making sure the best location was selected.

Let's say that you and your closest friends were going to plan to take a vacation together. However, there were a wide variety of opinions and disagreements about where to go. What statement best reflects how you would behave during the decision-making process?

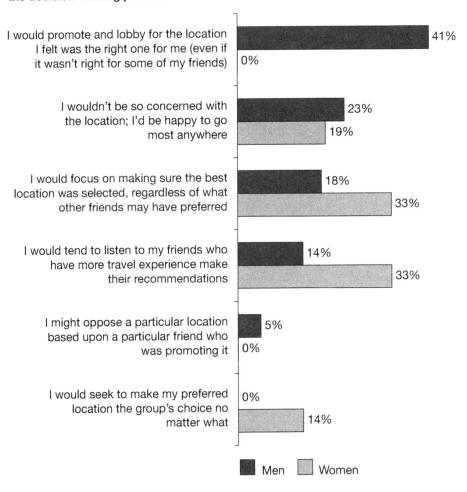

Figure 130.1 How gender influences decision-making among friends

The study results show gender influences the dynamics of decision-making committees at work. In the scenario shown in figure 130.2, the decision a committee makes will impact the person's ability to perform his or her job. Similar to making decisions among friends, men are more politically oriented and will take an active role in ensuring their best interest is protected. Once again, more men (64 percent) selected self-centered responses compared to women (38 percent). Women were more likely to maintain a positive attitude and listen to the recommendations of senior committee members.

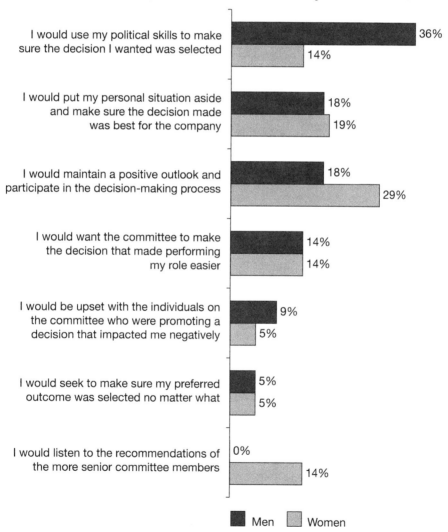

Figure 130.2 How gender impacts decision-making committee behavior at work

Now let's examine how gender influences vendor evaluation committee behavior. The results in figure 130.3 show that gender influence on evaluation committees mirrors that of a group of friends and committees at work. Again, men are more politically oriented and will take an active role in ensuring their best interest is protected. More men (39 percent) selected self-centered responses as compared to women (15 percent). Women were more likely to maintain a positive attitude and listen to the recommendations of others. Refer to chapter 76 for additional information on how evaluation selection committee members adopt different company buyer persona roles in order to influence their colleagues and the decision outcome.

Let's say you are part of an evaluating committee that is selecting between vendors for a $2,500,000 purchase that will enable a very important company initiative. There are six members on the committee from across different departments of the company. Therefore, this is a very political decision as committee members have vastly different points on which a vendor should be selected. Which role do you think you would take if you were on this evaluation committee?

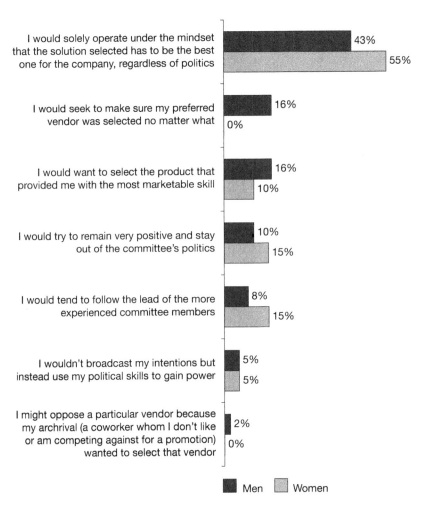

Figure 130.3 How gender impacts vendor evaluation committees

Do men and women have tendencies to select different vendors? Men and women made different selections when presented with three different vendor scenarios as shown in figure 130.4. Thirty-four percent of men compared to 9 percent of women selected the product that cost $50,000 from the largest, best-known company that is the well-

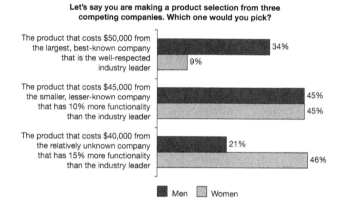

Figure 130.4 How genders select between products

respected industry leader. Forty-five percent of both men and women selected the product that cost $45,000 from the smaller, lesser-known company that has 10 percent more functionality than the industry leader. Forty-six percent of women versus 21 percent of men selected the product that cost $40,000 from the relatively unknown company that has 15 percent more functionality than the industry leader. As opposed to men, the results suggest women trend toward being value-sensitive buyers who are more interested in a bargain.

Personality Differences

Remember the last time you made a very important personal decision? Perhaps it was a major purchase such as a house, a car, or a particular stock. Maybe it was

a personal decision to get married, start a family, or change jobs. Whatever the case, many different factors influenced the decision you made. Ultimately, your decision was based upon the characteristics of your personality. Here are some findings from buyer personality testing.

Twenty-six percent of men compared to 12 percent of women consider themselves to be dreamers who envision achieving longer-term goals. Conversely, 39 percent of women versus 32 percent of men are more concerned with the "here and now" and concentrate on daily activities. Dreamers tend to fall in love quickly with a particular salesperson or the solution they believe will help them realize their fantasy soonest. As opposed to selling to the "here and now" buyer, emphasize the company vision and all the great new products that will be released in the future. Dreamers tend to be impulsive buyers, which can cause them to frequently change their minds. As a result, you need to continually qualify the opportunity.

Women (37 percent) have more emotional sensitivity than men (26 percent). This does not necessarily mean they're more emotional, but they are aware of their emotions more so than men. There's also a group of women who aren't necessarily wired that way. Whether because of their nature or a conscious choice, they ignore their emotions.

Preparation as a method to mitigate risk goes hand in hand with planning. By this measure, 49 percent of women will plan way in advance in order to achieve a more predictable outcome compared to 31 percent of men. It can be inferred that men are less willing to focus their time and energy to plan when compared to women. While an aggressive, high-energy strategy might be appropriate for certain buyer personas, it won't appeal to the "plan it way in advance" type of buyer.

Men and women are very different in many ways. For example, 63 percent of men compared to 43 percent of women consider themselves to be highly curious. Sometimes the differences are small but surprising. For example, women were twice as likely to be quick-minded decision-makers. These spur of the moment quick-minded decision-makers tend to be relationship-based decision-makers who befriend salespeople during the sales cycle as opposed to keeping them at arm's length. Ten percent more women than men were type A personalities who are always on the go. They're great to sell to because they operate with a sense of urgency, push themselves to meet deadlines, and are impatient with delays.

Thrill seekers long for excitement, and more men (30 percent) than women (19 percent) described themselves this way as shown in figure 130.5. These buyers are easily bored and more energetic than their counterparts who don't crave thrills. Their self-confidence drives them to take chances as opposed to playing it safe.

While many acts of kindness are motivated by the desire to feel good about ourselves, some people have an altruistic nature that inclines them to help others. Scientifically, women are more nurturing than men, which helps explain why 42 percent of women said they're eager to help people as opposed to 34 percent of men. Don't be misled by prospective buyers who talk to you on friendly terms and intimately offer their support. In many cases, they are extremely amiable people who are altruistically providing the same information to all the vendors competing for the business.

While humility is considered a good trait for salespeople to have, it may not be for buyers. Twenty-six percent of men consider themselves superior to most people while only 15 percent of women do. In addition, 37 percent of men are seldom embarrassed compared to 27 percent of women. And, women were more likely to classify themselves as habitual worriers. Peer pressure is a powerful influencer of decision-making dynamics because evaluators are constantly worried about how the purchase decision will reflect on them.

Your behavior is influenced by a complex combination of your personality, your experiences, and your biological

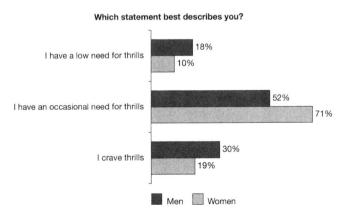

Figure 130.5 Thrill-seeking personality tendency

predisposition that has made you the person you are today. While it is definitely influenced by your gender, it is not the sole factor. Below, you will find summarized personality tendencies for men and women. However, these are only generalizations because human nature is far too complex to fit a simple characterization.

Women	Men
Are concerned with the here and now	Dream about the future
Have emotional sensitivity	Have a curious nature
Plan ahead	Are procrastinators
Are commitment oriented	Are outcome oriented
Are quick decision-makers	Are cautious decision-makers
Want to be leaders	Speak up when they have to
Are faster paced	Are more tolerant of risk
Are more trusting	Are more skeptical
Are more altruistic	Are more narcissistic
Worry	Are calm
Are more easily embarrassed	Are more stress resistant

One final thought on the subject of selling to men and women. During casual conversations over the years, I've asked hundreds of salespeople if they prefer to sell to men or women. The overwhelming majority of both salesmen and saleswomen said they'd rather sell to men. Perhaps it is because men are likely to spend more, as evidenced in this research. It could also be argued that there's a bias in business and men are still believed to have higher value than women in the business world. Or, it might simply be because salespeople are more comfortable selling with them; therefore they're easier to sell to.

Chapter 131. How to Cope with Losing

When we're closing a deal, life's great! When we're on the losing side of a deal, we're miserable and we sometimes feel as if our entire world has fallen apart. Losing is a subject that most salespeople don't like to talk about.

First, the only way to act after you receive the painful news is graciously and professionally. Although you might fantasize about annihilating the decision-maker's reputation and career, you must fight the urge for confrontation. By exiting on good terms, there's always a remote chance that the customer may call you back later when your competitor fails. But the real reason for maintaining your composure is your own mental health. Think of it in these terms: you've invested a great deal of energy into something you wanted badly and were counting on. In spite of your best efforts, you have been told that you weren't good enough. You have just been through a traumatic experience. The first step in dealing with any personal crisis is acknowledging it. By doing so, you will be able to get back to selling sooner. To help you get back into the winning frame of mind as soon as possible, here are four recommendations:

- *Commiserate with colleagues.* You will start to feel better by talking with fellow salespeople who have been in your position. Instead of repressing your pain and doubts, sharing your experience and venting your frustrations will help get you back on your feet. Catharsis enables you to let go of your negative thoughts and feelings. In addition, researchers have found that repeatedly uttering a swear word actually reduces physical pain![1]

- *Take a break.* After a big loss, we often think it's best to buckle up our feelings and put our nose right back on the grindstone. However, no matter how we act on the outside, we're often depressed, tired, and full of self-pity. Unfortunately, this message will be sent subconsciously to customers. As a sales manager, I learned the best way to rejuvenate the team was to give "mental health" days. Typically, it was the first business day after the close of a quarter. Regardless of whether you had a good or bad quarter, you were invited to disappear. As a result, everyone came back refreshed and ready to get back to a winning frame of mind.

- *Reanchor yourself to success.* An anchor is the premeditated association of a specific feeling to an object (described in more detail in the next chapter). After a particularly tough loss, you may have forgotten what it feels like to win. In this situation, go visit some "friendlies." These are customers who have purchased from you, like you, and appreciate your company. By doing so, you reanchor your mind to success.

- *Keep perspective.* I remember being on the road and receiving the bad news that I had lost an important deal to my archrival. On the plane flight from New York back home to California, I sat staring out the window. My mind was filled with destructive thoughts and other self-defeating prophecies. About halfway across the country I made a sudden realization. Not a single person in all the cities we passed over cared.

After you have missed your number, your first reaction is to think the sun has finally set on your career and your hot streak is over. However, you need to remind yourself that there's always next month, next quarter, and next year. As salespeople, our world is structured on a value system that is intimately tied to the production of a single revenue number. This number is how the rest of our world measures our contribution, and it is also how we tend to judge our own worth.

However, you will never be truly happy or satisfied if you measure your self-worth solely by the revenue you generate. You know you are not a good person because you make your number, just as you are not a bad person if you don't. Life is about being with your family and friends and, most importantly, having a relationship with your creator. These relationships are a true reflection of your life's significance.

Chapter 132. Conquering Nervousness

Sales is a profession based upon pressure: pressure from sales management to make your quota, pressure from competitors who are trying to defeat you, pressure you place on yourself to be number one, and pressure to perform well on every sales call. Pressure upon the salesperson during sales calls has a profound impact. It creates an emergency situation that triggers the body's fight-or-flight system.

Here are a few of the physiological changes that happen to a salesperson who is making a stressful sales call or conducting the critical presentation he hopes will land him a big deal:

- The eyebrows instinctively rise and the eyes widen. The iris muscles of the eye contract, causing the pupils to dilate. These actions enhance vision so that maximum visual information about the perceived threats can be sent to the brain.

- The brain's cortex interprets the visual information it is receiving and transmits messages to the brain's hypothalamus. The hypothalamus activates the adrenal glands, which instantaneously release adrenaline into the bloodstream. The hormone adrenaline activates the body's emergency response systems.

- The heart pumps at up to twice its normal rate. Breathing quickens so that the lungs can supply more oxygen to the blood. Oxygen-rich blood is sent to the brain for clearer thinking and to muscles for quick reactions. The liver releases sugar reserves for a quick boost of energy.

- On the outside of the body, perspiration forms as sweat glands are activated to reduce the body heat caused by the increased flow of blood. The nostrils widen so that air can be taken in faster. The face loses color and appears ashen as blood is diverted for more important uses.

The increase in bodily activity corresponds to the escalation of mental activity as well. Your internal dialogue speeds up, jumps from subject to subject, and second-guesses itself. Are they with me? What should I say next? This tension and fear are exposed in some salespeople's speech. They talk too fast, repeat themselves, stutter, or under extreme stress completely forget what they were going to say.

You must project a calm, cool, collected presence to customers at all times. To do otherwise would increase customers' stress levels. Nervousness and agitation may be misinterpreted and convince customers that you have something to hide. Verbal faux pas may be thought of as incompetence. Think about your last visit to the dentist. What would your reaction have been if the dentist had seemed nervous, agitated, or flustered before he or she started to work on your mouth? You would have been scared and had a very stressful appointment.

I still get nervous before I have to give a big presentation. In my opinion, nervousness is not only normal but positive because it drives you to better prepare yourself beforehand. However, once a meeting starts, you want your nervousness to stop. The tool I use to calm my nerves is a psychological anchor. Anchoring is the process of associating a premeditated feeling to an object.

Exercise: Now it's time to do one of the most interesting exercises of the entire book. Think of the best day of your business career. Have a very specific day in your mind. Stop and think about it. Remember how great you felt. Perhaps it was a day you received an award or were promoted. Whatever it is, try to relive the feelings, hear the sounds, and recreate a picture of it in your mind. While holding these thoughts, take your right hand and gently pinch the back of your left hand and hold it while you think of the memory until the back of your pinched hand starts to tingle, usually around thirty seconds or so. Now, repeat the process again. You have now created a psychological anchor.

Would you be nervous speaking in front of one thousand salespeople? Well, I am. That's why I use anchors. Now go ahead and pinch the back of your hand again. Did you feel the tingle again and a reassuring sensation? If not, repeat the entire process very slowly with single-minded concentration. Stop reading, relax, and concentrate.

There's no reason to be nervous when you meet with important customers. Regardless of how many people surround someone and how much fortune, fame, and power you think a person has, everyone is lonely in his or her own way. Loneliness isn't only about being alone. It is about feeling disconnected, isolated, alienated, unwanted, inadequate, self-conscious, unloved, and scared. Keep this idea in mind. The next customer you meet needs a friend.

The most important words you speak are the words you say to yourself. When we talk to ourselves internally, it's usually in the context of our shortcomings. Personally, I am more likely to tell myself that I am a failure at something than that I am great at something else. However, the congruence you emanate to anyone you speak with is based upon a positive perception of yourself, and anchors can help establish this mind-set.

Exercise: Now it is time for one final exercise that takes just a few seconds. Read the following statement slowly out loud, pause, and then repeat it again two times: "I am a success." Perhaps the only person who remains to be convinced that you are a success is you.

Chapter 133. Do You Have Congruence?

How people speak is a good indicator of congruence, the truthfulness of their communication. When people aren't telling the truth, their tempo speeds up or slows down, their volume gets louder or softer, and their tone is higher or lower than normal. For example, Visuals may slow down their speaking, Kinesthetics may speak faster, and Auditories may change their tone. In addition, people's choice of words will change when they are not telling the truth. People telling the truth will talk in a straightforward manner using ordinary terms. When creating misrepresentations, their word selection is more careful, and they tend to use more sophisticated words. They also speak with precision and are mindful not to repeat the same word twice, unlike in natural conversation.

Congruence is at the heart of persuasion. How can you improve your congruence? First, you should know your product inside out. This alone will build your credibility. You can't believe in what you don't understand. You need to understand your company: its history, what makes it unique, how it compares to others, and its future direction. You need to understand the customers you sell to and the problems they face, and you need to understand yourself. Why would someone buy from you? What are your strengths and weaknesses?

Congruence is attained when thoughts and language are aligned to communicate the same conscious and subconscious message. Do you have congruence? Here's a short exercise to test your congruence. Take a moment to answer the following questions:

• Do you honestly believe customers are better off when they choose your product over your competition's?

• Do you think your company is the best in your industry?

• Do you truly believe in yourself and that you are in the right profession?

What were your answers? Do you exude conviction about your product, your company, and your profession? If not, why would you expect someone else to believe in you?

Consider what motivates you. If your fundamental concern is fortune and fame, each of your various layers of communication will reek of it, regardless of how well you think you have concealed or camouflaged your motives from the customer. On the flip side of the coin, if you honestly put others' interests before yours, you will subliminally send this important statement about relationships. You can still be competitive, aggressive, and forceful, so long as you're acting in the customer's best interests.

Chapter 134. Personal Sales Strategy Checklist

We have been trained to think of customers and ourselves as rational decision-makers who use logic and reason exclusively. However, when you sell based solely upon logic, you are destined to be outsold. The successful influencer is the salesperson who understands and appeals to the emotional, political, conscious, and subconscious decision-maker. They bond with the customer's psyche. Use the following checklist to help you prepare for your next customer conversation. (Source chapters are referenced in brackets.)

What is my brand? [95]

How complete is my LinkedIn online persona? [95]

How will I establish situational dominance? [99]

How will I determine what the customer's benefactions are? [101]

What personal attributes and traits should I emphasize? [106]

What do I theorize is the customer's fantasy? [103]

How will I validate that the customer is telling me the truth? [104, 122]

What is the customers visual, auditory, and kinesthetic word catalog wiring? [110–113]

What is my visual, auditory, and kinesthetic word catalog wiring? [112]

How will I employ visual, auditory, and kinesthetic information to protect my price? [116]

How will I adapt my communication to the customer's word catalog wiring? [117, 125]

How will I interpret the customer's eye movements? [119–121]

What aspects of the customer's physical layer will I monitor? [124]

What's my communication level, and is it the same level as the customer's? [126]

How will I ensure my speech is clearly understood? [127]

What customer coping mechanisms should I be prepared for? [128]

Am I respectful of the differences between male and female buyers? [130]

Do I have congruence in front of customers? [133]

Never forget, you have developed sophisticated ways of cataloging the enormous amount of information you see, touch, and hear daily. You accurately interpret images, feelings, and sounds and store them for future reference. Your mind is able to aggregate unorganized reference points and derive meaning from seemingly nonsensical data as in this following example:

It denos't mtater waht oredr the ltteers in a wrod are, the olny iprmoatnt tihng is taht the frist and lsat ltteer be at the rghit pclae. The rset can be a total mses and you can sitll raed it wouthit nay porbelm. Tihs is bcuseae the huamn mnid deos not raed ervey lteter by istlef but the wrod as a wlohe.

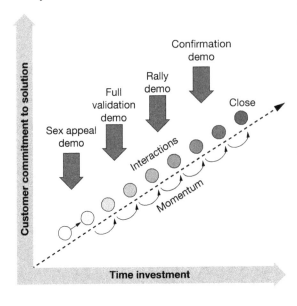

Figure 135.1 The four types of product demonstrations

Chapter 135. Key Questions Every Salesperson Should Know the Answers To

A smart salesperson knows how something works, while a clever salesperson knows how to get something done. While smart salespeople win some of the time, clever salespeople win most of the time. Knowing the answers to the key questions in this chapter make you not only smarter but even more clever. They summarize important findings based upon a detailed analysis of more than four hundred sales cycles. Thirty-six percent were renewal/add-on sales cycles where the salesperson was selling to an existing client. Forty-five percent were persuasion sales cycles where the salesperson was competing directly against the main competitors. Nineteen percent were creation sales cycles where the salesperson was selling to a new client and no decision was the main competitor. (See chapter 16 for more information on each of these sales cycles and the key moments they are lost or won.)

1. Do the Odds of Closing a Deal Increase with More Demonstrations?

The four different types of product demonstrations that occur as the sales cycle progresses are shown in figure 135.1. While each demo has a different purpose, they all are intended to increase your deal momentum. The goal of the "sex appeal demo" is to excite buyers and stimulate their thinking about how using your product will improve

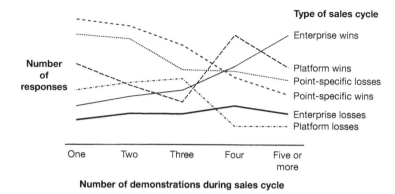

Figure 135.2 Impact of demonstrations on enterprise, platform, and point-specific sales cycles

their business. A key outcome of the sex appeal demo is the development of an internal coach, specifically a guide (see ch. 37). Next is the "full validation demo," where buyers conduct a detailed review of the product's operation. The purpose of this demo is to educate evaluators on all your product's capabilities and reinforce the value of your solution. The outcome of this demo is to validate the importance of your solution and continue to build more momentum. Because the decision-making process can take many months to complete, "rally demos" provide important customer touchpoints to keep the excitement level up about the anticipated benefits that will be enjoyed when the product is implemented and introduce the solution to other members of the company. Quite often senior-level decision-makers who weren't present at earlier demos will attend rally demos. Finally, "confirmation demos" calm nervous buyers and help analytical-minded evaluators document exactly what they are purchasing.

Certain patterns of winning or losing are associated with the number of demos. For example, larger enterprise and platform sales cycles share similar patterns. In general, the more demos that are performed, the higher the likelihood of winning. In over three-quarters of large enterprise sales cycles where a vendor was competing against the main competitors, the winning vendor conducted more product demonstrations than the losers as shown in figure 135.2. Simply put, the customer was more interested in one vendor and therefore evaluated that vendor with a higher level of due diligence.

However, this is not necessarily true for smaller point-specific sales. Winning point-specific sales is actually more likely to occur with fewer demos. These are see-like-buy sales cycles where the buyer immediately falls in love with the product upon seeing it. One way to think of this is that point-specific buyers react to the first demo with either a "Ahh— that's an interesting product" or an "Aha! We need it now!" In winning sales cycles, rally and confirmation demos are performed toward the end of the deal; however, in losing sales cycles, the salesperson conducts sex appeal demos over and over again because the buyer hasn't fallen in love with the product.

2. Where Do the Best Leads Come From?

Leads can be classified into four basic sources: inbound inquiries via the company's website or by telephone, leads generated by the inside sales team or telemarketing efforts, referrals from a partner or customer, and leads being generated directly by the salesperson. When analyzed by the probability of closing the business, the best leads were generated by the salesperson by a factor greater than three to one over inbound leaders, the second-best source. Therefore, if you have a DIY (do it yourself) approach to prospecting, you will reap rewards.

3. Should I Answer "Blind" RFPs?

As discussed in chapter 17, approximately 30 percent of the time the winner of an RFP-based persuasion sales cycle is determined before the "official" selection process even starts. Therefore, it seems logical that you wouldn't respond to a request for proposal when you haven't met the prospect and didn't have knowledge about the RFP beforehand. However, I have some surprising facts to share with you.

The decision to respond to blind RFPs should also be based upon your competitive position and whether or not you are the market leader in your space.

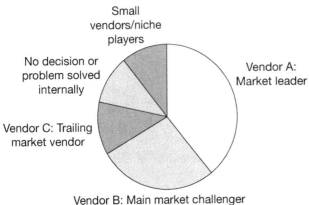

Figure 135.3 Mature market competitive landscape and the propensity for vendors to be selected by customers

Figure 135.3 represents the typical competitive landscape for a mature market and the propensity for vendors to be selected by customers. Vendor A is the market leader, vendor B is the main market challenger, and vendor C is the trailing market vendor. Please note that the exact market share percentages will vary by industry and this representation is for illustrative purposes. These three vendors will most likely be invited to participate in most every RFP process because of the nature of the market position in their industry. The next most formidable competitor is no decision or the customer's decision to solve the problem themselves using internal resources followed by small vendors and niche players.

Study results reveal that vendor A should respond to blind RFPs, as the market leader won an astonishingly high 57 percent of those they answered. Conversely, the blind RFP win rate for Vendor B was under 20 percent, and there weren't any reported wins for vendor C.

4. Should I Focus on Selling to Sophisticated or Less Sophisticated Buyers?

Sales success is profoundly impacted by the buyer's sophistication. The solution you sell has a sweet spot (see ch. 15) in the marketplace, and one aspect of fit is the buyer's sophistication level. While all products are marketed as being the most advanced and complete in their industry, buyers will gravitate to the solution they feel best matches their use case complexity (whether they need simple or robust functionality), knowledge level, and tolerance for difficulty.

Let's examine buyer sophistication using the example of a mature market and vendor A, the market leader, and vendor B, the main market challenger. Salespeople were asked to rate the sophistication of the buyer's evaluation team as extremely knowledgeable, moderately knowledgeable, or lesser knowledgeable. Vendor A was better able to

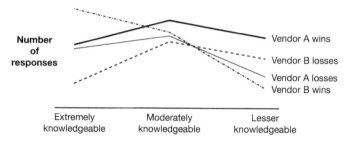

Figure 135.4 Win-loss patterns based on buyer sophistication

sell across all three categories but had the highest levels of success with moderately knowledgeable evaluation teams and performed far better with lesser

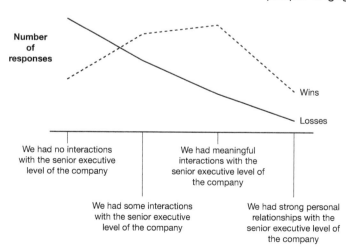

Figure 135.5 Win-loss patterns based on meeting with C-level executives

knowledgeable evaluation teams than vendor B. Vendor B enjoyed more success with sophisticated evaluators than less sophisticated evaluators as shown in figure 135.4.

5. How Does Meeting with Senior Executives Improve My Chance of Winning the Business?

There's a direct correlation between winning and the number of interactions the salesperson has with C-level executive decision-makers. The more C-level engagement touchpoints, the higher the likelihood of winning as shown in figure 135.5. The C-level engagement ratio (the percentage of times when the salesperson had C-level interactions) was 84 percent for wins and 59 percent for losses. In other words, the salesperson did not have any interactions with C-level executives in 41 percent of losses. In addition, the salespeople engaged the C-level executives earlier in the sales cycle, had more meaningful interactions, and more frequently built strong personal relationships.

6. Should I Introduce My Senior Executive Team Members to the Client?

There is a direct correlation between the probability of winning and the number of senior leadership team members a

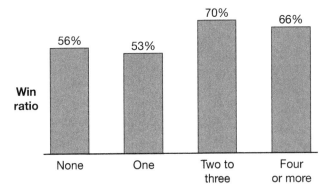

Figure 135.6 Win ratios based upon the number of senior executive team members involved from the salesperson's company

salesperson involves in an account. Overall, there were 30 percent more wins than losses reported when executive team members were involved in an account. Furthermore, the number of executives involved in an account impacts the likelihood of winning as shown in figure 135.6. Salespeople reported a 56 percent win rate where no members of their senior executive team were involved and a slight decrease to 53 percent where one member was involved. The win rate jumps to 70 percent when two to three members were involved and remains at a high level of 66 percent when four or more members were involved.

percent of sales cycles were decided early in the evaluation process. This means that more than half of all sales cycles are decided before the customer even starts the most intensive steps of the evaluation. Twenty-five percent of sales cycles were decided by the middle of the evaluation and only 23 percent at the end. This is a very important point because in about three-quarters of evaluations, the vendor is selected way before the customer publicly announces the decision. Salespeople who invest their time and company resources working a sales cycle to the very end, believing the evaluation is completely fair and open, are usually making a critical mistake. If you don't specifically know that you've won the deal by that point in the sales cycle, then you've likely already lost.

There were also distinctly different patterns in how evaluators made their decisions in won versus lost sales cycles. For example, winning salespeople described the evaluators as making their selection based upon product features and

7. When Does the Customer Actually Make a Decision?

You probably lose a deal much earlier than you think you do. In fact, salespeople reported that 20 percent of the time a favorite vendor won the business before the sales cycle even started as shown in figure 135.7. Another 32

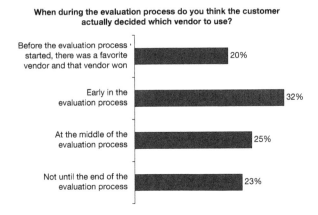

Figure 135.7 When the customer makes the vendor selection

functionality first, followed by state-of-the-art technology and product completeness, vendor strength and market position, initial and overall solution costs, and services and support as shown in figure 135.8. Salespeople who lost described the customer as being focused first on initial and overall solution cost, product features and functionality, vendor strength and market position, state-of-the-art technology and product completeness, and services and support.

How do you perceive evaluators made their final decision?	
Wins	**Losses**
1. Product features and functionality	1. Initial and overall solution costs
2. State-of-the-art technology and product completeness	2. Product features and functionality
3. Vendor strength and market position	3. Vendor strength and market position
4. Initial and overall solution costs	4. State-of-the-art technology and product completeness
5. Services and support	5. Services and support

Figure 135.8 Salespeople rank how evaluators made their final decision

There are three different ways to interpret these results. The first is from customers' point of view and whether they are strategically evaluating vendors or fixated on price. The second is from the perspective of salespeople, who may reflexively blame losing on price because it makes it easier to accept defeat. From my perspective, winners execute a better sales strategy than losers, which results in more meaningful customer conversations. In essence, that's the purpose of this book.

Ultimately, the quality of the vendor's relationship really comes down to the quality and work ethic of the account executive. My experience is the most important determination of whether we will have a successful relationship with the vendor than all the other things combined.

—Chief Information Officer

FINAL ADVICE

Most salespeople don't like to read. You see, your brain was built for talking. It was not designed for reading. While speaking comes automatically and is a natural part of the brain's development, reading is a skill that must be learned. It requires three different areas of your brain to work together in close coordination. So it's highly unlikely you'll read this reference guide in its entirety. Therefore, I would like to share my favorite chapters with you.

12. Seven Key Mistakes Salepeople Make According to Buyers
29. The Truth about Price and Decision-Making
36. Identifying the Bully with the Juice and the Emperor
37. Developing an Internal Coach
39. Flanking Strategies When You're Stuck at the Wrong Level
41. Logic versus the Human Nature of Customer Decision-Making
48. Why B2B Buyers Don't Like Salespeople
50. The Trusted Advisor Sales Goal
54. Speak the Business Operations Language with C-Level Executives
65. Positioning Value When Meeting with C-Level Executives
70. Closing Strategies
76. Company Buyer Persona Roles
78. Negotiation Strategy
99. Situational Dominance Is Your Ultimate Goal
111. How People Receive and Transmit Information
130. The Differences between Men and Women Buyers
135. Key Questions Every Salesperson Should Know the Answers To

What are your favorite chapters? Please connect with me on LinkedIn to let me know, and you'll also receive notification of my future sales research reports.

NOTES

Chapter 22

1. B. H. Liddell Hart, *Strategy* (New York: Frederick A. Praeger, 1954), 18.
2. Sun Tzu, *The Art of War,* ed. James Clavell (New York: Delacorte, 1983), 21.
3. "George S. Patton Quotes," Military-Quotes.com, http://www.military-quotes.com/Patton.htm.

Chapter 100

1. First Steps, "Your Child's Brain Development," http://www.firststeps.us/parents_brain development.shtml.
2. Speech Therapy Information and Resources, "Vocabulary," http://www.speech-therapy-information-and-resources.com/vocabulary.html.
3. Kevin Lee, "Strategies to Improve Vocabulary," http://www.ehow.com/info_7868824_strategies-improve-vocabulary.html.

Chapter 106

1. Carole Martin, "Nonverbal Message Speaks Louder Than Words," *Repertoire Magazine*, http://www.repertoiremag.com/Article.asp?Id=1667.

Chapter 119

1. Soichi Nagao, "Discovering the Source of Long-Term Motor Memory," MedicalXpress.com, November 15, 2010, http://www.MedicalXpress.com/news/2010-11-source-long-term-motor-memory.html.
2. Melinda Wenner, "Moving Your Eyes Improves Memory, Study Suggests," LiveScience, January 11, 2008, http://www.livescience.com/1473-moving-eyes-improves-memory-study-suggests.html.
3. Sara Goudarzi, "Where We Store What We See," *LiveScience*, August 29, 2006, http://www.livescience.com/7110-store.html.
4. Jim Phelps, "Brain Tours: Mood," PsychEducation.org, http://www. psycheducation.org/brain-tours/mood/.
5. Michele Solis, "Imaging Study Ties Brain Connection to Sociability," *Spectrum*, September 15, 2009, https://spectrumnews.org/news/imaging-study-ties-brain-connection-to-sociability/.

Chapter 131

1. Megan Gibson, "WTF? Study Shows Swearing Reduces Pain," *Time*, April 18, 2011, http://newsfeed.time.com/2011/04/18/WTFstudy-shows-swearing-reduces-pain.

INDEX